History after the Three Worlds

ọnyé ájụjụ́ ada efu ụzọ̀

اطلب العلم ولو في الصين

前車之覆，後車之鑒

जिन खोजा तिन पाया

History after the Three Worlds

Post-Eurocentric Historiographies

EDITED BY
ARIF DIRLIK
VINAY BAHL
AND
PETER GRAN

ROWMAN & LITTLEFIELD PUBLISHERS, INC.
Lanham • Boulder • New York • Oxford

ROWMAN & LITTLEFIELD PUBLISHERS, INC.

Published in the United States of America
by Rowman & Littlefield Publishers, Inc.
4720 Boston Way, Lanham, Maryland 20706
http://www.rowmanlittlefield.com

12 Hid's Copse Road
Cumnor Hill, Oxford OX2 9JJ, England

British Library Cataloguing in Publication Information Available
\
Library of Congress Cataloging-in-Publication Data

History after the three worlds : post-Eurocentric historiographies / edited by Arif Dirlik, Vinay Bahl, and Peter Gran.
    p. cm.
    Includes bibliographical references and index.
    Contents: Is there history after Eurocentrism? / Arif Dirlik—Archeologists and historians confront civilization, relativism, and poststructuralism in the late twentieth century / Thomas C. Patterson—Historiography in southwest Asian and North African studies since Sa'id's Orientalism, 1978 / R.A. Abou-El-Haj—Situating and rethinking subaltern studies for writing working-class history / Vinay Bahl—Reversals, ironies, hegemonies : notes on the contemporary historiography of modern China / Arif Dirlik—Conflict and connection : rethinking colonial African history / Frederick Cooper—The promise and dilemma of subaltern studies : perspectives from Latin American history / Florencia E. Mallon—Is world history possible? / Roxann Prazniak—Whither history? : encounters with historism, postmodernism, postcolonialism / Arif Dirlik.
    ISBN 0-8476-9341-4 (alk. paper) — ISBN 0-8476-9342-2 (pbk. : alk. paper)
    1. Historiography—History—20th century. 2. Historiography—Developing countries. 3. Developing countries—Historiography. 4. Postcolonialism. I. Dirlik, Arif. II. Bahl, Vinay. III. Gran, Peter, 1941–

D13 .H578 2000
9079.2—dc21
                                                                                00-033270

Printed in the United States of America

♾ ™The paper used in this publication meets the minimum requirements of American National Standard for Information Sciences—Permanence of Paper for Printed Library Materials, ANSI/NISO Z39.48—1992.

"As contact zones earlier presented Euro-Americans with a choice between civilizing mission and dissolution into 'barbarism,' the new contact zones present intellectuals of Third World origin with a choice between 'bridging' cultures that, given the persistent inequalities between societies, may mean further invasion of the rest of the world by the structures of power over which Euro-America continues to preside, or burning the bridges, so that alternatives might be thinkable to a Eurocentric vision of human future."

—Arif Dirlik

Contents

Part 1: The End of Eurocentrism?

1 Introduction 3
Vinay Bahl and Arif Dirlik

2 Is There History after Eurocentrism? Globalism, Postcolonialism,
and the Disavowal of History 25
Arif Dirlik

3 Archeologists and Historians Confront Civilization, Relativism,
and Poststructuralism in the Late Twentieth Century 49
Thomas C. Patterson

Part 2: Area Perspectives

4 Historiography in West Asian and North African Studies since
Sa'id's *Orientalism* 67
R. A. Abou-El-Haj

5 Situating and Rethinking Subaltern Studies for Writing Working-
Class History 85
Vinay Bahl

6 Reversals, Ironies, Hegemonies: Notes on the Contemporary
Historiography of Modern China 125
Arif Dirlik

7 Conflict and Connection: Rethinking Colonial African History 157
Frederick Cooper

8 The Promise and Dilemma of Subaltern Studies: Perspectives
from Latin American History 191
Florencia E. Mallon

Part 3: History at A(nother) Crossroads

9   Is World History Possible? An Inquiry   221
    Roxann Prazniak

10 Whither History? Encounters with Historism, Postmodernism,
    Postcolonialism   241
    Arif Dirlik

Index   259

About the Contributors   277

PART 1

The End of Eurocentrism?

1

Introduction

Vinay Bahl and Arif Dirlik

The contributors to this volume share a sense that a new world situation has brought with it problems that are not containable within known paradigms, especially that post–World War II paradigm of global organization around the concept of Three Worlds. These same problems seem to have contributed to a crisis in the practice of history, as they call for a rewriting of the past in order to account for the present. The present itself defies easy containment within accustomed spatial and temporal categories, lending credibility to a pervasive impression that knowledge of the past may not be relevant to understanding the present. What is at issue is history's epistemological status.

The writers in this volume are also motivated to affirm the relevance of history against its dismissal or marginalization in academia's current preoccupation with globalization, and against its attendant epistemologies, including postmodernism and postcolonialism, that invade the study of the past with the fictions of the present. The affirmation of history here is inevitably grounded in recognition that the present is best grasped as a reconfiguration of forces that have been shaping the world for centuries. The possibility that the relationship between the present and the past may be denied in the new world situation makes the study of history indispensable. Such a critical historical view is buttressed also by a conviction that new kinds of political practice, appropriate to the new configurations of domination, are necessary. The erasure of the past in contemporary ideologies is accompanied by a sense that there may no longer be an outside to capital in its contemporary, global, guise. And yet global capitalism in our day is torn by contradictions, and it is chaos rather than seamless domination that best characterizes the globalization of capital. It is these contradictions, which must be grasped in their historicity, that provide the spaces from which to think alternatives to the present.

To set the stage for what the essays have to say concerning these ideological and historical questions, this chapter elaborates on some problems presented by the larger global context for the contemporary crisis in historical thinking.

Among the many problems of contemporary societies worldwide, three are especially pertinent to the situation at the end of the twentieth century:

1. The predicament of global survival, anxiety over which pervades the utopianism of the present celebrations of global capitalism. A report from the Earth Summit, held June 29, 1997, concluded: "We are deeply concerned that the overall trends . . . are worse today than they were in 1992." Global warming is on the rise, fresh water is increasingly scarce, more than 50,000 square miles of forest are lost each year, the number of the absolutely poor—those living on less than a dollar a day—has edged above 1.5 billion, and 100 million women are unaccounted for in world population figures.

2. U.S. economists' response to the above situation. Jeffrey D. Sachs, a Harvard economist who is deeply involved in efforts to spread capitalism globally, suggests that to remove poverty in the "Third World," the West has to reinvent the worn-out "development" strategies to overcome deterrents to "growth." In other words, multinational companies should invest more to create sweatshops in poor countries so women and children can get jobs to survive. The economists think that even if these sweatshops exploit and abuse women and children, they are "better" alternatives than those where "destitute parents in India sell their children to Persian Gulf begging syndicates, whose bosses mutilate children for [in order to achieve a] higher take."[1]

3. Two tendencies in the field of ideas. One is the quite striking proliferation of U.S. television programs in which aliens, angels, and supernatural beings solve social and even individual problems in what is at the same time proclaimed to be a technology-driven scientific and rational society that is capable of landing a spacecraft on Mars. One is reminded that not too long ago, "Oriental" people's beliefs in the supernatural were seen as primitive, exotic, and backward. However, the phenomenon has historical precedents in other times of crisis that produced similar phenomena. The difference today may be that the whole world is in crisis.[2] Another interesting phenomenon is the increased intellectual colonization of the world through the use of English language on the Internet; it is predicted that this type of colonization could lead to the elimination of about two hundred languages by the end of the century. Anatoly Voronov, the director of Russia's best-known Internet provider, says of the use of English on the Internet: "It is the ultimate act of intellectual colonialism. The product comes from America, and we either adapt to English or stop using it. That is the right of business. But if you are talking about a technology that is supposed to open the world to hundreds of millions of people you are joking. This just makes the world into new sorts of haves and have nots."[3] So much for the democratization and localization of native cultures.

Thus, it seems that at the end of the twentieth century, poverty, colonialism, capitalism, and "orientalism" not only refused to vanish but also acquired new force from non-Western ideologies once deemed obstacles to capitalism. As the essays by Bahl and Dirlik suggest, Confucian and Hindu scriptures are being reinterpreted for the promotion of capitalism in China and India respectively.[4] Such culturalism is fickle, however, and easily returns to earlier "orientalist" devaluations of the Other. The Asian economic crisis in the late 1990s was followed by the derogation of the very same Asian value/belief systems, accompanied by the growing opinion that market culture and consumerism are the only means to achieve progress and economic growth. Despite the evidence that culture is subordinate to economic interests and phenomena, scholars in cultural studies continue to avoid confrontation of material realities out of an anxiety about "metanarratives" or "foundational" principles.

The emerging trends in the realm of ideas are reinforced not only through television and mass publications but through academic scholarship as well. Poor people (consisting of mostly women and children) living in Third World nations can survive only if they accept extremely exploitative and abusive conditions in the sweatshops. As Harvard economist Jeffrey D. Sachs writes, it is "not that there are too many sweatshops but that there are too few." He is opposed to child or prison labor and other outright abuses. "But many nations," he writes, "have no better hope than plants paying mere subsistence wages. Those are precisely the jobs that were the stepping stones for Singapore and Hong Kong and those are the jobs that have to come to Africa to get them out of their backbreaking rural poverty."[5] No wonder U.S. representatives have started wooing Africa once again with modernization projects that will enable Africans to compete with sweatshops in other poor areas.

Against such hopeless solutions that seek to bolster the very system that produces misery, progressive thinkers have been searching long for alternatives to capitalist modernity.[6] There is no shortage of critics of modernity; unfortunately, the most imaginative of such critics, mostly from Third World locations, go unheard because of an imbalance of power that continues to structure the world. Third World scholars and scientists suffer from the prejudices of media controlled by the powerful who deny a significant hearing to alternative visions of society, indigenous projects, and appropriate technologies as solutions to contemporary problems. Christopher T. Zielinsky, spokesperson for the World Health Organization, states, "The 2 percent participation in international scientific discourse allowed by Western indexing services is simply too little to account for the scientific output of 80 percent of the world."[7] Throughout the Third World, there are emerging alternatives to mainstream Western science and medicine that seek to alleviate general problems of survival and livelihood without the help of Harvard economists, sweatshops, and Western publishers. These alternatives indicate clearly that the problem is not a lack of scientific and technological knowledge in the Third World, but rather the unequal relationship between rich and poor countries, and alliances between neo-colonial forces and local elites that seek to marginalize or extinguish alternative ways of living and thinking. Armed with the power of institutions such as the World Bank and the International Monetary Fund (IMF), and those organizations' advanced technology and economic power, those who are in positions to control the global economy guarantee that the Third World poor will be driven into sweatshops stitching fashionable clothes for the consumers of rich countries and the emergent consumer populations of Third World societies. While looking askance at indigenous beliefs, moreover, the powerful do not hesitate to appropriate as their own such beliefs or ways of thinking, which they turn into commodities on a global market to serve not human needs but the greedy search for profits. Hence, while indigenous intellectuals seeking to put such knowledge at the service of human life are denied a hearing, indigenous knowledge produced through centuries of experience is filtered through the market and transnational corporations to be placed at the service of the rich and the powerful, further bolstering claims to Western scientific superiority.[8]

Critics of modernity who gain a hearing are those whose critiques may be contained within capitalist modernity, or serve to mystify it. Most prominent among them are postmodernists and their Third World progeny, postcolonialists, who have been all too successful in reinforcing the very project of modernity of which they are putative critics. Postcolonialists, including some members of the Indian subaltern school of historiography, have been embraced in Europe and the United States, because in their repudiation of "metanarratives," "foundational" concepts, and so on, they have contributed significantly to minimizing issues of structural oppression and exploitation implicit in such concepts as capital and class. Even more insidious may be a recently emerging tendency among erstwhile promoters of dependency and world system theories—for instance, Andre Gundar Frank—who, in repudiating Eurocentrism, have turned to erasing capitalism from history.[9] From a historical perspective grounded in the struggles over modernity, these so-called radical critics are most impressive for the manner in which they have hijacked, and erased the possibility of, social and political radicalism, displacing it to the realm of culture where it may be rendered harmless under slogans of multiculturalism.

These intellectual tendencies are products of complex circumstances, but surely one central factor in the warm reception received from all levels of culture is a resonance with "globalization." The contributors to this volume share an appreciation that globalization is a direct successor to modernization and is the project of a Western modernity, even where its agents are not necessarily Western by origin. Like modernization and modernization theory, globalization, as it is commonly articulated, seeks to disguise its parochial origins by a pretense that forces operating beyond human control are transforming the world. Any critical conception of globalization must, accordingly, insist that globalization is the direct consequence of human choices and of human control. Any such conception must also recognize that while there is significant transformation globally, such transformation does not automatically imply assimilation to a Western sense of globalization, partly because much of the world is noncapitalist, and partly because capitalism assumes so many forms, especially on the local level.

M. Waters suggests, "The degree of globalization is greater in the cultural arena, being facilitated by the economic [role of multinationals, trade, and international division of labor] and political processes both within each country as well as in the world arena."[10] It is with this concern in mind that this book takes notice of the real difficulty faced by a writer today who seeks to keep open the door to an alternative to "modernization and globalization."

It is essential, however, that the search for such alternatives take for a point of departure the contemporary world situation, which is no longer to be grasped in terms of past conceptualizations. While it is necessary to view contemporary ideologies of globalization critically, we can ill afford to overlook that they address contemporary challenges that are quite real. Especially important in this regard is the conceptualization of the world in terms of the Three Worlds idea. In past days, the Three Worlds idea provided a significant means to grasp global economic and political configurations. As late as the 1970s, the idea of the Third World pointed to certain concrete forms of economic exploitation and political struggle. By the 1980s, the struggle part of the meaning had lost its salience, rendering the Third World synonymous with backward or undeveloped, which also suggested a return to the original post–World-War-II use of the term. The Third World, which earlier had been a location of possible alternatives to both First World capitalist and Second World statist modernities, came increasingly to denote those areas in the world that were falling behind in the race of progress. At the same time, economic developments associated with globalization further scrambled the tenuous boundaries between the Three Worlds. The fall for all practices of statist socialist regimes in Eastern Europe in 1989 was the final event to render irrelevant earlier conceptualizations of global configurations. With global capitalism has emerged a situation that not only signals an end to the Three Worlds idea, but even more radically to the dichotomization of the world around East/West or North/South distinctions. What are gone are not only concepts for organizing the world, but also concepts that served to give coherence to projects of emancipation.

The irrelevance of the concepts, however, does not imply the disappearance of fundamental aspects of the situation that the concepts encompassed, especially the divisions between rich and poor, and the conditions of inequality, oppression, and exploitation, which are perhaps sharper today than in the past.[11] The problem with contemporary alternatives to the Three Worlds idea—globalization, postmodernism, and postcolonialism—is not that they do not articulate a new situation, but that they turn their backs on the persistent material and cultural problems created by the globalization of capitalism. Such Third World issues—which are no longer confined to a geographical Third World—are literally absent from discussions of modernity and postmodernity; as such discussions appear as "an all-Western debate; an Occidental quiz, with Western answers to Western questions."[12]

The problems these discussions present are not abstractly intellectual but profoundly pedagogical, with implications for everyday social ideologies. Students—
especially those who are nourished by Western academic culture—are often caught
in a situation where postmodern and postcolonial theories substitute for knowledge
about other countries, knowledge of languages, and most certainly knowledge of
other theories. To a degree this book is addressed to these students. The authors
must assume that "it is not possible for anyone to stand outside either their material reality (both human and nonhuman) or of the evolving context of ideas." Ide-
ally, "one must operate taking cognizance of how the available alternatives will
affect human beings living in the particular world of the present."[13] Postmodernism
and postcolonialism encourage preoccupation with identity and subjectivity, but
only by displacing into the realm of culture the kind of self-knowledge that comes
with the confrontation of historically circumscribed material realities. The end
result is, on the one hand, not so much self-knowledge as the denial of the possibility of knowledge of any kind and the re-reification of identities that produces a
liberal relativism, and on the other hand, murderous separation of human beings.
To overcome this new mode of culturalism in both its liberal and conservative manifestations, it is necessary once again to confront life in all its materiality, which
unites as well as divides humans across the globe. To this end, the various chapters
in this book reaffirm the historicity of the present to spell out the material context
that produces contemporary cultures and ideologies, including the contemporary
crisis of history. Similarly, the alternative historiographies the chapters propose insist
on the persistence of past problems while recognizing the changed circumstances
of the present; hence the title, *History after the Three Worlds,* which parts with the
Three Worlds idea but reaffirms it as the historical condition of the present.

It may be useful to spell out briefly, and in the most general terms, some of the
premises that run through this book, which should also indicate the ways in which
the authors share or depart from orientations that have been appropriated for globalism, postmodernism, or postcolonialism. One premise concerns the repudiation
of difference based on a "pure" and essentialist distinction between East and West.[14]
Not only are East and West constructed terms, but materially and culturally much
is shared in common these days by peoples around the world, including those orientations expressed in the terms globalism, postmodernism, and postcolonialism.
While postmodernism and postcolonialism (unlike globalism) are premised on the
affirmation of difference, they in their different ways also promote certain kinds of
sameness. In some ways, such shared orientations also make this volume possible,
where different histories may in fact be subjected to analysis around similar issues.
It is important, however, that the chapters also insist on structured differences both
culturally and materially. Such differences serve as critical reminders that the diffusion of certain epistemologies globally does not result in a so-called global village,
but on the contrary disguises the recolonization of the world under the guise of
globalism. In terms of destructured differences, postmodernism and postcolonial-

ism are complicit in the defusion of collective resistance to structured inequalities. The example of the Subaltern Studies, which emerged in India, is particularly pertinent. It is put to use as Third World ideology by the Third World bourgeoisie, because it offers the double advantage of appearing critical of the West and Western analytical categories, while in fact it is part of a Western discourse that marginalizes the mass populations of countries such as India. The advantages of "subalternization" have not been lost on establishment scholars in other locales as well, as Abou-El-Haj shows in his discussion of the appeals of Subaltern Studies in West Asian and North African studies.

Second is the related issue of Eurocentrism. Like many scholars in our day of various political persuasions, the contributors to this volume believe in the necessity of repudiating Eurocentrism. They also hold, however, that a thoroughgoing repudiation of Eurocentrism must include a critique of capitalism, for otherwise the repudiation of Eurocentrism must remain incomplete. More seriously, the repudiation of metanarratives in postmodern and postcolonial scholarship, including the metanarrative of capitalism, not only brings Eurocentrism back in, but also serves to disguise the continued hegemony of Eurocentric modernity through the agency of capitalism. This is quite visible in the so-called idea industry, which presently elevates knowledge over physical work or material wealth as a source of power. While knowledge is indeed power in an information-driven society, the control of information through the institutions of capitalism and class domination continues to be a reality of contemporary society.[15] It may not be coincidental that as public education continues to struggle for funding, knowledge is elevated in the diploma mills of capitalism. The Business Management Center at the University of California, Berkeley, created a chair for a "Professor of Knowledge." Such rendering of knowledge into an industry prompted a *New York Times* reporter to observe, "[K]nowledge seems like kind of a shaky industry."[16] Shaky or not, business schools around the country not only have elevated "knowledge" in their curricula but have begun to stress "culture" as a cornerstone of that knowledge. Cultural knowledge of this kind, however, is intended not to recognize and respect the culture of others, but to render more efficient the management of a "multicultural" workforce and the marketing of commodities.[17] The new recognition of non–Euro-American cultures, in other words, implies not an end to Eurocentrism, but appropriating Eurocentric modernity cultures that are rendered into capitalist commodities.

It is arguable from this perspective that postmodernist and postcolonialist culturalism serve not to subvert contemporary forms of power but provide an alibi for their operations. Howard Winant has suggested that consent, rather than domination, is essential to the efficient operations of capital. In order to achieve this consent "inequality has to be 'policed,' not only in the literal sense, but also in the cultural sense. Inequality requires constant interpretation. Why is there poverty amid plenty? How can the 'North' justify its excesses before the impoverished and increasingly desperate 'South'? How much responsibility do the poor bear?"[18]

Dismissing metanarratives in postmodernism and postcolonialism, in disguising the systemic nature of power, also makes it impossible to confront power systemically. It is not that postmodernist and postcolonialist arguments are irrelevant. The problem rather is that these arguments fail to articulate their position vis-à-vis the power structure that provides their context, a power structure that in its globalization finds in cultural hybridity an efficient means to manage people and things. While the postmodernist/postcolonialist argument claims that the abandonment of "fixed" identities provides a more radical means of resistance than earlier radicalisms, in its refusal to address questions of structural power (imbedded in questions of capitalism, democracy, privatization, and so forth), it in fact ends up disguising, if not celebrating, contemporary forms of power.[19] The preoccupation with identity, not to speak of affirmations of its fluidity and flexibility, coincide rather suspiciously with the efforts of capital to constantly remake and reconstruct identities in accordance with marketing needs. The outcome of the postmodernist/postcolonialist argument is at best to elevate the "nihilist face of the Occident, one which is also politically inconclusive and indeterminate." The repudiation of Eurocentrism through the reassertion of hybrid identities against structural paradigms of identity, informed by the history of Eurocentric domination of the world (capitalism, colonialism, nationalism, class, etc.), however, ends up in the very idea of hybridity in reifying pre-Eurocentric cultures. It is also a back-handed acknowledgment that Eurocentrism was indeed a formative moment in the construction of identities elsewhere—but now without any possibility of resistance to persistent power structures. No wonder that postcolonialists have found homes in First World business and educational institutions.[20]

A brief comment here on the recent attention Western media have given to selected South Asian intellectuals and scholars living in the West as well as South Asia: These scholars, who write in "Indian-English," have created a new "model" of scholars from the Third World. What they write in turn creates new models of writing not just for Third World scholars but also for First World scholars. It is not surprising that Salman Rushdie wrote, in response to his critics in India, that when Indians criticized such selective recognition, they were being parochial. He writes: "[Indian critics] do not deal with language, voice, psychological or social insight, imagination, or talent. Rather, they [are preoccupied] with class, power and belief." He points out further, "Western publishers and critics have been gradually more and more excited by the voices emerging from India. . . . British writers are often chastised by reviewers for their lack of Indian-style ambition and verve. . . . It feels as if the East were imposing itself on the West, rather than the other way around. . . . Literature has little or nothing to do with a writer's home address."[21] While the complex issues of literary identity that Rushdie raises are not to be denied, there is a profound irony in his statement concerning "the East . . . imposing itself on the West," even as he declares in the name of "Western" criteria of literature that the issues of concern to Indian writers are parochial and should be transformed to make Indian writers more acceptable to Western publishers.

These remarks are reminiscent of intellectual models in colonial India when a Bengali "babu class" was created, members of which were British in language, costume, and manners but Indian in skin color. This class of people helped the British colonial government rule the Indian subcontinent in the least expensive way and also assured the British of the existence of a social and cultural basis for their colonial rule. These babus became the role models for the upwardly mobile in colonial India. Today, in the context of a globalized capitalist system, it is not surprising that an international babu class, which includes postcolonialists and subalternists, is being created as a foundation for global hegemony and as a role model for other Third World intellectuals—all the more effectively because of the prestige and dollar signs attached to the names. The complicity of such intellectuals in global hegemony is an indication that far from being erased or "provincialized," Eurocentrism, in its appropriation of cultures globally, is being established on an even firmer foundation—at least where intellectuals are concerned.

New social theory is supposedly no longer Eurocentric, in that it does not use European categories and it seeks to "decenter" Europe. But even the effort to decenter or provincialize Europe may be infused with the legacy of Eurocentrism. Neither postmodernism nor postcolonialism is free from Eurocentrism. While postmodernism is replete with expressions about multicultural sensitivity, this is more than offset by an almost theoretical indifference to the knowledge of the world that is prerequisite to such sensitivity; a knowledge that the modernist historians, for all their faults, possess to one degree or another.[22] Equally debilitating is a feigned indifference to matters of power, as if access to e-mail and the Internet make us all equal in the age of multiculturalism. The hierarchies of disciplines, regions, and peoples survive in the age of multiculturalism. As Prazniak argues in her essay on world history writing, the inclusion of others in history, and even efforts to marginalize European modernity, continue to be done using Eurocentric modes of constructing the past.

Finally, the contributors share the conviction that complexity of social analysis categories, such as class and gender, must be recognized. All categories of social analysis are overdetermined, which is to say that they are manifested with different implications under different historical circumstances.[23] This is not to say, however, that they are irrelevant, or that they may be deconstructed to the point of irrelevance. The latter once again plays into the hands of dominant power structures, which has replaced "inequality" with difference, and parades "multiculturalism" in an effort to disguise continuing racial and ethnic problems. The many "posts" of contemporary social theory, from postcolonialism to "postgender" to "post-Marxism," connote that somehow the kinds of inequality imbedded in concepts of colonialism, gender, and class have been transcended, along with the political projects that they informed. Interestingly, questions of gender and class are increasingly interpolated into a "difference" marked by ethnicity, even as ethnicity as a principle of identity is co-opted by a supposed "multiculturalism" that, viewed in reverse from class and gender perspectives, "appears more than anything as an expression of intraclass struggles for self-assertion within a dominant class that now includes women and people of color."[24] By appropriating alternative historical trajectories into the spatiality of a globalized capitalism, moreover, multiculturalism also precludes the imagination of alternative futures to that of capitalism. The reassertion of historicity, and of alternative historical trajectories, therefore, becomes essential to the struggle against the hegemony of capital that nourishes the reification and commodification of cultures even as it admits into domain the previously excluded to create a sexually and ethnically more heterogeneous global ruling class. This concern appears in many of the chapters.

These attitudes toward contemporary theoretical and political problems are also relevant to understanding the ways in which the writers position themselves on questions concerning historical discipline. Chapter 4 by Abou-El-Haj, dealing with West Asian and North African studies, sets an appropriate framework in dividing the historians into two groups. One group includes those who reproduce old hegemonic paradigms without taking into account the changed global picture. The second group, taking "clues from postmodern and/or postcolonial discourses, seems to be willing agents of dead-end scholarship and nihilism," Abou-El-Haj writes. The ramifications of such historiographies are fleshed out in chapter 2 by Dirlik.

Historians on the whole have been resistant to reconsidering the problems of history in light of a new global situation and the new theoretical alternatives it has generated. Chapter 3 by Patterson shows that archaeologists and historians are in fact avoiding the use of theories consciously and are proud of their ignorance even though they steal from one another ideas and tools for the interpretation of their evidence and data. Dirlik, in chapter 6, identifies a group of historians from China who go so far as to deny the paradigms that guide their research even as they express suspicion of paradigms (and theory). Chapter 5 by Bahl makes note of Indian historians who disavow theory even as they continue to search for an untainted indigenous Indian culture.

Abou-El-Haj's chapter, linking craft with worldview, identifies four specific tendencies in scholarship within the field of West Asian and North African studies that have emerged since 1978. The first tendency has "an informing theory but is unable to muster the means" to test it and therefore "resort to secondary works." The second tendency "refuses to view history as a discourse or process" yet uses theory as a formula and fits evidence into an already given structure. These historians possess some language tools and have the potential capacity for testing their theories. But the problem for them is that they treat their sources as evidence without social bias. The third tendency is either outright Orientalist or neo-Orientalist. "The neo-Orientalist group, in spite of Sa'id's critique, continues to treat culture and Islam mainly in essentialist terms" while priding itself on its philological prowess. It is more thorough in the use of indigenous sources than were the Orientalist of yore but it is at core still made up of "empiricists who prefer their own unconscious theories to the latest theoretical or paradigmatic approaches in the social sciences." The fourth tendency adopts a postmodernist or a postcolonialist focus on culture and does not take into account the social context for its production. It ignores thereby the steps needed in setting up a research agenda for the study of colonial culture.[25]

Such groupings are not unique to West Asian and North African studies; indeed, it is possible to find parallels in the study of most of the countries of the world. Cooper (Africa), Mallon (Latin America), Dirlik (China), Bahl (India), and Patterson (archeology and history) also trace the development of different schools of historiography in their respective areas of study and many appear to overlap with each other and with those noted by Abou-El-Haj. Nevertheless, the authors handle the historiographies differently, in accordance with the different problem constellations that mark different historiographies. Some approach historical questions through the rise and fall of dominant paradigms. Cooper, for example, traces the history of different historical approaches in Africa from colonialist to nationalist to dependency school to Marxism, and finally to a growing recognition of the similarity of Africa's predicament to that of other Third World countries. In recent years, a few African historians have experimented with postmodernist and Subaltern Studies approaches, though Africanists in general have not found them useful in explaining the history of that continent.

Mallon also shows how Latin American scholars have used liberation theology, dependency models, and Marxist models and now are experimenting with Subaltern Studies type of historiography, mixed with a heavy dose of postmodern and postcolonial theories. Bahl shows much the same for Indian historiography. She traces the link of Subaltern Studies to the other main versions of history—colonialist, nationalist, secularist, Marxist, and now postmodernist. Dirlik covers the same ground for China, showing the rise of modernistic and neo-orthodox approaches against the earlier orthodox Marxist domination of Chinese historiography. Their experience with a state-enforced orthodoxy has made Chinese historians suspicious of paradigms, and yet this has resulted in an uncritical and articulated reassertion of paradigms that implicitly guide historical work, that resonate both with the ideological effects of China's incorporation into a global capitalism, and a chauvinistic response to the effects of the latter. Hence celebrations of Chinese tradition in facilitating capitalism are coupled with the reemergence of old mythologies. These trends also combine to erase the history of the modern revolution in China. Effects of contemporary theories are visible most prominently among nonprofessional historians, especially those of a literary bent.

Patterson shows how the concept of civilization emerged in nineteenth-century Europe, how it has been uncritically accepted by archaeologists and historians, and how scholars deploying such concepts as civilization have been able to accommodate the changing fashions of theory—postmodernism being a contemporary example—without ever abandoning their general conservative conformism to their respective fields.

Abou-El-Haj uses Edward Sa'id's *Orientalism* (New York: Pantheon Books, 1978) and Timothy Mitchell's recent book, *Colonizing Egypt* (Berkeley, 1988), to offer a critique of prevailing historiography in West Asian and North African studies. Cooper does it by taking on Subaltern Studies as well as postmodernism in the context of African historiography, as Bahl does for India.

The overall perspective that informs the critique of all the contributors in this volume is that postmodernist and postcolonialist (also now joined by the Subalternist Studies school) approaches are not able to achieve what they claim to in terms of emancipation from the mainstream approaches of the past. Instead they reinforce older projects, such as *Orientalism*. There is thus a need to create a new research agenda that will help us to move further ahead. Our proposal for a new agenda differs from the new group of historians that recently split from the American Historical Association.

A few years ago, Dirlik pointed out in an essay that postcolonialism represented the adjustment of Third World intellectuals to a new global power situation.[26] To illustrate this point in the realm of historiography, chapter 3 by Patterson, which is essentially on Western social science history, explores the implications of the technical division of labor between archaeologists searching for lost cities and historians searching for towns in archives. Patterson shows how both groups share similar concerns and even similar misconceptions. The major concern of both the archaeologist and the historian is the rise of civilization. In either case, a technical division of labor that emerged in the nineteenth century continues to guide research. Historians and archeologists both find it convenient to leave unexamined their most fundamental assumption, notably, that the real revolution in human history was that of writing, a phenomenon to which they point with great confidence as a boundary marker that separates something called prehistory from history. As Patterson writes, the two groups overlook the fact that literacy and writing always developed in particular societies and political contexts shaped by processes associated with class and state formation involving conquest abroad and repression at home. And both historians and archeologists prefer their theory implicit. It leaves unquestioned the meaning of civilization. Patterson then asks the question: Who stands to gain by this scholarship in the present time? His answer is that archaeologists and historians, by ignoring their theoretical premises, become complicit in the ruling-class agenda.

Extending on Patterson's concerns, Abou-El-Haj's chapter 4 deals with different groups of historians in West Asian and North African studies. Abou-El-Haj, however, begins with an account of the one book of real renown emanating from the postmodernist tradition, Sa'id's *Orientalism*. Abou-El-Haj points out that if *Orientalism* is to serve as a standard for history, then the "standard itself is a problem because Sa'id adopted an approach to scholarly literature which he himself criticized in other people. Orientalists read their texts in an unproblematized and unmediated manner as Sa'id often said; Sa'id, however, did the same." *Orientalism*

remains an ahistorical treatment of the orientalist scholarship that it seeks to criticize. Therefore, the question arises: What is the social utility of such projects, and
how do contemporary societies benefit from it? Abou-El-Haj alludes to another
area of weakness in Sa'id's approach, when he further points out that the analyses
of the scholarship of earlier writers should also be focused on the question of the
social uses to which this work was put by its contemporaries, because there are different motives, functions, and purposes in time and circumstances for every set of
scholarly productions. Abou-El-Haj thus contends that alternative approaches have
to be offered to replace the old scholarship of *Orientalism* but, as he also suggests,
"these do not have to be monolithic" final strategies. It would suffice if they could
provide a basis from which to critique future and existing research programs and
paradigms. In reflecting on the research carried out since *Orientalism*, Abou-El-Haj
suggests that most of the scholars in his field have "ceased to accommodate [the]
new social, economic, and political realities" and are proud of this fact.

Interestingly, Abou-El-Haj's concerns are not just a phenomenon in West Asian
and North African studies. Dirlik reaches similar conclusions about the direction or
at least the results of recent history writing in China. The crisis in Chinese historiography, he writes, can be connected with the intellectual crisis created by the
changes in China's historical development that in turn are bound up with changes
that are global in scope. The victory of modernization has rendered irrelevant
concepts, such as imperialism, Third World, or class, that were an integral part of
the analysis of modern Chinese history so long as the paradigm of revolution was
plausible.

Dirlik writes that during the revolution in China, the goal was to complete the
project of national formation and to disengage China from the world capitalist
economy. Today, it is capitalism that has abandoned in theory and in practice the
idea of the national economy as an autonomous unit, but instead proclaims the
necessity of internationalization or globalization as a condition of development. It
is possible, Dirlik writes, that our current view "of modern Chinese history is
shaped not by any development from within professional historical scholarship but
by this contemporary consciousness, which then projects upon the history of this
consciousness, as the revolutionary paradigm did earlier, without regard for
whether the present is structurally different from earlier phases of Chinese modernity." Whatever the case, Chinese historians today seem to think that there is no
paradigmatic assumption underlying their work. This leaves one skeptical. Silent
about their own conditions, are they not likely to "become complicit in the ideology of a contemporary developmentalism"? Is China-centeredness not a way to
render history useless for any real movement of change?

Dirlik's sentiments in connection with Chinese historiography are echoed in
chapters 5, 7, and 8, which deal with the Subaltern Studies school that originated in
India, including its rise in India and its integration in recent years into the Western
mode propagated by postmodernism and postcolonialism. Bahl's chapter situates

the Subaltern Studies school in its Indian context while assessing its contribution, especially to Indian working-class history. She includes the earlier critiques of Subaltern Studies writings and later challenges these writings and their supposedly liberating politics while discussing the issues of differences, agency, and empowerment. She asks: What should ex-colonial people do while waiting for the Subaltern Studies group to clean history of the colonial impact? Moreover, if this history can be cleaned, will the ex-colonial people really be able to achieve liberation after getting rid of the Western impact? Do ex-colonials live in a vacuum in which they can preserve their purity in a similar way to preserving the purity of food ingredients? Bahl raises these questions without overlooking the fact that culture and differences are as important to consider as the broader context of historical capitalism while understanding the history of people and society at large in modern times.

Chapter 7, by Cooper, is a critique of the Subaltern Studies school from within African historiography. Subaltern Studies, like much of traditional African history, Cooper finds, is simply reproducing the dichotomy of the colonizer and the colonized that has plagued the field for a long time. Both the colonizer and the colonized abuse such terms as resistance, terms that rarely ever get defined. In light of what has gone before, Cooper suggests that Subaltern Studies should concentrate more on the analysis of state and capital and abandon its attacks on metanarrative and modernity if it is to advance the study of Africa.

From the 1970s, Cooper notes, Africanists grew disillusioned with nationalist approaches and found Latin American dependency theory more useful, because it emphasized a wider range of determinants of economic and social problems. From using dependency theory, Africanists also became aware of Marxist approaches, in the process becoming more informed about the commonly shared features of the capitalist world system. Where the subalternists stress the importance of studying the unique authenticity of the community, Africanists are skeptical of "community" both for the reasons just given as well as because communities are in the process of killing one another off. Relationships, Cooper emphasizes, are complicated and cannot be reduced simply to difference. A port worker may work not just to seek European wages or to fight colonialism, but also to establish autonomy from his father, just as his wife may well have been acting within the urban commercial sector to attain a measure of autonomy from him. In this process they are remaking institutions as they use them. Subalternity does not satisfactorily categorize the experience of such people.

Cooper suggests "we should move beyond treating modernity, liberalism, citizenship or bourgeois equality as if they were fixed and self-contained doctrines unaffected by the appropriations and reformulatilons given to them by processes of political mobilization in Asia, Africa or Europe itself." Cooper maintains that Africa's crisis derives from a complex history that demands a complex analysis. Within such complex analysis the idea of "Provincializing Europe" will need a detailed and nuanced engagement with the vagaries of European history. But the argument is weakened when it slips into blanket dismissals of liberalism or assumptions that bourgeois equality is an unchanging construct.

Mallon raises the question of the alternatives available to progressive scholars in the face of recent changes in chapter 8. For some Latin American progressive scholars, the answer was Subaltern Studies. Mallon, however, finds Subaltern Studies problematic, because it leaves open the possibility for a reconstruction of a hegemonic postcolonial political order far more than it suggests change or emancipation. From a scientific point of view, the Latin American involvement with Subaltern Studies involved too much simplification. The original complex arguments of Ranjit Guha (the founder of Subaltern Studies), which involved methodological as well as political calls to action, are reduced by Latin Americanists to a project of recovering the cultural and political specificity of peasant insurrections. As Mallon points out, the subaltern project is defined as involving two techniques, first that of "identifying the logic of the distortions in the representation of the subaltern in official or elite culture," and second, that of "uncovering the social semiotics of the strategies and cultural practices of peasant insurgencies themselves." Mallon suggests that subaltern studies is thus being reduced to half of its complexity with the use of methods and techniques offered by postmodernism. That is why all the specificity of the Latin American Subaltern Studies' essays revolve around artistic and literary movements. As Mallon notes, "no wonder there is a 'poverty of historiography'" both on the side of Latin America and of Subaltern Studies. Furthermore, she adds that by reading existing documents "against the grain" and only against the grain, these scholars have moved away from history, perhaps to literature.

Mallon points out that the processes of production and preservation of archival versus published sources are distinct. The social relations that accompany the reading of the one and the other are also different. Mallon objects to the placing of textual analysis and literary source over the archival source and over fieldwork, as well as the tendency to assume that, because both are constructed texts, they can be substituted for each other. She states that ever-shifting alliances or confrontations are not deduced from specific, already existing subaltern identities of subject positions. They are constructed historically and politically, in struggle and in discourse. Furthermore, she asks: "Who gets to answer the question: 'Are we there yet?'" Why is it possible to gloss over hierarchies internal to the subaltern community? The work of Subaltern Studies scholars and others makes clear, "it is easy to privilege one tradition over another and to retire from the challenge of the contradiction between the two."

She thinks that the theoretical and methodological contradiction between Gramscian hegemonic politics and Foucauldian regimes of decentered power is great and can sometimes make research and analysis close to impossible. Referring to Gyan Prakash's observation (in a forum on Subaltern Studies in *American Historical Review* 1994) that the difficulty of this combination does not justify a mandate to choose between the two sides, Mallon suggests Subaltern Studies could take other possible directions as well as maintain the tension between the two no matter what.

Concluding chapters 9 and 10 by Prazniak and Dirlik address the contemporary ferment in the United States over the rewriting of history. Prazniak evaluates critically the claims of new world or global histories to overcome Eurocentrism in historical writing. Tracing the unfolding of Western civilization and world history teaching in the United States, Prazniak argues that these alternative modes of history have been implicated throughout in considerations of U.S. power. Rather than overcome Eurocentrism, world or global history as we have it seeks to contain the world by ruling out alternative ways of knowing and constructing the past. In chapter 10, on the other hand, Dirlik considers the challenge of new conceptualizations of the past to claims to historical truth. Associated broadly, if somewhat misleadingly, with the postmodern turn in historical studies, these challenges have forced new ways of thinking about the past. If the contemporary crisis in historical thinking is to be overcome, he suggests, rather than ignore these challenges, historians need to think through the problems they present to comprehend the past in more complex ways.

The old contact zones presented Euro-Americans with a choice between civilizing mission and dissolution into "barbarism." The new contact zones present intellectuals of Third World origin with a choice between "bridging" cultures and burning the bridges. The postcolonial rush to culture is an escape from building bridges. Postcolonialism finally is not just a matter of class, it is also a matter of a class relocated to the centers of capital. What has changed is location. In the new contact zones that serve as sites of negotiation, cultural differences may be asserted while sharing in the powers of the centers. Not surprisingly, today it is a new generation of "Third Worlders" firmly established in the structures of Eurocentric power who now speak for the societies from which they hail, while those back home are condemned to inaudibility or parochialism.

Thus at the end of the twentieth century there is a crisis in historical consciousness. As Dirlik writes in chapter 2, "We need a reaffirmation of history and historicity at this moment of crisis in historical consciousness. . . . It might serve at least to clarify the ways in which the present uses and abuses the past, and it might serve as a reminder of our own historicity. . . . It may be impossible . . . to think of spaces without at the same time thinking of the times that produced those spaces."

NOTES

1. *New York Times,* 22 June 1997. Paul Elins also points out that more than fifteen million children die each year as a result of poverty. Paul Elins, *A New World Order: Grassroots Movements for Global Change* (London: Routledge, 1992)

2. Sergei Kapitza, a prominent Soviet scientist, writing at the time of the breaking up of the former Soviet Union, points out that such tendencies had emerged in the past histories

of European countries at times of crisis. He traces the reasons underlying the current surge in the superstitions, cults, and antitechnological protests in his country, connecting it to seventeenth-century Europe. He writes:

A development in science, the emergence of capitalism and world trade, the decline of the authority of church and monarchy all happened in Europe at the same time. On all counts it was the great perestroika of Europe, the Reformation, with a [thirty]-year war—which ran on for most of the century. During this upheaval, superstitions of all kinds flourished . . . reportedly [fifty thousand] witches were burned alive or drowned, more than any other time. . . . The end of a millennium of medieval ideology and a way of life did not pass without these painful indications of social unrest and insecurity. On a lesser scale we see them reappearing in mesmerism before the French Revolution and in spiritualism and scientific superstitions during the profound and rapid changes in European society preceding World War I. . . . The extent to which outward manifestations of irrationality are socially indicative is also illustrated by the hippies in the [United States] at the time of the Vietnam War. . . . Superstitions, cults and mysticism appear with surprising consistency during a social crisis. Today it is ESP and UFOs, astrology and clairvoyance, mystic cults and mesmeric healers. The growth of interest in such things is a sure indicator of social unrest, personal uneasiness, frustration and loss of purpose. These symptoms are present in the West, particularly in the [United States] where they are more chronic: in the Soviet Union, however, we have an acute fever. . . . There is a strong correlation of antiscience and antitechnology trends with publications on sex, violence and extreme social ideas, such as rampant nationalism and fascism. . . . The regression into mythology in no way signals a new-science, an alternative science as some desire. . . . The authority of science is based on the power of the scientific method and resides in proof by experiment rather than by pronouncements of the learned or the vote of the people. . . . In the natural science, do we not now see a persistent craving for a mechanistic approach in our computer modeling, which promises to lead to magical insights, to forecasting and to resolving the complexities of the world? . . . At present, the limitations of human intelligence seem to be greater than the expectation of aid from an artificial one. We should keep in mind that social theory is much more demanding and complex intellectually than all our physics.

He stated that in 1991, the United States had fifteen thousand astrologers and only fifteen hundred astronomers. One can easily guess the implications of these numbers. Sergei Kapitza, "Antiscience Trends in the USSR," *Scientific American,* vol. 265, no 2 (August 1991).

3. Michael Specter, "World, Wide, Web: 3 English Words," *New York Times,* 14 April 1996, pp. E1, E5.

4. This reinterpretation's most interesting aspect is its effect on the lives of Western managers. *Times of India* (29 March 1996, Bombay) quotes from *The Times:* "Buddhist techniques are being introduced to the [c]ity of London by management consultants. Standard Chartered Bank has decided to teach its executives Japanese Kaizen teamwork and continuous self-appraisal. . . . This new Zen Buddhist method of motivating managers may triumph yet." On the other end, Japanese managers are joining monasteries for the weekend to learn how to relax and remain spiritually in touch with themselves. At the workplace, Japanese management is increasing productivity by using incense (Isabel Forsang, *New York Times,* 31 July

1992) and other subliminal methods to keep workers' moods pleasant while increasing productivity. The U.S. business community has devoted vast amounts of research funds to discover how to use subliminal messages through different types of music at different times of the day to induce customers to buy more. Using music and subliminal messages is a thriving industry now in the United States. In the wake of this development, is it possible to draw a line and claim indigenous identities without confusing it with capitalist market relationship?

5. *New York Times,* 22 June 1997. For more information on the inevitability of increased sweatshops in poor countries during and after the Asian economic crisis, see Nicholas D. Kristof, "Asia's Crisis Upsetting Effort to Reduce Sweatshop Blight," *New York Times,* 15 June 1998.

6. See an interesting survey of such literature by Patrick Wolfe, *American Historical Review* (April 1997).

7. W. Wayt Gibbs, "Lost Science in the Third World," *Scientific American* (August 1995).

8. See elaborate critiques of these issues in Daya Krishna, "New World Order and Indian Intellectuals," *Economic and Political Weekly* (hereafter EPW) (14 January 1995); Nirmal Sengupta, "Salvaging 'Traditional' Knowledges," *EPW* (16 December 1995); Suman Sahai, "Importance of Indigeneous Knowledge in IPR System," *EPW* (23 November 1996). Such arguments also inform the writings and activities of prominent intellectuals such as Ashish Nandy and Vandana Shiva.

9. This point is substantiated in the book *The Underdevelopment of Development: Essays in Honour of Andre Gunder Frank,* edited by Sing C. Chew and Robert A. Denmark (Thousand Oaks, CA: Sage Publications, 1996). One reviewer of the book comments, "This approach is the recent co-optation of the Western left with the neo-populism." G. K. Lieten "From Neo-Marxism to Neo-Populism," *EPW* (26 July 1997). He further points out that in this book "the idea of capitalism as a distinct system is rejected lock, stock and barrel." The editor of the book writes, "The call is to abandon the concept of capitalism as a distinct mode of production . . . and of transition between modes because these constructs are viewed as obstacles to understanding the essential unity of the world system that has existed for at least five thousand years." Lieten notes that words "imperialism" and "multinationals" hardly figure in the book. Instead, a "humanocentric" alternative to Eurocentrism is offered. It also omitted "class" from the long list of the multiple minorities that are making up the majority that is in line with commitment to "new social movements as the harbinger of a better world." Lieten seems to be correct in pointing out that [these] "authors . . . have ridden with the neo-Marxist view of the late 1960s and 1970s and . . . have now driven with the wave of neo-populism at various points aligning with post-modernism" (p. 1892). It is pertinent to note that while Andre Gunder Frank today is denying the existence of capital, another neo-Marxist scholar of the same generation, Giovanni Arrighi, has denied the existence of labor while writing about capital. Giovanni Arrighi, *The Long Twentieth Century* (New York: Verso, 1994).

10. M. Waters, *Globalization* (London: Routledge, 1995). See also J. Petras and Chronis Polychroniou, "Critical Reflections on Globalisation," *EPW* (6 September 1997). These two authors suggest, "Social movements working for radical change must reject the sharp distinction between state and civil society as they no longer exist . . . as well as the ideology of 'identity politics' and multicultural lifestyle politics—phenomena more akin to contemporary capital than to its subversion. The challenge to the competitiveness ideology must grow from the solidarity of competent and productive forms of social [organization], not from the escapist yuppie leisure culture nor from utopian intellectual nostalgia for countercultural styles."

11. Michael Geyer and Charles Bright, "World History in a Global Age," *American Historical Review* (October 1995). In this article, Geyer and Bright give a survey of the literature that avoids, or twists, the concept of "world history" according to their individual agenda. They suggest that silence against the world of "multiple modernities and globality needed to be broken by thinking and narrating the history of this existing world and how it has come about." Furthermore, they write "the promise and challenge of the twentieth century as an age of world historical transition that, in forging a world in which 'humanity' has become a pragmatic reality with a common destiny, we do not arrive at the end of history. World history has just begun" (p. 1060).

12. Jan P. Nederveen Pieterse, *Empire and Emancipation: Power and Liberation on a World Scale* (New York: Praeger, 1989), p. 52.

13. Gregory Bruce Smith, *Nietzsche, Heidegger and the Transition to Postmodernity* (Chicago: University of Chicago Press, 1996), p. 15.

14. See Jan Nederveen Pieterse, "Unpacking the West: How European Is Europe?" in Ali Rattansi and Sallie Westwood (eds.), *Racism, Modernity and Identity: On the Western Front* (Cambridge, Mass.: Polity Press, 1994).

15. A computer company has sued an employee for not writing down his ideas on the paper because, according to the job contract, the company owns all the ideas (as labor and labor power used to be under the manufacturing system) of its employees until they leave the job. The employee claims that his idea was formulated outside his job time. (Reported on CNBC evening business report.) Many students reported that such statements are now routinely part of the new job contracts, especially in the field of information industry.

16. *New York Times* 1 June 1997. For an eye-opener analysis of the diploma-mill industry, see David Noble, "Selling Academe to the Technology Industry," *Thought and Action* vol. 14, no. 1 (Spring 1998).

17. For an extensive discussion, see Arif Dirlik, "The Postmodernization of Production and Its Organization: Flexible Production, Work and Culture," in Arif Dirlik, *The Postcolonial Aura: Third World Criticism in the Age of Global Capitalism* (Boulder, CO: Westview Press, 1997), p. 186–219.

18. Howard Winant, "Racial Formation and Hegemony: Global and Local Developments," in Ali Rattansi and Sallie Westwood (eds.), *Racism, Modernity and Identity: On the Western Front* (Cambridge, Mass.: Polity Press, 1994).

19. The discussion here is based on Bjorn Hettene, *Development Theory and the Three Worlds* (New York: Longman, 1990).

20. Jan N. Pietrese, *Empire and Emancipation: Power and Liberation on a World Scale* (New York: Praeger, 1989), p. 68. In fact, recently various journals have started asking similar questions; see for example *Science and Society* (Spring 1997); *Radical History Review,* issues from 1995 and 1997; *American Historical Review,* since 1994 and more recently in April 1997; *Social Text* (Spring 1996); and *Gender and History* (April 1997). See especially Alan Sokal, "Transgression Boundaries: Towards a Transformative Hermeneutics of Quantum Gravity," *Social Text* (Summer 1996). Alan Sokal, "A Physicist Experiments with Cultural Studies," *Lingua Franca* 1996. Alan Sokal, "Truth, Reason, Objectivity and the Left," *Economic and Political Weekly* 16 (18–24 April 1998).

21. Salman Rushdie, "Damme, This Is the Oriental Scene for You," *The New Yorker* (23–30 June 1997).

22. Linda Gordon has observed recently a similar attitude in traditional historical fields within the United States toward previously ignored people's history. She wrote, "Those who do the history of previously ignored people must remain informed and current about traditional historical fields, but those who do traditional history are under no such obligation to go outside their specialties . . . and most male graduate students learn that doing so (including gender issues in their writings) is disadvantageous in the job market." "Race, Gender and Painful Transformation in the Field of American History," *The Chronicle of Higher Education* (11 July 1997).

23. For further discussion, see Arif Dirlik, *After the Revolution: Waking to Global Capitalism* (Hanover and London: Wesleyan University Press, 1994), especially pp. 8–15 and 100–105.

24. Another dimension to gender questions relating to feminism, which fits with recent trends in general, is that in its third wave in the United States, what has kept some women in feminism and identifying with it is "pleasure," and not ideology or debate on employment rights, abortion, child care, and whether feminism serves women of color. Lisa Jones, *Bulletproof Diva: Tales of Race, Sex and Hair* (New York: Doubleday, 1994). Jennifer Drake also points out that these "power [and pleasure] feminists . . . [do] not really understand how power works and [do] not recognize its own complicities. It has been co-opted by the media and labeled as the 'new' feminism because it shores up competitive individualism, the American work ethic, consumerism and catfighting all in feminism's name." She writes, "One task for Third Wave feminism is . . . clarify[ing] the connection between different forms of yearning, including the yearning to live [in] a more just world." Jennifer Drake, "Review Essay: Third Wave Feminisms," *Feminist Studies* 23, no. 1 (Spring 1997). Similar concerns are also raised in Vinay Bahl, "Cultural Imperialism and Women's Movements: Thinking Globally," *Gender and History* (April 1997).

On the issue of class in relation to gender inequality, Rosalinda Mendez Ganzalez explains why women's subjectivity cannot be understood without the class concept: "Women of the poor, slaves, or laboring classes do not tend to leave diaries. . . . To recapture the personal experience as Indian, Hispanic, black, Asian, and poor white women of the laboring classes, to find a conceptual interpretation of these diverse personal experiences, we must address the objective conditions of Western life. . . . [We] frequently forget that the position of the one is maintained only through the exploitation of the other and that such a relationship leaves little concrete room for sisterhood. [There is thus a] . . . gulf between the experiences of women of different classes. . . . To see through the eyes of the women on the bottom is to see not only the lives of the vast majority, but also to look upward through all levels of society; the flaws and contradictions of the upper classes and the social structure they maintain become exposed from this perspective." "Distinctions in Western Women's Experience: Ethnicity, Class and Social Change," in Laurel Richardson and Vera Taylor (eds.), *Feminist Frontiers III* (New York: McGraw Hill, 1993).

25. Eugene D. Genovese writes in a similar vein in his book *The Southern Frontier: History and Politics of Cultural War* (Columbia: University of Missouri Press, 1995), pp. 7–8. "Yes, our scholarly work, especially on subjects as explosive as slavery and racism, has an inescapable political implication, some of which may, however, contradict our intentions. Yes, a historian has the duty to make those implications clear. But, simultaneously, he has the duty to resist the imposition of his politics on the empirical record. Or to put it another

2

Is There History after Eurocentrism? Globalism, Postcolonialism, and the Disavowal of History

Arif Dirlik

Ours would seem to be another age of paradoxes. Localization accompanies globalization; cultural homogenization is challenged by insistence on cultural heterogeneity; denationalization is more than matched by ethnicization. Capitalism at its moment of victory over socialism finds itself wondering about different cultures of capitalism at odds with one another. There is a preoccupation with history at a time when history seems to be increasingly irrelevant to understanding the present. Worked over by postmodernism, among other things, the past itself seems to be up for grabs, as though it can be made to say anything we want it to say.

This chapter focuses on yet another one of these paradoxes: that of Eurocentrism. The repudiation of Eurocentrism in intellectual and cultural life seems to be such an obvious necessity that it may seem odd to speak of it as a paradox. Yet a good case can be made that Eurocentrism, too, has come under scrutiny and criticism at the very moment of its global victory. Whether we see the ultimate victory or the impending demise of Eurocentrism depends on what we understand by it, and where we locate it. The widespread assumption in our day that Eurocentrism may be spoken or written away rests on a reductionist-culturalist understanding of Eurocentrism. Rendering Eurocentrism into a cultural phenomenon that leaves unquestioned other locations for it distracts attention from crucial ways in which Eurocentrism may help determine a present that claims liberation from the past's hold on it. What is at issue is modernity, with all its complex constituents, of which Eurocentrism was the formative moment. Just as modernity is incomprehensible without reference to Eurocentrism, Eurocentrism as a concept is specifiable only within the context of modernity. Rather than define Eurocentrism from the outset, therefore, I seek to contextualize it in order to restore to it—and the many arguments against it—some sense of historicity.

If Eurocentrism is crucial to thinking modernity, we need to raise the question of whether it may be repudiated without a simultaneous disavowal of history. The question necessitates confrontation of Eurocentrism as a historical phenomenon against the background of other "centrisms"; in other words, the ways in which Euro-American production, dissemination, and domination of modernity differs in its values and processes from earlier forms of domination, such as "Sinocentrism." It is also necessary, in assessing Eurocentrism as a historical problem, to take account of earlier critiques of Eurocentrism. This latter is crucial especially to accounting for the historicity of contemporary critiques of Eurocentrism, both in terms of their relationship to the past and their relationship to contemporary configurations of power.

[I conclude that a radical critique of Eurocentrism must rest on a radical critique of the whole project of modernity understood in terms of the life-world, which is cultural and material at once] Modernity in our day is not just Euro-American, but is dispersed globally, if not equally or uniformly, in transnational structures of various kinds, in ideologies of development, and the practices of everyday life. It does not just emanate from a Euro-America that is understood geographically, nor are the agencies necessarily Euro-American in origin. A radical critique of Eurocentrism, in other words, must confront contemporary questions of globalism and post-colonialism and return analysis to the locations of contemporary struggles over the life-world. It should be noted that the critique of Eurocentrism is a diffuse characteristic of all kinds of critiques of power, from feminist to racial. On occasion, it seems as if the problems of the world would be solved if somehow we got rid of Eurocentrism. This, of course, is silly. It not only misses much about Eurocentrism; it ignores even more about the rest of the world. Not the least of what it ignores is that, while the agencies located in Euro-America may be the promoters of Eurocentrism, they are by now not the only ones, and possibly not the most important ones. Eurocentrism may not be global destiny, but it is a problem that needs to be confronted by any serious thinking about global destinies. These problems are too serious to be left in the hands of elites to whom Eurocentrism is an issue of identity in intra-elite struggles for power.

EUROCENTRISM: WHAT AND WHERE?

At one level, what Eurocentrism is and where it is located is sufficiently straightforward. Eurocentrism is crucial to understanding the spatialities and temporalities of modernity, not just in Euro-America but globally, from at least the late nineteenth century. [The spatial conceptualizations around which we have organized history—from nations to areas to continents and oceans to the Third World and beyond—are in a fundamental sense implicated in a Eurocentric modernity.] Even more powerful may be the reworking of temporalities by a Eurocentric conceptualization of the world, where the particular historical trajectory of Euro-American societies was to end up as a worldwide teleology in marking time. This was enunciated "theoretically" in the social sciences by the discourse of modernization, in its bourgeois as well as Marxist formulations. History itself, as Nicholas Dirks puts it succinctly, is "a sign of the modern."[1] For the last century, but especially since World War II, Eurocentrism has been the informing principle in our constructions of history; not just in Euro-American historiography, but in the spatial and temporal assumptions of dominant historiographies worldwide. Euro-Americans conquered the world; renamed places; rearranged economies, societies, and politics; and erased or drove to the margins premodern ways of knowing space, time, and many other things as well. In the process, they universalized history in their own self-image in an unprecedented manner. Crucial to this self-image was the European Enlightenment's establishment of a paradigm of the rational humanist subject as the subject of history. Armed with reason and science, they conquered time and space in the name of universal reason, reorganized societies to bring them within the realm of rationality, and subjugated alternative historical trajectories to produce a universal history ever moving forward to fulfill the demands of human progress. The paradigm rendered the Euro-American experience of history into the fate of humankind, which then could serve as the rationalization for the pain let loose upon the world by its transformative aspirations.

Let us ignore for the moment an immediate objection to such an account of Eurocentrism: that it recapitulates an ideological Eurocentrism worthy of a most unreconstructed Eurocentrist. There is no recognition in this account of the incoherence of Eurocentrism as a historical phenomenon, because it is oblivious to the historicity of Eurocentrism as well as to the contradictions that both made dynamic its history and limited its claims.

Culture and discourse would seem to be the most popular choices of location in contemporary answers to Eurocentrism, represented most prominently by postcolonialism and globalism.[2] While quite different, and perhaps even antithetical in their appreciation of the relationship of the present world situation to the past, postcolonialism and globalism would seem to be at one in their attitudes toward the location of Eurocentrism, or a Eurocentric modernity, which may account for their confounding by some cultural critics. The differences are deeply methodological and historical.

Methodologically speaking, postcolonialism in its most popular forms (in the United States, at least) eschews questions of the structurations of the world in terms of "foundational categories" and stresses local encounters in the formation of identities; it is in many ways driven by a radical methodological individualism and is situationist in its historical explanations.

Globalism, on the other hand, draws attention to the structurations of the world by forces that operate at the highest level of abstraction and, in some of its versions, finds in such abstraction the reaffirmation of the scientific promises of social theory.

Equally interesting may be their differences in the relationships they posit between the present and the past. Armed with the insights of the present, postcolonialists proceed to reinterpret the past with those very same insights. In this perspective, Eurocentrism, rather than having shaped history, appears to have been an ideological cover thrown over the past to disguise the complexity of local interactions; postcolonialism then offers a way to discover the past in its true complexity, more often than not expressed in the idea of "hybridity." In contrast to this presentist colonization of the past, globalism proclaims a "rupture" between a "present condition of globality and its many possible pasts."[3] Its consciousness is one of totality that must be distinguished from similar consciousnesses of earlier periods; what it does, however, is to deny to Eurocentrism its claims to the creation of such a totality ("its many pasts") and opens up the possibility that the Others of Euro-America may have been partners in its creation.

While I have no wish to reduce intellectual orientations that claim no coherence for themselves to one or another of their articulations, the differences mentioned above are illustrated through two statements by those who have gained some reputation as spokespeople of postcolonialism and globalism, respectively.[4] The editors of several influential volumes on postcolonial criticism write that:

> European imperialism took various forms in different times and places and proceeded both through conscious planning and contingent occurrences. As a result of this complex development something occurred for which the *plan* of imperial expansion had not bargained: the immensely prestigious and powerful imperial culture found itself appropriated in projects of counter-colonial resistance that drew upon the many indigenous and local hybrid *processes* of self-determination to defy, erode, and sometimes supplant the prodigious power of imperial cultural knowledge. Postcolonial literatures are a result of this interaction between imperial culture and the complex of indigenous cultural practices. As a consequence, postcolonial theory has existed for a long time before that particular name was used to describe it.[5] (Emphases in the original.)

Postcolonialism then is merely the current expression of forms of knowledge that have been around for a long time, except that there was no consciousness of it earlier. That those who are convinced of the discursive construction of knowledge should be oblivious to the positivistic implications of such an assertion is nothing short of remarkable.

By contrast, advocates of globalism leave no doubt about the break they seek to accomplish between the present and the past, including a break between a present condition and the factors that may have brought about such a condition. Roland Robertson, an enthusiastic advocate of globalization of social theory, writes:

> I argue that systematic comprehension of the macrostructuration of world order is essential to the viability of any form of contemporary theory and that such comprehension must involve *analytical separation of the factors which have facilitated the shift towards*

a single world—e.g., the spread of capitalism, western imperialism, and the development of a global media system—from the general and global agency-structure (and/or culture) theme. While the empirical relationship between the two sets of issues is of great importance (and, of course, complex), conflation of them leads us into all sorts of difficulties and inhibits our ability to come to terms with *the basic and shifting terms* of the contemporary world order.[6] (First emphasis is mine.)

The projects of postcolonialism and globalism are prima facie antithetical: the one repudiating all structurations but the local, the other aiming to uncover global structures; the one situationally historicist, the other seeing in complex empirical relations an obstacle to the formulation of grand theories; the one reenvisioning the past, the other proclaiming a break with it.

⌈And yet they stand to one another in the relationship of the local to the global and share in common a desire to break down the boundaries (or structures) that may intervene between the two.⌋ In the phraseology of one author who seeks to reconcile postcolonialism and globalism:

> [O]ne essential, underlying truth must be pointed out. Most of these peripheral post-modern effects and claims I have been recording stem directly from decomposition, under the contemporary phase of globalization, of the two fundamental assumptions of the three worlds theory. . . . The cultural borders authorized/enforced under that theory yield to perception of cultural interpenetration and transgression as the normal state in both the demystified past and the avant-garde present. And the evolutionary timeline along which the three worlds theory ranks cultures is cut up into discontinuously segmented, free-floating "realities," with even more transgressive an effect, making the primitive postmodern, and startlingly juxtaposing, not only different cultures and lifestyles, but even distinct epochs.[7]

In reading this statement, we need to remember that the "three worlds theory" was imbedded in the Eurocentric mapping of the world. For the immediate purposes here, Buell brings together postcolonialism and globalism in such a way as to articulate their common points in spite of the differences stressed above:⌈There is an assumption in both cases that culture is the site on which Eurocentrism needs to be challenged and also a disavowal of history in spite of differences toward the relationship between the present and the past.⌋While postcolonialists make no secret of the prominence they assign to culture in their stress on identity formations and negotiations, Roland Robertson is equally anxious in his discussion of globalization to separate "agency-structure (and/or culture) theme" from the forces that account for the emergence of globalization in the first place.[8] It may be that for globalists, no less than for postcolonialists, cultural boundaries are easier to negotiate than the boundaries of economic, social, and political power, which "inhibit" coming "to terms with the basic and shifting terms of the contemporary world order."

It may not be too surprising, in light of the culturalism implicit in such declarations not just of the autonomy but of the priority of culture, that postcolonialism and globalism also share in a disavowal of history. Anthony Smith observes that there is something "timeless about the concept of a global culture," which, "widely diffused in space . . . is cut off from any past."[9] Timelessness is clearly visible in the statement from Buell, which reorders many pasts into some kind of a postmodern pastiche. It is equally visible in the statement from Ashcroft, Griffiths, and Tiffin (see note 5), for whom the past was not in any way significantly different from the present, but they did not know it until the present articulated the past's potential consciousness.

The questions at issue here: Can Eurocentrism be grasped in its significance without reference to the structures of power that it implies? Conversely, can the present, with its many claims against and over the past, be understood in its full historicity, without reference to the past perspectives it seeks to erase, either through colonization or through assertions of rupture with the past? Both questions require consideration of Eurocentrism as historical phenomenon, its formations, and the agencies that have enabled it to serve as a formative moment in not just a Euro-American, but also a global modernity.[10]

EUROCENTRISM IN THE PERSPECTIVE OF HISTORY

The argument offered here may be stated simply: Eurocentrism as a historical phenomenon is not to be understood without reference to the structures of power Euro-America produced over the past five centuries, that in turn produced Eurocentrism, globalized its effects, and universalized its historical claims. Those structures of power include:

The economic: capitalism, *capitalist* property relations, markets, and modes of production, imperialism, and so on.

The political: a system of nation-states, and the nation-form, most importantly, new organizations to handle problems presented by such a reordering of the world, new legal forms, and so on.

The social: production of classes, genders, races, ethnicities, and religious forms as well as the push toward individual-based social forms.

The cultural: including new conceptions of space and time, new ideas of the good life, and a new developmentalist conception of the life-world.

The list is woefully inadequate, and the categorizations themselves are admittedly problematic, but it suffices to indicate the intractability of the problem of Eurocentrism. A culturalist appreciation of Eurocentrism that proceeds from a quite productive assertion of the autonomy of culture to an obscurantist isolation of culture and discourses from questions of political economy, and even renders culture into a privileged site that has priority over other aspects of life, may end up only with a dehistoricized, desocialized understanding of Eurocentrism that does not even come close to acknowledging the problems it presents. Does capitalism, regardless of the possibility of "different cultures of capitalism," nevertheless serve as an agent not just of new economic forms but also of certain fundamental values emanating from Euro-America? Does nationalism, as Partha Chatterjee argues, have imbedded in its "thematic" the most fundamental assumptions of a Euro-American Orientalism?[11] Does the very existence of certain forms of media, even apart from their content, introduce new values into everyday life globally? What may be said of "material" agencies as the carriers of Eurocentrism may be observed in reverse of the ways in which cultural constructs of Eurocentrism may acquire the power of material forces. Does it matter at some point that the current mapping of the world was a Euro-American construct when that mapping is internalized by others and shapes the goals and boundaries of life-activity? Especially important in this regard is the ideology of developmentalism, which will be discussed more below.

There seems to be some anxiety in contemporary thinking that to raise anew the question of these structures is to open the way to some kind of "functionalism" that once again reduces social phenomena to a few of its elements.[12] Let us leave aside the question that culturalist functionalism may be as much a functionalism as any other. To recognize a multiplicity of phenomena that coincide historically and appear in structural and structuring relationships of one kind or another requires neither a reduction of those phenomena to one or more of their numbers, nor a requirement that we ignore the relationships of contradiction between them—that in effect serve to undermine efforts to functionalize the structure. In fact, it is these relationships, in their totality and particularity as well as their functionality and contradictoriness, that enable a coherent grasp of differences in history, not self-referential localized differences that "result in an utter particularism in which history becomes a meaningless jumble of stories with no connection to each other."[13] This is the case in much of the postcolonial alternative, or deterritorialized totalities that have no clear spatial and temporal referents, as in the globalist alternatives.

The complexity of Eurocentrism becomes even more daunting if we note that Eurocentrism is hardly a Euro-American phenomenon. Much of what we associate with Eurocentrism is now internal to societies worldwide, so that to speak of "Europe and Its Others" itself appears as an oxymoronic distraction. Legacies of Euro-America are everywhere, from global structures to daily economic practices, from state formations to household practices, from ideologies of development to cultures of consumption, from feminism to the centering in politics of race and ethnicity. Ashis Nandy, as did Franz Fanon in an earlier day, locates them in the psyches of "Europe's Others."[14] These legacies are also in the ways we think about the world, from theorizations about society to thinking about history. Even where claims are made these days to premodern and, therefore, pre-"historical" ways of knowing, they fail to convince because their own efforts to refute a modernist historicism are conditioned by a self-consciousness about their own historicity. And how would we write the world without the legacies of Eurocentric mappings? Writing the world, no less than anti-Eurocentrism itself, may be incomprehensible without reference to those same legacies. If today we may find it impossible to think of the world without reference to classes, genders, and so forth, premoderns (and maybe even pre-postmoderns) would have been surprised that identities are as negotiable as are commodities in the marketplace.

The recognition of the pervasiveness of Eurocentrism in its various dimensions in many ways reveals the limitations of a preoccupation with "Europe and Its Others." That juxtaposition may still make sense with reference to the past, when a separation could be assumed between Europeans and others, which would play an important part both in the construction of others and in the construction of Eurocentrism. At the present, when more than ever the Others are most visible in their relocations to older colonial centers, they have, so to speak, come home. As Euro-American modernity long has been internalized in the rest of the world, the rest of the world has now entered the interior of Euro-America physically and intellectually—which, not surprisingly, is also the prime location for concern with Eurocentrism. Preoccupation with "Europe and Its Others" seems, under the circumstances, to be a distraction from the confrontation of the victory of Eurocentrism, which is evident above all in the rendering of Euro-America and its many products into objects of desire globally. ⌐The contemporary concern with Eurocentric constructions of the Other, interestingly (and with some irony), seems to provide endless occasion for speaking about Euro-America, perpetuating the Eurocentrism it would formally repudiate—which may be the form this desire takes among intellectuals. At the risk of simple-minded psychologism, anti-Eurocentrism strikes me above all as the mirror image of this desire, not so much as a

negative compensation for it but rather as a demand for admission of non–Euro-American cultural elements into the interior of a world that has been shaped already by its historical legacy in a Eurocentric modernity.⌐What, after all, is multiculturalism that calls for the recognition of cultural relics or heritages without challenging the structures of power that are the products of Euro-American domination of the world, and imbued through and through with its values? These same circumstances may have something to tell us about why globalism and postcolonialism, in their very contradictoriness, have caught the imagination of many as ways to deal with such a contemporary situation—even though in their different ways they may evade the most fundamental and pressing question:⌐whether there is an Outside to Eurocentrism in a world that has been worked over by the forces of modernity.⌐

If Eurocentrism, understood as a cultural phenomenon, is insufficient as a critique of Euro-American domination of the world—which was hardly just a "discursive" domination but has been imbedded in structures of power—the power of Eurocentrism itself is not to be grasped without reference to these same structures. This is not to say that culture and discourses are insignificant, but only to reiterate that they are insufficient as explanations of the world; the separation of culture and discourse into realms apart from the material is itself very modern. For the same reason,⌐to argue for a reconnection of culture and discourse to the materiality of everyday life is not to argue for a return to an earlier privileging of political economy, but rather to open up new ways of thinking the connection under contemporary circumstances—which implies also rethinking the connections that were repudiated under the regime of modernity. Eurocentric modernity then appears as a way to connect modes of living and cultures, rather than establish a "scientific" and, therefore, forever valid, causal relationship between the two. The problem, as a historical problem, then is to question why Eurocentric ways of representing this relationship have acquired such power. Eurocentrists may suggest that it is the power of Euro-American cultures. I would like to suggest here that it is power, which has little to do with culture, which then makes dynamic the claims of culture. The issue here is not one of ethical judgment or choice. The issue rather is ethical domination. And cultural domination is hardly its own justification. Neither Eurocentrism nor the contemporary challenges to it may be understood without reference to elements outside of the strictly cultural—which, needless to say, raises significant questions about what we mean by the cultural.

To recognize Eurocentrism as a historical phenomenon, it is necessary to view it within the context of other instances of domination, of which Eurocentrism was neither the first nor is likely to be the last. Such a historical perspective may also provide clues for a more thoroughgoing critique of power and domination than is currently available.

Eurocentrism is a complex term that disguises all manner of struggles within Euro-America over the meanings of "Europe" and "modernity" but more importantly over the belief that Eurocentrism was the product of a historical process, if not itself a historical process, that is inextricable from the invention of Europe's "Others." While at the level of power there may be little question that by the end of the nineteenth century Euro-Americans had more or less conquered the whole world and proceeded to produce ideological legitimations for the conquest, as a cultural orientation, Eurocentrism itself is a hindsight invention of the Europe/Other binary, not the other way around.[15] Clichés about Enlightenment rationalism, unilinear histories, and so forth that are quite common these days in the critiques of Eurocentrism overlook the ways in which historical processes mediated the understanding of such ideological products within a Euro-American context. Euro-America itself is still within this historical process of invention. Globalism, explicitly, and postcolonialism, inadvertently, may well be constituents of the process in its contemporary phase.

Without the power of capitalism, and all the structural innovations that accompanied it in political, social, and cultural organization, Eurocentrism might have been just another ethnocentrism. It is rather remarkable in an age of proliferating ethnocentrisms such as ours that so little attention should be paid to ethnocentrism as a legacy, not just of Eurocentrism (although that may have contributed to it in significant ways), but as a condition of the world at the origins of modernity, more often than not expressing the centrality in a variety of world-systems of the cultural assumptions of those who dominated those world-systems. This may be stating the obvious, but it needs to be stated nevertheless since considerations of political correctness have led to shyness about criticizing ethnocentrisms other than Euro-American (or blatantly murderous expressions of it in such places as Bosnia, Rwanda, or Turkey). Spheres of cultural hegemony that more or less coincided with economic and political domination have been present all along, defining a "Chinese" world, an "Islamic" world, "Arabic" and "Indic" worlds, and so on. In spite of real or imagined hegemonies over vast territories, however, none of these worlds were in the end able to match Eurocentrism in reach or transformative power. The statement may seem foolhardy when the end of history is not yet in sight. What seems safe to say is that if these other cultural hegemonies are ever globalized and universalized in the same manner as Eurocentrism, it will be on the basis of a world globalized and universalized through Eurocentrism and in their articulations to this new world. There are presently efforts to discover an early "modernity" in East and Southeast Asia, but it did not occur to anyone in those regions to even raise the question of modernity until modernity had been established as a principle of history. Similarly, East Asian societies may claim a Confucian heritage that explains their recent success in capitalism, but this heritage is one that has been reinterpreted by the very requirements of capitalism.

Eurocentrism is the one centrism that historically has encompassed the globe and reached levels of life that were not even of much concern to its competitors; it revolutionized lives around the globe, relocated societies in new spaces, and transformed their historical trajectories—to the point where it makes no sense to speak of history without reference to Eurocentrism. There may have been no shortage of "cultural hybridities" earlier; what is interesting and compelling about Eurocentrism is that by the time its globalizing aspirations neared (for the aspirations could never be reached) their geographical boundaries, Eurocentrism was to become a constituent of most people's hybridities—which is not to be said of any of the other centrisms, which were regionally limited and historically unstable.

The question is, then, what accounts for this power? The Eurocentric answer is clear enough: the superiority of Euro-American values. It is an answer that is convincing only to Eurocentrists themselves. It is also the cultural level at which most critiques of Eurocentrism proceed and run into dead ends. The problem with the culturalist critique of Eurocentrism is not only that it provides no explanation for the hegemony of Eurocentrism in contrast to other centrisms, but that it is also for the same reason incapable of addressing normative questions of value. The values of the dominant (such as human rights) are not prima facie undesirable because of the fact of domination, just as the values of the dominated are not to be legitimated simply by recourse to arguments of cultural difference. If capitalism is as much an agent of Eurocentrism as the advocacy of human rights, it does not make much sense to laud the entry into capitalism of other societies while also collaborating in their abuse of human rights on the grounds of cultural difference. The conflict between history and value is nowhere better illustrated in the historicist (culturalist) affirmations of difference, which then proceed nevertheless to discover in these different societies civil and other societies without any awareness that the latter might be products of Eurocentric teleologies, imbedded in the very terms themselves, that contradict the notions of difference.

I suggest here that such contradictions are products of the isolation of cultural questions from those of political economy. Eurocentrism was globalized not due to any inherent virtue of Euro-American values but because those values were stamped on activities of various kinds that insinuated themselves into existing practices (such as trade) and proved to be welcome to certain groups in non–Euro-American societies, or, when there was resistance to them, were enforced on the world by military power. In other words, the globalization and universalization of Eurocentrism would have been inconceivable without the dynamism it acquired through capitalism, imperialism, and cultural domination. One of the most remarkable pieties of our times is that to speak of oppression is to erase the subjectivities of the oppressed; however, not to speak of oppression, but still operate within the teleologies of modernist categories, is to return the responsibility for oppression to its victims.[16] Alternatively, it is to make a mockery of any notion of resistance to oppression, by identifying resistance with any kind of deviation from "normalcy." The result, in either case, is the evasion of any significant and historically determined notion of politics by turning all such encounters into instances of cultural politics.[17] What is also remarkable is the resonance between the political conclusions of contemporary culturalism with the culturalism of an earlier modernizationism, that what is at issue is not politics or political economy but culture.

Recognition of Eurocentrism as a historical phenomenon that differs from other centrisms, in terms of the totalizing structures that served as its agencies, returns us to the question raised above. If Eurocentrism globalized a certain ethnocentrism and rendered it into a universal paradigm, is there then an outside to Eurocentrism? An outside to Eurocentrism may be found in places untouched and marginalized by it, which are fewer by the day, or it may be found in its contradictions, which proliferate daily. The universalization of Eurocentrism must itself be understood in terms of the ways in which Euro-American values were interpellated into the structures of societies worldwide, transforming their political, social, and economic relations, but not homogenizing or assimilating them to the structures and values of Eurocentrism. Questions of homogenization versus heterogenization, sameness and difference, assimilation and differentiation, are in many ways misleading, for they confound what are historical processes with the apportionments of identity into ahistorical, static categories. The universalization of Eurocentric practices and values through the Euro-American conquest of the world implies merely the dislodging of societies from their historical trajectories before Europe onto new trajectories, without any implication of uniformity, for the very universalization of Eurocentrism has bred new kinds of struggles over history, which continue in the present. It also implies that these struggles took place increasingly on terrains that, however different from one another, now included Euro-American power of one kind or another as their dynamic constituents. That distinguishes what we might want to describe as a modernity defined by Euro-America from earlier forms of

domination, which were regionally, politically, and socially limited by the technological, organizational, and ideological limits of domination. Sinocentrism, however effective in East and Southeast Asia, was nevertheless limited to those regions.
Eurocentrism as compared to earlier "centrisms" is universal in three senses:

1. The omnipresence globally of the institutions and cultures of a Euro-American modernity. While the effects of this modernity may not be uniformly
   or equally visible, as implied by global, it is nevertheless everywhere forcing
   widely different peoples into parallel historical trajectories (which does not
   imply identity).
2. Eurocentrism may be diffused through the agencies of non–Euro-Americans, which underlines the importance of a structural appreciation of Eurocentrism.
3. While Eurocentrism may not be universal in the sense that it permits no outside, nevertheless it has become increasingly impossible to imagine outsides
   to it, if by outside we understand places outside of the reach of Euro-American practices. It is not that there are no outsides but that those outsides must
   of necessity be conceived of as post-Eurocentric, as products of contradictions generated by the dialectic between a globalizing Euro-America, and
   places that struggle against such globalization.

What this implies is a common history that, of necessity, provides the point of
departure even for imagining outsides or alternatives to Eurocentrism. Eurocentrism, in other words, is not to be challenged by questioning the values that emanate
from Euro-America. It requires challenging values and structures that are already
part of a global legacy.

In a world that does not operate according to the norms of functionalism but
rather of contradictions, the globalization of Eurocentrism inevitably brings multifaceted contradictions into the very interior of a Eurocentric world, undermining at every moment the integrity of that world, beginning with the notion of
Eurocentrism itself. The contemporary critique of Eurocentrism is driven not by
victimization by Eurocentrism but by empowerment within it. Foremost among
modern critics of Eurocentrism are those who are not marginalized by Eurocentrism or left out of its structures of power, but those who claim "hybridities" that
give access to both Eurocentrism and to its Others, probably more of the former
than the latter. If Orientalism was a product of Euro-Americans located in "contact zones" outside Euro-America on the margins of non–Euro-American societies, anti-Eurocentrism is a product of contact zones located at the hearts of Euro-
America or in transnational structures and circuits of power. As contact zones earlier
presented Euro-Americans with a choice between civilizing mission and dissolution into "barbarism," the new contact zones present intellectuals of Third
World origin with a choice between "bridging" cultures that, given the persistent
inequalities between societies, may mean further invasion of the rest of the world

by the structures of power over which Euro-America continues to preside, or burning the bridges, so that alternatives might be thinkable to a Eurocentric vision of human futures.

The contrast between building and burning bridges offers a convenient way to identify differences between contemporary and past radicalisms in their attitudes toward Eurocentrism. As late as the 1960s and '70s, radical evaluations of Eurocentrism insisted on intimate ties between questions of cultural domination and political economy, more often than not encompassed by the term imperialism. Third World national liberation struggles, synthesizing in local, particular ways goals of national independence and socialized economies, sought to "delink" national economies from the global markets of capitalism, to reorganize those economies in accordance with local needs, and to achieve cultural revolutions against Euro-American cultures of capitalism that would create citizenries responsive to national needs. In First World social sciences, insistences to consider political economy became the means to challenge the culturalism of modernization discourses that blamed "backwardness" on the native traditions and cultures of Third World societies.

From a contemporary perspective, both these earlier radical movements and their articulations in new social science theorizations (such as "world-system analysis") appear, contrary to their claims, to have been dominated by the master narratives and "foundational" assumptions of Eurocentrism. This is plausible to a large extent. In spite of the revolt against capitalism, national liberation movements for the most part remained wedded to the developmentalism of Euro-American modernity. They also remained within the spatial webs of Eurocentrism in taking for granted the spatial arrangements of modernity, most prominently the idea of a Third World itself. The nation-form was taken for granted, with the consequence that the nation was rendered into the location for culture, ignoring the idea that a national culture could be realized only through the colonization of diverse local cultures.

Other aspects of contemporary critiques of past radical assumptions seem a great deal more problematic and may have more to say about the present than the past. The charge of essentialism is a favorite weapon in the arsenal of postcolonialism. It has been brought to bear on ideas of the Third World, Third World nationalism, and so forth, which says less about the historical unfolding of these ideas than about efforts to create straw targets against which to validate postcolonialism. While Third World may have carried essentialist connotations in modernization discourse, this was hardly the way it was understood by the "Third Worlders," to whom Third World connoted anything but the identity of the societies so described; rather, Third Worldness was a condition of national situations, contingent on relationships between capitalist and noncapitalist societies. In revolutionary nationalisms, national cultures were not the givens of some tradition or other, but were seen as cultures yet to be created through national struggles for liberation. Foundational categories were anything but foundational; in the context of a guerilla revolution in China, for instance, there was considerable attention to the overdetermined and locally contingent nature of social categories, especially of class.[18] That these revolutions worked from a Euro-American spatiality means only that present realities provided the point of departure for thinking alternatives to them. Most bizarre is the idea, rather common these days, that to speak of oppression and imperialism as determinants of these revolutions is to ignore or suppress the subjectivities of the oppressed,[19] when these movements themselves represented nothing short of the reassertion of native subjectivities and sought to create new revolutionary subjectivities. This silly charge elides questions of whose subjectivities are at issue and what kinds of subjectivities we are talking about.

Questions of this nature imply that there is much to be gained from viewing the present in the perspective of the past. The world has changed, indeed, and the radicalism represented by immediate postcolonial struggles in the Third World truly appear to belong to a distant past, no longer relevant to contemporary politics. The question is how the world has changed, whether what we witness in the present is a rupture with the past or a reconfiguration of the relationships of power that have facilitated the globalization of earlier forms of power, while eliminating earlier forms of resistance to it. New economic, political, social, and cultural spaces are now being formed. Do these new spaces mean that the earlier spatializations of the globe are no longer relevant, or are they superimposed on those earlier spaces to provide more complicated arrangements of domination? There are now assertions of temporalities (including reassertions of traditions). Does that mean that the temporalities of Eurocentrism have disappeared? Consumerism, culture industries, the production of signs, seem to have moved to the forefront of economies, replacing political by discursive economies—at least for those situated in postmodernist First Worlds. Does that mean that production and political economy are no longer relevant? The diffusion of markets and market mentalities has rendered the production of cultures and identities into a matter of negotiation. Does that mean that there are no longer inequalities in the market place? The list could go on, but this much will suffice.

That these questions are missing from much of the contemporary discussion of globalism and postcolonialism may not be too surprising, because for all their claims to radicalism and significant differences between them, both globalism and postcolonialism represent accommodations to contemporary configurations of power in which they are complicit. This is quite evident in the case of globalism, which is promoted by capital and its institutions and for which globalization is anything but a matter of culture. In this perspective, globalism is little more than a recognition that capital is no longer just Euro-American, that there are successful participants who hail from other locations, and that cultures other than Euro-American must be incorporated into the structures and operations of capital because transnationalism itself implies the interiorization of difference—so long as they recognize the primacy of those structures in the first place. In social science theory, or history for that matter, these Others must be recognized in the fullness of their "traditions" and indigenous subjectivities, which are denied in discourses of imperialism and oppression. Never mind that social science theory itself, into which differences are interpellated, represents a kind of thinking about the world grounded in Eurocentric structures of power. Hence it becomes possible to speak of different "civil societies," grounded in different social configurations, as if the term civil society were innocent in its political implications. And, of course, "rational choice theory" represents a transcending of cultural differences in its "scientificity," as if science as a mode of comprehending the world had nothing to do with "culture." One foundation representative remarks, in support of globalization, "Western theories" are not "for the rest of the world to adopt."[20] There is no indication in the statement that "Western" itself might be redundant, as it may be implicit already in the term "theory."

Unlike globalization, which is founded in the developmentalist assumptions of capitalism, postcolonialism seems to me to be more of an accommodation with a current structure of power than an apology for it. In an earlier writing, I suggested that the present situation is better described as postrevolutionary rather than postcolonial, because while the immediate response to postcoloniality as historical phenomenon was revolution, contemporary postcolonialism eschews revolutionary options for accommodation to the capitalist world system. The postcolonial rush to culture is an escape not only from the structures of political economy but more importantly from revolutionary radicalisms of the past, which are now denied not only contemporary relevance but even past significance.

Postcolonialism's complicity with contemporary configurations of power rests in its explicit repudiation of structures and "foundational" categories, which obviate the need to address the question of structured power in considerations of change but also in its culturalism. Localized encounters and identity politics seem to serve in postcolonialism not as a refinement of, but as a substitute for, structured inequalities and struggles against it. More significant may be the rereading of the past with such a "methodology," which also serves to erase the memory of more radical struggles for culture and identity and renders localism into a metanarrative that postcolonialism supposedly repudiates. What is remarkable about postcolonialism methodologically and conceptually is that, for all its objections to "essentialism," it is based on presumptions of essentialized identities, which is implicit in notions of "hybridity," "third space," and so on. Repudiation of foundational categories also relieves it of the obligation to confront "differences" along the fault lines of classes, genders, races, and so forth, which all become subject to negotiations of one kind or another. Postcolonialism, repudiating Eurocentric spatializations, ironically also returns us to pre–World War II spaces, where spaces established by colonial empires are acknowledged on unguarded occasions to provide spaces for theorizing about culture and identities.[21] Most importantly, however, may be that in its repudiation of the structures of political economy in the name of discourses and culture, postcolonialism returns us past an earlier concern with political economy to the culturalism of modernization discourse. Its own discourse on culture is quite different, needless to say, than the spaceless and timeless cultures presumed by modernization discourse, but it is at one with the latter in elevating culture to primacy in social and cultural theory.

The parallel has interesting implications. Culturalism in modernization discourse served to conceal inequalities in the realms of economy and politics and to shift the blame for problems in development from the dominant to the dominated—all the time assuming a certain teleology of development. Postcolonialism eschews teleology, and it eschews fixed, essentialized notions of culture. But what are we to make of its isolation of questions of culture from those of political economy? Does it also serve as some kind of a cover for inequalities and oppressions that are no less a characteristic of the present than they were of the past? Postcolonialism itself does not provide an answer to these questions, because it refuses to address them in the first place. Clearly, the present represents not a rupture with the past but a reconfiguration. If the transnationalization, and transnational domination, of capital is a prominent feature of the contemporary world situation, another is the transnationalization of the class structures associated with capitalist domination. Postcolonialism, as Aijaz Ahmad observes, may be a "matter of class."[22] But it is not just a matter of class. It is also a matter of a class relocated to the centers of capital, in the new contact zones mentioned above, which serve as sites of negotiation—"in the belly of the beast," as Gayatri Spivak once put it. Spivak knows better than to say that this is the whole story, but for most postcolonialists who do not share in her radicalism, that does seem to be the whole story. The contact zones at the heart of Euro-America provide locations where cultural difference may be asserted while sharing in the powers of the center, in which culture serves as a means to evade questions of inequality and oppression in interclass relations but is a useful means to identity in intraclass negotiations for power. Contact zones located on the boundaries of societies of the "Other" produced earlier Orientalisms; contact zones at the core produce "self-Orientalizations."[23] Unlike the former, which distanced societies from one another, the latter produces multiculturalist redefinitions of global power—as is indicated in the idea of "ethnoscapes," or the stipulation of diasporic identities, regardless of place, class, gender, and so forth. Interestingly, it is a new generation of Third Worlders, firmly established in the structures of Eurocentric power, that now speaks for the societies from which its members hail, while those back home are condemned to inaudibility—or parochialism.

HISTORY AFTER EUROCENTRISM

Much of what has been discussed above may seem to have little to do with history as a discipline, for historians have been notably absent from recent discussions over history as epistemology. It is probably not too much of an exaggeration to suggest that a crisis of historical consciousness is one of the markers of life at the end of the twentieth century. The crisis refers to the ways in which we think of the relationship between the present and the past, and, therefore, the relevance and validity of anything we may have to say about the past. A sense of a break, not just with the immediate past but also with the whole history of modernity, calls into question anything history might offer to an understanding of the present. Historians might have a significant part to play in reasserting the significance of past perspectives in a critical appreciation of the present; but they seem to have adjusted with remarkable speed to the contemporary rewriting of the past. It is a professional disease of historians, especially of positivist historians, and a limitation on their imagination, that they may blame everything on the limitations of archives. A conviction that the only obstacle to truth lies in the limitations of archives helps historians avoid the challenges of historical crises by allowing them to fall back on those limitations. If things did not go the way a previous generation of historians had indicated, or if the problems of a previous generation no longer seem relevant, the historian can always claim that it was not in the archives.

In the field of modern Chinese history, changes in China call for an urgent consideration of historical paradigms and an evaluation of competing paradigms. Two generations of historians of China (in China and abroad) have taken revolution to be the paradigm around which to write modern Chinese history. That paradigm now lies in ruins, not because the paradigm itself was wrong necessarily, but because the revolution is a thing of the past in a China where leaders may pay lip service to the revolution in their very nonrevolutionary and nonsocialist turn to incorporation into capitalism. Rather than observe the turn critically, historians have been quick to deny that there was a revolution, that what had been considered a revolution was really nothing more than the perpetuation of backwardness, and that it was the archives that were responsible for their failure to foresee the fate of the revolution. The denial of revolution, not surprisingly, is accompanied by a shift of attention to pasts that may be more consonant with the self-images of the present. The question here is not just a question of ideology in history; it is also a question of bad history that refuses to acknowledge the ways in which the revolutionary past, having failed to achieve its putative goals, nevertheless served to shape the present.[24]

A reasonable alternative to this rapid adjustment to the present that also requires a disavowal of the past (both the past in actuality and the past in historiography) might be to acknowledge the crisis and turn to a revaluation of the past—not by an abandonment of the paradigm of revolution but by inquiring into the meaning of revolution.[25] Radical historiography does not consist of the abandonment, or rewriting, of the past every time a new historical situation presents itself—in which case it cannot overcome a continuing adjustment to the present, which is hardly a claim to radicalism, as it makes it impossible to differentiate what is radical from what is mimicry of the demands of power. Rather, it is informed by a principled defense of autonomous political positions that question ever-shifting claims to reality, not by denying reality but by critically evaluating its claims on the past and the present. If the past has no relevance to understanding the present but is merely a plaything at the hands of the latter, there would seem to be little meaning to any claim of validity for history as epistemology, or for that matter, to any truth imbedded in the archives of the past.

The proposition that "history is a sign of the modern" would suggest only to the most naive that the moment we have gone postmodern we may abandon history. The posts of our age, to those who would read them with some sense of reality, should suggest that what comes after bears upon it the imprint of what went on before, and that we are not as free as we might think of the legacies we have consigned to the past. The same goes for postrevolutionary, and for what has been my primary concern in this discussion, post-Eurocentric. Our conceptions of the world face the predicament of turning into ideologies the moment that they forget their own historicities. And awareness of historicity requires attention both to transformations and the presence of the past in such transformations.[26]

To affirm the historical role Eurocentrism has played in shaping the contemporary world is not to endow it with some normative power, but to recognize the ways in which it continues to be an intimate part of the shaping of the world, which is not going to disappear with willful acts of its cultural negation. One aspect of Eurocentrism that infused both earlier revolutionary ideologies and the accommodationist alternatives of the present seems to be especially important, perhaps more important for the historian than for others because it is complicit in our imagination of temporalities: developmentalism. The notion that development is as natural to humanity as air and water is one that is deeply imbedded in our consciousness, and yet development as an idea is a relatively recent one in human history. As Arturo Escobar has argued forcefully in a number of writings, development as a discourse is imbedded not just in the realm of ideology but also in institutional structures that are fundamental to the globalization of capital.[27]

If globalism is a way of promoting these structures, by rendering their claims into scientific truths, postcolonialism serves as their alibi by not acknowledging their presence. Historians meanwhile continue to write history as if attaining the goals of development were the measure against which the past may be evaluated. That, I think, is the most eloquent testimonial to the implication of our times in the continuing hegemony of capital, for which the disavowal of an earlier past serves as disguise. It also indicates where the tasks may be located for a radical agenda appropriate to the present: in questioning contemporary dehistoricizations of the present and the past and returning inquiry to the search for alternatives to developmentalism. However we may conceive such alternatives, they are likely to be post-Eurocentric, recognizing that any radical alternatives to modernity's forms of domination must confront not just the cultures but also the structures of modernity. At any rate, it seems that we need a reaffirmation of history and historicity at this moment of crisis in historical consciousness, *especially* because history seems to be irrelevant—either because of its renunciation at the centers of power where a postmodernism declares a rupture with the past, unable to decide whether such a rupture constitutes a celebration or denunciation of capitalism, or contradictorily, because of an affirmation of premodernity among those who were the objects of modernity, who proclaim in order to recover their own subjectivities that modernity made no difference after all. A historical epistemology will not resolve the contradiction or provide a guide to the future, but it might serve at least to clarify the ways in which the present uses and abuses the past and serve as a reminder of our own historicity—why we say and do things differently than they were said or done in the past. Ours is an age when there is once again an inflation of claims to critical consciousness. These claims are based often on an expanded consciousness of space. We need to remind ourselves, every time we speak of the constructedness of some space or other, that it may be impossible, for that very reason, to think of spaces without at the same time thinking of the times that produced those spaces.

NOTES

I am grateful to a number of people for reading and commenting on this chapter. My cocontributors to this volume, Vinay Bahl and Ali-Rifaat Abou-El-Haj, read it with special care and an eye on the volume. Leo Ching, Michael Hardt, Roxann Prazniak, and Orin Starn contributed to it significantly in reminding me of all that I had overlooked; I appreciate their comments. I am also grateful for their encouragement and comments to the participants at the conference "Colonialism and Its Discontents: An Interdisciplinary Forum"(Institute of Ethnology, Academia Sinica, 8–9 July 1997), where this chapter was presented as a conference paper. What remains is my responsibility.

1. Nicholas Dirks, "History As a Sign of the Modern," *Public Culture* 2.2 (1990): 25–32

2. This is not to say that culture and discourse are the popular choices *only* for postcolonialism and globalism. What I describe here as a new culturalism is characteristic of contemporary critical thought in general and has its origins in the turn from the 1970s to culture and discourse in varieties of poststructuralism, postmodernism, cultural studies, feminism, and so on.

3. Michael Geyer and Charles Bright, "World History in a Global Age," *American Historical Review* (October 1995): 1034–1060, p. 1042

4. As I have remarked elsewhere, postcolonial criticism covers a wide political (and, therefore, intellectual) range, from the Marxist feminism of Gayatri Spivak to the near-libertarianism of Homi Bhabha and, more recently, Stuart Hall. That it is the more libertarian versions of postcolonial criticism that have caught the imagination of post-Reagan/post-Thatcher scholars in the United States and the United Kingdom may not be very surprising, as it points merely to the importance of context in the reception of ideas. The same may be said of globalism, which also covers a wide range of intellectual and political orientations, from leftists who look to a cosmopolitan world to rational-choice political scientists who would make sure that cosmopolitanism lives up to the demands of scientific ways of knowing the world (read, Euro-American hegemony). The problem is not quite novel. Capitalists have long sought globalization. So have leftists, but not quite in the same way. What seems to be different about our times is the willingness of leftists to buy into the visions of globalization offered by capital.

5. Bill Ashcroft, Gareth Griffiths, and Helen Tiffin (eds.), *The Post-Colonial Studies Reader* (London and New York: Routledge, 1995), p. 1. I have offered more sustained critiques of the problems of postcolonialism elsewhere and draw on those earlier critiques in much of the discussion below. These critiques may be found in Arif Dirlik, *The Postcolonial Aura: Third World Criticism in the Age of Global Capitalism* (Boulder, CO: Westview Press, 1997). Of special interest from the perspective of questions of history may be the Introduction ("Postcoloniality and the Perspective of History"), "Three Worlds or One, or Many: The Reconfiguration of Global Relations Under Contemporary Capitalism," and "Postcolonial or Postrevolutionary: The Problem of History in Postcolonial Criticism."

6. Roland Robertson, "Mapping the Global Condition: Globalization As the Central Concept," in Mike Featherstone (ed.), *Global Culture: Nationalism, Globalization, and Modernity* (London: Sage Publications, 1994), pp. 15–29, p. 23. For a somewhat more elaborate critique, see Arif Dirlik, "Globalization, Areas, Places," Center for Asian Studies—Amsterdam (CASA) Working Papers (1997).

7. Frederick Buell, *National Culture and the New Global System* (Baltimore and London: Johns Hopkins University Press, 1994), pp. 336–337.

8. For an even more uncompromising argument for the priority of culture, see Rob Boyne, "Culture and the World-system," in Featherstone, pp. 57–62, where Boyne attacks Immanuel Wallerstein for speaking of culture in conjunction with economic and political analysis.

9. Anthony D. Smith "Towards a Global Culture?" in Featherstone, pp. 171–191, 177.

10. That we should be more attentive to modernity rather than Eurocentrism is a view I share with John Tomlinson, *Cultural Imperialism* (Baltimore: Johns Hopkins University Press, 1991). I do not, however, share Tomlinson's conclusion that Euro-American agency may be taken out of the picture by such a shift of attention.

11. Partha Chatterjee, *Nationalist Thought and the Colonial World: A Derivative Discourse* (Minneapolis: University of Minnesota Press, 1993).

12. In a rather ill-conceived essay, Stuart Hall brings a charge of ("primitive," as well as "primeval") "functionalism" against me (along with Robert Young). See Hall, "When Was 'the Postcolonial'? Thinking at the Limit," in Iain Chambers and Lidia Curti, *The Postcolonial Question: Common Skies, Divided Horizons* (New York: Routledge, 1996). The charge does not call for comment, except to note that it is rather below the potential of such a distinguished cultural critic, to whose formulations I would myself acknowledge a debt. Rather than methodological problems of culturalism and functionalism, Hall's attack may have something to do with the post-Thatcherite turn in British Marxism. For this turn, see Chantal Mouffe, "The End of Politics and the Rise of the Radical Right," *Dissent*: 498–502.

13. Ken Armitage, "The 'Asiatic'/Tributary Mode of Production: State and Class in Chinese History," Ph.D. dissertation, Asian and International Studies (Australia: Griffith University, 1997), p. 3.

14. Ashis Nandy, *The Intimate Enemy* (Oxford: Oxford University Press, 1983).

15. Samir Armin analyzes this with brilliant pithiness in his essay *Eurocentrism* (New York: Monthly Review Press, 1989). Historians of Europe have also demonstrated that Europe, and "nations" within Europe, were products of an internal colonization that paralleled the "European" colonization of the world. For Europe, see F. Braudel, *Civilization and Capitalism, 15th to 18th Century*, 3 vols., trans. Sian Reynolds (New York: Harper and Row, 1984), especially vol. 3, *The Perspective of the World*. For an outstanding study of internal colonization in the creation of nations, see Eugen Weber, *Peasants into Frenchmen: The Modernization*

of Rural France, 1870–1914 (Stanford, CA: Stanford University Press, 1976). Societies such as the United States, Canada, Australia, and others, themselves colonial creations, interestingly provide the most explicit examples of such colonization in the creation of modern nation-states.

16. I am referring here to certain kinds of writing that assume categorical teleologies and then proceed to judge other peoples for having failed to live up to them. An example of this kind of teleology, on the issue of class, is Dipeh Chakrabarty, *Rethinking Working Class History* (Princeton, NJ: Princeton University Press, 1989). Equally prominent are writings on feminism, including writings that attack the condition of women in China and not only ignore what Chinese women might or might not want but also have encouraged attacks on the socialist program for women, which has certainly accomplished a great deal for women. It is interesting that feminists who attack the socialist program for what it has failed to achieve are often oblivious to what socialism has achieved, because it has not achieved what they think ought to have been achieved. This is not to say that women's questions should be reduced to what is of concern to women under socialism, but that women under socialism or under precapitalism may have a great deal to teach women who have discovered their "womanness" under capitalism and, regardless of what they may claim, are conditioned in their feminism by the mode of production that is their context.

17. Blatant examples of the dangers implicit in the new culturalism are provided by Samuel Huntington's by now infamous "The Clash of Civilizations?" (*Foreign Affairs* 72.3 [1993]: 22–49) and his subsequent "The West: Unique, Not Universal" (*Foreign Affairs* 75.6 [1996]: 28–46). Huntington's views of "civilizations," his approach to the question of culture, and the conclusions he draws from those are diametrically opposed to those of postcolonialism and globalism. He reifies civilizations into culturally homogeneous and spatially mappable entities, insists on drawing impassable boundaries between them, and proposes a fortress Euro-America to defend Western civilization against the intrusion of unmodernizable and unassimilable Others. What is remarkable about his views, especially in the second article, is his disavowal of Western involvement in other civilization areas. His is a conception of the contemporary world that divides the world into several "civilization" areas, where each hegemonic power should be responsible for the achievement of order in its area. Huntington sustains this remarkable view of the world by refraining from any reference to the structures of political economy (he does not even say that a goal of fortress Euro-America is to withdraw its transnational corporations from the rest of the world); by taking out of the definition of culture any element of material culture; by confounding ethnicity, culture, race, and civilization; by questioning the significance of the nation; by an erasure of colonialism and an insistence that whatever has happened in other societies, has happened as a consequence of their own indigenous values and cultures; and, at the most general level, by a disavowal of history. His divisions of the world may be a far cry from the insistence in globalism and postcolonial criticism on the abolition of boundaries, rejections of cultural reification, and negotiations of cultural identity. His reinstatement of the power of indigenous "cultures," understood not in terms of nations but "civilizations," his erasure of colonialism and the reinstatement of persistent native subjectivities, his obliviousness to questions of political economy, and his disavowal of modernity's history, however, resonate with globalist and postcolonialist arguments. This is not to suggest that they are "identical," therefore, or even operate out of the same paradigm (Huntington's is a paradigm of top-down order) but that they are contemporaneous. Huntington's writings do not offer an explanation of contemporary structures of power so much as mystify them; they are also symptomatic of a

contemporary antimodernist ethnicism that seeks to reconceive the world as it might have been at the origins of modernity. He, in fact, may be representative of a contemporary conservatism against the contemporary liberalisms represented by globalism and postcolonial criticism (Euro-American and Third World, respectively), the one advocating bounded ethnocentrisms while the others aim at the multiculturalist pluralisms of placeless globalism or postcolonialism, but both foregrounding ethnicity to mystify the transnational structures of unequal power that are their context.

18. Arif Dirlik, *After the Revolution: Waking to Global Capitalism* (Hanover, NH: University Press of New England, 1994), chap. 2, and Arif Dirlik, "Mao Zedong and 'Chinese Marxism,'" in B. Carr and I. Mahalingam (eds.), *Companion Encyclopedia of Asian Philosophy* (London: Routledge, 1997), pp. 593–619.

19. Bueller provides an egregious example of this tendency. The volume opens up with an attack on Herbert Schiller for his views on cultural imperialism.

20. Quoted in Jacob Heilbrunn, "The News from Everywhere: Does Global Thinking Threaten Local Knowledge? The Social Science Research Council Debates the Future of Area Studies," *Lingua Franca* (May–June 1996): 49–56, pp. 54–55.

21. Stephen Slemon, "Unsettling the Empire: Resistance Theory for the Second World," in Ashcroft, Griffiths, and Tiffin, pp. 104–110, where Slemon suggests that postcolonialism may be most relevant to societies of the British Commonwealth.

22. Aijaz Ahmad, "The Politics of Literary Postcoloniality," *Race and Class* 36.3 (1995): 1–20, p. 16.

23. I am referring here to the reification of cultures at the level of diasporas, an egregious example being the idea of a "cultural China." For an extended discussion, see A. Dirlik, "Confucius on the Borderlands: Global Capitalism and the Reinvention of Confucianism," *Boundary 2*, 22.3 (Fall 1995): 229–273. Attention to diasporas points to a second aspect of the part culture may play in intraelite struggles. Preoccupation with Eurocentrism occludes the struggles among "native" elites over the definition of cultural identity. As diasporic populations may be denied their cultural "authenticity" by those in the societies of departure, the repudiation of "authenticity" and the reaffirmation of "hybridity" provide obvious strategies in countering such denial.

24. These questions are discussed at length in Arif Dirlik, "Reversals, Ironies, Hegemonies: Notes on the Contemporary Historiography of Modern China," *Modern China* 22.3 (July 1996): 243–284.

25. For a gender-based argument that advocates adjustment to contemporary struggles while insisting on the immediate relevance of the past to the structuring of the present, see Vinay Bahl, "Cultural Imperialism and Women's Movements: Thinking Globally," *Gender and History*, 9.1 (April 1997): 1–14.

26. A note is in order here on the many writings of Dipesh Chakrabarty who, at least in his more theoretical writings, shares many of the arguments advanced in this chapter. Some of his relevant writings are: "Postcoloniality and the Artifice of History: Who Speaks for 'Indian' Pasts?" *Representations* 37 (1992): 1–26; "History as Critique and Critique(s) of History," *Economic and Political Weekly* (14 September 1991): 2162–2166; and "Radical Histories and the Question of Enlightenment Rationalism: Some Recent Critiques of *Subaltern Studies*," *Economic and Political Weekly* (8 April 1995): 751–759. In these and other writings, Chakrabarty argues for a position that is very similar to the one I voice here: Eurocentrism is everywhere, including the very writing of history. He is also unwilling, unlike in some more atavistic versions of Eurocentrism, to repudiate either the legacy of the Enlightenment,

or that of the nation, in the writing of history (indeed, he sees the nation as the location for historical consciousness, which is threatened by the consumerism of capital). Finally, he is quite willing to speak of history in relationship to the cultures of capitalism. Against this seemingly invincible hegemony of history (read, Eurocentrism), Chakrabarty, in a direction very similar to the one here, finds in "fragmentary and episodic . . . knowledge-forms" a promise of a more democratic knowledge (*Economic Political Weekly* [8 April 1995], p. 757). However, it is not at all clear from Chakrabarty's arguments whether his own project includes anything beyond challenging Eurocentric "knowledge-forms" or to "provincialize Europe," as he put it in another context. The "fragmentary and episodic . . . knowledge-forms" he speaks of, judging by his argument, are intended mainly to undermine Eurocentric claims to universality and not to privilege the lives or modes of living that produce those knowledge forms. In the same vein, Chakrabarty has little to say on the questions of development, capitalism, and so on, except as they relate to colonialism's knowledge. It is not very surprising, therefore, that under his editorship, *Subaltern Studies* has abandoned its original concern for giving voice to the "subalterns" to "deconstructing" representations of India and the Third World. (For the basis for these remarks, see the essay above by Vinay Bahl.) At any rate, I question the preoccupation with Eurocentrism here to redirect attention from "culture" to structures: that Eurocentrism resides in the structures of everyday life, which must be transformed if Eurocentrism is to be challenged. "Knowledge-forms" are important but not as an end in themselves; they are most important for showing the way to different kinds of living. I would like to think that the project implied here is quite different from the postcolonial, multiculturalist thrust of Chakrabarty's culturalist criticism.

27. See, especially, *Encountering Development: The Making and Unmaking of the Third World* (Princeton, NJ: Princeton University Press, 1994). What kind of radical historical agenda this may call for is discussed in Dirlik, "Reversals, Ironies, Hegemonies," and "Place-Based Imagination: Globalism and the Politics of Place"(unpublished paper, forthcoming).

3

Archaeologists and Historians Confront Civilization, Relativism, and Poststructuralism in the Late Twentieth Century

Thomas C. Patterson

Archaeologists, so television shows on PBS, Discovery, and other networks tell us, mount expeditions to remote corners of the earth in search of lost cities or the buried tombs of ancient rulers. Historians, by contrast, spend their time in archives, hunched over documents or manuscripts deciphering the often barely legible handwriting of some deceased scribe or bureaucrat. This chapter will explore the implications of this technical division of labor and consider some of the concerns archaeologists and historians share—such as the rise of civilizations or the dual specters of radical relativism and poststructuralism.

A DIVISION OF LABOR

Archaeologists and historians study past societies for diverse reasons. Both tend to believe that the societies of yesterday are linked in some way to what is happening now—that is, that the past shapes the present. Even though both groups try to understand and explain what happened in the past, it is clear that most archaeologists are not historians and that most historians are not archaeologists.[1] The one difference that stands up under close scrutiny is that the two groups examine different kinds of evidence and, consequently, have developed different techniques for analyzing the kinds of information they study. While archaeologists rely primarily on material remains and, more importantly, their spatial associations with one another, historians deal with written records. Another way of saying that they have

different epistemologies and methodologies is that both participate in a technical
division of labor that emerged in the nineteenth century.

This division of labor has several important consequences. First, both groups
have more sharply honed and narrower objects of inquiry and have experienced
the deskilling that accompanies increased specialization in the modern world; each
group now knows much more about much less.[2] Second, both archaeologists and
historians sometimes overlook the real significance of writing when they point to
literacy and writing as a boundary marker that separates prehistory from history.
This perspective either overlooks or trivializes the fact that literacy and writing
always developed in particular socioeconomic and political contexts—ones that
were always shaped by processes associated with class and state formation, which
always originates with "conquest abroad and repression at home."[3]

In spite of their methodological differences, archaeologists and historians are very
much alike in several respects. First, regardless of whether they are from the capitalist West or were trained there, or whether they are from the socialist, former
socialist, or Third World, they share many ideas and concerns about society and
history. One of these shared concerns is the rise of civilization—that is, the formation of class-stratified, state-based societies. Historians of the West and classical
archaeologists are typically concerned with the rise of Western civilization, whereas
those who focus on Mexico or Peru are interested in the development of state-
based societies in those regions. That archaeologists and historians from different
parts of the world share ideas and concerns should not be surprising since students
and professionals in different countries are likely to have read or been exposed to
many of the same writers—a canon that probably includes large or small doses of
Aristotle, Hobbes, Locke, Marx, Darwin, Spencer, and Freud, for example, all of
whom had something to say about society and history.

Second, archaeologists and historians are empiricists who like their data and usually prefer their theory implicit rather than open to critical examination. By empiricism, I mean that direct observation of the archaeological and historical records
constitutes the sole source(s) of knowledge about the past and that abstract concepts, such as social class, provide no window to domains of reality that cannot be
directly experienced. As a result, the empiricists in the two disciplines believe that
the artifacts or archival documents will reveal what actually happened or what a
particular premodern society was like. More importantly, they usually do not consider the premises underlying the questions they ask of the artifacts or documents
or those that shape the interpretive frameworks they use to organize the information they glean from those interrogations. When pressed about the theoretical
underpinnings of their work, they often answer that their interpretations follow
from a judicious application of common sense and that their analytical framework,
while not specified clearly, is eclectic (i.e., confused) and draws the best from
diverse sources of theoretical inspiration, which only seem to be at odds with one
another.[4]

The third way in which archaeologists and historians are alike is that, while they are very respectful of disciplinary boundaries established in the late nineteenth century, they occasionally, and usually quite uncritically, will appropriate ideas or interpretive frameworks from one another.[5] In other words, they behave like muggers who randomly select their victims, steal their ideas or methodologies, and retreat with no regard for the identities of the victims, their place in social discourse, or the implications of such acts, and then sell the stolen goods in the next issue of a scholarly journal. Archaeologists and historians, I should add, are not the only ones who mug innocent bystanders and unsuspecting victims in other fields of inquiry.

Civilization is one of the ideas (concepts) archaeologists and historians share. In fact, they have appropriated and reappropriated the concepts of civilization from each other so many times that it is almost impossible to determine the identity of the first mugger or victim. But this question is not as interesting as either the idea of civilization itself or why it has become such a popular and useful term in politically sensitive discourse at the end of the twentieth century. This chapter will look at the idea of civilization in order to consider what it is that archaeologists and historians have actually appropriated. Besides pointing out the dangers inherent in indiscriminate mugging, it will examine who benefited in the past from their theft and who stands to gain as they sell these stolen goods at the present time.

Civilization is not only an idea but also a way of organizing a particular understanding of social reality.[6] The idea of civilization was a major part of the ideology that accompanied and buttressed the rise of the modern European state. The modern state emerged within the crisis of feudalism—a crisis that was characterized by declining incomes among the ruling class even in a period of economic expansion. The appearance of the modern state began during the Renaissance and gained momentum in the 1500s after enormous quantities of plunder began to arrive from the Americas. The formation of modern states was also connected with the emergence of social classes that marked new relations among monarchs, nobles, and their subjects, and this influenced the idea of civilization.[7]

Civilization always involves hierarchically organized social relations and cultures. As part of the civilizing process, the politically dominant groups in an emerging European state portrayed themselves as polished, refined, and cultured. They sought to distinguish themselves socially and culturally from the members of subordinated classes and external communities that they always depicted in oppositional terms—such as uncivilized, barbaric, savage, crude, rustic, or wild. From their perspective, they were the mainsprings of civilization, superior in every way to the peasants, masses, and barbarians whom they despised, distrusted, and feared. In the back of their minds were questions: What would happen if their subjects refused to comply with their demands? What would happen if their subjects resisted threats and coercion? What would happen if their claims to legitimacy were challenged?

Archaeologists and historians have tended to focus entirely on the civilizing process and have ignored questions that lurk in the minds of the ruling classes. They have viewed civilization largely in terms of education, the advantages of writing, the culture of the city, or the aesthetic qualities of state architecture and royal tombs. As a result, they have accepted the claims of ruling classes and states as their own. Thus, the institutions and practices of the ruling classes and the state are desirable and essential because they maintain social order and/or underwrite the conquest of nature. The values and practices cultivated by them promote reason and the rationality required to overcome the limitations imposed by nature and tradition. The culture created by the ruling classes and the state is authentic, superior, and preferable to the essentially acultural condition of the masses. Civilization, which was brought about under guidance of the ruling classes and the state, marks the highest stage of social development—the end of history as it were—and the civilizing process has definitely made the world a better place in which to live.[8]

Buoyed by the economic prosperity and position of the United States in the late 1940s and 1950s, U.S. anthropologists provided new evolutionist accounts of the rise of civilization. They argued that human society had developed through a linear progression of stages from hunters and foragers to civilized city-dwellers who satisfied their needs by buying and selling goods and services in markets. They had a base-superstructure or layer-cake image of society. The base was narrowly economic—that is, subsistence technologies and strategies separated the human world from nature and, furthermore, shaped or determined the social, ideological, and cultural layers of the superstructure. Such economistic formulations, of course, had their origins in the writings of such Scottish Enlightenment social critics as Adam Ferguson or Adam Smith.[9]

In the late 1940s, the anthropologist Julian Steward, a liberal state functionary, interpreted the rise of early civilizations in both the Old and New Worlds in terms of an evolutionist framework. His assessment of the processes involved was, in fact, a very elaborate theory of human history:

> The rise and decline of the kingdoms in the ancient centers of civilization in Egypt, Mesopotamia, India, China, Meso-America, and the Andes is often described as the rise and fall of civilization. It is true that the particular kinds of societies found in these centers did not survive, but most of the basic cultural achievements, the essential features of civilization, were passed on to other nations. In each of these centers both culture and society changed rather considerably during the early periods, and everywhere the developmental processes were about the same. At first there were small communities of incipient farmers. Later the communities cooperated in the construction of irrigation works and the populations became larger and more settled. Villages amalgamated into states under theocratic rulers. . . . Finally culture ceased to develop, and the states of each area entered into competition with one another.
>
> [A]n era of cyclical conquest followed. The conquests conformed to a fairly stable pattern. . . . Each state began to compete with others for tribute and advantages. One or another state succeeded in dominating the others, that is, in building an empire, but such empires ran their course and collapsed after some . . . years only to be succeeded by another empire not very different from the first.

For the historian this era of cyclical conquests is filled with great men, wars and battle strategy, shifting power centers, and other social events. For the culture historian the changes are much less significant than those of the previous eras when the basic civilizations developed or, in the Near East, those of the subsequent Iron Age when the cultural patterns changed again and the centers of civilization shifted to new areas. . . .

The industrial revolution brought profound cultural change to Western Europe and caused competition for colonies and for areas of exploitation. Japan entered the competition as soon as she acquired the general pattern. The realignments of power caused by Germany's losses in the first world war and by Italy's and Japan's in the second are of a social order. What new cultural patterns will result from these remains to be seen.

The general assumption today seems to be that we are in danger of basic cultural changes caused by the spread of communism. Russia acquired drastically new cultural patterns as a result of her revolution. Whether communism has the same meaning in other nations has still to be determined.[10]

Steward's account of the rise of civilization shaped subsequent discussions of this issue during the 1950s and 1960s.[11] What anthropologists debated was not whether civilization was the culmination of a cultural evolutionary process marked by increasing complexity, but rather whether the motor of the civilizing process was located in the economic, political, ideological, or cultural realms of society. For example, in the 1960s, anthropologist Clifford Geertz, following Émile Durkheim's lead, rejected Steward's materialist conception of history:

Referring to that part of culture "most closely related to subsistence activities and economic arrangements" as the "core" of culture, while denoting the rest of culture as "secondary" indeterminately shaped by accidents of random innovation and diffusion, means begging the question. There is no *a priori* reason why the adaptive realities a given sociocultural system faces have greater or lesser control over its patterns of development than various other realities with which it is also faced.[12]

In the early 1970s, archaeologist Kent Flannery, adopting the language of systems theory, indicated that the flow of energy or information in a society was regulated by a hierarchy of specialized components, "[t]he highest, most abstract, and most unchanging of these . . . lie in the highest-order (or governmental controls), which deal in policy more often than commands."[13] In this Durkheimian perspective, as Flannery pointed out, the superstructure determines the economic base, and the *natural* role of the state is to maintain equilibrium and to protect society from systemic pathologies that promote instability and threaten the existing social order.[14]

By the 1970s, archaeologists were revising their understandings of the rise of civilization. Excavations in various parts of the world—for example, the Andes and southern Mexico—revealed that the earlier stages of the process were more complicated than Steward's interpretation allowed. Many of the early foraging and farming societies manifested variations of socioeconomic and political organization that did not mirror the political and economic categories embedded in the stagist analytical categories of cultural evolutionist theory. In order to support and salvage the theoretical underpinnings of cultural evolutionism in a way that would allow them to deal with the diverse social and political-economic forms exhibited by these anomalous precivilized societies, archaeologists introduced the idea of complexity.[15] They argued that later societies were more complex or heterogeneous than earlier ones in the archaeological record of particular regions, like southern Mexico. In their view, the evolution of civilization was a gradual, continuous process that reflected the unfolding of some potential inherent in the very core of society. It was a process marked by steadily increasing social differentiation, as Herbert Spencer and Émile Durkheim had suggested in the late nineteenth century.

The idea of increasing social differentiation created difficulties for those archaeologists, who had observed rather rapid and dramatic changes in the archaeological records of various areas. In their view, the crashes or catastrophes that led to the "dark ages" they observed—e.g., the collapse of Minoan and Mycenaean civilizations in the Aegean, and the disappearance of the Harappan civilization in the Indus Valley—represented neither slow, steady growth nor increasing social differentiation. They realized, "For some human societies, stability (in the sense of peace and prosperity) is assured only by continued growth. Zero growth does not for them represent a stable state, and negative growth can accelerate to disintigration" [sic].[16]

In attempting to resolve this dilemma, the archaeologists followed Adam Smith's arguments in *The Wealth of Nations*. The rise of civilization, they claimed, was a complex phenomena that involved the interaction of societies in contiguous regions.[17] Their theory implied that, while the development of civilization might be blocked for some reason in one region, it might continue unabated in others. In effect, the proponents of this view fine-tuned their definition of civilization. In the new version, civilization was a spatially organized cluster of interconnected, self-governing, politically autonomous state-based societies. This redefinition allowed them to retain the basic premise of the evolutionist perspective: The rise of class stratification and the state was a directional, natural process of social development that involved the gradual unfolding of certain core institutions and practices.

Many archaeologists, and the historians who have mugged them, have adopted a ruling-class perspective and characterization of civilized society. These boosters of civilization claim that the social and cultural hierarchies of civilized societies are natural, that hierarchical social relations are inevitable, that oppressive social relations and violence are the immutable, natural outcome of history, and that other kinds of social relations are not possible.

> [Their] assertions that civilization is desirable, beneficial, or superior to societies that lack similar hierarchical social relations merely perpetuate and promote the views of the powerful, self-proclaimed bearers and arbiters of culture and knowledge. Such assertions ultimately distort history. They trivialize the accomplishments of subordinated communities and classes and deny their members roles in making their own his-

tory. Recognizing the existence of subordinated groups, acknowledging their contributions and the historical roles they have played, and understanding their views about life ultimately challenges the validity of accounts that disregard them or deny them agency in shaping their own lives.[18]

As boosters of civilization, these historians and srchaeologists have joined a club that includes Aristotle, José de Acosta, Jean Bodin, Adam Smith, Herbert Spencer, Émile Durkheim, Samuel Huntington, and Newt Gingrich, to name only a few.

By ignoring the fact that civilizations—class-stratified, state-based societies—are fraught with inequalities, exploitation, alienation, immiscibility, and the repression of desire, archaeologists can minimize, or even overlook altogether, the issues raised by critics of civilization, such as Michel de Montaigne, Jean-Jacques Rousseau, Karl Marx, Friedrich Nietzsche, Sigmund Freud, and Stanley Diamond. Furthermore, they do not confront the observations that the members of the subordinated classes and communities, the uncivilized peoples created by ruling elites—such as Sojourner Truth, Chief Joseph, or W. E. B. DuBois—have made about everyday life in civilized society.[19]

ARCHAEOLOGISTS' INTERPRETATIONS

Merely recognizing that civilized societies contain oppressed and repressed classes, that the members of these subaltern groups do speak, and that they often have very accurate understandings of the structures of power and repression they confront in everyday life, does not automatically resolve the problems inherent in the way archaeologists and historians have usually deployed the idea of civilization. Furthermore, it is certainly not an invitation to adopt the radical relativism of those archaeologists who claim that, since meaning is culturally constructed, different cultures, even those in the same society, are not comparable and, hence, their relations cannot be understood by present-day observers who create stories about the past that accord with their own culturally constructed systems of meaning.[20] It does not matter how skilled these observers are in the arts of interpretation (*Overseen*) and cultural translation, because archaeology and history are culture-bound activities that are always carried out in the present. In the words of one archaeologist who has flirted with radical relativism:

> Archaeology is not so much about reading the signs of the past but writing these signs into the present. Correct stories of the past are dependent on a politics of truth linked to the present because all interpretation is a contemporary act. This interpretation is active. There is no original meaning to be textually recreated in an analysis of a set of artifacts.[21]

Such statements obscure the nature of archaeological evidence and the constraints imposed by the archaeological record on interpretation.[22] The objects excavated by archaeologists, their spatial relations with one another, as well as the processes by which these associations were formed, constitute the facts of the archaeological record. They are the raw materials, the data archaeologists interrogate in different ways as they strive to establish evidence of the past—that is, the facts about some ancient society and how it changed through time. Such interrogations involve complex inferential processes—including the use of analogies and comparisons and exploiting multiple strands and diverse types of data, as well as moving back and forth between them—to assess, support, or reject particular hypotheses about society and change that are, in fact, constructed in the present and informed by particular bodies of social theory.[23]

Thus, the facts of the archaeological record that become foundations for evidence of the past are mediated by middle-range practices as well as by social theoretical concerns. The significance of many facts of the record only becomes apparent after they have been interrogated; they acquire meaning in the context of the beliefs held by the particular archaeologist interrogating them. However, this does not mean that the interpretations constructed by different archaeologists are incommensurate. During the past century, they have interrogated the archaeological record in various parts of the world and, as a result, they have made statements about the structure, formation, and development of past human societies. Archaeologists have good reason to assert, for example, that societies with hunting and foraging economies were widespread ten thousand years ago, that some of these hunting and foraging societies added agricultural and/or pastoral production to their economic foundations, that there was a gendered division of labor in the hunting and foraging societies of coastal Peru during the fourth millennium B.C.E., or that class-stratified, state-based societies regularly fall apart. They do not have good reasons to claim, for example, that the rise of civilization was a consequence of the arrival and generosity of aliens from outer space, or that the collapse of Teotihuacán, a city in central Mexico, was mysterious.[24] In other words, the evidence sets certain constraints on what archaeologists can say about the past. While they may not always be able to provide unambiguous reason for preferring one hypothesis over another, they often have excellent grounds for excluding certain statements about human history.

This does not mean that archaeology is not a thoroughly political-economic and social enterprise that is shaped by the various contexts in which it is practiced. It is.[25] However, if we want to examine the various political-economic and social factors that shape the practice of archaeology in some particular national context, then we do have to call into question all of the results archaeologists have achieved. The theoretical pluralism advocated by feminist writers, such as the philosopher of science Sandra Harding, becomes especially useful in this regard.[26] They argue that constructivist critiques, opposed to other viewpoints, provide space for developing new understandings of the discipline, its often unstated premises, and its political-economic and social foundations. For purposes of investigation, the authors of such critical studies have typically treated their object of inquiry independently from what archaeologists have written about the past. As Alison Wylie, a feminist philosopher of science, observes:

> The common thread in these analyses is a concern to articulate an account of knowledge production that recognizes its own contingency and standpoint specificity, that repudiates any quest for a unitary ("master") narrative and any faith in context-transcendent "foundations," and that yet resists the implication that any comparison or judgment of credibility is irreducibly arbitrary, that "anything goes."[27]

The advantage of such constructivist critiques is that they do not conflate issues or problems emerging from the interpretation of the archaeological record with those that arise from particular theoretical foundations or the practice of archaeology in particular national contexts. At the same time, they afford archaeologists an opportunity to examine the interplay between theory and practice, on the one hand, and interpretations of the archaeological record, on the other. Such critical inquiries are illuminating to say the least, and some archaeologists have found it useful to reconsider both the theory and practice of the discipline, as well as various interpretations of past societies, in light of what they suggest or show.[28]

Constructivist critiques also have the capacity to counteract the historical amnesia that afflicts postmodern and postcolonial literary critics.[29] They do not have to separate contemporary practices and interpretations from their historical development. They do not have to treat the interpretive texts written by archaeologists as a literary genre. They do not have to accept claims about the assets and/or liabilities of certain transcendental analytical categories. They do not have to accept claims that assert that, since meaning is culturally constructed, different cultures, even those in the same society, are incommensurate and certainly cannot be understood by a Western observer, even one skilled in the art of interpretation (*Verstehen*) and cultural translation. They also do not have to accept the claim that, since all knowledge is subjective, all efforts to discover objective knowledge are doomed to fail.

By this, I do not mean that archaeologists and historians are not susceptible to certain themes that echo the claims of poststructuralist writers.[30] I do mean, however, that archaeologists and historians are amazingly unaware of the historical development of their disciplines—that is, many suffer from severe cases of historical amnesia. They are also amazingly unaware of the theoretical perspectives that buttress their interpretations of the empirical evidence with which they work; in fact, they are proud, often stridently so, of their ignorance. Theory and theoretical discussions are, in their view, disconnected from empirical reality; since they are largely divorced from historical reality, they have little or nothing to do with historical interpretation. This view provides an incredibly rich medium for the adoption and growth of poststructuralist ideas. It allows archaeologists and historians to support a trendy new theoretical stance without ever changing what they actually do or considering what it is that they actually believe.

Let me provide a few examples of how ideas that echo the claims of poststructuralists have oozed into the views of archaeologists and historians. A few years ago that learned neoliberal social theorist, Margaret Thatcher, said that there was no such thing as society; societies were, in reality, nothing more than aggregates of individuals who competed with one another in the marketplace of life, and some clearly competed more successfully than others, because of their natural endowments or the fact that they were just plain lucky enough to live in an English-speaking capitalist state. Neoliberalism promotes a number of misconceptions about the world, but let us focus our attention on one: Social relations are always built on market exchange. An archaeologist who is exceptionally clear about his theoretical views described prehistoric Europe as follows:

> In order to gain profits, entrepreneurs [that is, individuals who seek profit] change the status quo. An entrepreneur might encourage a community to produce more wool for export by promising imported luxury goods, and that surplus wool could then be used for trade at profit. The economic organization of the community would thereby be altered.[31]
>
> I assume . . . that the principal motivating factor at work in creating change is self-interest—the desire of individuals to accumulate wealth for its own sake, for the security it can bring, and for its use in gaining status, prestige, and sometimes power. This desire seems to be a virtually universal human drive. This idea is well suited to archaeological investigation, since wealth is well documented in the material evidence.[32]

More than a century ago, Frederich Engels described with clarity and precision what was involved in the construction of this view:

> The whole Darwinian theory of the struggle for existence is simply the transference from society to animate nature of Hobbes's theory of war of every man against every man and the bourgeois economic theory of competition, along with the Malthusian theory of population. This feat having been accomplished . . . the same theories are next transferred back from organic nature to history and their validity as eternal laws of human society declared to have been proved.[33]

In other words, the social relations characteristic of capitalism are proclaimed to operate in the natural world, and this "fact" is used to buttress claims that capitalist social relations are the transcendental expression of natural relations between individuals. Furthermore, the social relations characteristic of merchant capital, which has occurred as an appendage to tributary modes of production, is conflated with the capitalist mode of production that is rooted in industrial capitalism, based on the creation of a waged labor force and the extraction of surplus value as opposed to the extraction of surplus labor or surplus product.[34]

A corollary of this view is the claim that consumption is the motor driving the development of modern society, which is characterized as postindustrial and increasingly global.[35] Advocates of this position recognize that consumption is socially constructed, which explains what and why people consume what they do. This assertion is often tied to the works of Gabriel Tarde or George Simmel, who argued that the masses emulate or imitate the behavior and consumption patterns of the upper classes.[36] This implies that the upper classes' inspirations and demands for luxury goods eventually trickle down and ultimately form the foundations for mass production and markets. It also means that class relations are harmonious rather than antagonistic. The consumption theorists argue that Marx was mistaken, because he did not adequately appreciate the significance of

> the central contradiction of capitalism in which the laborer represents, in his or her other role as consumer, the market necessary for the goods produced by capitalism. However opposed capital and labor may appear in the struggle of wages against profit, for capitalism to achieve its goals, and its sales, it is necessary for the laborer to buy and to continue to desire more goods. When the labor force does not represent the market, the interests of the two groups are totally antagonistic, but when the labor force is the market the relationship becomes more ambiguous. . . . When this happens, a certain identity of interests between capital and labor may appear.[37]

Archaeologists view class struggle as virtually erased except when the workers do not constitute a market for the goods they produce. This perspective led one post-processual archaeologist, whose identity I will not reveal in order to protect his job, to proclaim that, "when progressive folks go out and buy foreign commodities, they are really waging class struggle against the U.S. capitalist class!"

The two examples just discussed share several other features that echo postmodernist concerns. They portray the economic base of society not in terms of the relations of production or how surplus is pumped out of the direct producers, but rather in terms of constant, transhistorical desires to exchange, accumulate, and consume. By viewing exchange and consumption, but not production, as parts of a transcendental human nature, they dismiss any concern with modes of production or production relations as mere economic reductionism or economic determinism, both of which have been proven erroneous in the post-Marxist world marked by the political disintegration of the Soviet Union.

It also leads archaeologists and historians to approve of Émile Durkheim's contention that the real problems of modern industrial society are not economic, since capitalism had excluded economic life from processes of communication by which the state regulated the rest of society. Economic relations were not part of the real foundations of modern society, which rested instead on a substrate composed of religious faiths; legal and moral regulations; political, literary, and occupational associations; and, curiously, financial systems.[38] This position is reinforced by their penchant for repeating the theoretical views of late–twentieth-century Durkheimians.

By naturalizing socially constituted categories, such as class, archaeologists and historians, many of whom usually have not read Friedrich Nietzsche since their days as freshmen in Western civilization courses, find it easy to adopt Michel Foucault's

Nietzschean claim that, since all social relations are based on power and domination, societies that lack exploitative social relations are not possible.[39] Denying the existence of kin-organized societies with nonexistent or poorly developed exploitative social relations flies, of course, in the face of numerous ethnographic accounts of communities, such as the San or the Iroquois.[40] Nevertheless, such instances of primitive communism have been easily forgotten or dismissed in light of the evolutionary arguments of Durkheim, Herbert Spencer, and others who portrayed the increasing social differentiation and exploitation as natural features of society.[41]

In each of the examples described above, ideas with other sources of inspiration have become easily associated with or enveloped by the claims of poststructuralist or postmodernist writers. And on these points, some archaeologists and historians have found themselves in agreement, even though they have not necessarily appreciated the obtuse literary styles and language games of the poststructuralists. Instead of exploring the origins and implications of the shared viewpoints in some critical manner, they are either repelled or seduced. However, repulsion and seduction have the same effects: Neither promotes constructivist critiques of the theory and practice of the two disciplines, and both allow the mugging of social theory to continue. The difference is that those who are appalled by social theory deny that they are still mugging it, while those who have become enamored, either through self-deception or fascination, extol the virtues of their paramour, even as they search his or her pockets for validation and new ideas.

Where does this leave archaeologists and historians concerned with the formation and development of one or another ancient civilization? Recognizing that civilized societies contain oppressed classes whose members had understandings of power and everyday life that differed from those of their rulers is certainly movement in a productive direction. Archaeological investigations away from palaces and royal tombs in rural peasant homesteads, workers quarters, or workshops have begun to provide insights into the nature and extent of class, ethnic, and gender-based differences in particular civilizations. Another move in the right direction has been the use of data derived from such inquiries to clarify and refine the theoretical assumptions and frameworks—the ideas about society, change, and culture—archaeologists employ to explain the formation of these civilizations. Finally, examining how particular national contexts and class interests shape the practice of archaeology and its theoretical underpinnings is also beginning to bear fruit at this time.

NOTES

1. There are some exceptions to the rule. For instance, Marc Bloch, Karen Spalding, Moses Finley, and Jalil Sued Badillo are historians who have used archaeological data in sophisticated ways, and Elizabeth Brumfiel, Bruce Trigger, and Christine Hastorf are archaeologists who appreciate the value of historical information and recognize its limitations.

2. Thomas Jefferson, who is often hailed as the "father of American archaeology," was

not, of course, an archaeologist. He and his contemporaries were concerned with practical issues; when they employed archaeological and historical evidence, their goal was not to reconstruct the past as it had been in order to satisfy some antiquarian curiosity but rather to illuminate the constant and universal principles of human nature. As I pointed out in *Toward a Social History of Archaeology in the United States* (Ft. Worth, TX: Harcourt Brace, 1995), nineteenth-century U.S. writers examined the archaeology of classical antiquity, the Holy Land and the Bible, and America's past for different reasons. Classical antiquity represented civilization, a set of images that could be, and were, appropriated for the emerging nation state—e.g., the Roman eagle, the Senate, classical styles of architecture, and place names, such as Rome and Athens. Biblical history and archaeology were important, because they linked missionary activity and the adoption of Christianity as necessary features of the process of becoming civilized. Archaeological evidence from the Americas was deployed by settler-colonists in arguments that sought to deny or limit the property rights of native peoples whose everyday lives were being transformed by civilizing processes such as commerce, dispossession from their homelands, the destruction of their customary institutions and practices, genocide, and resistance.

3. Stanley Diamond, *In Search of the Primitive: A Critique of Civilization* (New Brunswick, NJ: Transaction Books, 1974), p. 1. For an informed discussion of the relation between literacy and state formation, see Mogens Trolle Larsen, "Introduction: Literacy and Social Complexity," in *State and Society: The Emergence and Development of Social Hierarchy and Political Centralisation,* ed. John Gledhill, Barbara Bender, and Mogens Trolle Larsen (London: Unwin Hyman, 1988), pp. 173–191.

4. For a discussion of a recent trend in archaeology, popular in the anglophone world but not elsewhere, see Thomas C. Patterson, "History and the Post-processual Archaeologies," *Man,* vol. 24, no. 4 (1995), pp. 555–556; Philip L. Kohl, "Limits to a Post-processual Archaeology (Or, the Dangers of a New Scholasticism)," in *Archaeological Theory: Who Sets the Agenda?* ed. Norman Yoffee and Andrew Sherratt (Cambridge: Cambridge University Press, 1993), pp. 13–19; and Bruce G. Trigger, "Archaeology and the Integrated Circus," *Critique of Anthropology* vol. 15, no. 4 (1995), pp. 319–335, and "Hyperrelativism, Responsibility, and the Social Sciences," *Canadian Review of Sociology and Anthropology* vol. 26, no. 5 (1989), pp. 776–797. 5. For example, readers might recall the opening chapters in most world history textbooks that borrow heavily from archaeologists to describe the rise of civilization in Mesopotamia and Egypt. Written evidence becomes increasingly important in the narratives of these authors once civilization, in their view, shifted to Greece and Rome and after it reappeared in northwestern Europe and achieved full fluorescence in the United States.

6. Thomas C. Patterson, *Inventing Western Civilization* (New York: Monthly Review Press, 1997).

7. To counter postmodernist claims that civilization is a wholly Eurocentric concept that cannot be used elsewhere, let me point out that each class-stratified, state-based society invents its own version of civilization. For example, Chinese intellectuals of the third century B.C.E. defined the social order of the Han world and civilization in terms of four concentric zones. The king extracted daily revenues from the royal domain at the core of the civilized world, monthly tribute from the noble zone, quarterly tribute from the pacified zone that lay beyond it, and annual tribute from the tamed barbarians who lived in the frontier zone. Beyond the civilized Han world lay the wild lands occupied by barbarians who perhaps paid tribute once in a lifetime. The Incas who ruled a conquest state in the Andes

during the fifteenth century C.E. viewed themselves as an island of civilization surrounded by a sea of barbarians (see Patterson, ibid., pp. 18–19).

8. Only the Australian archaeologist V. Gordon Childe recognized that civilized society was fundamentally oppressive to its direct producers. See his *Man Makes Himself* [1936] (New York: New American Library, 1983), pp. 117, 130–133, 173–178.

9. Ronald L. Meek, *Social Science and Ignoble Savage* (Cambridge: Cambridge University Press, 1976).

10. Julian H. Steward, "Area Research: Theory and Practice," *Social Science Research Council Bulletin,* no. 63 (1950), pp. 1–164, pp. 103–105.

11. In "Julian Steward and the Construction of Area Studies Research in the United States," in *Julian Steward and the Great Basin,* ed. Richard Cemmer, L. Daniel Myers, and Mary E. Rudler (Salt Lake City, UT: University of Utah Press, 1999), pp. 219-241. Thomas C. Patterson and Antonio Lauria-Pericelli argue that the weaknesses of Steward's broader research program began to emerge after 1952 when the locus of U.S. foreign aid shifted to Asia, Africa, and the Middle East, and questions of decolonization and modernization rather than economic reconstruction came to the fore. The weaknesses became more apparent in 1955 after the Bandung Conference of nonaligned nations and the emergence of the Soviet Union as a source of foreign aid. His evolutionist model of society driven by a narrowly defined economic base said nothing about how to identify, and support, those groups that would promote capitalist economic development in the Third World.

12. Clifford Geertz, *Agricultural Involution: The Process of Ecological Change in Indonesia* (Berkeley: University of California Press, 1963), pp. 10–11.

13. Kent Flannery, "The Cultural Evolution of Civilizations," *Annual Review of Ecology and Systematics,* vol. 3 (1972), pp. 399–426, p. 409.

14. Ibid., pp. 413–414.

15. Sander E. van der Leeuw (ed.), *Archaeological Approaches to the Study of Complexity* (Amsterdam, the Netherlands: Universiteit van Amsterdam, 1981); and Douglas T. Price and James A. Brown (eds.), *Prehistoric Hunter-Gatherers: The Emergence of Cultural Complexity* (New York: Academic Press, 1985).

16. Colin Renfrew, "Systems Collapse As Social Transformation: Catastrophe and Anastrophe in Early State Societies," in *Transformations: Mathematical Approaches to Culture Change,* ed. Colin Renfrew and Kenneth L. Cooke (New York: Academic Press, 1979), pp. 481–506, p. 489.

17. The clearest statements of the neo-Smithian "trade thesis"—that is, the motor driving the development of civilization is exchange or commerce—are Barbara Price, "Shifts in Production and Organization: A Cluster Interaction Model," *Current Anthropology,* vol. 18, no. 2 (1977), pp. 209–234, and Colin Renfew, "Introduction: Peer Polity Interaction and Socio-political Change," in *Peer Polity Interaction and Socio-political Change,* ed. Colin Renfrew and John F. Cherry (Cambridge: Cambridge University Press, 1986), pp. 1–18.

18. Patterson, *Inventing Western Civilization,* p. 136.

19. Ibid., pp. 59–135, provides a concise summary of their critiques of civilization. Social historians and anthropologists who have paid close attention to subaltern voices, placed them in a social context, and looked carefully at processes of class and state formation are: Karen Spalding, *Huarochirí: An Andean Society under Inca and Spanish Rule* (Stanford, CA: Stanford University Press, 1984); Christine W. Gailey, *From Kinship to Kingship: Gender Hierarchy and State Formation in the Tongan Islands* (Austin: University of Texas Press, 1987); and Kathy Le Mons Walker, *On the Road to Modern China: Local Society and Semicolonial Process, Nantong*

County and the Northern Yangzi Delta (ca. 1450–1930) (Stanford, CA: Stanford University Press, forthcoming).

20. For recent commentaries on the implications of relativism, see Trigger, "Archaeology and the Integrated Circus"; Frances E. Mascia-Lees, Patricia Sharpe, and Colleen B. Cohen, "The Post-Modernist Turn in Anthropology: Cautions from a Feminist Perspective," *Signs,* vol. 15, no. 1 (1989), pp. 7–33; and Melford E. Spiro, "Postmodern Anthropology, Subjectivity: A Modernist Critique," *Comparative Studies in Society and History,* vol. 38, no. 4 (1996), pp. 759–780.

21. Christopher Tilley, "Michel Foucault: Toward an Archaeology of Archaeology," in *Reading Material Culture,* ed. Christopher Tilley (Oxford: Basil Blackwell, 1990), pp. 281–347, p. 338.

22. Alison Wylie, "The Constitution of Archaeological Evidence: Gender Politics and Science," in *The Disunity of Science: Boundaries, Contexts, and Power,* ed. Peter Galison and David J. Stump (Stanford, CA: Stanford University Press, 1996), pp. 311–343.

23. Thomas C. Patterson, *The Theory and Practice of Archaeology: A Workbook* (Englewood Cliffs, NJ: Prentice Hall, 1994); and Alison Wylie, "Facts of the Record and Facts of the Past: Mandelbaum on the Anatomy of History 'Proper,'" *International Studies in Philosophy,* vol. 17, no. 1 (1985), pp. 71–85, and "Archaeological Cables and Tacking: The Implications of Practice for Bernstein's 'Options Beyond Objectivism and Relativism,'" *Philosophy of the Social Sciences,* vol. 19, no. 1 (1989), pp. 1–18.

24. Archaeologist René Millon, "The Last Years of Teotihuacán Dominance," in *The Collapse of Ancient States and Civilizations,* ed. Norman Yoffee and George L. Cowgill (Tucson: University of Arizona Press, 1988), pp. 102–164, pp. 146–158, used archaeological data to discuss the active role played by urban dwellers in the demise of the ancient city: They set fire to several hundred public buildings and murdered the members of the ruling elite who resided in the main palace.

25. See, for instance, Thomas C. Patterson, *Toward a Social History of Archaeology in the United States* (Ft. Worth, TX: Harcourt Brace, 1995); Alison Wylie, "Gender Theory and the Archaeological Record: Why Is There No Archaeology of Gender?" in *Engendering Archaeology: Women and Prehistory,* ed. Joan M. Gero and Margaret Conkey (Oxford: Basil Blackwell, 1991), pp. 31–54; and the various essays in *Making Alternative Histories: The Practice of Archaeology and History in Non-Western Settings,* ed. by Peter R. Schmidt and Thomas C. Patterson (Santa Fe, NM: SAR Press, 1996).

26. Sandra Harding, *The Science Question in Feminism* (Ithaca, NY: Cornell University Press, 1986), esp. pp. 136–162, and *Whose Science? Whose Knowledge? Thinking from Women's Lives* (Ithaca, NY: Cornell University Press, 1991).

27. Alison Wylie, "Alternative Histories: Epistemic Disunity and Political Integrity," in Schmidt and Patterson, *Making Alternative Histories,* p. 270.

28. Patty Jo Watson and Mary C. Kennedy, "Gender, Space, and Food in Prehistory," in Gero and Conkey, *Engendering Archaeology,* pp. 15–31; Joan Gero, "Socio-Politics and the Woman-at-Home Ideology," *American Antiquity,* vol. 50, no. 3 (1985), pp. 342–350; and Stephanie Moser, *Archaeology and Its Disciplinary Culture: The Professionalization of Australian Prehistoric Archaeology,* Ph.D. dissertation in archaeology (Sydney, Australia: University of Sydney, 1995); and Thomas C. Patterson, "Conceptual Differences between Mexican and Peruvian Archaeology," *American Anthropologist,* vol. 98, no. 3 (1996), pp. 499–506.

29. Aijaz Ahmad, "The Politics of Literary Postcoloniality," *Race and Class,* vol. 36, no.

3 (1995), pp. 1–20; Carol A. Stabile, "Postmodernism, Feminism, and Marx: Notes from the Abyss," *Monthly Review,* vol. 47, no. 3 (1995), pp. 89–107.

    30. Here, I am arguing that poststructuralist writers—such as Jacques Derrida and Michel Foucault, who have resurrected Friedrich Nietzsche—provided, during the 1970s and 1980s, the philosophical underpinnings for postmodernism, which is typically defined in vague, internally inconsistent, and contradictory terms. See Alex Callinicos, *Against Postmodernism: A Marxist Critique* (New York: St. Martin's Press, 1990), and Thomas C. Patterson, "Post-Structuralism, Post-Modernism: Implications for Historians," *Social History,* vol. 14, no. 1 (1989), pp. 83–88. 31. Peter Wells, *Farms, Villages, and Cities: Commerce and Urban Origins in Late Prehistoric Europe* (Ithaca, NY: Cornell University Press, 1984), p. 31.

    32. Ibid., pp. 34–35.

    33. Frederick Engels' letter to Lavrov, 12–17 November 1875, in Karl Marx and Frederick Engels, *Selected Works in Three Volumes,* vol. 3 (Moscow: Progress Publishers, 1970), pp. 477–480.

    34. For example, see Thomas C. Patterson, "Merchant Capital and the Formation of the Inca State," *Dialectical Anthropology,* vol. 12, no. 2 (1987), pp. 217–227.

    35. Daniel Miller, *Material Culture and Mass Consumption* (Oxford: Basil Blackwell, 1987), and Arjun Appadurai (ed.), *The Social Life of Things: Commodities in Cultural Perspective* (Cambridge: Cambridge University Press, 1986). For a critical discussion of consumption theories, see Ben Fine and Ellen Leopold, *The World of Consumption* (London: Routledge, 1993).

    36. George Simmel, *The Philosophy of Money,* 2nd ed. (London: Routledge, 1990), and Gabriel Tarde, *Les lois de l'imitation: étude sociologique,* 2nd ed. (Paris: Félix Alcan, Editeur, 1895).

    37. Miller, *Material Culture,* p. 184.

    38. Émile Durkheim, *The Rules of Sociological Method* [1895], ed. George E. G. Caitlin. (New York: Free Press, 1938), pp. 3–4.

    39. For example, Michel Foucault, "Nietzsche, Genealogy, History," in *Language, Counter-Memory, Practice: Selected Essays and Interviews by Michel Foucault,* ed. by D. F. Bouchard (Ithaca, NY: Cornell University Press, 1977), and Friedrich Nietzsche, *On the Genealogy of Morals* (New York: Random House, 1967).

    40. The articles in Eleanor Leacock and Richard Lee (eds.), *Politics and History in Band Societies* (Cambridge: Cambridge University Press, 1982) provide a useful introduction.

    41. Émile Durkheim, *The Division of Labor in Society* [1893] (New York: Free Press, 1964).

PART 2

Area Perspectives

4

Historiography in West Asian and North African Studies since Sa'id's *Orientalism*

R. A. Abou-El-Haj

It has been more than two decades since Edward Sa'id published *Orientalism* (New York: Pantheon Books, 1978), in which he addressed the work of Western Orientalists who had essentialized views of Arab and Islamic society, and found their approach odious, if not sinister. The source for Sa'id's observations was specifically Western European and U.S. literary and scholarly production on the "Orient" and the "scientific" (scientistic?) tradition that went with it. The scholarly response to Sa'id's critique has been quite positive, so far that the scholarship, especially concerning the study of West Asia and North Africa, has felt obligated to measure itself in terms of its distance and proximity to the critical parameters set by the book.

Making Sa'id's critique the standard by which to place one's scholarship poses a problem of its own. It does not pay enough attention, for example, to the fact that Sa'id's assessment of the scholarly literature was mainly carried out by adopting the approach that he himself had condemned. In the same way that Orientalists read their texts in an unproblematized and unmediated manner, not allowing themselves any kind of self-conscious transcendence, so did Sa'id as he read, approached, and analyzed the intellectual output of the field. Since the Orientalists' approach to reading texts was unmediated, it follows that what guided their understanding, analyses, and explication was not a consciously chosen theory or model. Some Orientalists had even expressed pride in being guided simply by the facts in the presentation of their narratives. But, unlike their approach, a model or a theory has known assumptions and values and is therefore subject as much to argumentation as to falsification.

Since Orientalist scholarship has generally been innocent of any conscious theory, it was mostly guided by the writer's aesthetic sensibility (or free association) and unconscious assumptions about the society whose "primary" texts the scholarship examined and directly read. A transcendent view would allow for the ambivalence of the sources. Orientalists, on the other hand, project a picture, using the texts they read as evidence, that reflects and fulfills their unconscious and predetermined values—that is, their prejudices.

In a similar fashion, because he did not consciously provide an alternative model by which to evaluate and critique Orientalist scholarly works, Sa'id's treatment falls back on unconscious assumptions and aesthetic sensibilities, notwithstanding his defense of his position as one of "adversarial critique."[1] Sa'id can be chided for lumping together Orientalist scholarship into one body of knowledge. On the macro level, the scholarship is treated as if it were all the same, with no differentiation in its historical meaning, thereby collapsing time, place, and occasion of its production. However, in microstudies focused on the specificities of the scholarship, it is possible to achieve this differentiation, which can explain the scholarship in terms of its context and also allow us to examine it in light of its social utility. By not taking into account the various historical metamorphoses of this scholarship, *Orientalism* remains an ahistorical treatment of the scholarship.

For example, Western societies that produced scholarship as Orientalism in the seventeenth century are treated on a par with those same societies that produced it in the eighteenth, nineteenth, and twentieth centuries. No account is taken of the lapse of time and disparity of societies, let alone the individuality of those who produced the various forms of scholarship. Accordingly, Sa'id's approach would render the same judgment on *Geschichte des Osmanischen Reiches* (ten volumes, Pest, 1827–1835), nineteenth-century Habsburg author Joseph von Hammer-Purgstall's treatment of Ottoman history, as he would of Stanford Shaw in *History of the Ottoman Empire and Modern Turkey,* vol. 1, (Cambridge: Cambridge University Press, 1976), in the twentieth century. These writers come from different times and places and therefore their writings serve different social purposes. Our analyses of their scholarship should be focused instead on how their contemporaries put their work to social use.

Similarly, French scholarship on North African Islam that was produced at the height of Western imperialism will have quite a different meaning from French scholarship on the same subject appearing in the 1990s. Analysis of the Islamic culture of North Africa as a means to help France control Algerian society (one of the purposes of the earlier scholarship) should not be equated with French scholarship on Islam that was aimed at the control of Muslim immigrants to France (in the late twentieth century). In other words, there are different motives, functions, and purposes in time and circumstance for the two sets of scholarly production. Similarly, one should view differently the understanding of Islamic culture by the late Algerian-born Roger La Tourneau, a French scholar of North Africa who was publicly against granting independence to Algeria, and the more recent analysis by Gilles Kepel (in *Muslim Extremism in Egypt,* Berkeley: University of California Press, 1985). Kepel is a French scholar who has written several books on Islamic movements, especially in Egypt and the Arab world, and on North African Muslim immigrants in France. He is also a member of the Paris-based Institute of Political

Studies. It is conceivable, theoretically, that some scholars study Islam and West Asia and North Africa out of pure, strictly scholarly, and scientific motives. But any analysis of a study's purposes should address the motives of the individual creators of the scholarship and the issue of its contemporary social function and purpose.[2]

Sa'id, by his own acknowledgment, did not intend to provide a methodological alternative to Orientalism. In an article published ten years after the appearance of *Orientalism,* he pleaded that his work should be viewed as an "adversarial critique."[3] The specification of an alternative method was for him fraught with the very same traps to which Orientalism or any scholarly production is likely to succumb. Nevertheless, his work has helped clear the path for more complex approaches to West Asian and North African studies. In the last two decades, new scholars have been trained and they, in turn, have been weaned on the critique that is in *Orientalism.*

As scholars in the field, we will have to come to grips with the epistemological questions critiqued in *Orientalism.* One of these is an alternative approach to the question: "How do we get to know West Asia and North Africa?" By denying this to be the purpose of his critique, as indicated earlier, Sa'id could not help spawning alternatives.[4]

One consequence of leaving to dangle the alternative approach to studying West Asia and North Africa, as Sa'id's approach had done, though unintentionally, is to leave a vacuum into which many alternatives to the one he criticized insinuate themselves.[5] (These alternatives will be discussed in a separate part of this chapter.[6]) Alternative approaches to research have to be offered to replace the old scholarship of Orientalism. These research projects do not have to be monolithic or presented as final strategies. One could argue that even a research project outline could provide an ideal against which to critique future and existing research programs and paradigms. Such a research program could also take into account evidence that on its own would not be deemed historically relevant. For example, in looking at the question, "Was there a civil life autonomous of the state in early modern West Asian history?" we look at the space between society and state. Scholars who postulated that civil life did not exist in early modern times were blinded by their assumptions and therefore unable to see the evidence that was there. As soon as the concept of civil life was postulated, evidence could resurface and be used to support the hypothesis of civil life. In a similar fashion, Philip Huang has recently challenged the restrictive and exclusive use of the term "civil society" to European societies and postulated and discussed it for Chinese history.[7]

The second part of this chapter will focus on the alternative scholarship that filled the vacuum left in the wake of the deconstruction of Sa'id's Orientalist scholarship. The occasion and time for the new scholarship's production should be noted before treating it under separate schools. The 1980s and mid-1990s represent a period of change in the realities of power and hegemony on the global level. The epistemological stance that informed scholarly knowledge, that once supported as it legitimated the wielding of hegemonic power, was proving inadequate to the new task of explaining the changed power relations on the global level. Scholarly production was divided in terms of First, Second, Third, and Fourth Worlds. Instead of facing the change in political and economic relations on the global level and, therefore, effecting a change in the assumptions that informed their approach to the production of scholarly knowledge, some scholars resorted to reproducing the same scholarship and paradigm while others covered it with a postmodern label. Thus modern epistemology was dismissed as being inadequate to the task of explaining social reality instead of being reconstructed to accommodate change. As the rest of the world builds its half of the bridge to the First World, its efforts are consistently being undermined by self-pitying Eurocentric intellectuals whose worldview ceased to accommodate new social, economic, and political realities. There is an ironic twist to the continuity of this form of epistemology. As the First World states turn to realism in their relations with the new global power structure, most scholars in the fields of West Asian and North African studies seem divided into two groups: one is content with the reproduction of the old hegemonic paradigms without taking into account the changed global picture[8]; the other, taking its clues from postmodern and/or postcolonial discourses, seems to be a willing agent of dead-end scholarship and nihilism.

At first glance the latter position seems puzzling, unless one were to see it as a tactical move in the transition from national to global capitalism. A full discussion of the implications of this new discourse and its epistemological ramifications will have to be postponed. However, in his contributions to this book, Arif Dirlik has fleshed out some of the profound issues involved in arriving at some form of resolution. The rest of this chapter addresses the specific schools of scholarship that have emerged since 1978. This scholarship can be divided into at least four schools.

SCHOOL NUMBER 1: THEORY

The first school on this list is based primarily on theory. In the main, this school consists of a number of scholars who, while having an informing theory, are unable to muster the means to actually test their theories first hand; instead they resort to secondary works. By not taking into consideration the orientations of the secondary sources that they had not generated themselves, they abdicate both the assumptions and the designs of their own studies. In the process, these scholars present the approach and the results of their secondary sources as their own, often quite unconsciously, while including, in many instances, their secondary sources' prejudices, biases, and contradictions. In the end, no matter how sound the practitioners' theories are, these are vitiated by assumptions underlying the unconsciously adopted discourse and the commensurate highly selected evidence that was used to test the theories. The dilemma for these scholars is perhaps further compounded, since their main contribution to the field of knowledge is merely a theoretically informed approach. The consequence is a static theory that floats uncomfortably independent of the evidence and cannot be used to explain new patterns or synthesis. In other words, there is a lack of synchrony between evidence and the theory that often results in fragmented pieces of insight searching for coherence. Examples of scholars from outside the field who are most representative of this group are Perry Anderson, especially in his treatment of the Ottoman Empire,[9] and, more recently, Jack Goldstone.[10] From within the field itself, the recent work by Karen Barkey can be cited.[11]

The inability of practitioners to test their theories using primary research often leads them to arrive at totally opposite conclusions than would have been warranted by their newly minted theories. This tautology is especially well spun by Perry Anderson in his treatment of the Ottoman Empire. In *Formation of the Modern State* (Albany, NY: State University of New York Press, 1992), I carried out an extended analysis of his challenge of the thesis that the Ottoman Empire represented an example of Asiatic mode of production (AMP).[12] After close examination, however, we find Anderson offering an alternative that, when examined systematically, brings us back to observations that are reminders of AMP. The Ottoman Empire is then saddled with all the attributes of an AMP, which Anderson had so assiduously denied in earlier paragraphs of his book. The underlying assumptions of his secondary sources particularly emerge when he conveys the specificity of Ottoman society into the "other," accentuating mainly Ottoman society's "unnatural" presence in Europe. Instead of enlightenment, we are presented with prejudice that is informed by culturally hegemonic assumptions, constructed in a scientist language, though sometimes quite eloquently.[13]

SCHOOL NUMBER 2: PROCESS

Scholars who use theory but refuse to view history as a discourse or process represent the second school. The theory itself is not seen as something that must be tested for its validity by means of primary and other sources. Instead, theory is used as a formula at which evidence, even that which is generated by research in the primary sources, is thrown in haphazardly, whenever it fits the established structure set forth by the theory.

The advantage that this group exhibits over the first one is in its possession of some language tools. Here, scholars have the potential capacity to test, from first-hand research, the validity of the theories that they advance for their research. This advantage is soon invalidated by their approach to theory strictly as a formula. Their research mainly consists of a mechanical exercise that views evidence as a checklist of essential, undifferentiated, and simple attributes. Furthermore, the practitioners compound their problems with an uncritical reading of primary sources, usually limited and scattered, which they treat as if the sources represented a database of available evidence. Not only is the unsystematic research of the parts made to represent the whole, but also their conclusions are sometimes projected to the level of civilization, without taking into account all the other mediating stages. For example, the social bias, timing, and occasion for the production of the primary sources are overlooked. Since no historical analysis was involved in the scrutinization of primary sources, the uncritical reading (an anachronistic direct reading of the

sources without taking into consideration the time of the writing or its social mediation) adds to a formulaic view of theory, resulting in a scholarship that is short on
specifics, simplistic in its conception and application, repetitive, undynamic, and
wooden, if not outright boring. What is the intellectual efficacy of this scholarship
for its practitioners, let alone for their readers who have to suffer their way through
it? How can scholars with this orientation toward sources and theory sustain themselves intellectually, let alone morally?

The most dramatic example that illustrates the uncritical reading of sources is
from D. Crecelius ("Ahmad Shalabi ibn 'Abd al-Ghani and Ahmad Katkhuda 'Aza-
ban al-Damurdashi: Two Sources for al-Jabarti's *'Aja'b al-'Athar fi' l-Trajim wa'l-
Akhbar,*" 1987), which was initially presented as a lecture at a conference in Tunis
and then again in Los Angeles.[14] In the lecture, Crecelius took "personal offense"
at the well-known early modern chronicler from Egypt, al-Jabarti, for having mis-
used contemporary sources. According to Crecelius, this eighteenth-century
chronicler lied, cheated, and plagiarized certain parts of his eighteenth- and
nineteenth-century chronicle of Egypt, sometimes even verbatim. Instead of
addressing the problem of the nature of the "originality" of a scholar's work in early
modern times, Crecelius approached his subject of study as a moralist; therefore, he
thought that he would be following double standards if he were to contextualize
what was a cultural, albeit scholarly tradition. Al-Jabarti had taken information from
other sources without acknowledgment, and that was plagiarism! That this took
place in the eighteenth century and has sociohistorical and sociological implications
is not part of Crecelius' analytic vision.

Al-Jabarti has been dead for nearly two hundred years. He cannot be addressed
or be held accountable directly, nor should he be treated by twentieth-century standards of scholarship. (The historical assumptions and the scholarly apparatuses under
which we operate today had not come into common use until the nineteenth century.) All of us have been faced with the question of originality of sources—what
is original in that which is reported by an author, chronicler, artist, or literary
researcher. However, some scholars are left unperturbed, for they have other
research agendas to engage them; others have made originality the center of their
scholarly preoccupation. It did not occur to Crecelius that other scholars of al-
Jabarti's time accepted plagiarism as a normal phenomenon of the cultural production of that period, Instead, he made an issue of it with all the connotations of copy-
rights private ownership of ideas. Is this not the case, perhaps, because other scholars
late in the twentieth century were familiar with the normality of heavy "borrowing" in the cultural production of early modern times?

Perhaps the best way to approach the problems of direct interpretation and analysis, as in the futile search for originality, is to test an interpretation's usefulness by
comparison with another interpretation. In other words, does it lead us to the next
level of thinking and research or does it, in fact, end up in a blind alley? The worst
scenario occurs, however, when we try to test comparatively the anachronistic
question of originality against modern standard historical methodology.

In previous publications, I have suggested various ways out of this impasse by treating the issue of originality in terms of the time and context of the occurrence and reconfiguration of a particular phenomenon, concept, treatise, or historical episode. For example: the reconfiguration in use of the "feudal" term *emin* by Defterdar Mehmed Pasha, an early modern chronicler and experienced financial officer, to stand for a new office he proposed for a salaried tax collector in the late seventeenth century.[15] Another example of cultural recovery for new uses can be argued from evidence from the sixteenth- and seventeenth-century nasihatnames—mirrors to princes. Their primary recovery facilitated their use in the expression of political discourse. In several instances of this second example, the originality of the treatise can best be analyzed not in terms of the language in which it was produced, precedents cited, or style of writing, but by looking at how concepts, terms, and precedents that came from different times, social contexts, and discourses are used. In other words, such a cultural recovery is one of the means through which a society reconfigures concepts, texts, and forms from its cultural and intellectual heritage and puts them to new social uses. J. G. A. Pocock, in *Virtue, Commerce, and History* (Cambridge: Cambridge University Press, 1985), discusses the early modern European literary genre suggestive of similar social utility.

Among the scholars who belong to this second school are economic historians, those who claim to approach history from a neo-Marxian or political economy position, labor historians, and specialists in the communist and socialist movements in West Asian and North African history.

Scholars in schools one and two have two characteristics in common: first, a lack of awareness of the ambivalence and fluidity of the available evidence; second, their treatment of theory as dogma, in other words, as fixed, unchangeable, indeed almost "sacred." The structure that they construct accommodates evidence that is thrown at it randomly; whatever does not stick, falls by the wayside, often burying evidence that could vitiate their interpretation.

SCHOOL NUMBER 3: LANGUAGE

A third school of scholars consists of those who are either outright Orientalists or neo-Orientalists who produce similar kinds of scholarship. They blame Sa'id's critique of Orientalist scholarship for all the ills of the social scientific alternatives that have appeared since 1978 (for instance, theory oriented but lacking or deficient in language training). We sometimes find that natives of the regional languages who subscribe to both the Orientalist and neo-Orientalist views base their positions on the premise that knowledge of the languages, in and of themselves, is sufficient to the scholarly enterprise.

The neo-Orientalists, in spite of Sa'id's critique, continue to treat culture and Islam mainly in essentialist terms. During the past two decades, a concourse of factors has helped to reinvent the Orientalist paradigm. At its center is the revival of

Islam as a structural alternative to modernity, which appeared to most observers as the resurgence of fundamentalism. The most dramatic realization of this process has been the Iranian Revolution of the late 1970s, but it is also occurring in South Lebanon and Algeria, among other countries. These historical movements have reignited the scholarship focused exclusively on the study of Islam and have received financial, official, semiofficial, and private support from the United States and France. Examples include the U.S.-based Fulbright Fellowships, which are devoted to such studies, and Georgetown University's newly endowed center for the study of Islam. Schools are scrambling to appoint scholars who can teach Islam, even though no standard of teaching or scholarly parameters has been set. With this new interest in Islam, yet another justification for the production of neo-Orientalism comes into play.

An added incentive for the study of Islam has been occasioned by the decreased challenge from the former Soviet Union. Islam has filled the vacuum that resulted from that federation's dissolution and is now considered the main threat to Western Civilization. This perception is reiterated by no less an authority in the social sciences than Claude Levi-Straus. In an interview with the *New York Times* ("The Paris Journal," December 21, 1987), he declared, "I have the concern . . . to defend a certain number of values which are those of my society and which . . . are threatened by the Soviet Union, by Islamic fundamentalism and by the demographic growth of the third world."[16]

Also of interest is the media's depiction of "Islamic practices" as illogical and barbaric. Islam—the whole of its mentality—is shown to be inhabited by dangerous, nasty fundamentalists. Thus no attempt is made to analyze or explain the cultural phenomenon associated with Islam in the time of its historical occurrence, let alone to specify its social contexts. An example that best illustrates this distortion is the controversy associated with interpreting the publication of Salman Rushdie's *Satanic Verses* (New York: Viking, 1989). Reactions to this work have emerged from professionals in fields ranging from theology to sociology. Perhaps the best example of an attempt to historicize the discussion of Rushdie's work is in Talal Asad's *Genealogies of Religion: Discipline and Reasons of Power in Christianity and Islam* (Baltimore: Johns Hopkins University Press, 1993), in which the author discusses the reception of the novel by Muslim immigrants in England and that of the "host society." For Asad, the novel is best understood not in terms of Islam the religion, but in terms of how the Muslim immigrants to the United Kingdom view their culture as a shield against the exploitive and assimilationist policies of the British government in its handling of the Muslim minority working class.

The third school of scholars detaches itself from the first one by faulting its practitioners for their innocence in the use and knowledge of primary and other sources of the region. It faults the second school for its rudimentary command of the region's languages. The practitioners of the third group thus take special pride in their philological prowess. Although not trained in the social sciences (their training is either philological or linguistic in departments and institutes at which the primary function is teaching Near Eastern languages), most members of this group end up teaching in the social sciences. So through this pedagogical path, the "method" of Orientalism, now appearing as neo-Orientalism, is thus reproduced and perpetuated.

The scholars of the third school fault Sa'id for the license his critique has given some scholars to ignore the languages and primary sources of the field. The critique has been accused of having given license, if not licentiousness, to these practitioners, as well as to a new crop of scholars, the postmodernist and postcolonial scholars.

A redeeming quality of the third group of practitioners is to be found in its members' greater thoroughness in the use of indigenous sources than the earlier Orientalists. But at the core, the third school scholars are empiricists who prefer their own unconscious theories to the latest theoretical or paradigmatic approaches in the social sciences. They choose to remain uninformed by theory in the social and humanistic sciences and are unwilling to examine their unconscious, individual assumptions, while priding themselves on the individuality and singularity of their ad hoc interpretations. They insist on reading their sources uncritically, as did the earlier Orientalists, without taking into consideration the mediations of social context or the social processes out of which these sources are but partial structural manifestations. Their claim is that they are able to make the primary sources speak to them and, therefore, to us. They are unwilling to consider how the structures that inform their method of selecting evidence, or their analyses and approaches to the primary sources, are social constructs. Since they do not hypothesize social processes behind change, they end up with the anomalous assumption of structures as dynamic forces, as in several studies by Carter Findley, for example, *Bureaucratic Reform in the Ottoman Empire: The Sublime Port, 1782–1922* (Princeton, NJ: Princeton University Press, 1980). Here institutions are seen as having a monopoly on instigating social change, whereas they should be viewed as structures that invite access to power for society's ruling social groups.[17]

One of the best examples of this approach is that of Cornell Fleischer in his study of Mustafa Aali, a late sixteenth-century Ottoman bureaucrat and man of letters.[18] Fleischer's methodology is one of collecting and reading the extant works of a historical figure (which in Aali's case meant a considerable number of works in three languages) and then writing a study, in this case a biography. Since in Fleischer's approach Aali is not viewed as a product of a historical process that generates culture as well as the available genres that Aali puts to use in his own works, the reader is at a loss to place Aali and his literary-historical works in the historical context of his time.[19]

In the past, Orientalists often attributed their reluctance to provide any significant interpretation of a particular historical topic or subject to the incompleteness of the sources. In other words, there was always another source to be explored before a particular interpretation could feel comfortable. In Fleischer's study, all the available primary sources have been exploited.

Fleischer's approach, however, remains one of narrative history based on the extant primary texts. As already indicated, the author does not adopt a conscious theory that guides the reconstructions of time, place, and social context for the production of these extant cultural expressions, on which is based the construction of the modern text. With this approach the scholars in this school arrogate for themselves the roles of judge, prosecutor, and jury. They resort to anachronisms instead of addressing the complexity inherent in the construction of the social context for the historical texts they are analyzing. Finally, the approach allows authors to claim objectivity in their approach, meanwhile maintaining an Olympian transcendence as facilitators of a dialogue between texts.

Cemal Kafadar's *The First Ottoman State* (Berkeley: University of California Press, 1996) is a recent example that illustrates the consequences of direct dialogue between sources.[20] Perhaps the most serious consequence of analyzing only the extant cultural products, the texts, while shunning conscious theory, is that this precludes a comparative study. Kafadar gives the reader the impression that he is doing the opposite as he cites, in passing, Eleanor Searle's *Predatory Kinship and the Creation of Norman Power 840–1066* (Berkeley: University of California Press, 1988), which could have served as an uncanny parallel to the early Ottoman experience. While Searle consciously emphasizes theory through a model that hardly emphasizes religion (Christianity), Kafadar gives an essentialized Islam a much wider scope in his narrative. He goes further in suggesting, though without any effort at implementation, a comparative approach to his study by citing Americo Castro's ideas (through the collected studies edited by J. R. Barcia, *Americo Castro and the Meaning of Spanish Civilization* [Berkeley: University of California Press, 1976]) on social bridging between the "disparate" Muslim and Christian communities, who in al-Andalus occupy the same social space. A detailed emphasis on the "predatory" nature of early Ottoman history, and the parallels between Andalusian and Ottoman societies in social bridging, would have served as the basis for an enlightening and provocative debate.

Another aspect of works produced by the third school of scholars reveals a split approach within the scholarship: on the one hand, a discrete synthetic approach that is inconsistent in its theoretical orientation, and on the other, an empirical approach. The theory implied in the syntheses turns out to be an afterthought to the empirical work. The syntheses sometimes appear in the form of separate publications and usually appear in a single volume devoted to collections of articles written over several years. These articles often reflect contradictory theoretical orientations, as for example, in some of Suraiya Faroqhi's collected essays. These contradictions are not found in her strictly empirical book monographs, such as *Towns and Townsmen of Ottoman Anatolia* (Cambridge: Cambridge University Press, 1984) nor in *Men of Modest Substance* (Cambridge: Cambridge University Press, 1987).

Other writers combine the empirical and synthetic in the same volume, hoping that the combination will somehow form a monograph. But the two parts sit side by side uneasily since they are neither organically nor methodologically integrated.

Linda Darling's *Revenue-Raising & Legitimacy: Tax Collection and Financial Administration in the Ottoman Empire, 1560–1660* (Leiden, Holland: E. J. Brill, 1996) is a sterling example of this effort.

This book represents an exercise that illustrates a transition in methodology between the theoretical-synthetic and the "substantial," or empirical. Of the nine chapters in Darling's work, the middle seven empirical ones do not constitute a well-argued monograph but are best described as a handbook to guide scholars through the technical intricacies of handling the Ottoman financial archives. The first and last chapters represent, however, a different methodological trajectory from the "how to read the financial registers" chapters. They purport to synthesize the secondary literature on the issues covered in the other chapters. Thus, the theme of legitimation through financial registers is taken up first, which is then followed by the theme of "decline," both themes having become standard historical issues for discussion in the field.

In Darling's work, the problem of legitimation and decline are stated, but they are only tangentially discussed. When the two problems are mentioned in the empirical chapters, they are not resolved through a substantial argument using evidence from the financial records; instead, the author declares them to be resolved directly by the marshaled evidence. However, the problem of these two historical issues are nowhere systematically discussed or illustrated in either of the two parts (the first and last chapters, and the seven middle chapters) of the book. Therefore, a tenuous relationship exists between what is discussed in the synthetic chapters on the issues of Ottoman legitimation and decline, and their illustration in the empirical chapters. Furthermore, while the question of legitimation of state authority is discussed as a theme and a question in the synthetic chapters, in the empirical chapters it is presented as direct evidence that the Ottoman system was equitable and just. In a similar fashion, Darling tries to tackle the daunting question of "decline." Here, the author finds direct evidence from the financial records in support of the opposite of decline for the period 1560–1660.

Darling's flagrant flaunting of historical method thus takes the form of direct intervention in history. Without apology, the scholar declares her partisanship, usually in the guise of efforts to rectify what she considers unfair assessments by other scholars. As illustrated earlier with Crecelius' (mis)treatment of Jabarti, Darling makes direct judgments on the historical issues at hand, foregoing complex explanations for "common sense" ones.

Amy Singer in *Palestinian Peasants and Ottoman Officials: Rural Administration around Sixteenth Century Jerusalem* (Cambridge: Cambridge University Press, 1994) finds something positive about the Ottoman state's treatment of peasants. As does Darling, she analyzes official state documents to assess the performance of officialdom. In the meantime, the author justifies her direct intervention in history by the fact that other scholars in the past had mostly maligned the Ottoman state as an insensitive exploiter of peasants.

A direct and single-minded intervention in history to rectify an historical "injustice" can be found in Bishara Doumani's *Rediscovering Palestine: Merchants and Peasants in Jabal Nablus* (Berkeley: University of California Press, 1995). For Doumani, the exclusion of the Arabs from the history of modern Palestine represents such a case. The author takes it upon himself to directly repair the damage and in doing so, he commits an anachronism. He describes as "Palestinians" the eighteenth-century inhabitants of Jabal Nablus. Whereas Singer finds direct evidence for equity in what is considered otherwise an exploitative system of land management, Doumani rectifies the perceived injustice perpetrated by Israeli scholarship on the residents of the south Syrian subprovince of Jabal Nablus. After all, it is this scholarship that has deprived the Arab Palestinians of their political identity.

By using the term "Palestinian" for the inhabitants of an Ottoman *sanjak* or (sub)province, Singer injects herself into history by giving the peasants in Jerusalem and its surrounding region a wider political identity. But this designation has a different use from the one found in Doumani. The appropriation of the charged term "Palestine" in Israeli scholarship has as its goal the identification of a coherent, recognizable geographical and political entity, starting from at least 1948, to which the modern state of Israel could lay claim. (After the Oslo agreements, U.S. newspapers began to use the expression "prestate Israel" for this same political entity. Dropping the term "Palestine" for the political entity that existed before 1948 is perhaps a contestation of the legitimacy of Palestinian Arabs' claims for the same land.) That the scholarly competition over this political "space" is neither illusory nor irrelevant can be illustrated further with similarities found in the same monograph by Singer and an earlier one by Amnon Cohen and Bernard Lewis, *Population and Revenue in the Towns of Palestine in the Sixteenth Century* (Princeton, NJ: Princeton University Press, 1978). Both works use the term "Palestine" anachronistically in their titles. In the indexes for both books, however, the expression "Arab" is hardly used in acknowledgment of the culture and language of the overwhelming population of the southern Syrian districts (estimated by the latter work at 300,000). Furthermore, although the term "Muslim" is referred to in the Cohen-Lewis book nineteen times, the terms "Christian" and "Jewish" are accorded forty-four annotated references each. Similarly, in the index for Singer's book, the same imbalance in allusion prevails with no reference to Arabs, but eighteen to Christians and eight to Jews.

In conclusion, the approach adopted by this group is one that distinguishes itself from others that are merely theoretically informed or only partially informed scholarship. The neo-Orientalists show competence in one or two of the languages of the field as opposed to the minimal competence of its counterparts.[21] The authors in this group participate in the writing, rectifying, and modifying of history that they write most directly, or anachronistically, as they eschew most of the known norms in the social and humanistic sciences.

SCHOOL NUMBER 4: POSTMODERNIST

The fourth school of scholars has adopted a postmodernist, or a postcolonial, stance. The scholarships that best exemplify this group are Timothy Mitchell's *Colonizing Egypt* (Berkeley: University of California Press, 1988) and, more recently, Zeynep Çelik's *Urban Forms and Colonial Confrontations* (Berkeley: University of California Press, 1997). Both works share a common approach in their focus on "culture," through the examination of the colonizing culture of Europe for Egypt, and urban architecture of the city of Algiers under French rule.

Perhaps the most glaring feature of Mitchell's work is that the focus on culture does not take into account the social context in Egypt or that of the European colonizers, France and England. It would seem then that one would first have to get to understand these two sets of societies in order to provide the history and specifics of the culture of colonization.

Mitchell, by doing neither, omits the required steps in setting up a research agenda for the study of colonial culture. The agenda would involve an approach that starts with the idea that there is an interdependence between the colonizer and colonized. Mitchell, by not taking into account these societies' roles in creating and receiving the colonizing culture and by not revealing the bridges that illustrate their interdependence, shows a lack of awareness of the assumptions underpinning scholarship on the historical phenomenon of colonialism.

Using these same assumptions separates and gives autonomy to the two societies. By maintaining his perception at the level of old assumptions, subject and prey remain unequal in valuation, let alone as scholarly subjects of analysis and discussion. This bias is consistently maintained throughout, since the book proposes to study Egypt by something other than its own culture (language, practices, history). Nowhere in the book is Arabic, let alone the specific culture, demonstrated as a key to understanding Egyptian society in the second half of the nineteenth century. This is asserted, even though there are parts of *Colonizing Egypt* in which Mitchell analyzes changes in relation to the modernization of Arabic as a language.[22]

Had Mitchell started by studying the societies and their contexts, he could have hypothesized the social processes that produced the specific colonial culture of the nineteenth century (in terms of time, place, and people or class). Instead, Mitchell starts with the colonial culture, analyzes it without specifying agencies (motives) or the varieties of production of colonial culture, and does not assess the various social contexts in which they had operated, in particular the "recipient" society.

Mitchell could have tackled the languages of power and hegemony that had permeated colonial culture. In other words, in place of his perception of the world as one divided into tiers of priority such as, for example, first or third worlds, he would have needed to start with the premise that societies are equal. This would have come closer to what is needed at this stage of research on the question of colonial culture and its meaning today; there is, then, a place for deconstruction. (Thus, for example, the effect on both the colonizer and colonized of the appropriation of human and material wealth would have to be assessed.) In this fashion, the two sets of societies would be perceived as interdependent but equal. At the very least, Mitchell would have had to alter his approach to what he is studying to the point that he would recognize his own Egyptianness as much as his own Europeanness—seeing the other in himself as much as seeing himself in the other.[23]

The appropriate and relevant time (political and perhaps even in social scientific terms) to bash empire and colonialism, as Mitchell does, is when empire and colonialism are in place, and not in 1988. Such an approach is appropriate to a radical agenda, as is illustrated by the stand Jean-Paul Sartre took in support of the Algerian War of Independence. It therefore is necessary to question the relevance in terms of time, if not social utility, of carrying out this type of scholarship by Mitchell in a postcolonial setting. By analyzing the language of the culture of colonialism, without providing the social context and the time of the creation of that culture, through an analysis of the materiality and reality of colonialism, Mitchell seems to have managed to strike two birds with one stone and to kill them both. His liberal stance (posed as radical, since it does not account for change over time) is held intact by condemning colonialism. But by using colonialism as culture, he has only substituted words for action. Meanwhile, Mitchell does not tackle the processes of colonialism and their disastrous consequences on the colonies and ex-colonies, and the colonizing and then ex-colonizing countries alike. In Mitchell's conception, the hegemony of the then-colonial powers is left untouched. His liberal, humanistic credentials notwithstanding, Mitchell's commitment to change his as well as others' perception of colonialism, let alone to change the consequences of colonialism, rings false.

To put it in other words, the postcolonial critique that Mitchell's work represents does not arise from the necessity of changing the standard approach to the subject: that there were unequal power relations between the colonizer and colonized. Indeed, his perception of the topic is based on the very same assumptions that inform a hegemonic European approach, one that remains unchanged and therefore undiminished. This is Mitchell's stance when the required research program is a postcolonial critique that accepts, as it hypothesizes, the interdependence of the various components of the present world as this program gives equal weight to the social contexts of an historically based colonialism.

Çelik's study shares with Mitchell the same set of historiographic problems. However, in addition, she neither pretends to be able to nor is capable of independently assessing the "validity" of the claims made in the French secondary sources she uses in her study. For example, in her treatment of "The Indigent House," Çelik uses the work of French ethnographers who discussed the "Muslim," or indigenous house. But at no point is there a critical evaluation of the qualifications that these scholars brought to their studies. Therefore, Çelik's readers are left uninformed as to why each group, at different points, wrote, advocated, or went as far as to implement their plans in a particular manner. By not evaluating or problematizing the issues found in her secondary sources, Çelik focuses primarily on the study of French urban developmental policies, while neglecting their impact on the lives of colonized peoples. As with Mitchell, Europe or France is the primary object of study, and the colonies remain, at least in these two studies, of marginal and secondary significance and importance.

Throughout this study, I have intentionally refrained from offering any alternative models for scholarship to those that were analyzed. In refraining from providing a model, I was guided by my perception that the focus of this chapter, as that of the book, was to subject the various approaches in the historiographies covered to a close examination in light of a commonly perceived need for a revisionist, future research agenda. This constraint was meant to leave the shaping of the agenda to those scholars who are concerned with the issues raised by the book.

NOTES

This version was written in 1996–97 when I was the Ahmet Erteğün Visiting Professor at Princeton University. I thank Petry Kievit-Tyson for copyediting the final text, and dedicate this chapter to Marriam and Sara.

1. Edward Sa'id, "Representing the Colonized: Anthropology's Interlocutors," *Critical Inquiry,* 15 (Winter 1989), pp. 205–225.

2. A hint on the relationship of a particular paradigm, or approach in scholarship and its immediate social utility, can be best apprehended by surveying which scholarly proposals in the social sciences obtain funds and which do not. When the quality and ingenuity are equal, then the differentiating line for what is funded by official or semiofficial agencies in particular is the perceived relevance of the scholarship to the current policies. A survey of such trends, especially concerning the National Endowment for the Humanities and National Endowment for the Arts evaluation of proposals for support was published July 14, 1991 in the *New York Times.*

3. Sa'id, "Recognizing the Colonized."

4. By the 1980s, the critique of Orientalist scholarship was overdue, and therefore would have taken place with or without Sa'id's contributions. Well before the publication of Sa'id's book, some scholars were already thinking and writing with alternative approaches to the prevalent paradigm. This should not come as a great surprise, since the reception of Sa'id's work is in great measure due to the existence of a spontaneous contemporary air of disaffection with the prevalent Orientalist paradigm. Indeed, this was the specifically prepared ground that eventually proved receptive to aspects of Sa'id's work. A personal note: By the mid-1950s, while Edward Sa'id was an undergraduate student at Princeton University, some graduate students in the West Asian and North African field were already voicing such disaffection. For what it is worth, and for the historical record, I recall that Ibrahim Abu-Lughod was the center of quite a striking and colorful critique of Orientalist scholarship.

5. When it came to intent, motives, and goals for the scholarship, first it needs to be asserted here that some of us who are engaged in thinking, researching, and writing in West Asia and North Africa, as in other social scientific endeavors, cannot afford the luxury of the virtual nihilism to which deconstruction without a social goal or purpose seems to lead, by what Sa'id calls adversarial critique. This is asserted in the light of one premise, which is at the same time a commitment. The following are some of the disclaimers that guide this study: scholarship, in the social sciences as in all other fields of human endeavor, should not be done for its own sake, or primarily and simply for the purposes of the narcissistic satisfaction of its practitioners. If it were that subjective, scholarly endeavor would hardly have any support, either by governments or private foundations.

Given the global picture, there are some scholars today who are guided by the premise that scholarship in human and other sciences should be assessed in light of the contributions these can make toward the preservation and survival of humankind, the continuity of the human species, and the improvement of living conditions. For a recent critical analysis of the academic defense of the autonomy of science from social scrutiny, mounted in the aftermath of the nuclear bombing of Japan, and calculated to dissuade laymen from analytical evaluation of the role of science in society, see Steve Fuller, "Being there with Thomas Kuhn: A Parable for Postmodern Times," *History and Theory,* 31.3 (1992). In this article, Fuller places the timing of the publication of Thomas Kuhn's book, *Structure of Scientific Knowledge* (Chicago: University of Chicago Press, 1962), within this historical context. These goals are the more urgent in a world that is nearly totally interdependent, global in every sense of that term, and at the same time one that is equally adept at self-destruction.

For a discussion of the question of cardinal values and some of the epistemological issues raised in this study, see Ramkrishna Mukherjee, *Society, Culture and Development* (New Delhi: Sage, 1991).

6. Sa'id himself is not immune from implicitly supporting an alternative. On the occasion of the American Historical Association meeting in December 1988 in Cincinnati, Ohio, in what appears as a contradiction of his innocence in trying to provide an alternative, he chaired a panel revealingly called "After Orientalism: The Third World Writes Its Own History." Sa'id is part of the revisionist culture reflecting certain trends in West Asian and North African scholarship. Thus, distancing oneself from the "Orientalist" approach is used as a legitimating argument for the new scholarship that has emerged since at least the publication of *Orientalism.*

Again, when taken strictly from the point of view of one who subscribes to the assumption that there are purposes to scholarship of the region, as for all scientific research, what I propose is that in order for deconstruction to be useful for the next stage of research and appreciation, there will have to be a critique or assessment of the extant body of knowledge, and viable, credible, and significant alternatives will have to be offered in the form of research agendas. Albert Einstein would not surrender to others the issue of epistemology in his field. He was of the opinion that "the physicist cannot simply surrender to the philosopher the critical contemplation of the theoretical foundations: for he himself knows best and feels most surely where the shoe pinches." Quoted from Gerland Hold, "Constructing a Theory: Einstein's Model," *The American Scholar,* 48.3 (1979), p. 309.

7. Phillip Huang, "'Public Sphere'/'Civil Society' in China," *Modern China,* 19.2 (April 1993), pp. 216–240; and "Between Informal Mediation and Formal Adjudication," *Modern*

China, 19.3 (July 1993), pp. 251–298. The sociologist Zygmunt Bauman has some thoughts on the civil space that early modern society had available and that modern society does not, due to occupation of most civil space by the nation-state. From recent reevaluation of notes of local archival materials that I had collected in the mid-1960s, I also note that the absence of direct Ottoman control in most of the civil space of Jerusalem society of the early and later sixteenth century suggests a similar space of autonomy to the one Zygmunt Bauman postulates in *The Holocaust and Modernity* (Ithaca, NY: Cornell University Press, 1991).

8. See the debate within the Social Science Research Council appearing as a discussion concerning area studies programs and their relevance to the changed global realities. Discussed in *The Chronicle of Higher Education* (April 1991).

9. Perry Anderson, *Lineages of the Absolutist State* (London: Verso, 1974 [1979]).

10. Jack Goldstone, *Revolution and Rebellion in Early Modern Times* (Berkeley, CA: University of California Press, 1991).

11. Karen Barkey, *Bandits and Bureaucrats: The Ottoman Route to State Centralization* (Ithaca, NY: Cornell University Press, 1994).

12. Rifa'at Ali Abou-El-Haj, *Formation of the Modern State* (Albany: State University of New York Press, 1992).

13. Anderson, in *Lineages of the Absolutist State,* characterized the Ottoman Empire's presence in Europe as a foreign intrusion.

14. Daniel Crecelius (ed.), *Eighteenth Century Egypt: The Arabic Manuscript Sources* (Claremont, CA: Regina Books, 1990). A recent work on the history of the footnote and scholarly citations is Anthony Grafton, *A History of the Footnote* (Princeton, NJ: Princeton University Press, 1997).

15. As for example, the question of the meaning of "emin" in Defterdar Mehmed Pasha. See Abou-El-Haj, *Formation of the Modern State.*

16. Etienne Balibar and Immanuel Wallerstein, *Race, Nation, Class: Ambiguous Identities* (London: Verso, 1991). In one of his essays, Balibar discusses Levi-Strauss' position on these issues. Talal Asad discusses the case of Muslims in Europe in "Europe Against Islam: Islam in Europe," *The Muslim World*, vol. 87. no. 2 (April 1997).

17. Carter V. Findley, *Ottoman Civil Officialdom: A Social History* (Princeton, NJ: Princeton University Press, 1989).

18. Cornell Fleischer, *Bureaucrat and Intellectual in the Ottoman Empire: The Historian Mustafa Ali (1540–1600)* (Princeton, NJ: Princeton University Press, 1986).

19. R. A. Abou-El-Haj's review of Fleischer's study in *Middle East Studies Association Bulletin* 21 (1987).

20. Reviewed by R. A. Abou-El-Haj, *American Historical Review* 59:2 (December 1996), pp. 156–157. Kafadar has a problem with the shape of the primary sources he uses. Most of the primary Ottoman Turkish sources he examined appear as translations and/or transliterations. Sidestepped is the problem that these renditions may have turned them into secondary sources. The author concedes too readily to some of the authorities whose scholarship should have been subjected to critical revaluation. He appraises the reader of one scholar's "brilliant suggestion" (p. 132); of another's "masterpiece of Ottoman political history" (p. 190, n. 58); of a third's "masterful demonstration" (p. 143); and of a fourth's "brilliant article" (pp. 170–171, n.31). One of the unstated assumptions that informs Kafadar's approach associates the origins of the Ottoman state with Europe, paradoxically through Rum, in other words, Byzantium. Europeanness is further emphasized by the *devshirme* (collection of Christian

boys), which became the basis for janissary recruitment. This is in differentiation of the early "Ottoman Turkish" from other historical experiences of Turks and Muslims elsewhere.

21. The social utility for the production of neo-Orientalism seems to parallel the favorable reception of subaltern studies by First World academic circles, the object of critical analysis by Arif Dirlik, "The Post-Colonial Aura: Third World Criticism in the Age of Global Capitalism," *Critical Inquiry* 20:2 (1994), pp. 328–356; and Ramkrishna Mukherjee, "Illusions and Reality: Review of R. Guha (1983) *Elementary Aspects of Peasant Insurgency in Colonial India,*" *Sociological Bulletin* 37.1–2 (March–September 1988), pp. 127–139.

22. On this point, see especially the review by Charles Hirschkind in *Critique of Anthropology* 11.3 (1991), pp. 279–298. Another reviewer comes closest to the appreciation of Mitchell's book when she characterizes it "neither as 'research' nor as 'prophecy' but rather as interesting and on the whole challenging fiction." Ursula Wokoeck, "Mythology of Representation, Power, and Truth: Timothy Mitchell's *Colonizing Egypt,*" *Asian and African Studies,* 23 (1989), pp. 271–288.

23. Ashis Nandy, *The Intimate Enemy: Loss and Recovery of Self Under Colonialism* (Delhi: Oxford University Press, 1983), suggests that there is a historical, cultural, and psychological interdependence between colonizer and colonized.

5

Situating and Rethinking Subaltern Studies for Writing Working-Class History

Vinay Bahl

In the last fourteen years the Subaltern Studies school has produced a fairly large quantity of literature on peasants and working-class history,[1] and its impact has been felt beyond India. At the same time, this literature has been widely criticized in India, Great Britain, Latin America, and the United States.[2] The inadequacy of the Subaltern Studies approach, especially on the issue of the working-class "emancipation," became apparent to me while I was completing a case study of the Indian working-class struggle[3] during the colonial period. Twenty years ago, under the influence of Marxism, "working-class history" and "class analysis" were the dominant subjects of study. Such studies contributed to the then-ongoing debate about the roles of "structure" and "agency" in the formation of working-class consciousness. In recent years, however, the analytical separation of "structure" from "action" has changed, as shown in studies of these subjects and specifically in U.S. sociology. Indeed, Marxian concepts, such as "class," "structure," and "agency," have come under severe attack not only from the right but also from the left. In the 1980s, the "New Right" in Britain and the United States, represented respectively by Thatcherism and Reaganomics, gained electoral victories. These victories coincided with the restructuring of Western economies (as well as technological developments) that brought about a decline of the manual working class.[4]

The emergence of the New Right and the restructuring of the Western economies profoundly affected the world of business management and the working masses, both materially and culturally. Business management schools increasingly recognized "culture" (Western and non-Western) in their theories and practice. The new managerial classes offer courses on non-Western culture and work ethics based on various non-Western religions (which are reinterpreted and reinvented for the use of capitalism). The need to understand non-Western cultures has arisen because a large number of people have migrated to the West from non-Western countries since World War II in search of a better life. These working-class immigrants have become confused about their social and cultural identities in the face of massive consumerism in the West and now, increasingly, in non-Western countries.

Now that multinational companies are expanding their role in the non-Western world, many people are moving back to their countries of origin, but their return has created another identity crisis. Expatriates find it difficult to identify with people in their mother country, and in fact identify themselves with the country from which they are returning.[5] In the new world (dis)order, it has become increasingly difficult to define social reality according to old categories that now include the boundaries of countries as well.

These historical, social, political, and economic changes that have occurred since World War II also have affected Western academia. The academic community feels inadequate in the face of the new social reality. Scholars such as E. P. Thompson and Eric Hobsbawm began to change the old categories of analysis in the 1970s by including the role of culture in the writing of working-class history. Because of their initiative, the ideas of "history from below" and the "role of agency" became popular and gained wide acceptance. Theodore Koditschek points out that it is too often forgotten that the turn toward language was originally taken not by the post-structuralists of the 1980s but by Thompson in 1963. "It was Thompson who first repudiated economic reductionism, focused on workers' cultural expressions, and showed us how to use poems and placards as historical sources and read riots and rituals as though they were texts."[6] Since then, much has been written in this vein on the role of agency and structure, metanarrative, and culture.

With this new surge of writings about the roles of agency and structure, Western academic debates underwent a major shift. A "plurality of voices from the margins" insisting on "differences" challenged the academic mainstream (for example, the tradition of the universalistic metanarrative). Furthermore, the old categories of class and class formation were rejected, along with the "grand theory" of Marxism. These challenges were concerned with finding the source of meaning; the production of meaning, as it occurred historically in relation to power, became the new object of academic inquiry. As a result, the role of external or objective class structure was marginalized within these inquiries.

In this search for the source of meaning, three explanations have emerged. One group of scholars believes that meaning lies in the relations with power and authority. Another group believes that every meaning is arbitrary. According to the third group, it is the consumer who creates meaning while consuming a product.[7]

In light of these new interpretations of social reality (collectively called postmodernism), many scholars started to write history as a politics of the particular or of difference; they did so by focusing on "cultural" history. Such histories generally concern racial or ethnic groups or gender, and often are based on individual stories. These authors believe that by writing such histories, based as they are on individual stories, folklore, indigenous languages or mythologies, or other non-conventional sources, they can give voice to silent, subordinated groups. These scholars also have attempted to show that subordinated people do not experience their circumstances passively but negotiate their positions in society. Thus the subordinated groups are agents in making their own history.

Very soon the impact of this "new" historiography was felt in India as well. In India, however, the challenge to Marxist categories in history writing was not a mere intellectual exercise; it was closely related to actual political situations and to people's movements against the legitimacy of the state. Since independence, Indian historians had been trying to undo the British colonial version of Indian history, which emphasized India's "backward culture" and the so-called benevolence of the Raj. Modern Indian historians thus have been rewriting Indian history and have done so in nationalist, communal, secular, and Marxian frameworks.

During the 1970s, the Indian Marxist scholars and historians lost their credibility when they supported the ruling party in its repression of people's movements.[8] This bankruptcy of intellectuals in Indian left-wing circles facilitated the rise of the Subaltern Studies group and its challenge to the adequacy of Marxist categories (which was also in vogue, one might note, in the Western academic world). Despite resistance by established historians on the left, the Subaltern Studies school made inroads into the Indian academic world and influenced the writing of history.

In a wider perspective, the birth of Subaltern Studies can be attributed to the historical conjunction of various forces: the new international economic and social conditions after World War II; conditions rendering inadequate the earlier categories of analysis; the emergence of the "history from below" approach; the crisis of the Indian state during the 1970s; the emergence of people's movements in India; and, of greatest concern here, the bankruptcy and hypocrisy of the left-wing Indian historians and intellectuals.

WHAT IS SUBALTERN STUDIES?

Subaltern Studies originated in India in 1982. The founding members of the group challenged Indian Marxist historians and their claims to write the people's history. In doing this they responded to a genuine need for a new methodology, epistemology, and paradigm, a need felt not only in India but also worldwide. Borrowing from Gramsci the concept of "subaltern" and drawing on the prevailing Western ideas about the historiography of mass culture, Subaltern Studies tried to provide new interpretations and methodologies for writing Indian working-class history. Subalternists maintained that colonialist, nationalist, and Marxist interpretations of Indian history had denied the role of the common people and their agency. To rectify this situation, Subaltern Studies announced that its new approach would restore history to the subordinated. In addition, the group theorized that the

elite in India played a dominant part during the colonial period, not merely a hegemonic role. With the logic of this new interpretation, the Subalternists were able
to show that subordinated people (subalterns) were autonomous historical persons
who acted on their own because they were not led by any elite group.

Subaltern Studies also claims that it can find Indian subalterns' voices, despite
problems with sources: Indian peasants and workers have not kept diaries, as British
workers have done. This absence of "workers' authentic voices" led to a shift in
the methodology of the Subaltern Studies. To find these voices, Subalternists had
to use different methods of reading the available documents—that is, to read them
"against their grain." For this purpose they found the postmodern and postcolonial
methodology useful. Ironically, this method led these scholars to concentrate more
on what constituted subalternity than on finding subaltern voices. The focus of the
group shifted, which brought another change in their focus of study: the Subalternists have now begun to critique Western "Enlightenment" thought,[9] a project
already in progress in the West, led by postcolonialist and postmodernist scholars.
With these shifts in the Subaltern Studies approach, initial concerns have become
secondary.

Using postmodernist methodology, Subaltern Studies now concentrates on how
the knowledge of history was produced and how its construction can be "decolonized." In raising these "new" questions, the Indian Subalternists realized that they
could write history only from a position of subalternity, because India, as a British
colony, itself (as a subcontinent and its people, but irrespective of class structure)
was a subaltern. Furthermore, the postcolonial subordination of India can be illustrated by the following example. To write history, a non-Western scholar must read
and know "good" Western scholars and historians,[10] whereas a Western scholar
does not have to know any non-Western works. In fact, Indian economic historians and nationalist leaders R. C. Dutt, D. Naoroji, and M. G. Ranade, in the last
quarter of the nineteenth century developed a "drain theory," claiming that India's
poverty was due to the drain of its resources (material and physical) and wealth by
British colonial rulers. This point, however, is rarely discussed or mentioned in the
dependency theories that arose after World War II as part of Western thought.
Today people in the West know about dependency theory as a recent pioneer idea;
the "drain theory" propounded by Indian economic historians remains virtually
invisible in Western theories.[11]

In spite of criticisms concerning Western concepts and methodology, the Subaltern Studies school depends heavily on postmodernist ideas (which emerged in
the West) and on other Western methods for textual analysis. The group interestingly claims to work toward the goal of "provinciali[zing] Europe and its history,"[12]
"push[ing] history to its limits, and rewrit[ing] history from the grounds of ambivalence and contradictions."[13] In these efforts, the Subaltern Studies collective insists
that subalternity remains the vantage point of its critique.

Dipesh Chakrabarty, a leading Subaltern Studies spokesperson, recently
expanded the responsibility of Subaltern Studies to include "differences" as a tool

for producing possibilities for action.[14] Since the Subalternist school's project is to challenge old universal categories, Chakrabarty thinks that by emphasizing "difference" it will be possible to remove the "problem of universality" in history. Yet, Chakrabarty does not wish to give up either Marx (remember, Subaltern Studies initially was critical of Marxist categories and kept a distance from Marxism) or differences because he finds Marx's category of "real labor" useful in developing the idea of differences.[15] The goal of Subaltern Studies, in his view, is not to achieve political democracy or to promote the equal distribution of wealth but to keep alive the philosophical question of differences, because according to him, egalitarian and universalist concepts are insensitive to such matters. Therefore, Subalternist scholars are not writing to describe how some group in Asia, Africa, or Latin America resisted the penetration of colonialism; instead, as Chakrabarty claims, they are trying "to take history to its limits" in order to "make its unworking visible."[16]

To sum up various shifts in their focus, the Subaltern Studies started with the idea that subalterns were autonomous in the Indian nationalist movement and actively participated in negotiating their situation. To prove their theory, this school needed to find subaltern voices, which could be done only by reading the documents "against the grain," a method borrowed from the then-dominating Western ideology of postmodernism and postcolonialism. In the process of finding the subaltern voices, they realized their own status as subaltern Indian historians and asked, "How was the colonial knowledge produced?" This questioning removed them from their initial project of finding subaltern voices in order to discover how to "provincialize Europe" and "take history to its limits" so that they could find out how colonial knowledge was produced. Chakrabarty's recent focusing on "difference" is a logical outcome of these shifts in Subaltern Studies school focus. Chakrabarty correctly admits that he and other scholars are not interested in finding an "egalitarian society" or "political democracy," because the real issue now for this school is to "provincialize Europe" and deconstruct history. Thus, Subalternists are able to make a complete turn around from the issue of the subaltern's agency.

It appears from the above discussion that the goal of Subaltern Studies is to keep the "discourse of truth" alive, which means, in their view, that some "real" truth exists out there that can be uncovered. This assumption is a "powerful medicine" as Friedman puts it.[17] Yet, the Subalternists' statements do not make clear who has the right to say what is "real" and what is "truth." This question of "truth" is not unique to Subalternists. This question of "truth" has arisen globally because, as Friedman explains, the hegemonic structure of the world is no longer a reality, and its cultural form is also dissolving.[18]

It is in this new situation that both the Subalternists (progressive scholars) from the Indian subcontinent and the "New Left," which emerged in the West, are abandoning the concept of class and instead concentrating on the production of meaning. The New Left considers "[a]n 'objective' class interest [as] . . . illusionary and with it a politics based on class."[19] With such an assumption, it was possible to change the social analysis based on the production of goods to one based on the exposure and critique of the production of meaning. "Thus conceived, it (class) is cut off from a clear-cut social base from which it is deemed to originate."[20]

As discussed below, the Subaltern Studies group followed postmodernist and New Left thinking and practice. Therefore, it is important to understand why the Subaltern Studies school, which emerged in the context of the Indian people's movement challenging the legitimacy of the state, accepts the structural changes in a society as given rather than challenging those structural changes. Why have the members of this group abandoned the question of class and the related issue of class-consciousness? Their historical and political roots may provide an explanation.

THE ORIGIN OF THE SUBALTERN STUDIES GROUP

The Subaltern Studies group was founded in India in 1982 by Ranjit Guha, an Indian historian[21] who now lives in Australia (Australia seems to be a place of residence and postdoctoral research center for many members of the school). Guha edited the first six volumes of the series of publications bearing the group's name. A biographical sketch[22] shows that during 1979–1980, Guha and a number of younger historians, then living in England, held a series of intense discussions on Indian colonial history; this led to the formation of their group in 1982. The group published its first volume in 1983. In 1971, during a visit to India, Guha became involved with the Maoist students' movement in Delhi;[23] some of these students subsequently went to study in England. Perhaps it is no coincidence that most of the founding members of the Subaltern Studies group had connections with the Maoist groups in Delhi and Calcutta. Today, most of them have close connections with the academic communities of England, Australia, and the United States.

It is also no coincidence that the Subaltern School rejects the concept of class struggle, as did the Naxalites (during the 1970s) in India, and that it promotes cultural particularism. As explained by Tom Brass, a well-known English historian of peasant studies in south Asia, the "Naxalites not only mobilized tribal support on the basis of cultural particularism, claiming that no difference existed between present struggles and those of the 1855 tribal insurrection, but also organized guerrilla activity on the basis of existing tribal and kin group authority at the village level. Therefore, by the late 1980s the Communist Party of India (ML) [also called Naxalites], was engaged not in a class but a caste struggle." Brass states further that this point is significant, because "this strategy both legitimizes and creates a space for communal discourse and practice, which can then be reappropriated by the parties of the political right in order to undermine any class solidarity that has been achieved."[24] As discussed below, many scholars criticize the Subaltern Studies school on grounds similar to these.

Given the political roots of the Subaltern Studies founders, it is curious to note that Gyan Prakash, a well-known historian, recently joined the Subaltern Studies group.[25] His association with this school introduces a leftist political background that opposes the Naxalites (as they were in the 1970s; in recent years Naxalites have revised their social analysis) and their theoretical analysis.[26] The puzzle is that Brass,[27] one of Prakash's critics, regards him as a postmodernist, whereas another scholar[28] finds him a critic of Subaltern Studies. It may be simply that Prakash has the ability to "ride two [or may be three or more] horses at the same time," as O'Hanlon[29] pointed out.

What, then, of progressivism? Isn't progressivism an exercise in how to remain noncommittal—not to take sides, as one student put it[30]—and to be a radical left-ist at the same time? One wonders how a progressive scholar can produce such apparently "noncommittal" writings about nonelite people's history while preserving the aura of progressivism!

Contrasting examples could clarify this question. Historians such as E. P. Thompson and Eric Hobsbawm, who also began to challenge old categories, did not depoliticize the writing of history or class analysis; the Subaltern Studies group, however, did do this. This fact is important, although obviously the Subaltern school emerged as a voice for the oppressed in the concrete context of the Indian people's movements. Before pursuing this theme, however, the Subalternists' themes must be examined more carefully.

THEMES OF SUBALTERN STUDIES

Since 1983 the Subaltern Studies collective has produced nine volumes[31] and several monographs. Ranjit Guha edited the first six volumes (1982), which had various themes, including critiques of elite historiography, uncovering peasant belief systems, peasant movements, peasant revolts, Indian nationalism, sectarianism, the colonial construction of communalism, power relations within the community, peasant insurgency, subaltern consciousness and politics, the people's perception of Gandhi, Gandhi's politics, the mentalities of the people, the character of the state, the ecological dimension of peasant protest, tribal protest, patterns of liquor consumption, Western medicine and caste, critique of feminist writings, crime in the context of the nationalist movement, and even a few critiques of Subaltern Studies. These volumes include very few themes related to the working-class movement, or to work, or to production. Most of the studies concern peasant and tribal people protests but have no connection with the broader context in which they occur.

Beginning with volume 7 (1993), the role of series editor shifted from Ranjit Guha to Partha Chatterjee and Gyanendra Pandey. The themes in volume 7 and 8 are different from those in the previous six volumes. They revolve mainly around the nation, the community, the Bengali middle class, forest people, colonial prisons, India's partition and historiography, and Indian religion and language. This difference in themes was noted by one reviewer for volume 8, who commented, "The contents of this volume, like those of its immediate predecessor, seem to confirm a marked shift of emphasis in the project of Subaltern Studies. . . . Over the years, most members of its editorial collective have moved from documenting subaltern dissent to dissecting elite discourse, from writing with (Socialist) passion to following the (postmodernist) fashion. Intellectual history, reframed as 'discourse analysis' . . . is emphatically not subaltern studies."[32]

Given the influence of Subaltern Studies among the younger generation of scholars in India and abroad, some such challenge seems justified, because intellectuals' writings do affect the real lives of people, often as public policy.[33] This is a matter of further concern because, as Tom Brass again points out, "when any idea, analysis or perspective become academically in vogue, it is not because the ideas are themselves intrinsically right ([meaning] theoretically acceptable) but rather because the times are right ([meaning] politically acceptable) in both senses of the term."[34]

Therefore, if we wish to remove the elitist bias from history and to empower the people, as Subaltern Studies claimed it wished to do, where do we turn? We must ascertain what our politics are when we raise questions about people's history: Why might we prefer some methods of analysis and not others? For a school that claims to be writing for the oppressed, it should be a matter of concern that it has gained wider acceptance in the United States at a time when political life there has taken a sharp turn to the right. Before discussing such concerns in greater detail, let us widen the discussion and expand on other aspects of the Subaltern Studies project.

ISSUES RAISED IN PREVIOUS COMMENTARIES

Sociologists, historians, economists, anthropologists, and those who combine the methods of history and sociology have produced commentaries on the Subaltern Studies collective and on the monographs produced individually by some of its members. It seems appropriate to begin with the views of well-known Indian sociologist and historian Ramkrishna Mukherjee on the writings of Ranjit Guha,[35] the founder of Subaltern Studies, because the unifying principles of the Subaltern School are found in Guha's *Elementary Aspects of Peasant Insurgency in Colonial India* (Delhi: Oxford University Press, 1983).

Mukherjee's critique hits two major flaws in the assumptions of the Subaltern Studies founder:

1. Guha's use of "peasant" category is not appropriate, because it is devoid of real life variations among peasants and their contemporaneous social base.[36] Thus, this categorization is ahistorical and on astructural basis.
2. Guha draws parallels among countries by the sweeping use of a large span of time (four hundred years) in history across the universe.[37]

In contrast to Guha's second flaw, the Subalternist writers insist on the "moment of suffering" (or oppression) and particularity, so as to achieve a more textual "truth." But this focus on the moment of suffering, or grief, is equally problematic because in reality it works like a "linguistic oxymoron," because, as one scholar wrote, "it [is] a psychological impossibility"[38] in real life. Once the moment of grief is over, people try to cope by rationalizing it in the ways available to them at that point of time. How can historians find that particular "moment of suffering" as "truth"? In the end it will be the people who will reconstruct that "moment" for the historian. Thus, the assumptions of both the founder of the Subaltern Studies and the collective are basically flawed.

Mukherjee also thinks that Guha's exclusive cultural analysis is based on Weberian appraisal of reality and reminds one of similar efforts made by British imperialism "for a cultural understanding of contacts among conflicting groups."[39] In several subsequent commentaries on the Subaltern Studies volumes, others echoed Mukherjee's concerns. For example, Rosalind O'Hanlon and David Washbrook wrote the following in a critique of Gyan Prakash's discussion on "Writing Post-Orientalist Histories of the Third World: Perspectives from Indian Historiography."[40]

> What all this begins to look very like, in fact, is a new form of that key and enduring feature of Western capitalist and imperialist culture: the bad conscience of liberalism, still struggling with the continuing paradox between an ideology of liberty at home and the reality of profoundly exploitative political relations abroad, and now striving to salvage and re-equip itself in a postcolonial world with new arguments and better camouflaged forms of moral authority.[41]

Similarly, Indian scholar Darshan Persuk points out:

> Subaltern social history, in the final analysis, suffers from the same kind of "politically anesthetized idealism" that the Genoveses note in the account of the liberal history of slavery in the old South (in the United States), which, in its celebration of black cultural achievement in slavery, "abstracts the slave experience almost completely from its political conditions of incipient violence and from that work experience which consumed so many of the slaves' waking hours . . . and, in doing so 'denies the decisive importance of the master-slave dialectic—of the specificity and historically ubiquitous form of class struggle.'"[42]

Other scholars have accused the Subaltern School of implicitly promoting fascism.[43] Sumit Sarkar, a well-known Indian historian[44] and the son of Sushobhan Sarkar, the mentor of Ranjit Guha,[45] wrote the following in an essay on the "fascist" nature of the Hindu right: "An uncritical cult of the 'popular' or 'subaltern,' particularly when combined with the rejection of Enlightenment rationalism . . . can lead even radical historians down strange paths." It is from this stance that Dipesh Chakrabarty drives his conclusion that Sarkar stopped just short of calling him and Gautam Bhadra (a member of the Subaltern Studies editorial team) "fascist."[46]

Similarly, Chakrabarty reports that Tom Brass[47] and K. Balagopal, an Indian activist,[48] have "express[ed] similar misgivings." For Brass, "The real importance of

Chapter 5

postmodernism lies in its theoretical impact on political practice; it forbids socialism, encourages bourgeois democracy and allows fascism."[49] Balagopal wrote on the dangers of neo-Hinduism. Chakrabarty responded by claiming that Balagopal "blames 'postmodernists" and 'subalternists" alleged rejection of the possibility of 'objective' analysis for the inadequacies of Left resistance to the fascistic Hindutva push."[50]

Chakrabarty wrote in reply, "[O]ur critics are seldom as well-read in post-structuralist philosophy as [Christopher] Norris but the sentiment they express is the same." He seems to suggest that Indian historians should stop being Eurocentric, because:

> [Leftist intellectuals in] the west have ceded to the fascists all moments of poetry, mysticism, and the religious and the mysterious in the construction of political sentiments and communities . . . [whereas] ours [Indian] are cultures rich in these elements. . . . It would be sad if we ceded this entire heritage to the Hindu extremists out of a fear that our romanticism must be the same as whatever the Europeans produce under that name in their histories. . . . What, indeed, could be a greater instance of submission to a Eurocentric imagination than that fear?[51]

It is agreed that the cultural heritage of a country should not be allowed to be a monopoly of any specific group. But one wonders if non-European countries, by simply being less Eurocentric, could enjoy a happier state of affairs despite economic globalization and increased global communication. So much for the efforts of erasing Eurocentricism in a changing global culture.

Ananya Reed Mukherjee also criticized Partha Chatterjee's analysis with similar accusations. She writes that the analysis of Subalternists, such as Chatterjee's,

> bears an uncanny resemblance to the revisionist phase in the development of psychoanalytic theory in Europe: as Marcuse has so eloquently summarized in his epilogue to *Eros and Civilization,* this revisionism helped in many ways to justify and diffuse the true colors of fascism in Europe.[52]

In addition to pointing out similarities between Subaltern Studies and imperialist/fascist and liberal ideologies, many scholars have criticized the idea of subaltern autonomy. An Indian critic observes that the Subaltern School represents a significant divergence from the Gramscian idea of the subaltern, because, for Gramsci, subaltern groups by definition cannot possess autonomy.[53] Similarly, O'Hanlon[54] writes that to portray "the figure of the subaltern as self-originating, self-determining, in possession of a sovereign consciousness . . . is [in effect] to readmit through the back door the classic figure of Western humanism—the rational human subject." Mallon, a Latin American historian, points out, "[C]omplicity, hierarchy and surveillance within subaltern communities . . . make clear that no subaltern identity can be pure and transparent, most subalterns are both dominated and dominating subjects."[55] In the words of Ortner, a U.S. scholar, this insight, "offered repeatedly by structural Marxism and feminist studies in their different ways, by and large elude[s] Subaltern Studies."[56]

Along with the issue of subaltern autonomy, scholars have criticized the school's inconsistencies. Sivaramakrishnan's critique is particularly trenchant in this regard. When Prakash claims to reject traditional foundational categories, it is acceptable that he create new ones[57]:

> [S]ubalternists, particularly those dealing with peasant movements in adivasi (indigenous people) areas, have mechanistically applied the categories of elite and subaltern to their material, without attending to the actual power relations they were intended to signify or examining the historical formation of important sociological categories like tribe and caste, shifting cultivator, pastoralist, laborer, petty producer and so on.[58]

Similarly, Darshan Perusak[50] commented:

> The actual works of the subaltern group itself have been, at best, problematic, at worst, tediously neo-antiquarian and remarkably unremarkable in their banality. These problems derive from the contradictions and confusions inherent in the very concept of subalternity as a socio/political category. . . . The first problem has to do with the proposition regarding the "autonomous terrain" of subaltern consciousness and political activity . . . there seems to be greater emphasis in subaltern historiography on the limitations of the mentality of the poor as a factor in the explanation of their failed struggles than on the fact that they also lack the instruments of coercion that their adversaries in the struggle own.[60]

Jene Lerche, a scholar in South Asian studies, points out other contradictions in Subaltern Studies writings.[61] She remarked that they concentrated mostly on the conflicts between tribal and nontribal people, and not on landless groups (which are work-related): "It is mainly (but not only) when struggles can be understood within contexts other than the work relation, such as conflicts between tribal and non-tribal peoples, or questions of ethnicity and religion that they have become foci for subaltern enquiries." Similarly, Ortner[62] states: "[T]he lack of an adequate sense of prior and ongoing politics among subalterns must inevitably contribute to an inadequate analysis of resistance itself."

Darshan Persuk,[63] however, goes beyond a comment on the important issue of the Subalternists' contradictions. He writes:

> What seems to have little or no place in this [Subalternists'] historiography is the institutions and structures of power and economic exploitation which, in their very real and bloody exchanges with passive or insurgent masses, break bones and spirits equally effectively. . . . It is not enough for subaltern historians to prove, by recounting "peoples' revolts," that the oppressed have never liked being oppressed, or to show that, when they did not, their deviations from the rituals and symbols of the dominant culture contained seeds of "incipient" revolt. The primary question . . . is, to what extent

did these revolts and deviations pose a challenge to the ruling class? . . . The powerless cannot, just by virtue of their indubitably heroic struggles, become subjects of uncritical admiration, nor can their cultural achievements, because they are the achievements of the oppressed, be idealized without noting their inadequacies.

Quoting from the Genoveses, Persuk points out: "Marx viewed any attempt to cover the blemishes or exaggerate the virtue of working masses not only as romantic nonsense but as counter-revolutionary politics."[64]

It is not surprising that the concept of "class" evoked so much controversy, because the Subalternists reject Marxist categories. The exclusion of this concept from Subaltern Studies has not gone unnoticed. Rosalin O'Hanlon and David Washbrook point out that by excluding the concept of class, the Subalternists deny the underclass the ability to present itself as a victim of exploitation—for example, the universalistic, systemic, and material deprivations employed by capitalist exploitation. Such strategies, say these authors, if widely adopted "would give new credence to the well-known hostility of American political [science] culture to any kind of materialist or class analysis."[65]

Chakrabarty, coeditor of the series since 1994 and its main spokesperson, has promoted the idea of "difference" rather than "class." Sivaramakrishnan, Bagchi, and others, however, argue that these "differences," as promoted by Subaltern Studies, do not exist in the writings of this group. Sivaramakrishnan asserts that one can notice in the Subaltern analyses a "movement from Levi-Strauss to Ricouer-Geertz, culture as text and as neo-romanticism, and finally there are glimpses of Foucault. Part of the problem appears to be the creation of new binarisms in place of old ones, and the reification of power, as a result of which Subalternists analyze power in a way that does not raise the specter of disunited subalterns," or differences.[66]

Some scholars also have noted that the place of women in a Subalternist history is contentious, because "while some critics like Spivak have critiqued the subaltern project for a certain degree of insensitivity to the problem of women, others like Chatterjee have optimistically contended that women's writings, as well as their sheer presence, in (their own and others') letters, autobiographies and fictions, preserved a crucial place for traditional values during a period of embattled nationalism."[67] Rukmini Bhaya Nair, however, raises this question in connection with her own project about the accounts of rural women, asking how one can recover the agency of these women in the written medium when "they are and have always been kept at a safe distance from any kind of even elementary literacy."[68] One can add to Nair's predicament that written texts can give information only about those women who were from well-off families and had some opportunity to be literate.

The issue of literacy is highly pertinent because Subaltern Studies emphasizes the written "text" and has extended the analytical domain of history, as Gyan Pandey has suggested, to include poetry.[69] But "if poetry is admitted as historical evidence, why not fictionalized history? Should short stories, novels, docudramas about the Bhagalpur blindings, the partition, the Lalur earthquakes be privileged as 'history' because they describe affect in a manner the historian cannot avail of?"[70] On this subject Nair remarked perceptively, "The alleged 'failure' of the philosopher to produce satisfactory deductive generalizations about emotion, and that of the historian to produce empirical generalization about 'suffering' are . . . comparable because they center on the same paradox . . . [because] history . . . involves numbers. . . . But in order to render emotion, you need the individual mode, which can only be literary and artistic. That is the paradox."[71]

As noted earlier, the members of the Subaltern School also produced individual monographs. One of these monographs, Chakrabarty's *Rethinking Working Class History*,[72] has drawn the attention of A. K. Bagchi,[73] V. Bahl,[74] and Ramchandra Guha.[75] Bagchi, a well-known Indian economist, critiqued *Rethinking Working Class History,* linking the authors' arguments to those of the Royal Commission on Labour in India MCMXXX, which published its report in 1930, and saying that both, in effect, discuss the Indian mill workers as "uprooted" Indian peasants. In addition, Bagchi observes that Chakrabarty treats the "uprooted peasants as an undifferentiated mass liable to be governed by 'primordial' loyalties, and [liable to] break out into primeval violence from time to time." Bagchi also points out, "Most students of society, whether trained in political economy or not, would find it surprising to be told that the experience of living perilously close to the margins of subsistence and of being exposed to the threats of disease and death or of living away from their nearest family members year in and year out should somehow not enter into the consciousness of these people."[76] Bahl and Ramchandra Guha also share with Bagchi a concern about the Subaltern School's lack of sensitivity to historical processes and to historical dynamics, as well as its insistence that "there is no such thing as a social system such as capitalism or colonialism with its own systemic exploitation and oppression."[77]

Ramchandra Guha, who writes as a one-time Subalternist insider,[78] finds in volume 8[79] of the *Subalternists' Studies* a shift toward the study of the *bhadralok* (genteel people) class. Therefore, he suggests that Subaltern Studies now should be called *Bhadralok* Studies or, "in deference to the spirit of the times, post-subaltern studies [or the Sub-Studies of postmodernism]."[80] Elaborating on this shift, Ramchandra Guha also criticizes Gyan Prakash for promoting the writing of "desk history" by urging scholars to look inside elite discourses. This process calls for a "complex and deep engagement with elite and canonical texts." Quoting Prakash's observation that "the project of subaltern study has helped bring about the relocation of subalternity in the operation of dominant discourse," Guha exclaims, "Wonderful: Read James Mill and Jawaharlal Nehru . . . to learn about the subaltern. It all makes it very easy for the historian."[81]

In this "age of globalism" the ideas of Subaltern Studies have spread to progressive Latin American scholars, especially those who challenged the relevancy and validity of using Marxism and its concepts of progress, modernity, and revolution. Such scholars are seeking an alternative to traditional thought but hesitate to embrace postmodernism or poststructuralism. They question its applicability to an area of the world not yet "modern," as well as its ahistorical approach. Can post-modernism facilitate political engagement and commitment? To such scholars, Subaltern Studies seems to be a perfect compromise because it was formulated by a group of intellectuals belonging to the non-Western world. Better yet, it speaks the politically radical language of anticolonialism but also is informed by the newest Western academic textual analysis and postmodernist methods.

The Latin American Subaltern Studies group contains only one historian; the other members are literary critics. The latter had been borrowing from postmodernist methods and techniques (despite initial suspicion), and they believed they benefited from Subaltern Studies by "simplifying their fields." In the words of one observer, however, this simplification of literature and history has led to the "poverty of historiography." The borrowing and application of the original Indian Subaltern Studies became a "simplified misrepresentation in the hands of Latin Americans."[82]

In African historiography, Subaltern Studies' impact has not been felt strongly except by Terence Ranger. Although scholars increasingly mention Subaltern Studies in African historiography, Frederick Cooper[83] points out that it is mainly South African historians who do so. Most South African historians, however, do not agree with the concept of subaltern autonomy, because in South Africa, boundary lines between race and class are clearly and sharply defined. Another difference between Indian Subalternists and African historians is that Indian scholars have been trying to dismantle the idea of an essential "India" by insisting on differences within communities and identities. In contrast, Cooper says, "African scholars have felt, they had to put together 'Africa' in the face of general perceptions of everlasting and immutable division. Therefore, Subaltern Studies seem less appealing to African historians."

Moreover, Africanists do not find the Subalternists' ideas new or earthshaking.[84] For example, Subaltern Studies focuses mainly on the problems of recovering histories while understanding how colonial documents construct their own colonialistic versions of those histories. This methodology appears to the African historians to be more of a sound practice than a methodological breakthrough. In the 1960s, African historians learned that colonial sources distorted history; they found a solution by using oral sources as well as reading colonial documents against the grain. In addition, in the process of writing a people's history, African scholars place more emphasis on showing that Africans had a history than on asking how the African's history making is implicated in establishing or contesting power.[85]

African and Africanist scholars are sympathetic to the Subalternists' critique of a colonial state's controlling project and of the continuation of that project during independence. Yet, they are skeptical about ideas such as autonomous "communities"[86] based on the "politics of location," as suggested by Prakash. Their skepticism is based on their bitter experience in contemporary Somalia and Rwanda: The role of the state in these regions was highly damaging to the "communities," and today the state itself has become a prospective trophy of battle between rival groups.

Under these circumstances, and with the increasing availability of automatic weapons, some "communities" are wiping out other communities.[87] Overall it seems that African historians will not find much to borrow from Subaltern Studies, whether by deconstructionism or any other feature.

Here it is necessary to point out that there is a difference between the Subaltern Studies concept of "autonomous communities," the "politics of location," and Arif Dirlik's notion of "place based"[88] resistance movements. The Subaltern Studies concept of "autonomous communities," according to Dirlik, applies to those communities that seek to reaffirm some "authentic" local culture in an ahistorical context with no regard for the conjunctures that produced it. This type of community, Dirlik maintains, is doomed to failure in its resistance movement because "authentic" local culture is daily disrupted and reorganized by the global forces (e.g., "guerrilla marketeers") that seek to reconstitute it and are to assimilate it into global homogenization.[89] Whereas "place based" resistance movements arise in a historical context in a particular place where people (despite their cultural differences in race, gender, nationality, language, and so on) come together to fight hegemonic forces. This clarification is important in understanding the issue of "difference."

CULTURE, DIFFERENCE, AND THE NARRATIVES OF GLOBAL CAPITALISM

The following exchange between a philosophy teacher and his student sums up the main criticism of the Subalternists' search for the "real, authentic voices of the people" and their rejection of metanarrative.

Teacher: Si Fu, name the basic questions of philosophy.
Si Fu: Are things external to us, self-sufficient, independent of us, or are things in us, dependent on us, nonexistent without us?
Teacher: What opinion is the correct one?
Si Fu: There has been no decision about it.
Teacher: Why has the question remained unresolved?
Si Fu: The Congress, which was to have made the decision, took place two hundred years ago at Mi Sant Monastery, which lies on the bank of the Yellow River. The question was: "Is the Yellow River real or does it exist only in people's heads?" But during the Congress the snow thawed in the mountains and swept away the Mi Sant Monastery with all the participants in the Congress. So the proof that things exist externally to us, self-sufficiently and independently of us, was not furnished.[90]

We should begin with our concern about the issue of working-class "emancipation," because this was an important project for progressive-minded scholars and for most of the Subalternists. The general concern about subalterns implied a commitment to the notion of social justice for oppressed and subordinated people. Because of this concern, I wish to evaluate the Subalternists' role by asking the following questions:

- Does Subaltern Studies, as it has evolved to this point, bring us closer to the goal of social justice for all?
- What type of collective actions would be possible when "differences" are promoted as with Subaltern Studies, against what forces?
- Does this historiography help us understand people's lives, their actions, and their histories more meaningfully in terms of developing strategies for future action?
- In order to develop strategies, do Subaltern Studies develop a historiography, which help to create an emancipatory politics for the subalterns?

To understand the Subalternist commitment to people's history, let us begin with their claim of finding subalterns' voices. Most of their writings display an emphasis on individual subalterns' stories, which presumably give subalterns a voice. Yet, as one Indian anthropologist pointed out, the subalterns' stories tend to lose their punch if not situated in context.[91] Quoting from Comaroff and Comaroff, this scholar states, "[I]mproperly contextualised, the stories of ordinary people . . . stand in danger of remaining just that: stories. To become something more these . . . have to be situated in wider worlds of power and meaning that give them life."[92]

Furthermore, by decontextualizing subaltern stories, the project somehow misses some of the basic realities of human life—that is, an account of how the social order and social institutions articulate in forming the individual subject. How is the link between social and psychic reality to be spelled out?[93] How should it be theorized? In short, Subaltern Studies, by emphasizing only the subalternist nonmaterial culture (values, consciousness, and identity), has failed to consider aspects of the material culture[94] such as clothes, food, furniture, living and working conditions, housing, technology, the financial system, political institutions, trade, and the impact of these features on people's lives. Furthermore, the Subalternists do not examine how the human agency produces the material culture (physical objects) while people interact socially with other people and with specific conditions. These processes are important for the existence of any society and for the production of the material culture, in which people's bodies are located (including the brain, which processes human emotions). These material conditions affect people's psychology (the nonmaterial culture) as strongly as psychological conditions influence their material choices. In short, Subalternists, by avoiding the discussion of material culture and conditions of people, are able to avoid the question of emancipatory politics as it is closely linked with material life.

The Subaltern Studies' emphasis on "culture," as discussed above, creates even further confusion for scholars who wish to comprehend the notion of culture. In commenting on this point, Sivaramakrishnan observes that this "school seems to stand uneasily between the 'invention of tradition' argument, which basically says that culture is the organization of the past in terms of the present, and the historical anthropology of Sahlins, who says that 'culture is the organization of the current situation in the terms of the past.'"[95] He adds that Subaltern Studies fails to specify how past and present interpenetrate in constituting culture.

Chakrabarty, for example, in his studies of jute workers, found the workers' backward primordial values to be a hindrance to developing their class consciousness.[96] He does not explain why the nationalist ideas prevailing at the time and the project of modernity did not affect these jute workers' "primordial values." Is it possible that it did not? He rejects an understanding of the nature of this "community" (workers) in terms of an economic conception of class, claiming instead that their "sense of identity as 'workers' or 'poor people' was always enmeshed in other narrower and conflicting identities such as those deriving from religion, language and ethnicity."[97] According to Chakrabarty, the class identity of the jute mill workers "remained remarkably fragile and easily gave way to the other identities created by race and religion."[98] In this analysis Chakrabarty thus identifies the Indian workers' inegalitarian values as the basis of their "backwardness"[99] (meaning not being revolutionary). Interestingly, in contrast to Chakrabarty's complaint about the "backward" values of the Indian working class, some Chinese scholars are creating the myth that the "values of Confucianism" are useful for promoting a capitalist economy in China.[100]

In view of these scholarly efforts to disapprove or approve of Indian or Chinese ancient culture for the benefit or denial of capitalism, it is ironic that the managers of the multinational corporations themselves acknowledge that they now have the power to appropriate the local for the global, to admit different cultures into the realm of capital, only to break them down and remake them in accordance with the requirements of production and consumption. Today, multinational capital has the capacity even to constitute subjectivities across national boundaries, to create producers and consumers more responsive to the operation of capital.[101] In such a situation, and if we are truly concerned with people's history, how can we, in our analysis, separate the formation of subjectivity from the metanarrative (as it was constructed in the past as well as in the present)?

Jan Nederveen Pieterse has elaborated on this point. He writes, "Confucianism used to figure as a reason why east Asian countries were stagnating, while in the later [twentieth] century it is presented as the reason why the 'Tigers' have been progressing. In the process, Confucianism has been re[mis]interpreted, recoded. Part of this recoding owes to a cross-cultural translation of the Weberian thesis of the Protestant ethic as the 'Spirit of modern capitalism.'"[102]

This misinterpretation of Confucianism for the use of modern capitalism did not occur by accident. Today, international business managements are seeking to understand other (especially non-Western) cultures and to integrate them into their organizational structures. This development has encouraged business academics to address issues of culture. Scholars and authors of management best-sellers postulate that even ancient religious values have contributed to contemporary management practices. In India, a recent book speaks of the contributions to management of Vedic insights.[103] Managers are taught ideas such as that of *shresta dharma* (supreme ethics) to extol the virtues of judicious management; factory workers are introduced to notions of *tat tvam asi* ("thou art that," a formula that is the keynote of *Upanishads,* an ancient Hindu scripture of teachings; the fundamental doctrine of the *Upanishads* is the identity of the individual soul with the world soul) and to *Vishwakarma puja* (worship of instruments or machines, an age-old religious practice dedicated to the God *Vishwakarma* in Bengal) so that they will relate well to equipment and will increase production.[104] More recently the Indian Oil Company has started experimenting with the idea of using dreams to improve their managers' creative thinking for generating new ideas as well as to increase their crisis-solving capacity in the workplace.[105]

This incorporation of non-Western culture is important in this time of global economy, because increased consumerism creates the need for more marketing rather than more manufacturing as the central source of profit for business management. In this context, culture is seen as a "source for capitalist activities, the very plurality of which can be integrated in multiple ways in either production (as in employment of a certain ethnic group, or women for particular types of work), marketing (as in the integration of local cultural preferences), or organizational activities (as in the recruitment of local personnel). With culture becoming a capital itself, the new business managers are prepared to address, assess, integrate, and create a range of cultures," selectively, of course.[106]

Elaborating on the above issue, Bauman states that the "market seems to thrive on cultural diversity: there is hardly a cultural idiosyncrasy the market cannot take in its stride and make into another tributary of its power."[107] In the process of expanding the market, however, the market managers generally observe and recreate the preferences of the middle class, especially the urban middle class. Then they propagate these preferences throughout the wider audience through advertisements and other marketing strategies. In this context, the studies of culture (not of anthropology per se) are being incorporated into the business management schools. It seems that the "definition of 'culture' in the [twenty-first] century will be influenced by the role of business management in an age of transnational multicultural capitalism,"[108] and not by intellectuals debating cultural studies.

In this context of the making and remaking of culture and the future of cultural studies, we inquire about a specific use of the term "culture" in Subaltern Studies. The problem with the Subaltern Studies school is that it does not apply the heading of culture to material relationships in its analysis of subalterns, as if the one has little to do with the other. "Such a focus diverts criticism from capitalism to the criticism of Eurocentrism as a cultural or ideological problem (reducing it as one of the ethnocentrisms) that blurs the power relationships that energized it."[109] This approach fails to explain why this particular ethnocentrism, Eurocentrism, was able to define modern global history and to make itself the universal object of aspiration.[110] In fact, the arguments of Subaltern Studies mystify the relationship between power and culture, and in the process help the ideology of global capitalism to achieve its goal.

Furthermore, Subaltern Studies promotes the idea of differences based on ethnicity, religion, region, race, and gender identities. Before accepting these differences, we must understand how these identities are created and promoted in the real world. Let us take the example of the United States, where the capitalist system and the "democratic" structure of the state seem to go together. Workers who are constantly struggling to improve their wages and living conditions keep alive the democratic structure. The capitalist system occasionally must concede a little to workers' struggles to keep social tension low and thus to maintain its profit margin. For example, in the course of their struggles U.S. workers have compelled capital to restructure itself and share its profits. In the United States, the welfare system and affirmative action are the result of workers' struggles. After 1945, U.S. workers wanted automobiles, college educations for their children, vacations in the sun, and adequate health facilities.[111] Achieving better and better living conditions is the norm in the United States, although recently this norm has weakened under the pressure of capital flight.

If democracy is to survive in the United States, the system must be changed so as to give people better material conditions. Workers in the United States, as elsewhere in the world, are not interested in overthrowing the system; they merely demand higher wages and better living conditions. Today, however, capital cannot give more because of economic globalization. In this crisis of the capitalist system, the proven "divide and rule" policy is attractive to those who wish to continue multiplying their profits in the transnational economic system while encountering the least possible social tension at home, where their headquarters are located. In this context, the U.S. working classes are directed to seek individual solutions for a better life within their "communities" (as also defined by Subaltern Studies), and in ethnic, religious, national, racial, and gender differences.

The above statement is not a figment of the imagination or the expression of a conspiracy theory. Recognizing the grim, explosive situation in the United States today, Jeremy Rifkin, a well-known writer,[112] recommended in 1995 that an improvement in the country's "social economy"—churches, communities, and charities—should play an important role in forming individual subjectivity (and individual responsibility). Not surprisingly, a law was enacted to that effect in September 1996: Churches will receive more grants with no strings attached to support charity work for the poor, because local and federal governments can no longer supply welfare. This approach is now promoted officially in Baltimore by the Maryland state government.[113]

In support of the official line, conservative columnist Cal Thomas, while chiding church leaders, writes, "[R]eligious bodies are about the business of changing the direction of people's lives. . . . The state grants certain tax breaks to religious bodies expecting them to perform work that the state cannot do or should not do. If church leaders think government ought to be the primary provider for the poor, perhaps the state ought to be asking the churches to help foot the bill." Thomas believes that federal and state governments are providing places of worship with an opportunity to reclaim their mandate[114]—at the time of financial crunch, one should add. Thus churches are being pushed to increase their control over the poor, because these poor people soon will lose support from the government. Then they may join other "dangerous classes" in threatening the legitimacy of the state.

On February 6, 1997, President Clinton said in his budget statement that churches and charities should take on the burden of welfare recipients. Churches are now responding under protest, making the issue of poor people and welfare recipients a struggle between state and religion rather than an outcome of restructuring the economy. This process (the capitalists hope) will help to control those millions who have lost their jobs because of the restructuring of the U.S. economy, as well as repress social and political tension.[115] Meanwhile, the capitalists will continue to benefit from the "favorable market conditions."

Should historians and scholars help to promote these differences based on community, race, nationality, and religion, and legitimize the efforts of the corporate world by disguising the real problem? Or should they try to explain the processes that are creating those conditions? I propose that historians should not deprive themselves of the analytical tools necessary to study capitalism and its effects around the world in all their complexities, contingencies, and limitations: "Instead of seeing them simply as metanarrative and modernity, capital and state should be made the object of an analysis that is nuanced and also interactive."[116] In fact, historians need to find a method of analysis that does not snatch away the role of agency but rather sheds light on it—on the role of the state, the world capitalist system, other international historical forces, elite groups, small merchants and traders, the complicity of subalterns, their oppression, and the pursuing of subaltern men over subaltern women. Historians must understand the history of people, with all its complexities, as well as the complexities of the ruling classes, within those of the colonial state and those of capitalism, which are as much part of people's lives as is their own subjectivity.

Three decades before Subaltern Studies came into existence, African historian K. Onwuka Dike[117] attempted to write history from an African perspective. His work clearly illustrates how not to essentialize agency or resort to metanarrative. Africans do not appear in this text as either resisters or collaborators in the face of European involvement. Europeans, indeed, appear as actors in the universe of various actors in the region; all are trying to work with the opportunities and constraints of overseas trade and regional political structure. In short, Dike succeeded in giving an account of African agency intersecting with a European agency at a crucial moment of history.

In contrast to Dike's approach, Subaltern Studies promotes the problematic idea of "differences"[118] but fails even to differentiate between peasants, tribes, or other subalterns. How can the Subalternists lump together all the "subalterns" as one oppressed mass of people and write about "differences" at the same time? In the world outside the academy, differences can be used to instigate murderous ethnic conflict[119] and to perpetuate inequalities between and within societies, classes, and genders. Therefore, when scholars define "differences" between people, they should be careful not to become part of that rationalization.

Before promoting "differences," ask the following questions:

- Are perceptions of differences in a given context a basis for affirming this diversity, or do these perceptions act as a mechanism for exclusionary and discriminatory practices?
- How are different categories of people represented in such discourses? How and why do people construct or represent the specificity of their experiences?
- Under what circumstances does difference become the basis for asserting a collective identity?
- By what process does the social order articulate with the formation of the subject?
- To return to an earlier point, how is the link between social and psychic reality to be theorized?
- What qualities, characteristics, and aspects are compared in determining the differences?
- What is the nature of the comparison?[120]

One should be careful not to reinvent "differences" between people by undermining their commonalities. Differences are not static; therefore, attention must be given to the "operations of differences" (the mechanisms by which differences are promoted) and to the insistence on differences (including material differences), whether in a complex or a simple substitution of multiples for binary differences (as in race, caste, religion, and nationality). Such substitutions will pave the way to pluralism and conservatism. Is it not true that most people, most of the time, find ways to relate to one another and to work together in the same place and environment, despite apparent "differences"? Over a period of time these people develop human bonds based on similar experiences in the workplace. What then becomes of difference?

Moreover, identities are historically conditioned. Kumkum Sangari wrote:

> Our cultural identities are simultaneously our cultures in process but they acquire specific meanings in each given context. Sometimes, depending upon the context, one ethnic group may legitimize class or caste divisions by proclaiming and stressing only the unity of an otherwise heterogeneous group. They may also take recourse to constructing essentialist differences to save themselves from the hegemonic forces of the time. This can especially be a problem for women if the cultural values that the groups in question excavate, recast and reconstruct are those that underscore women's subordination.[121]

Furthermore, we must not minimize the effects of translocal communication systems, as developed in recent years on the poor peasants and farmers of near and remote areas. Pieterse correctly points out:

[F]armers and peasants throughout the world are wired, directly or indirectly, to the fluctuations of global commodity prices which affect their economies and decision making. The ecologies of agriculture are local, the cultural resources are translocal. . . . Does that . . . imply that the new social technologies of translocal communication—from transport to electronic media—are surface phenomena only that do not affect deep-seated attitudes? If so, the implications would be profoundly conservative . . . [because] [c]ultural differentialism translates into a policy of closure and apartheid.[122]

As Pieterse further explains:

Growing awareness of cultural differences is a function of globalization. Increasing cross-cultural communication, mobility, migration, trade, investment, tourism, all generate awareness of cultural differences. The other side of the politics of difference is that the very striving for recognition implies a claim to equality, equal rights, same treatment—in other words, a common universe of difference. In this sense differences do not lead to a closure but to a demand for more democracy, democratic rights and equal participation in policy-making.[123]

While agreeing with Pieterse, I add that when the Western powers advocate "differences and cultural diversity," they have in mind the fear that the South will overtake the North, thus causing ecological economic disaster. Hans May, director of the Protestant Academy, made the following statement in a conference on the New World (dis)order, held in Germany in 1992: "The impossibility of achieving a standard of living in the South which is approximately equal to that in the North leads us to conclude that human rights must be differentiated and regionalized." In this connection Saral Sarkar quotes May's caution "against discrediting religious fundamentalists."[124] In 1997, no more needed to be said on this subject, with the rise of religious fundamentalism everywhere, along with emphasis on "differences," "diversity," and "multiculturalism" in both political and academic worlds.

The above discussion shows that the notion of "difference" can be promoted in different agendas or with different meanings for organizations, institutions, or individuals. Yet if the common people are to achieve equal rights, participate in policy making, and create strategies for change, they must understand the "differences" within different groups as well. Take as an example the women in the most oppressed group in India, the *dalits* (also called "untouchables").[125] Recently, many external and internal factors prompted *dalit* women to organize themselves separately from *dalit* men, because *dalit* leaders have always subordinated and sometimes suppressed independent political expression by *dalit* women. In the cultural field as well, *dalit* women have criticized their male counterparts for dominating the literary scene and not taking serious note of the women's literary output; the women also protest at their exclusion from the top positions in *dalit* literary conferences and institutions.

Because not all *dalit* women have achieved the same levels of education and employment, another type of exclusion is created. For example, *dalit* women from Maharashtra are better educated and better employed than their counterparts from

Karnataka; therefore, the Maharashtra *dalit* women represented all Indian *dalit* women at the Fourth World Conference on Women, held in 1995 in Beijing.[126] Here too, then, a certain segment of *dalit* women was rendered anonymous.

Most important of all, *dalit* women are dependent on the state to create a space that enables them to challenge *dalit* male dominance in politics. This dependence complicates the situation for *dalit* women's associations because these associations are also challenging the state and state-mediated *dalit* patriarchy. For example, *dalit* women in Bodh Gaya in Bihar opposed the state's decision to hand over land in the name of *dalit* men. This assumption for transfer of land action would further marginalize *dalit* women. In Maharashtra (a western Indian region) *dalit* women in the Bahujan Mahila Aghadi and Shetmajur Shetkari Shramik Aghadi organizations are opposing the process of liberalization. Most interestingly, *dalit* women, particularly at the grassroots level in Maharashtra, are exhibiting a strong, spontaneous solidarity across caste and regional lines against the violence created by the Hindutva (Hindu fundamentalist) forces. They are also participating in the ongoing struggle over pasture lands and are organizing campaigns against Hindutva (Hindu fundamentalism) in Bangalore.[127]

In this example of *dalit* women, we see multiple differences within the same oppressed caste group—between women and men, between grassroots-level and educated and employed women, between regions and languages, as well as in their struggle against global forces and their demand for modernity (equality), their fight against the primordial religion-based values of Hindutva, their ability to transcend caste and regional identities, their use of the state for their empowerment, and their struggle against state policies of liberalization. Can the complexities of such issues and the struggle of *dalit* men and women across India (or anything similar in other countries) be understood by construing *dalits* as an ethnic group, a "community," a caste, or a collection of primordial values?

If historians wish to keep the concept of "difference" alive—and we do—it must be related to some context, because every individual is part of a context. At the same time, the context itself changes constantly as it is conditioned by the world around it. "In a highly segregated and stratified society the overall context is reflected in a stratified way in the consciousness of individuals." This context is reflected in the responses of each segregated group to other groups when each group responds to another in similar movements with its own subjective notions.[128]

The relationship among the three major organized efforts in India in the 1990s—the feminist movement, the *dalit* movement, and the tribal movement led by the Naxalites—illustrates this point.[129] All three are the outcome of an objective situation that subjects individuals to varying levels of exploitation. Mass movements born in one context interact with other mass movements (one might suppose) on the level of diversity. Such movements appear to be hostile toward one another. For example, *dalits* perceive the Naxalite movement as elitist because it is led by the upper caste. The Naxalites view the *dalit* movement as bourgeoisie because the *dalits* raise questions of self-respect and of capturing power, while leaving the land question unanswered. Similarly, Naxalites perceive feminist movements as elitist because they treat all women within the same parameter of gender. Feminists, on the other hand, argue that when atrocities are committed on *dalits* or when police raid villages in search of Naxalites, the women are subjected to torture and rape: They suffer the worst atrocities, all of which originate in gender, not in caste or class. Thus, each segregated movement can perceive other segregated movements more as competitors than as allies, more as enemies than as friends. In this manner, each movement works as a check on the growth and success of the others; stagnation by one is perceived as a fault on the part of the others.[130]

The fact is that the agendas of all three movements—land for the tribals, gender equality for women, and caste rights for *dalits*—reflect genuine exploitative experiences. Yet, to achieve their goals, all three, while pursuing their own separate priorities, also should work together in complementary fashion in order to achieve overall emancipation. Furthermore, because the general context remains the same for the three movements, it seems inconceivable that any one of them could succeed in achieving its goals unless all three achieved their goals at the same time. The result of much current thought, seen in this light, is that "diversity proves more a fetter than a potential transformer."[131] Similar situations probably exist in other countries, where different groups of people have different goals and each movement wrongly perceives the other as an enemy rather than as an ally.

POLITICS AND THE POLITICS OF HISTORY

As stated earlier, progressive writings are usually taken to reflect scholars' politics. It may be asked, therefore, what politics can be found in the writings of Subaltern Studies? What is this group trying to achieve by writing the history of differences? This question was pertinent in the 1980s, and is even more so today. When Subaltern Studies first came into being, the people's movements in India were being repressed. At that time speaking for oppressed people appeared to be an intellectual trend. By the 1990s, this was not the case; the Subalternists' voice had become the voice of "differences" only, leaving no hope for a better future for the oppressed. Poor people in effect are now told that to be "different" (unequal access to resources and "indigenous" culture) is natural; they should live with it, celebrate it, and by no means try to change it.

Ironically, the celebration of "differences" as a strategy for people's empowerment is very similar to the World Bank's strategy to "empower" poor Indian women. Mary E. John explains that new situations sometimes can be interpreted in progressive terms while in fact they hide the reality of powerlessness. She writes that through a

> crucial shift in signification, the World Bank has been able to rework the findings about the range of tasks poor women perform, their often greater contributions to household

income despite lower wage earnings, their ability to make scarce resources stretch further under deteriorating conditions, all of which were documented and debated in the past. The shift in interpretation converted the argument about exploitation into a proof of efficiency. . . . [A]s the World Bank report concludes, poor women are clearly more efficient economic actors, with greater managerial and entrepreneurial skills than men . . . references in the literature to women as "household managers" and to self-employment schemes as "micro-enterprises" point to a peculiar middle classification . . . of the poor, especially poor women. The message of the times seems to be that if poverty cannot be eradicated in, as they say, the medium-to-long term it can perhaps be endured better through more efficient management. And poor women, as we have seen, are made out to be more promising managers of poverty than their men.[132]

Though women are seen as better managers it does not automatically translate into their having more money or better life conditions. Instead they are only glorified, creating an illusion of empowerment, for what they have always been doing all these years. According to John, "[V]iews such as these are feeding into that moment in Indian history when production itself is no longer definitive for national identity."[133]

Along similar lines, Tom Brass points out that the notion of the "Third World" has been reconstructed as an empowering form of "cultural differences."[134] In this way, Brass explains, there is no need to perceive the "Third World" as alienated or exploited but merely as organizationally "other." Thus, the economic differences between the "Third" and the "First" Worlds are made invisible (with no need for explanation) by being declared as cultural differences; such differences, according to these new interpretations, should be celebrated. Brass writes:

The "new" populist/"new" right discourse is accordingly a relativistic analytical framework in which it is possible to assert that the rich and powerful are simply culturally "different" from the poor and powerless, and the economic "difference" of the latter is not merely part of their culture but much rather a form of empowerment. Both the fact of economic "difference" and its cause are thereby banished from this discourse.[135]

Brass points out that by explaining the differences as being empowerment, and by banishing the fact of economic differences, it is simpler to recategorize the rural population of the poor countries in a discourse, which the "new" right shares with the "new" populism, as "other"/different. Once these poor people are re-created in the "new" discourses as "different," they automatically become the unknown and the unknowable. As is well known, such treatment of the Third World is nothing new; as Brass points out, that has been the center of conservative philosophy for a long time.[136]

While promoting the notion of "difference," Subaltern Studies also emphasizes the idea of "resistance," though what is being resisted is not necessarily clear. As Carol Upadhaya stated in another context, "By interpreting all manner of things as resistance, from songs to petty theft, there is an inclination [in Subaltern Studies] to view systems of power as ineffective."[137] Another scholar, Paul Willis, has shown that the "development of a counter-culture among working-class youth does not necessarily lead to a radical consciousness, but may only reinforce [the existing] class status."[138] This "tendency to trivialize the degradation experienced by subordinated groups by stressing their 'cultures' of resistance and the maintenance of social identity even under conditions of extreme exploitation, [indicates the] need for more careful exposition of what is meant by both power and resistance."[139]

In the absence of explanations of existing power structures, the notion of resistance becomes jejune and may even narrow our understanding of history rather than expand it. The working masses struggle daily to make ends meet and improve their lives through various available means. Generally, poor people's starvation and near-subsistence existence is regarded as natural (the World Bank sees it as such), as a result of a culture of poverty, or (worse) as resistance (as promoted by recent ideologies) whenever they are able to survive their plight. With such thinking it is easy to be convinced that poor people do not need help or money to improve their living conditions; they know how to be "efficient" managers of their lives and should "celebrate" their strength for survival. In this way, capitalism can continue to justify its exploitative tactics without any sense of "guilt" or "social responsibility."[140]

Without understanding the context in which resistance takes place, the Subalternists, despite their attraction to the term postcolonial discourse, ignore the complexity of the role of colonialism in a capitalist context. In their analysis, "colonialism [sometimes] appears as a force whose nature and implications do not have to be unpacked."[141] Subalternists' refusal to consider class as a category in a colonial context frees the capitalist society from the stigma of "classness." In such a "classless" society, people's resistance can never be directed against capitalist or imperialist forces. In this way, Subalternists can easily keep intact both worlds—capitalism/colonialism and resistance—while at the same time remain "committed" to "people's history."

The above discussion makes it clear that Subaltern Studies does not capture the intricacy of the integration of the world economy into a capitalist system.[142] Although globalization is frequently characterized as a homogenizing force, actually it fuses with local conditions in diverse ways, thereby generating rather than eroding differences among social formations. The Subaltern Studies group seems to promote those differences that are generated and reinforced by world economic forces. Group members ignore the fact that their philosophical question of "differences" is useful only to the right-wing ideologues who wish to control the "dangerous classes" by appropriating the ideas of individual responsibility, the role of race, and "community" in eradicating poverty. It is not surprising that the slogans and agendas of the U.S. Republican Party sound very much like the ideas of the postmodernists and Subalternists.

In this regard, Brass's discussion of conservatives, and their promotion of diversity, is very pertinent.[143] He observes, "[C]onservatives not only emphasize variety, they also love it. . . . Conservatives usually accuse radicals of wishing to destroy existing variety—expressing what is old and familiar—by implementing the precepts of an abstract and uniform rationalism. . . . The conservative view of the world affirms in theory (not always in practice) the existence of a plurality of competing values."[144] Thus it does not seem a coincidence that "those who used to mock the backwardness of 'savages' in the name of progress and civilization are now (verbally) the fiercest defenders of primitivity and archaic value."[145]

Managers of multinational corporations, who function through transnational links generally treated as stateless, also promote this defense of "other" (exotic) cultures. These links are created with the mobility of capital. Capital mobility, which is made possible by flows of commodities (both labor and material), in fact helps to structure new class configurations and power relations, using the prevailing religious, gender, and racial inequalities in a community or a country. Discussion of this dimension of culture, and its exploitation, is absent from Subaltern Studies.

In this new world context some leaders in a "nation-state" may contest the reality of globalization and may try to fan the flames of economic nationalism or build competitive trading blocs. Such resistance inevitably creates social conflict. One can see it in India, where the Bhartiya Janta Party (Hindu fundamentalists) is fighting against economic liberalization and against the entry of the multinational corporations in the name of the essential India. It is happening in Russia, the United States, and probably many other countries as well. In the United States, the main political agenda is either to support corporate America or to return to a protectionist policy, in either case acting in the name of saving U.S. jobs.

The social and political conflicts arising in such processes cannot be thought to issue from people's "primordial values." The fact is that working-class identity changes continually, because of changing economic and technological conditions, both international and national. These changes are confused with the visible racial, ethnic, and sexual divisions of labor.[146] As mentioned above, however, these changing conditions in fact are restructuring the classes with new configurations and power relations.

On the basis of the above discussion, one can conclude that it is impossible to "declare a sudden, dramatic deglobalization" of capitalist knowledge because that knowledge is deeply entrenched in our day-to-day life, which interacts constantly with global markets and global wiring. Most of the theoretical conceptions of Subalternist Studies seem to "amount to little more than a hallucination whenever they are brought face to face with the concrete exigencies of society structured in dominance."[147] As Bourdieu and Wacquant have pointed out, "[T]o denounce hierarchy does not get us anywhere." Instead, "[w]hat must be changed are the conditions that make this hierarchy exist both in reality and in minds."[148] In the same vein, Cooper has remarked, "It is easy to privilege one tradition over the other and retire from the challenge of the contradiction between the two. The original tension in Subaltern Studies did not go away; instead of addressing that tension Indian Subaltern Studies practitioners chose to adopt postmodernist methods."[149]

In regard to the Subaltern Studies' call to "provincialize" European history,

Cooper has correctly observed that a detailed and nuanced engagement with the intricacies of European history must first be made.[150] Furthermore, it must be understood that the histories of all societies are also histories of links between societies. There is no single, permanently rooted, static society. Some societies may take a long time to change during a certain period, but none are static; those that remain static disappear. Change occurs not because of internal or external forces alone, but through both at the same time, and thereby creates something new in all societies. Thus, in modern times each society is linked to others; they are interdependent, sometimes are even shaped, by the processes of societalization (interaction between societies) that are common to them.

Such insights would not serve the agenda of those who focus only on "differences." Yet, is it not true that today all of us, including those in the Western world, experience the pressure of contemporary global circumstances? This pressure affects every society and brings changes both intended and unintended, peacefully or violently, depending on the situation. From this perspective it seems illogical and unrealistic to echo some of the critiques of anthropological literature that interprets and analyzes the experiences of people and societies as a process only of internal conditions (and therefore different from other conditions), and to dwell on that process, thereby creating merely these "differences." Instead, we should try to understand the contemporary hegemonic powers and forces, and their various mechanisms of control.[151] Only then can we begin to explore how these forces interact with different societies and with different classes and groups within a society, and how they create particular conditions that shape people's lives, culture, and consciousness.

We must also learn how people respond to these interactions with new hegemonic forces inside and outside each society. People do not absorb everything passively as helpless beings. In fact, they resist these hegemonic influences and develop survival techniques—sometimes as individuals or as social groups, and sometimes as a "nation," and not in the mindless ways suggested by Subaltern Studies. Most members of the Subalternist groups in India, and now of a Subaltern group in Latin America as well, come from progressive backgrounds. Unfortunately, however, as Chakrabarty has recently stated, their aim is still to keep the idea of "difference" alive as the philosophical question of our times. As Chakrabarty pointed out, "[H]aving an egalitarian society and political democracy may be laudable thoughts in themselves but these thoughts are not as important or as sensitive to the philosophical questions of differences."[152] Therefore, "better" histories can be written only on a clean slate (by removing reality); this can be done only by pushing history to its limits.

If we follow this strategy of Subaltern Studies, we will not be able to write "better" histories for a long time—and perhaps never. Will the world historical forces stop functioning and wait until we can clean the slate? Who benefits from this strategy? One cannot hope that political democracy and egalitarian societies can be achieved, because these, according to Subaltern Studies, are Eurocentric ideas; the slate must be cleaned and the people's history found. What are the poor working masses, subalterns, and their agencies to do in the meantime? What should they hope for while they wait for the slate to be cleaned of colonial constructs? Are we better equipped to improve our collective human experience by pondering the philosophical question of "differences"?

In light of these questions, we should start thinking about the relevance of Subaltern Studies so that it can be restored to its original purpose: creating an emancipatory politics.[153] We should not waste time in finding out whether the Yellow River is reality (which turned yellow because of the huge amount of soil it carried due to deforestation in the highlands), and exists in our minds or autonomously outside our minds, because the river of historical forces, such as transnational capital, will not wait for our answers. All of us will be swept away by its force. If we truly believe in the role of agency, we should not allow historical forces to subsume us but should take charge of our lives and act now, making our own history to the best of our abilities before it is too late.

NOTES

An earlier brief version of this chapter was presented December 1, 1995, at the Center for Studies on Social Change, The New School for Social Research, in New York City. I am grateful to Professor Eric Hobsbawm and Professor Louise Tilly for inviting me to share my ideas on Subaltern Studies. A second version of this chapter was presented in November 1996 at the Labor History Workshop, held at the History Department of Pennsylvania State University, University Park. I thank the Labor History Workshop organizers and discussants for their comments. I am also very grateful to Rifa'at Abou-El-Haj, Arif Dirlik, and Peter Gran for their valuable comments and for patiently reading many drafts. Last but not least, I would like to thank Anne Simpson of the Netherlands Institute for Advanced Studies in the Humanities and Social Sciences for her editorial assistance. 1. Ranjit Guha and Collective (eds.), *Subaltern Studies 1982–1997,* nine volumes (Delhi: Oxford University Press).

2. Rosalind O'Hanlon, "Recovering the Subject: Subaltern Studies and Histories of Resistance in Colonial South Asia," *Modern Asian Studies* 22(1) (1988); Rosalind O'Hanlon and David Washbrook, "After Orientalism: Culture, Criticism and Politics in the Third World," *Comparative Study of Society and History* 30(1) (1992); "Subaltern Studies III and IV: A Review Article," *Social Scientist* 16(3) (March 1988); K. Sivaramakrishnan, "Situating the Subaltern: History and Anthropology in the Subaltern Studies Project," *The Journal of Historical Sociology* 8(4) (December 1995); Ramchandra Guha, "Critique of Subaltern Studies Vol. VIII," *Economic and Political Weekly* (19 August 1995); R. Mukherjee, "Illusion and Reality," *Sociological Bulletin* 37 (1–2) (March–September 1988); Darshan Persuk, "Subaltern Consciousness and Historiography of Indian Rebellion of 1857," *Economic and Political Weekly* (11 September 1993); Florencia E. Mallon, "The Promise and Dilemma of Subaltern Studies: Perspectives from Latin American History," *American Historical Review* 99 (5)

(December 1994); Vinay Bahl, "Class Consciousness and Primordial Values in the Shaping of the Indian Working Class," *South Asia Bulletin,* vol. 12, (1–2) (1993); Ranjit Das Gupta, "Indian Working Class and Some Recent Historiographical Issues," *Economic and Political Weekly* (24 February 1996); A. K. Bagchi, "Review Article: Working Class Consciousness," *Economic and Political Weekly* (28 July 1990); Frederick Cooper, "Conflict and Connections: Rethinking Colonial African History," *American Historical Review* 99 (5) (1994); Arif Dirlik, "The Postcolonial Aura: Third World Criticism in the Age of Global Capitalism," *Critical Inquiry* 20 (2) (Winter 1994).

3. V. Bahl, *The Making of the Indian Working Class: A Case of Tata Iron and Steel Co.1880–1946* (New Delhi: Sage, 1995).

4. The information in this section is borrowed from the "Introduction" in Patrick Joyce (ed.), *Class* (Oxford: Oxford University Press, 1995).

5. It is interesting to note that nonresident Indians (known as NRIs), who have returned to India to settle down, have built their separate colonies and are sending their children to schools meant for U.S. citizens living in India. These Indians do not feel at home in their mother country and they nostalgically identify themselves with North America and its culture. (Madhu Jain, "NRIs: Nervously Returning Indians," *India Today* [14 May 1996], pp. 116–151.) How should one explain the "identity" of these people? Should it be based on their place of origin, or adopted country, or the mobility of labor and capital in different periods of time and the conditions that allow the mobility of both to take place?

Another trend among some rich Indian families is to get each member of the family (if they have a large number of children) to become citizens of different countries in the North so that in case global capitalism creates some unexpected turn in one country the whole family can be saved (both persons and their assets) by moving with other family members to another safe country. How should we explain this trend with the postmodernist concept of "identity"?

6. Theodore Koditschek, "Gendering of the British Working Class," *Gender and History,* vol. 9, no 2 (August, 1997). See also Theodore Koditschek, "The Marxist Interpretation of British History: From Engels to Thompson, to Deconstruction and Beyond," in *History, Economic History and the Future of Marxism,* ed. Terry Brotherstone and Geoff Pilling (London: Porcupine, 1996).

7. Discussion on these three trends within the postmodernists is based on the following books: Simon Frith and Howard Horne, *Art Into Pop* (London: Methuen, 1987), p. 169; Madan Sarup, *An Introductory Guide to Post-Structuralism and Postmodernism,* 2nd ed. (Athens: University of Georgia Press, 1993); and Thomas Docherty (ed.), *Postmodernism: A Reader* (London: Harvester Wheatsheaf, 1993; New York: Columbia University Press, 1993).

8. I personally witnessed this phase of Indian history and the role of the Marxist and leftist historians while working for the Indian Council for Historical Research, where the "famous" capsule containing the whole of the Indian history for the posterity was produced by these "leftist" Marxist historians eulogizing only the Nehru family and Indira Gandhi's rule (it was later dug out by the opposition parties).

9. This information is based on Gyan Prakash, "Subaltern Studies As Postcolonial Criticism," *American Historical Review* 9 (5) (December 1994).

10. As remarked by Dipesh Chakrabarty, "Postcoloniality and the Artifice of History: Who Speaks for Indian Past?" *Representations* 37 (Winter 1992). Chakrabarty is the most prominent spokesperson of the Subaltern Studies group at the moment.

It is interesting to note that the Western mainstream scholars feel exempt (without feeling inadequate) from reading histories of the "Third World" countries as well as the history of previously ignored people. In "Race, Gender and Painful Transformations in the Field of American History" (*The Chronicle of Higher Education* [11 July 1997]), Linda Gordon commented on this issue pertaining to the field of U.S. history:

> Those who do the history of previously ignored people must remain informed and current about traditional historical fields, but those who do traditional history are under no such obligation to go outside their specialties. Even today, only exceptional and rather brave men bring women or gender into their work to any significant degree; and most male graduate students learn that doing so is disadvantageous in the job market.

11. The Indian economic historians and nationalist leaders and their books are as follows: R. C. Dutt, *The Economic History of Early British Rule* (London: B. Franklin, 1901); R. C. Dutt, *India in the Victorian Age, An Economic History of the People* (London: B. Franklin, 1904); D. Naoroji, *Poverty and Un-British Rule in India* (London: G. A. Nateson and Co., 1901); M. G. Ranade, *Development of Iron Industry in India* (New Delhi: National Archives of India, 1892) and M. G. Ranade, *Essays in Indian Economics* (Bombay: Thacker, 1898).

12. Chakrabarty, "Postcoloniality and the Artifice of History."

13. Dipesh Chakrabarty, "Marx After Marxism: A Subaltern Historian's Perspective," *Economic and Political Weekly* (29 May 1993). Chakrabarty reinforced his ideas on these issues in his presentation, "The Time of History and the Times of Gods," at the University of Pennsylvania in November 1995.

14. Ibid.

15. Chakrabarty "Marx After Marxism." Patrick Wolfe's remarks are appropriate in pointing out the dilemma of Subaltern Studies when he writes, "[R]ather than viewing the incompatibility between Marxism and poststructuralism as necessitating a choice between them, diasporan postcolonialism [Subalternists] has derived much of its disruptive energy from a strategically provisional juggling of the two." Patrick Wolfe, "Review Essay: History and Imperialism. A Century of Theory, from Marx to Postcolonialism," *American Historical Review* 102 (2) (April 1997).

16. Chakrabarty "Marx After Marxism."

17. Jonathan Friedman, *Cultural Identity and Global Process* (London: Sage, 1994), p. 140.

18. Ibid., 141.

19. Discussed in Joyce, *Class,* p. 5.

20. Ibid.

21. Ranjit Guha, *Elementary Aspects of Peasant Insurgency in Colonial India* (Delhi: Oxford University Press, 1983).

22. Biographical Sketch of Ranjit Guha, published in *Subaltern Studies Volume VIII* (Delhi: Oxford University Press, 1993), pp. 222–225.

23. Information in this section is based on ibid. Aijaz Ahmad, in his article "Between Orientalism and Historicism: Anthropological Knowledge of India," (*Studies in History,* 7, 1, n.s. [1991]), has also mentioned, "Original Subalternists . . . initially wanted to retain some relation with Marxism; for some of the founders at least, the Communist Movement itself—Maoism as romance, CPI(M) as adversary—had been a point of reference; for virtually all of them, the issue of 'agency' presumed oppositionality and subalternity" (pp. 158–159).

24. Tom Brass, "Post Script: Populism, Peasants and Intellectuals of What Is Left of the Future?" *The Journal of Peasant Studies,* vol. 18, no. 2 (1991), pp. 262–263.

25. Dipesh Chakrabarty claims this in his article "Radical Histories and Question of Enlightenment Rationalism: Some Recent Critiques of Subaltern Studies," *Economic and Political Weekly* (8 April 1995).

26. Gyan Prakash was the leader (president) of the All India Student Federation (a student wing of the Communist Party of India) at Jawaharlal Nehru University in the mid-1970s.

27. Tom Brass, "Old Conservatism in 'New' Clothes," *The Journal of Peasant Studies* 22(3) (April 1995), p. 523.

28. Sivaramakrishnan, "Situating the Subaltern."

29. O'Hanlon and Washbrook, "After Orientalism," pp. 141–167.

30. An Indian student studying Indian history in the United States, after reading the following articles written by Prakash, commented, "Now I have learnt how not to take sides and remain leftist at the same time": Gyan Prakash, "Writing Post-Orientalist Histories of the Third World: Perspectives from Indian Historiography," *Comparative Studies in Society and History* 32 (April 1990); and Gyan Prakash, "Can the 'Subaltern' Ride? A Reply to O'Hanlon and Washbrook," *Comparative Studies in Society and History* 34(1) (1992).

31. *Subaltern Studies Series, Vol. 1–8* (Delhi: Oxford University Press).

32. Ramchandra Guha, "Critique of Subaltern Studies Vol. VIII."

33. For example, the writings of ecofeminist writer Shiva Vandana have been very influential in making environmental policies in India. An example is Jeremy Rifkin's book, *The End of Work: The Decline of the Global Labor Force and the Dawn of the Post-Market Era* (New York: Putnam Books, 1995), suggesting the use of social capital to remove social tension in the United States. A law was passed in September 1996 to that effect. For details, see notes 109–112 and the related discussion within the text.

34. Brass, "Old Conservatism in 'New' Clothes."

35. Ranjit Guha, *Elementary Aspects of Peasant Insurgency in Colonial India*

36. R. Mukherjee, "Illusion and Reality," *Sociological Bulletin* 37 (1–2) (March–September 1988), p. 132.

37. Ibid.

38. Ludwig Wittgenstein, *Philosophical Investigations,* trans. G. E M. Anscome (Oxford: Basil Blackwell, 1976), p. 174. Quoted in Rukmini Bhaya Nair, "Acts of Agency and Acts of God: Discourse of Disaster in a Post-Colonial Society," *Economic and Political Weekly* (15 March 1997).

39. Mukherjee "Illusion and Reality."

40. Gyan Prakash, "Writing Post-Orientalist Histories of the Third World."

41. O'Hanlon and Washbrook "After Orientalism," pp. 141–167.

42. Darshan Persuk, "Subaltern Consciousness and Historiography of Indian Rebellion of 1857," *Economic and Political Weekly* (11 September 1993), p. 1936.

43. This accusation is mentioned in Chakrabarty, "Radical Histories and Question of Enlightenment Rationalism."44. Sumit Sarkar, "The Fascism of Sangh Parivar," *Economic and Political Weekly* (20 January 1993).

45. This information is mentioned in *Subaltern Studies* volume 8 in the biographical sketch of Ranjit Guha.

46. Chakrabarty "Radical Histories and Question of Enlightenment Rationalism."

47. Tom Brass, "A-away with Their Wor(l)ds: Rural Labourers through the Postmodern Prism," *Economic and Political Weekly* (5 June 1993).

48. K. Balagopal, "Why Did December 6, 1992 Happen?" *Economic and Political Weekly* (24 April 1993).

49. Brass, "A-away with Three Wor(l)ds," p. 1163.

50. Chakrabarty, "Radical Histories and Question of Enlightenment Rationalism," p. 751.

51. Ibid., pp. 758–759.

52. Ananya Mukherjee-Reed, "The State As Charade: Political Mobilization in Today's India," in Leo Panitch (ed.), *Ruthless Criticism of All That Exists: Socialist Register* (London, New York: Merlyn Press, Monthly Review Press, Fernwood Pub., 1997), p. 253. For another critique of Partha Chatterjee's analytical approach, see Akeel Bilgrami, "Secular Liberalism and Moral Psychology of Identity," *Economic and Political Weekly* (4 October 1997), pp. 2527–2540.

53. David Arnold, "Gramsci and Peasant Subalternity in India," *The Journal of Peasant Studies* 11(4) (1984), pp. 155–177. Quoted in Sivaramkrishnan.

54. Rosalind O'Hanlon, "Recovering the Subject: Subaltern Studies and Histories of Resistance in Colonial South Asia," *Modern Asian Studies* 22 (1) (1988), pp. 189–224, p. 191.

55. Mallon, "The Promise and Dilemma of Subaltern Studies."

56. Sherry Ortner, "Resistance and the Problem of Ethnographic Refusal," *Comparative Studies in Society and History* 37(1) (1995), pp. 173–193.

57. G. Prakash, "Writing Post-orientalist Histories of the Third World: Perspectives from Indian Historiography," *Comparative Studies in Society and History* 32(3) (1990), 383–408.

58. Sivaramakrishnan, "Situating the Subaltern."

59. Darshan Perusak "Subaltern Consciousness and Historiography of Indian Rebellion of 1857," *Economic and Political Weekly* (11 September 1993).

60. Ibid.

61. Jene Lerche, "Is Bonded Labour a Bonded Category?" *The Journal of Peasant Studies* 22(3) (April 1995), pp. 484–515.

62. Ortner, "Resistance and the Problem of Ethnographic Refusal," p. 179.

63. Perusak, "Subaltern Consciousness and Historiography of Indian Rebellion of 1857."

64. Ibid. He is quoting from Elizabeth Fox-Genovese and Eugene D. Genovese, "Political Crisis of Social History," in *The Fruits of Merchant Capital: Slavery and Bourgeois Property in the Rise and Expansion of Capitalism* (New York: Oxford University Press, 1983), pp. 196–197.

65. O'Hanlon and Washbrook, "After Orientalism," pp. 141–167.

66. Sivaramakrishnan, "Situating the Subaltern," p. 413.

67. Nair, "Acts of Agency and Acts of God," p. 538.

68. Ibid.

69. Quoted in Nair, "Acts of Agency and Acts of God."

70. Nair, "Acts of Agency and Acts of God."

71. Ibid.

72. Dipesh Chakrabarty, *Rethinking Working Class History* (Princeton, NJ: Princeton University Press, 1989).

73. A.K. Bagchi, "Review Article: Working Class Consciousness."

74. V. Bahl, "Class Consciousness and Primordial Values in the Shaping of the Indian Working Class," *South Asia Bulletin,* vol. 13, no. 1–2 (1993).

75. Gupta, "Indian Working Class and Some Recent Historiographical Issues."

76. Bagchi "Review Article: Working Class Consciousness."

77. Dipesh Chakrabarty's reply to A. K. Bagchi, in "Discussion—Rethinking Working Class History," *Economic and Political Weekly* (27 April 1991), p. 118.

118 *Chapter 5*

78. Ramchandra Guha, "Critique of Subaltern Studies Vol. VIII," p. 2057, and Shahid Amin, *Memory and Metaphor: Chauri Chaura 1922–1992* (Delhi: Oxford University Press, 1995).

79. Ramchandra Guha, "Critique of Subaltern Studies Vol. VIII."

80. Ibid.

81. Ibid., p. 2057, note 3.

82. The discussion on Latin American Subaltern Studies is based on Mallon, "The Promise and Dilemma of Subaltern Studies."

83. The discussion on African historiography is based on Cooper, "Conflict and Connections: Rethinking Colonial African History."

84. Cooper, "Conflict and Connections: Rethinking Colonial African History."

85. Ibid.

86. Ibid.

87. Ibid.

88. Arif Dirlik, *After the Revolution: Waking to Global Capitalism* (Hanover, NH: University Press of New England, 1994), p. 112. See also Arif Dirlik, "Place-Based Imagination: Globalism and the Politics of Place," forthcoming.

89. Ibid.

90. W. Suchting, "On Materialism," *Radical Philosophy* 31(1) (1982). Cited in Brass, "Old Conservatism in 'New' Clothes."

91. Sivaramakrishnan, "Situating the Subaltern," p. 399.

92. Ibid. Sivaramakrishnan quoted from Jean Comaroff and John Comaroff, *Ethnography and the Historical Imagination* (Boulder, CO: Westview Press, 1992), p. 17.

93. Especially now that the 900 telephone numbers in the United States are making big money out of people's need to get psychic security in the face of such mass uncertainty in the job market. AT&T and other big communication companies are involved in this effort. Many cases have been reported of people losing track of time while calling 900 numbers and ending up with bills of up to $3,000. The project of psychic security is useful for big business and keeping people's minds diverted from real problems and issues, while telephone companies are making big money. In an age of information, it is not difficult to find the personal history of people, with credit card numbers, who are talking to the psychics on the telephone. In 1997, it is also noted that the TV programs showing angels and aliens who are solving individual and social problems have increased more in number in comparison to other types of programs in the United States.

94. Material culture is one part of the total culture of any society. Culture in a sociological understanding consists of material culture and nonmaterial culture for the sake of comprehension, though both are dialectically related. Nonmaterial culture relates to values and norms of a society, whereas material culture is produced by the people of a society in the process of interacting with nature while fulfilling their basic needs for survival; examples include housing, furniture, clothes, food, and other objects of daily use.

It is important to explain what culture means because culture is the "fountain of our creativity," as well as of material progress. Amartya Sen writes in this regard: "[C]entral to culture is freedom, and in particular, the freedom to decide what we have reason to value, and what lives we have reason to seek. . . . The instrumental, the evaluative and the constructive roles of culture are all related, ultimately to this freedom." (In "A Matter of Choice," *Little India* 7[2] [February 1997]. Reprinted from *UNESCO Courier* September 1996.)

95. Sivaramakrishnan, "Situating the Subaltern."

96. Chakrabarty, *Rethinking Working Class History*. For a critique of Chakrabarty's book, see among others Bahl, "Class Consciousness and Primordial Values in the Shaping of the Indian Working Class."

97. Chakrabarty, *Rethinking Working Class History*, pp. 194–195.

98. Ibid., p. 198.

99. Ibid.

100. Arif Dirlik, "The Postcolonial Aura."

101. Ibid.

102. Jan Nederveen Pieterse, "Globalisation and Culture: Three Paradigms," *Economic and Political Weekly* (8 June 1996). For a detailed discussion on the phenomenon of reinventing Confucianism, see Arif Dirlik, "Confucius on the Borderlands: Global Capitalism and the Reinvention of Confucianism," *boundary* 22(3) (1995), pp. 229–273.

103. S. K. Chakrabarty, *Ethics in Management: Vedantic Perspectives* (Oxford: Oxford University Press, 1994). Quoted in A. R. Vasavi, "Co-opting Culture Managerialism in Age of Consumer Capitalism," *Economic and Political Weekly* (25 May 1996).

The Business Times Bureau of India also reported on June 7, 1995, that Maharashi Mahesh Yogi, the internationally known guru of Transcendental Meditation (TM), has opened an institute for business management with "Vedic" business theory. The president of the Indian branch of the Chicago-based Maharishi University of Business Management in Noida, Delhi, claimed that the university had developed new knowledge that could cure sick industries and prevent others from falling sick. One wonders why the same efforts are not dedicated to resolving the issue of poverty in the world. Is it possible that spiritual forces care only for the industrialists?

104. Mentioned in *Outlook,* November 15, 1995. Quoted in Vasavi, "Co-opting Culture Managerialism in Age of Consumer Capitalism." It is relevant to point out that Subalternist spokesperson Dipesh Chakrabarty also discussed *Vishwakarma puja* in one of his papers, "The Time of History and the Time of God," at the University of Pennsylvania in November 1995. (This paper was published in Lisa Lowe and David Lloyd (eds.), *The Politics of Culture in the Shadow of Capital* [Durham, NC: Duke University Press, 1997].) D. Chakrabarty writes that workers treat *Vishwakarma puja* as an insurance policy against accidents, which shows the context and need for this feeling, or to relate with God Vishwakarma.

By the same token, one can also explain that the context of these workers is the factory work and health hazards at the work place in a country where few managers are interested in workers' health or related problems. Therefore, workers rely for their physical security on a mystical "insurance policy" through the ritual of *Vishwakarma Puja*. In this sense, one cannot separate a worker's psychological need to perform a ritual from the nature and condition of his work and workplace at a particular historical time. Today, this ritual has gained extra importance in the context of "indigenous" cultural awakening and is now promoted by the company and factory owners to increase productivity and discipline.

It may be pointed out that today, many people in India are forming organizations to help people get rid of blind faith in superstitions. The major questions for scholars are: Should we condemn such efforts because people's faith in superstitions are "untainted" by European influence? Should we not worry about the consequences of such blind faith that generally affect women's conditions? It is well known by now that witch hunting in Europe came into being to get rid of female healers (doctors). By the same token, should we bring back the custom of *Sati* (widow burning) in India, because the British Raj abolished it? The male population in India can probably promote it, as it does not affect them. In fact, one state minister publicly said in 1987 that the state economy could be uplifted if each village observed one *Sati* ceremony and built a *Sati* temple, as it would bring in additional tourists. Should we support such "untainted" ideas in the name of "economic growth" or "subjectivity" or "identity" or "religion," "indigenous," and "tradition"? This important issue is being ignored. Meera Nanda, a science scholar, has systematically developed this idea in her essays, "Restoring the Real: Rethinking Social Constructivist Theories of Science," in Panitch, *Ruthless Criticism of All That Exists: Socialist Register,* pp. 302–352.

105. Anjali Hazarika, *Daring to Dream: Cultivating Corporate Creativity through Dreamswork* (New Delhi: Response Book, Sage, 1997).

106. *Business Week* (12 December 1994). Quoted in Vasavi, "Co-opting Culture Managerialism in Age of Consumer Capitalism."

107. Zygmunt Bauman, *Intimation of Postmodernity* (London: Routledge, 1992).

108. Ibid. See also Ashis Nandy, "The Politics of Application and Social Relevance," in Upendra Baxi and Bhikhu Parekh (eds.), *Crisis and Change in Contemporary India* (New Delhi: Sage, 1995).

109. Cooper, "Conflict and Connections: Rethinking Colonial African History."

110. Ibid.

111. A body of literature exists dealing with the issues of the U.S. working class, for example, journals such as *Monthly Labor Review* and *Labor History*. For books on changing labor conditions and culture in the United States, see Curt Tausky, *Work and Society: An Introduction to Industrial Sociology* (Itasca, IL: F. E. Peacock, 1984); U.S. Bureau of Labor Statistics; Richard C. Edwards, Michael Reich, and David M. Gordon, *Labor Market Segmentation* (Lexington, MA: Lexington Books, 1975); Richard Sennett and Jonathan Cobb, *The Hidden Injuries of Class* (New York: Random House, 1972); Berch Berberoglu, *The Legacy of Empire: Economic Decline and Class Polarization in the United States* (New York: Praeger, 1992); Mike Davis, *Prisoners of the American Dream: Politics and Economy in the History of the U.S. Working Class* (London: Verso, 1986); David R. Roediger, *The Wages of Whiteness: Race and the Making of the American Working Class* (New York: Verso, 1991); Ava Baron (ed.), *Work Engendered Toward a New History of American Labor* (Ithaca, NY: Cornell University Press, 1993); and David R. Roediger and Philip S. Foner, *Our Own Time: A History of American Labor and the Working Day* (London: London University Press, 1989).

112. Rifkin, *The End of Work.*

113. *Williamsport Sun Gazette,* March 8, 1997. Church leaders are making statements that welfare plans are unrealistic. Pastor David Beckmann, who runs Bread for the World, a Christian organization that fights hunger, said, "There is no way that churches and charities can pick up the tab for what the government is walking away from. I have yet to find one church that is taking the president up on that." Rev. Try Hammond, coordinator of urban ministry for the Presbyterian Church (U.S.A.) and a former Dallas minister, said, "It assumes that just a little TLC [tender loving care] and pat on the head and everything will be all right."

114. Cal Thomas, "Some Churches Evade Responsibility to Poor," in *Williamsport Sun Gazette* (18 December 1996).

115. For a discussion on the restructuring of the U.S. economy and a strategy for promoting social economy in the United States to ease the social tension among the millions of people thrown out of their jobs, see Rifkin, *The End of Work.* In pursuing the idea of social economy, President Clinton and former President Bush, along with state governors, met in Philadelphia in May 1997 to promote volunteerism as a way to resolve social problems in the United States. Volunteerism has not broken down in the United States. The problem is

that people are doing two or more jobs and do not have the time to volunteer. The people in power and with money find it difficult to pay for the upkeep of the poor in the United States. Therefore, struggling people are asked to work for free by taking care of social needs. "Such a system . . . shifts the cost of labor to the people with hearts or consciences . . . and it is cheaper," Robert Muir writes. "Can any society as immersed in the games of marketing and advertising as ours is, a society that has raised persuasion to the level of a satanic art, claim, nay even suggest, that the volunteers it seeks will make free informed choices—fully aware they don't have to do it. . . . They do not give a damn what happens to the volunteers in the course of their experiences. . . . It is a cop-out of the lowest order. . . . And to have a summit on volunteerism is to have a summit to lend government support to the sale of snake oil. . . . [It is an] ill-disguised exercise of naked power that unbalances the civic order. . . . [I]n the midst of our affluence we have to ask people to work for nothing in order to get the job done." Robert Muir, "Is Volunteerism Necessary? Yep, and This Is Why," *Williamsport Sun Gazette* (24 May 1997). On this issue, also see James Petras, "United States: Volunteerism—The Great Deception" in *Economic and Political Weekly* (5 July 1997).

116. Cooper, "Conflict and Connections: Rethinking Colonial African History."

117. Onwuka K. Dike, *Trade and Politics in the Niger Delta 1830–1885: An Introduction to the Economic and Political History of Nigeria* (Oxford: Oxford University Press, 1956). Quoted and discussed in Cooper, "Conflict and Connections: Rethinking Colonial African History." Also see Steven Feierman, "African History and World History," in *Africa and the Disciplines,* ed. Robert H. Bates, V. Y. Mudimbe, and Jean O'Barr (Chicago: University of Chicago Press, 1993).

118. D. Chakrabarty, "Marx After Marxism."

119. Cooper, "Conflict and Connections: Rethinking Colonial African History."

120. These questions are also raised by Avtar Brah, "Difference, Diversity and Differentiation," in James Donald and Ali Rattansi (eds.), *Race, Culture, and Identity* (London: Sage, 1992).

121. Kumkum Sangari wrote the following ("Politics of Diversity; Religious Communities and Multiple Patriarchies," *Economic and Political Weekly* [23 and December 1995]) on the issue of differences and the feminist movement:

The idea of difference seems to be based on an active deferral or denial of commonality. . . . A diffuse, over encompassing notion of postcolonial, non-Western modernity combines with the inadequacies of enlightenment rationality to tacitly preclude "non-Western" women from any other horizon of self-definition but their "own" culture . . . dismantling the as yet incomplete project of modernity for egalitarian, feminist social movements run the danger of political quietism, parochialism and anti-feminism . . . how the question of rights of women can be posed from within a claim to infinite pluralization or from outside the parameters of the nation-state. . . . Cultural diversity is formed in a complex play of power, resources, geography and political systems. Ideas of "essential" difference have been a notorious basis of discrimination. So "differences" produced on the basis of class, caste, race or gender, the products of systemic inequality now need to be preserved as indices of cultural diversity? Can plural practices resulting from the discriminations or exclusions of caste and gender usefully be called diversity and if so is it a desirable diversity? While we cannot afford to politically confuse cultural diversity with social disparity, we have to simultaneously recognize that in our history disparities have indeed produced specific forms of diversity. . . . Unless cultural diversity is confronted with such questions it runs the danger of becoming a localized replay of the angst of colonial anthropologists or of the bad faith of bourgeois anxiety vacillating between destroying and preserving its "others."

122. Nederveen Pieterse, "Globalisation and Culture."

123. Ibid.

124. Saral Sarkar, "Development Critique in Culture Trap," *Economic and Political Weekly* (22 July 1995). Sarkar is quoting Hans May, about the conference, from *Frankfurter Rundschau* (27 April 1992).

125. The example and narrative is taken from Gopal Guru, "Dalit Women," *Economic and Political Weekly* (14–21 October 1995), pp. 2548–2550.

126. Ibid.

127. Ibid.

128. Ibid.

129. This example and narrative is taken from G. Vijay, "Discussion: Mass Movements and Marxist Method," *Economic and Political Weekly* (4 November 1995).

130. Ibid.

131. Ibid. My ideas on collective actions are further confirmed by the fact that the National Alliance of People's Movements (NAPM) has emerged in India, focusing attention on such common public concerns as unemployment and inflation. While representing various local struggles across the subcontinent, the varied constituents of NAPM all share a common identity as victims of the process of development and modernization in India. (Mentioned in Rajni Bakshi, "Development, Not Destruction: Alternative Politics in the Making," *Economic and Political Weekly* [3 February 1996].) Similar trends are noticeable in connection with the phenomenon of the people who work at home, a trend that has increased in the Western world as well. It has led to the formation of "homenets," connecting women all over the world and compelling the ILO to change the definition of "worker." These women from different countries are coming together in spite of different subjectivities and identities. For details, see Sheila Rowbotham, *Homeworkers World Wide* (London: Marlin Press, 1993), as well as in my comments in "Cultural Imperialism and Women's Movements: Thinking Globally," *Gender and History* (April 1997).

132. Mary E. John, "Gender and Development in India, 1970s–1990s: Some Reflections on the Constitutive Role of Contexts," *Economic and Political Weekly* (23 November 1996).

133. Ibid.

134. Tom Brass, "The Agrarian Myth: The 'New' Populism and the 'New' Right," *Economic and Political Weekly* (25 January 1997).

135. Ibid.

136. Ibid.

137. Carol Upadhaya, "Discussion: On Anthropology," *Economic and Political Weekly* (30 November 1996).

138. Paul Willis, *Learning to Labor: How Working Class Kids Get Working Class Jobs* (New York: Columbia University Press, 1981).

139. Upadhaya, "Discussion: On Anthropology."

140. Similar arguments are used in employing migrant workers in the United States at 30 cents to $1 an hour, justifying that these workers are such efficient managers of money that they save even out of that pittance and become rich back in their own country by buying land.

A similar argument is used within the antiwelfare movement in the United States as a way to control the minority population. According to this way of thought, if immigrants and other poor people who are not on welfare can manage their lives working at McDonald's or similar low-paying jobs, then those on welfare should be able to manage without government assistance. Based on this logic, the people in power do not see any need to keep welfare going or to increase wages. According to the people in power, the poor should learn efficient management of their resources and not be dependent on the state. It is a very convenient logic that relieves the rich and government from a sense of "guilt," if there is any, saves money for the rich, and ideologically blames the poor for being inefficient managers of their meager resources. Thomas Sowell's article, "Serving Is Not Servitude," in *Forbes* (March 1993), seems to point in that direction. He is an African-American, an economist, and a senior fellow at Stanford University's Hoover Institute. These credentials are sufficient to convince people in power to promote these ideas among poor African-Americans.

I am reminded of encounters I had in the academic arena of a similar nature in both the United States and in India. In the United States, I was told on three different occasions (once denying me financial assistance for studies), "You do not seem to need money as you are able to manage efficiently without resources." When I was able to find a job, I was told, "You will not know what to do with the money as you never had it in your life." And when I received an outside fellowship (barely $5,000 of support) to go to India to conduct my research, I was told, "You will save so much money from this fellowship that you could live the rest of your life on it." The message obviously was that it is the rich who do not know how to manage without money and it is they who really need help because they will collapse for want of it. The poor will never collapse, as they know how to manage and survive without money. Similarly, in India I was denied help (financial and moral) in the academic world with the message, "You are brave and independent-minded so we do not see the need for helping you." I wondered what the difference was between these arguments and those made by the World Bank or by the academic community to justify discrimination, depriving people of their rightful income and support. I also wondered about these arguments and those my mother (an illiterate woman) used to say to justify discrimination against baby girls, that God has made them strong, therefore they can be neglected, whereas baby boys need extra care as God did not make them strong. We all know the consequences of such discrimination against baby girls in India, where the ratio of women to men is 932:1000 (and growing).

141. Cooper, "Conflict and Connections: Rethinking Colonial African History."

142. Ibid. For a discussion on the transformation of the state in the globalization era, the emergence of nonstate agencies, and the redefinition of citizenship under the new realities of transnational capital, see Saskia Sassen, "On Governing the Global Economy, *The 1995 Leonard Hastings Schoff Memorial Lectures* (New York: Columbia University Press, 1996). Saskia Sassen very kindly allowed me to read the draft of these lectures.

143. Brass, "The Agrarian Myth."

144. Ibid.

145. Ibid.

146. Cooper, "Conflict and Connections: Rethinking Colonial African History."

147. R. Radhakrishnan, "Towards an Effective Intellectual: Foucault or Gramsci?" in *Intellectuals, Aesthetics, Politics, Academics,* ed. Bruce Robbins (Minneapolis: University of Minnesota Press, 1990), pp. 77–95.

148. Pierre Bourdieu and Loic J. D. Wacquant, *An Invitation to Reflexive Sociology* (Chicago: University of Chicago Press, 1992), p. 88.

149. Cooper, "Conflict and Connections: Rethinking Colonial African History."

150. Ibid.

151. Ibid.

152. D. Chakrabarty, "Marx after Marxism."

153. On similar lines, Patrick Wolfe wrote at the end of his review essay on "History and Imperialism" (*American Historical Review* [April 1997], p. 420), "[D]iscursive distinctions . . . only make sense in relation to the material conditions that historically shaped the different colonial relationships concerned. If we wish to produce histories that tell us enough about imperialism to suggest ways of resisting it, we should start with these conditions."

It is pertinent to point out the example of white North American society that came into being by exterminating the native population. But within a few years, North America will be dominated by people of color: Africans, Asians, and Latinos. Can we define the identities of these people without understanding the colonial (neocolonial) relations between the United States and the Third World? Can we understand their histories without knowing about British imperialism, colonialism, local responses, their complicity, and resistance to these relations? Can we understand all these imperialisms without understanding the flow of capital and labor, initially to the West and today to the East? These questions cause us to think about creating a "World History" in which all cultures are intertwined and have contributed to the formation and shaping of various historical forces. These historical forces have enveloped in its fold today most of the regional and cultural focus on "identity." It is in this new context that it is difficult to understand the identities and writing of histories. If we really wish to know our identity and subjectivity today, one thing is clear: It cannot be achieved in a vacuum and ahistorically, because they are made, unmade, and remade in the historical processes of the areas we come from or adopt.

6

Reversals, Ironies, Hegemonies: Notes on the Contemporary Historiography of Modern China

Arif Dirlik

This chapter will focus on problems in the historiography of modern China that have come to the fore in recent years. The concern is not with specific areas, or with a specific collection of texts. Rather, a number of broad interpretive questions in their relationship to economic and political changes in China and globally will be addressed. The discussion is not intended to be exhaustive, or even particularly systematic. The questions are those that illustrate significant shifts in historical thinking on China from previous years. Where I refer to texts, I do so for illustrative purposes, without ascribing to them representative paradigmatic status.

The mode in which my thoughts are presented is dictated by my understanding of the contemporary state of historiography on China: a move away from totalizing interpretations, and a proliferation of approaches in which the historical field appears most prominently in its disjunctures. The chapter will suggest that disjunctures in historical interpretation point to new hegemonies, as well as new critical possibilities in our consciousness of the past.

THE PRESENT AND THE PAST: REVERSALS, REVIVALS, IRONIES IN CONTEMPORARY CHINA HISTORIOGRAPHY

Paradigms and "a paradigm crisis" would seem to be on the minds of historians of China these days. It seems appropriate, therefore, to begin this chapter with some observations on this topic.

In late summer 1993, I was invited to meet with historians at the Institute of

Modern History of the Chinese Academy of Social Sciences in Beijing for an informal exchange of views on problems of modern Chinese historiography. I went prepared to address the question of a paradigm crisis, which had been on my mind for some time. When I raised the question and suggested that a new paradigm is needed to replace the now-defunct paradigm of revolution, I received an unexpectedly heated negative response from some of the historians, not because I had questioned the paradigm of revolution, but because I had called for a paradigm at all. To the historians, the call for a paradigm was all too reminiscent of long-standing controls over the field of history from which, they believed, they had just been liberated to pursue in freedom historical questions of their choice.

Chinese historians may be free (or freer) today; whether that also means that they are free of paradigms is another question. The immediate issue here is the question of paradigms in historical work. Chinese historians' response to my suggestion points to an aspect of paradigms that rarely enters into discussions of paradigms and "paradigm crises": the relationship between paradigms and control over intellectual work, or more generally, the relationship between paradigms and power. Paradigms are not just innocuous models of explanation that guide intellectual work. Paradigms are also expressions of social ideologies—narrowly within professions but also, since professions may hardly be isolated from their broader social contexts, within the broader context of social relations. The supremacy of one paradigm over others does not rest merely on a superior ability to explain available "facts"; it is also an ideological supremacy that expresses power relations within a context of social relations and ideologies. Paradigms do not just guide inquiry; they also control it, excluding alternative explanations, and, therefore, those who favor or promote alternative explanations. With their experiences of the direct relationship between political power and historical explanation, Chinese historians are more sensitive to the implications of paradigms than we may be, with our idealized notions of professional freedom and the free interplay of ideas.

It is not only Chinese historians who face a paradigm crisis in modern Chinese historiography. The foremost journal of modern Chinese history, *Modern China,* since 1991 has published four special issues addressing the question of new paradigms in modern Chinese historiography.[1] These articles in some ways provide the point of departure for this discussion. Unlike those earlier treatments, which focused on specific historiographical issues and dealt with those issues as if they were internal to historiography, this chapter will inquire into the broader political and cultural context of historians' work so as to elucidate the extra-historiographical forces that impinge on the ways in which we do history.

If there is a paradigm crisis in contemporary China historiography, this crisis may not be viewed apart from the intellectual crisis created by changes in the direction of China's historical development, which in turn is bound with changes that are global in scope. These changes have had two consequences that are directly relevant to historical work—the undermining of temporal teleologies and the scrambling of spatial teleologies—with a corresponding problematization of notions of inside and outside.

The Disruption of Temporalities:
Revolution and Modernization in Modern China

The central event of the last decade was the repudiation in China of revolution in the name of modernization, in other words, of socialist in the name of capitalist modernization. The repudiation of revolution entails several dimensions. At the most basic level, revolution measured in terms of criteria of development has been judged a failure. The impressive economic development in China since the early 1980s lends powerful empirical support to this judgment. Secondly, not only did revolution not deliver its developmental promise, but it also obstructed progressive developments in Chinese society, such as its abortion of a civil society. In this view, a civil society asserting the priority of society against the state had begun to emerge by the late Qing Dynasty, gathering strength in the first two decades of the republic, only to be aborted after 1949, when the all-powerful Communist state was established. The Communist revolution, in other words, extinguished the democratic promise of the earlier years of the revolution. Finally, revolution caused or contributed to the overall ethical degeneration of Chinese society. First applied to the Cultural Revolution, this idea of ethical degeneration has been extended in some of the literature to the whole history of the revolution.[2]

The Chinese Revolution has even been denied its historicity; Roderick Mac-Farquhar described it on one occasion as a "historical aberration." In works published the last two to three years, the only things that appear important about the recent years of the revolution are the personal corruption of the leadership, chief among them Mao Zedong, with his penchant for teenage girls, and the primitive practices the revolution engendered, such as cannibalism.[3]

The repudiation of the revolution has been accompanied by reversals of judgment concerning historical events and currents, which had been deemed regressive so long as the revolution held center-stage as the progressive phenomenon of modern Chinese history. Guomindang rule in China is subject to reevaluation for its positive contributions to China's development; perhaps more enthusiastically in China than in the United States. An element here may be the backward projection of Guomindang developmental success on Taiwan after 1949. Also under reevaluation are contributions to China's development of the Chinese bourgeoisie; a Chinese publisher has launched an ambitious series of biographies of Chinese businessmen. As the civil society discussions suggest, even late Qing gentry and merchants appear more progressive these days than the Communist revolutionaries. Most striking, however, may be the reversals of judgment concerning imperialism and Chinese tradition. Earlier regarded as an obstacle to China's development, imperialism (and its Chinese outposts, the Treaty Ports) now is reinterpreted as a motive force of Chinese modernization. The restoration of tradition is most obviously evident in the Confucian revival. Placed in the museum of history by Joseph Levenson three decades ago, Confucianism has reemerged from the museum "to advance toward the twenty-first century with a smile on his lips," to quote a recent article in the *Renmin ribao*. But there have been other revivals as well, less justifiable historically than Confucianism, including the myth of the Yellow Emperor as the historical ancestor of the Chinese people, whose ancestry still binds together Chinese around the world.

Modernization as paradigm has been the beneficiary of these reversals. In competition with the paradigm of revolution from the early 1970s (in the United States), the modernization paradigm has been declared to be "victorious" over revolution.[4] Even the revivals of tradition feed the modernization thesis, although they also present problems to the latter that are rarely acknowledged. At the same time, "the victory of modernization over revolution" has rendered irrelevant concepts such as imperialism, Third World, or class that were an integral part of the analysis of modern Chinese history so long as the paradigm of revolution was plausible.

A number of works in earlier years described the republican period in modern Chinese history as a "transitional period," or as an "interregnum," between the integration that prevailed under the empire and the reintegration under the Communist regime, comparable to the interregna between dynasties in the past.[5] The analogy may not have had too much merit, but its contrast to the present is instructive nevertheless. The Communist regime, where peasant rebel leaders with imperial pretensions cavorted with teenagers, now appears as an interregnum. The temporal framework is provided now not by an analogy with dynasties of the past, but with modernization: China launched itself on the path of modernization consequent on foreign contact, was interrupted by a backward-looking Communist regime, and once again is on the way to modernization with the abolition of that regime. The problem is, of course, that the regime has had to cope not just with Chinese tradition but with the revolutionary tradition as well, which, far more than an aberration, was an integral part of modern Chinese history. And it is not very surprising that as China reembarks on the path of modernization, problems have surfaced that are quite reminiscent, at a crude level of analysis, of the earlier days of "modernization." Not only are severe class differences reemerging, but so also are social phenomena reminiscent of an earlier day, from regionalism, to banditry, to warlordism (now under Communist cadres). The revival of traditions, reminiscent of the Guomindang regime in the 1930s, has the same fascist overtones that it did in an earlier day. If modernization is indeed "victorious" over revolution, the victory is no guarantee of a temporal teleology. But the present is not the past. The reasons to be suspicious of the teleology of modernization are even stronger today than they were in the past. This should become clearer when one looks at the problem of spatiality, which undermines the assumptions both of revolutionary and modernizationist historiography.

The Disruption of Spatial Teleology: Diasporas, Fragmentations, and the Nation

If the scrambling of temporalities is a prominent feature of present-day consciousness of China, one reason is the disappearance of the spatial teleology of the nation-state, which has been assumed by both revolutionary and modernizationist historiography; the assumption, in other words, that development in either its revolutionary or modernizationist versions would result in an increasing homogenization (economically, socially, and culturally) of the nation. It will be useful to recall here that, early on, while analysis based on imperialism was in vogue, one fundamental reason Chinese revolutionaries sought a revolutionary alternative against capitalist modernization was a belief that, under conditions of imperialism, national economic, cultural, or political integration would be impossible. Rather, development under imperialism would inevitably create economic and cultural bifurcation, with parts of the nation absorbed into an international capitalist economy and culture, while other parts would be marginalized or become the objects of exploitation. A basic goal of the revolution, then, was to complete the project of a national formation.[6] Efforts in post-1949 China to "delink" the Chinese from the world economy for a nearly autarkic development were closely bound with this goal.

The situation in China in post-Mao years, rather than invalidate this view, confirmed it. Few would deny that, at present, China is in a state of disintegration, this time consciously engineered by the state itself. It repeatedly bemoans the situation it has created with its own policies, and although is ready to use coercion to contain centrifugal tendencies, by now even its ability to do so is questionable. That I assume the present to be different from the past should be evident in my description of the situation as one that is engineered by the Communist state itself. The capitalism into which Chinese society is being integrated presently is vastly different in both structure and ideology from the capitalism that earlier Chinese Marxists spoke of: It is a capitalism that has abandoned in theory and practice the idea of the national economy as an autonomous unit and proclaims the necessity of internationalization or globalization as a condition of development. In practice, this shows in the replacement of an earlier developmental model based on "import-substitution" by a developmental model based on "export-orientation." Global integration (or homogenization) is accompanied here by local fragmentation (localities in competition to attract developmental resources). In spite of ideological claims to the contrary, uneven and unequal development is a premise of the new economy.

In the case of China, this new situation is apparent in a number of developments, some of which are universal in scope while others are peculiar to Chinese society. As China has opened to the world, several phenomena have appeared that call into question the boundaries of what we mean by China, from both the inside and the outside. Some of these phenomena are novel to the contemporary situation, while others appear as the reinforcements of tendencies that have their origins in the past. Here I may only enumerate these phenomena, which I think are integral parts of the same situation but without necessary causal connections.

Viewed from the inside, two phenomena are prominent: economic localization and the reemergence of ethnic consciousness. Economic localization may be viewed at several levels, from transprovincial regionalism (South China, Eastern China, Yellow Sea, and so on) to provincial and even urban/township levels. In every case, however, rather than being merely a revival of earlier localisms, the new localism is tied in with patterns of involvement in the global economy.[7] Similarly with ethnicity: While ethnicity is not to be reduced to an economic phenomenon, it may be viewed as one form of localized consciousness. There is evidence that so-called ethnic groups in China, which were defined earlier through political classifications, are increasingly beginning to perceive themselves also as "natural" economic units.[8] In either case, the boundaries claimed by economic regionalism and ethnicity disrupt the spaces defined by national boundaries.

The view from the outside is similar. The current Communist regime has accomplished what earlier revolutionaries feared the most: the bifurcation of China into developed coastal and underdeveloped interior areas. Zhao Ziyang's dream, expressed in 1987, of converting all of coastal China into a special economic zone, has been realized by his opponents, who deposed him in 1989. In this case, however, even the coastal areas are fragmented according to the economic ties they establish with the outside world. What this fragmentation implies may be illustrated through one such region, the Yellow Sea Economic Zone. While on Chinese maps this zone appears as part of China, needless to say, a recent Korean map includes it in a "Greater Korea."[9] Where other such regions may be headed is equally problematic: whether Southern China is more Hong Kong than Beijing, for example.

In the case of China, the disruption of spatial teleology is complicated by two other elements. First is the existence of Chinese societies outside of the mainland, the so-called Greater China that encompasses Taiwan, Hong Kong, and Singapore. It is possible to argue that as these other Chinese societies, models in the contemporary world economy, get more heavily involved in the mainland economy, what is at issue is what role they will play in defining the nature of the borderlands and, therefore, the national boundaries of the People's Republic. Even more troublesome is the problem presented by Chinese in diaspora, who are also included presently among the "Children of the Yellow Emperor," which the Chinese state seeks to involve in China's development. Diasporic Chinese, even more so than those in Taiwan, Hong Kong, and Singapore, are culturally different from the Chinese on the mainland by virtue of their different historical trajectories in different locales around the world. Encompassed recently in the notion of a "Cultural China," diasporic Chinese make their own claims on a Chinese identity. Tu Weiming, the foremost advocate of Cultural China, views the dynamic of a new Chinese identity formation as the recapturing of the center from the periphery.[10]

The disruption of national space implied by these developments calls into question the very idea of "Chineseness." While a powerful state capable of coercion is still very much alive in Beijing, the state's own policies have created a situation where it is no longer possible to take for granted the idea of China as a nation marked by homogeneity of space. The latter is no longer even part of a national project economically. Under the circumstances, resorting to a primordial Chinese cultural unity appears not so much as an expression of homogeneity but rather as an ideological effort to contain fragmentation and the very dispersal of Chineseness into local spaces. Spatial fragmentation coincides with, and reinforces, the fragmentation of temporalities.

If the scrambling of temporal teleology has confounded our understanding of then and now, the disruption of spatial teleology has done the same for our notions of inside and outside. The dislodging of revolution from a place of preeminence may be viewed as a salutary development, for it has enabled us to see problems so long as the teleology of revolution held sway. Same for the notions of inside/outside imbedded in the nation. The proliferation of boundaries implies that there are many insides and many outsides, depending on where one stands, which is not very different from saying that the outside has disappeared or has become very problematic. This may enable us to see the past differently also, dislodging history from its identification with the boundaries of the nation.

These phenomena provide the conditions for our consciousness of China presently. They are important to a discussion of historical paradigms for two reasons. First, it is possible that our consciousness of modern Chinese history is shaped not by any developments from within professional historical scholarship but by this contemporary consciousness, which then projects upon the history of this consciousness, as the revolutionary paradigm did earlier, without regard for whether the present is structurally different from earlier phases of Chinese modernity. It is possible, for instance, that a concept such as imperialism may be quite irrelevant today without, however, losing its significance to understanding an earlier phase of modern Chinese history. Cognizance of this new situation, and its implications for historical consciousness, is crucial to critical self-consciousness in historical work. To return to the Chinese historians mentioned at the beginning of the discussion, while they are suspicious of the notion of paradigms, they seem to think that there is no paradigmatic assumption that underlies so much of the historical work in China today: the paradigm of modernization as defined by Deng Xiaoping, which all of a sudden has swept from the field the study of classes, peasants, workers, imperialism, and so on, in the name of the united front with the Guomindang, patriotic businessmen, and warlords, chambers of commerce, and others.

The second reason, related to the first, is that such cognizance enables a critical evaluation of the alternative approaches to modern Chinese history that have recently come to the fore. To the extent that these approaches are silent about their own conditions, they become complicit in the ideology of a contemporary developmentalism. Rather than enable a new critical historiography, or historiographies, in other words, they appear as partners in the perpetuation of ideological notions of modern China. These approaches, to which I will now turn, have acquired prominence in recent years.

POSTREVOLUTIONARY HISTORIES

For all its apparent diversity, contemporary historiography of China shares a basic ideological orientation that I will describe here as "postrevolutionary." There are two aspects to my use of the term "postrevolutionary." First, for all the repudiation of the revolution, the historical legacy of the revolution continues to shape much of this work, for the simple reason that the revolution as an historical event was, and is, crucial to modern Chinese history. Second, much of this historiography is also antirevolutionary, not just in the sense that it is in opposition to the Chinese Communist Revolution, as we have understood it, but more fundamentally in opposition to revolution and revolutionary transformation as concepts in history. I will focus on three historiographical tendencies of some prominence in recent years: modernizationism, which occupies a hegemonic paradigmatic status presently; the antimodernizationist paradigm enunciated in Paul Cohen's notion of a "China-centered history"; and the antiparadigmatic historiography that has found a voice in the periodical *Positions,* which began publication in 1993.

Modernizationism Victorious

It is arguable that the narrative of modernization all along has provided the criteria for thinking and writing about modern Chinese history. While "modernization" as a social science concept has served more often than not as a euphemism for the processes of capitalism, the modernization narrative is arguably integral to Marxist historiography as well.[11] What distinguishes the present from the past is the apparently seamless paradigmatic hegemony of that version of the modernization narrative that is inscribed in the history of capitalism. While Marxism and the revolutionary paradigms it inspired have receded from the field with the victory of capitalism over socialism, however, it is not clear what the "victory" of modernization over revolution means politically or historiographically. I suggest that this assumption of "victory" for modernization is sustained by suppressing both the past and the present of the modernization narrative.

In the immediate years after World War II, when modernization first made its appearance as a social-science concept, modern Chinese history viewed in terms of the modernization narrative appeared to be a failure. The very victory of Communism in China provided prima facie evidence of the failure of modernization. Unabashedly Eurocentric and culturalistic in this first historiographical phase, historians of China looked for the reasons for this failure. Chinese culture, inconsistent with the liberal political and cultural assumptions of modernization, obstructed the formation of a modern society. However, there seemed to be something about the cultural and the institutional legacy of the Chinese past that favored Communism. Communist victory, rather than signal a Chinese modernity, underscored the alienness and remoteness of China from modernity. The significant exceptions to this "orthodox" view were the works of Joseph Levenson and Benjamin Schwartz, which stressed China's break with the past.

This view was challenged in the late 1960s, when revolutionary movements around the world (including China's Cultural Revolution) empowered a paradigm of revolution against the narrative of modernization. The revolutionary paradigm, too, acknowledged a failure of modernization, but shifted the causes for the failure from the realm of culture to the realm of social and economic relations—imperialism externally, and class relations internally. Modern Chinese history was rewritten in terms of the revolutionary struggle to overcome the obstacles thrown in the way of China's modernization by these relationships. In this renarrativization, the failure of traditional society was accompanied by the success of the revolutionary struggle, which also promised an alternative modernity. Revolutionary historiography was premised on a break between the present and the past. It also challenged both the Eurocentrism and the culturalism of previous historiography as it shifted attention to the material conditions of change. This new historiographical trend is best exemplified in the two new periodicals that were the products of these years: *Bulletin of Concerned Asian Scholars* and *Modern China*.

I suggest that the revolutionary paradigm reworked, rather than broke with, the modernization narrative. Work inspired by this paradigm was able to render respectable the possibility of modernization by means other than that in the bourgeois-liberal model of modernization. It was limited in this regard, but not therefore insignificant. It challenged Eurocentrism in modernization. It dislodged culturalism to the point where questions of culture and ideology nearly disappeared from work on the history of modern China. It brought into the field and rendered respectable the terminology of national liberation struggles, such as imperialism, Third World, and class, and, eventually, gender.

By the late 1960s, the paradigm of revolution had acquired such power globally that even modernizationists of the bourgeois-liberal camp felt an obligation to incorporate revolution (and socialism) into the modernization narrative as possible alternative modes of development to capitalism. At the same time, the challenge of revolution led to a perceived need to modify modernization theory itself. The foremost example of this was Samuel Huntington's influential *Political Order in Changing Societies,* which recognized the process of modernization itself as a destabilizing process that resulted in revolution and, in order to forestall such eventualities, offered authoritarianism as a substitute for the liberal notions of modernization that had hitherto dominated the understanding of the modernization process.[12] Huntington's work was important because it integrated revolution into the modernization process. His work also broke with the assumption of the liberal modernization narrative that there was a necessary connection (in the short term, at least) between economic modernization and modernization at the levels of politics, society, and culture. His "conservative" answer was that for non–Euro-American societies, authoritarian modernization provided an alternative to revolution.

In the early 1970s, the modern/traditional dichotomy that had been a staple of the modernization narrative earlier was also challenged. An influential article by Dean Tipps stressed the contemporaneity of the modern and the traditional and argued that the "traditional" itself was an integral part of the modern world and was produced by it. Other work further scrambled notions of the modern and the traditional. Lloyd and Susan Rudolph argued (for India) for the "modernity of tradition." Scholars from the left, developing various versions of "world-systems analysis," pointed to the structural interconnectedness of the world under capitalism, arguing that the "underdevelopment" of the Third World was itself a product of the development of Euro-America.[13] While the bourgeois-liberal narrative remained strong in the historiography of modern China, for two decades it had to share the field with these alternatives.[14]

This situation began to change in the mid-1980s, once again in connection with global events, mainly the recession of socialism and of Third World revolutions. In the background, however, were also new developments within capitalism, which in hindsight may have had close connections with the decline and fall of socialism. The disappearance of revolution (and socialism) has made possible once again the separation of revolution from modernization, which is the condition for recent declarations of the "victory" of modernization over revolution. But what kind of victory is it?

Declarations of such victory presuppose an unbroken narrative of modernization, from its beginnings (in China) in the nineteenth century to the present. If the account above has any validity, however, this narrativization is plausible only to the extent that it suppresses the history of the modernization narrative itself; in other words, the modernization narrative, in order to erase memories of revolution, also has to erase the complexity of the notion of modernization itself, which in a previous period assimilated revolution as part of a modernization narrative.

This is what is meant when referring to the suppression by the modernization narrative of its own past. But what about the present? Is the modernization to which we have returned the same as the modernization that dominated the field in an earlier day? Do declarations of victory suppress the present as well?

The answer is an unqualified yes, for the simple reason that contemporary capitalism is vastly different than what it had been for a century before the emergence of "modernization theory" in the 1950s. The single most important difference, as noted in the last section, is the disappearance of the temporal and spatial teleology of modernity. This has to do, above all, with the emergence of a global capitalism that, in erasing memories of revolution, seeks also to erase its history of imperialism and global pillage. It also has something to do with the legacy of revolution. Indeed, it is arguable that recent developments in capitalism are in part products of efforts to deal with the challenge of socialism and revolution, made possible by new technologies. This renders simplistic the divorcing of modernization from revolution. It also disguises much about the present.

Capitalism, by overthrowing socialism, has succeeded in unifying the globe. What it has failed to do is to achieve any kind of homogenization; in fact, in its very operations, it has introduced new kinds of fragmentations, sometimes along the old fault lines, sometimes along new ones. Socialism as we have known it may be a thing of the past, but the idea of an alternative mode of development, which is its legacy, is still very much alive within the context of capitalism. This is quite evident in the case of the People's Republic of China (PRC), which, having opened its gates to capitalism after 1978, continued to insist on a "socialism with Chinese characteristics." What is important here is not the socialism part but "Chinese characteristics." Since 1978, but especially during the 1990s, little pretense has remained in China of "socialism," but the insistence on "Chinese characteristics" remains. Indeed, as the PRC has abandoned pretensions to socialism, it has become more receptive to the so-called Confucian revival, which from the beginning has argued for Confucian-style capitalism.

Important as the legacy of revolution is, the new fault lines have much to do with the reconfiguration of the globe under a new global capitalism. After all, the Confucian revival itself was nourished from the beginning by the success of East Asian societies in general and the Chinese societies of Hong Kong, Singapore, and Taiwan in particular. Having achieved success in capitalist development, these societies are now in a position to assert themselves ideologically against a Euro-American cultural hegemony that earlier denied to them any kind of a subjectivity in modernity. On the contrary, their success makes them available as models for emulation by the older centers of capital in Europe and North America.

Two observations of significance are to be made. First, while the modernization narrative persists in its culturalism, the cultural explanation is vastly different than in the past. Chinese culture, viewed in the immediate postwar years as an obstacle to modernization and somehow held responsible for Communism, has been converted now into some kind of progressive force that breathes new life into a capitalism plagued by contradictions. It is now Communism, viewed in the late 1960s and '70s as an alternative modernization, that has been rendered into an obstacle to China's modernization. Not the least important aspect of this reversal in cultural explanation is its class basis. The culture of the elite, Confucianism, is now a progressive force. Peasant and working-class cultures, hailed earlier as the sources of a progressive revolutionary identity, have been reconstructed as the locations for a backward, feudal culture that created the Chinese version of socialism.

Second, the very possibility that "traditions" other than the Euro-American may serve the cause of capitalism has undermined the Eurocentric teleology of an earlier modernization narrative. Modernization, in other words, has broken down into a variety of temporalities and spatialities. This is apparent in the increasing attention devoted in recent years to the so-called cultures of capitalism.[15] This is the case not just for China. The "traditional societies" that informed an earlier modernization narrative, from Confucianism to Islam, have now been converted into different cultures of capitalism. The products of the globalization of capital have turned now into threats to the capitalist order. Samuel P. Huntington, ever mindful of power relations, predicted in 1993 a coming war between civilizations.[16] What Huntington overlooks is that these "civilizations" are not the older civilizations but products of the globalization of capital, that they are not just divided from one another but also tied together in their partnership in global capitalism. The conflict, in other words, is not between civilizations as they once were, but within a capitalist world-system. His prediction goes to show, nevertheless, that modernity has been fragmented even as it has been universalized. Some victory!

One final note is necessary on the question of the nation. The modernization narrative of an earlier day was premised on the nation as the unit of analysis. Modernizationist culturalism took the national culture as the criterion by which to judge national suitability to modernization. As noted in the last section, global capitalism has confounded the idea of the nation by scrambling national boundaries; in the case of China, the nation is now a site of contestation among diasporic, national, and a variety of local cultures. The obliviousness to the structural conditions responsible for such scrambling in the culturalist insistence on national culture makes the contemporary claims of the modernization narrative less convincing than ever before. What has disappeared with the appearance of multiple boundaries is any clear notion of inside/outside, or of self and the Other. Dominations and hegemonies have not disappeared, but they now appear at a multiplicity of levels that are not to be contained along older national boundaries.[17]

What all this implies historiographically is that the contemporary modernization narrative is founded on an untenable historicism—that the "victory" of modernization over revolution represents the culmination of a 150-year struggle for modernity. Such a narrative is no more plausible than the narrative of revolution over which it claims victory, because it suppresses different phases in the transformations of Chinese society and of its global context that need to be distinguished structurally. The contemporary narrative of modernization is very much a postrevolutionary narrative that is empowered by global capitalism. The present may illuminate the past, as the past may offer critical perspectives on the present, but that may well be due to difference, rather than to some narrative continuity.

If narrative continuity presents one set of problems, narrative erasure of past alternatives presents another set. Projecting present conditions on the past, or reading the present from the past, may serve ideological affirmations of contemporary capitalism but it does little service to the various historical contexts within which modern Chinese history is to be comprehended. Narrative historicism, in other words, betrays historicity in its very obliviousness to the structural contexts that endowed historical events with concrete meaning, either temporally or spatially.[18] It also conceals its present: that modernization may be a teleology without a future, for the future lies shrouded in the uncertainties of the present.

"China-Centered History"?

In spite of the challenges to it during the past three decades, the modernization narrative remains Eurocentric. Talk of different "cultures of capitalism" hardly disguises that capitalism bears upon it the imprint of its European origins, and its transformation of societies globally has established globally the hegemony of Euro-American culture, even where these societies have challenged the domination of Euro-American capitalism. To appropriate capitalism, non-European societies must first assimilate themselves to the demands of capital. This is quite evident in the Confucian revival, which, to gain a voice for a native Chinese culture, first has articulated Confucianism to the values of capital to prove that Confucianism is as suitable to the values of contemporary transnational corporations as the "Protestant ethic" that Max Weber perceived in the origins of capitalism.[19] It is against this ineluctable Eurocentrism of the modernization narrative that I place Paul Cohen's challenge to modern Chinese historiography in his *Discovering History in China,* which, on the surface at least, has rejected a variety of modernization narratives for looking at China from the "outside."[20] Cohen writes in his preface:

> The Book is a critical appraisal of some of the major approaches that, since World War II, have shaped American writing on recent Chinese history. By "recent" I mean, in general, the nineteenth and twentieth centuries, a span of time often referred to as the modern era. For reasons that will become plain, I have developed serious misgivings about the application of the term "modern" to Chinese history, even for purely nominal purposes, and where possible have used labels like "recent" or "post-1800" instead.[21]

Cohen gives us a reason for his uneasiness: "After Vietnam, there could be no more easy assumptions about the goodness of American power, no more easy equating of being 'modern' with being 'civilized.' "[22]

Cohen's appraisal of historiographical literature, however, takes as its target not just those modernization narratives that equated being "modern" with being "civilized," but also those that asserted Euro-American modernity with a new kind of barbarism—in other words, those narratives informed by a revolutionary paradigm that saw in Euro-American modernity the sources of the imperialism that oppressed Third World societies and obstructed their development. These latter narratives, no less than bourgeois-liberal modernizationism, posed questions of modern Chinese history from the "outside."

Against these narratives, Cohen offered his version of a "China-centered history." According to Cohen, this "China-centered history" had four characteristics:

> (1) It begins Chinese history in China rather than the West and adopts, *as far as humanly possible,* internal (Chinese) rather than external (Western) criteria for determining what is historically significant in the Chinese past; (2) it disaggregates China "horizontally" into regions, provinces, prefectures, counties and cities, thus making regional and local history possible; (3) it also disaggregates Chinese society "vertically" into a number of vertical levels, facilitating the writing of *lower-level history, both popular and nonpopular;* and finally (4) it welcomes with enthusiasm the theories, methodologies, and techniques developed in disciplines other than history (mostly, but not exclusively, the social sciences) and strives to integrate these into historical analysis.[23] (emphases mine)

Cohen's critique of the tradition/modernity dichotomy in earlier modernization narratives was well taken but hardly original by 1984. His critique of imperialism-based explanations had some insights into the problem but was not without a kind of intellectual inconsistency, as in his deployment of "Chinese tradition" against arguments that imperialism had been responsible for China's woes—after having argued against the very idea of tradition in the previous context.[24] It is possible that having risked offending major figures in the field by criticizing their approach to the tradition/modernity problem, Cohen was anxious to make up for it in the very next chapter by defending their views against radical scholars. He also focused almost entirely on the moralistic aspects of the imperialism argument, avoiding questions it raised concerning a new world context. By the time Cohen reached the middle of his book, he seems to have forgotten what he says in the Preface was the source of his dissatisfactions: the war in Vietnam!

The major problem with *Discovering History in China,* however, lies with the counter-paradigm Cohen offers, the so-called China-centered history. Seemingly uneasy about the idea himself, Cohen qualifies his China-centered history in so many ways that his paradigm is exhausted even before he is finished laying it out. What he has to say is worth quoting at some length:

> The idea that the China-centered approach tries to encompass is that there is an internal structure or direction to Chinese history in the nineteenth and twentieth centuries that proceeded from the eighteenth and earlier centuries. . . . What we have is not a "traditional" order going no place, marked by "inertia," definable largely if not exclusively in terms of its incapacity to cope with the West, but rather a genuine historical situation, bristling with tensions and problems that countless Chinese are trying to deal with in countless ways.
>
> Enter the West. The West creates new problems—and this is the aspect that until recently has mesmerized American historians (Fairbank and Levenson being prime examples). But it also creates a new *context,* a new *framework* for the perception and understanding of old problems, and finally, it offers for the solution of problems both old and new a radically different stock of ideas and technologies. *Throughout, however, although the context is increasingly influenced by the West, the internal history remains Chinese.* [Emphasis in the last sentence is mine; the previous ones are in the original.] My use of the term *China-centered* is not intended to describe an approach to this history that ignores external determinants and treats China in isolation from the rest of the world; nor, certainly, do I mean to revive the old concept of "Sinocentrism," with its connotations of a world centering on China. Rather, *China-centered* is intended to delineate an approach to recent Chinese history that strives to understand what is happening in that history in terms that are as free as possible of imported criteria of significance . . . as long as the practitioners of China-centered historiography are Americans, no matter how hard we try to get "inside" Chinese history, we will still end up insinuating into this history vocabulary and concepts that are American.

This is true—up to a point. But it is also false in that it lays too much stress on a particular kind of outsideness and in so doing betrays a fundamental misconception of the limitations under which historians *in general* operate in their efforts to retrieve the truth about the past. The fact is, all historians—not only Americans approaching Chinese history from without but also Chinese historians approaching it from within—are, in some sense, outsiders.[25]

This reasoning in defense of a "China-centered history" is neither very rigorous nor particularly illuminating. "China-centered history" recognizes the crucial part "Western" history played in modern China but reaffirms nevertheless that the "internal history" remains Chinese. Cohen insists on separating the text (of Chinese history) from its context (in global history), even though he recognizes that the latter shapes and redirects the trajectory of the former. Even though a "new stock of ideas" has entered Chinese history to offer new understandings and solutions of problems old and new, the historian must keep out of analysis imported vocabulary, concepts, and criteria of significance. Most significantly, it turns out by the end that an "insider's" history is impossible after all because all historians are "outsiders" to the past; recalling the wonderful title of a book by Richard Lowenthal, *The Past Is a Foreign Country*. All we are left with at the end is a pious (and somewhat arrogant) reminder to historians that they cultivate an awareness of this problem of history.

More than twenty-five years ago, I concluded an article on Chinese Marxist historiography with the line, "Chinese history, having its own past, would be the arbiter of its own future."[26] What I meant by that line was that Marxist historians, having grounded Chinese history in the material circumstances of Chinese society, had shown (in spite of themselves) the falseness of writing Chinese history after imported models, bourgeois or Marxist. Cohen's "China-centered history," I assume, overlaps with this sentiment. What Cohen argues for, however, goes beyond the question of models. In spite of his defensive statements about the "outsideness" of U.S. historians, and his call to make use of all available social-science concepts and methodologies in the writing of a "China-centered history," he is obviously troubled by the intrusion of foreign concepts into Chinese historiography. In blatant contradiction to his statements at the end of the book is the statement with which he begins it, which questions the "Chineseness" of Chinese historians to the extent that they make use of foreign concepts.

> The supreme problem for American students of Chinese history, particularly in its post-Western impact phase, has been one of ethnocentric distortion. One source of this problem is the obvious fact that the West—our West—has played a direct and vitally important part in recent Chinese history. *Another source, somewhat less obvious, is that the Chinese themselves, both Marxist and non-Marxist, in reconstructing their history, have depended heavily on vocabulary, concepts, and analytical frameworks borrowed from the West, thus depriving Western historians of compelling insider-produced alternatives to our own outsider perspectives.*[27] (emphasis mine)

Modern Chinese, who have "borrowed" extensively from the West intellectually, in other words, are not to be considered "insiders" to Chinese history. They are tainted.

Equally problematic is Cohen's notion of "China" in "China-centered." The inside/outside distinction that he insists on results in a reification of China and

Chineseness that contradicts his project for a "China-centered history." If we recall this project in the statement above, Cohen is cognizant of a variety of geographical differentiations in what constitutes China. He also seems to be cognizant of what he calls "vertical" differentiations (stated vaguely as "upper" and "lower," "popular" and "nonpopular" histories). It is all the more surprising, therefore, that he does not pursue what these differentiations might imply for a conceptualization of "China." Viewed from the perspective of these various differentiations, histories grounded concretely in different circumstances would be expected to reveal different "Chinas." Cohen presumably eschews other possible differentiations based on classes, genders, and ethnicities, because they are of "foreign" origin (as if William Skinner's marketing analysis were not!). Had he included those in his project, the constructedness of China as a category might have come into even sharper focus, raising the question of "what" and "whose" China. The questions are equally relevant diachronically, in constructions of China in the past and the present. Why is imperialism an outside force when its effects are felt in the restructuring of Chinese society, as well as in the Chinese perception of self and other in an entirely new spatial and temporal mapping of the world? Why are Chinese constructions of China in the modern period any less valid than constructions of China in the past? The answer (for Cohen) is in some ways obvious: because the former have been tainted by Western concepts. It is here that we may begin to perceive the implication of "China-centered history": its denial of historicity to Chinese to the extent that they have become modern. The question then is: Can we deny historicity to modern Chinese without a denial of history to the past? Are Chinese tainted by Buddhism, and are they less Chinese than those who are not tainted by Buddhism? The denial of history is implicit in the very reification of China.

Cohen's protestations over the issue of "Sinocentrism" to the contrary, the underlying implication of a "China-centered history" is an advocacy of a self-referential history that indeed presupposes a "China" that is a world unto itself. This is quite obvious in some of the work that has been inspired by "China-centered history." One example is John Schrecker's *The Chinese Revolution in Historical Perspective,* which the author describes as an attempt "to bring the story of the nineteenth and twentieth centuries into accord with what might be called the traditional version of earlier Chinese history as portrayed by American specialists on that era."[28] Less subtle than Cohen, Schrecker has no qualms asserting that the task is to be performed by foreign scholars, because the Chinese themselves are "out of touch with the dynamic side of [their] traditions." The tradition Schrecker wishes to restore is the Confucian tradition. His analysis takes the form of rewriting modern Chinese history in terms of the concepts of *fengjian* and *junxian,* seemingly unaware that he transforms the content of these terms drastically in order to enable them to serve as substitutes for something akin to Marxist modes of production.

Another example is to be found in Frank Dikotter's *The Discourse of Race in Modern China.*[29] Along with Schrecker, Dikotter acknowledges the inspiration to him of a "China-centered history." And as with Schrecker, his is a self-referential history that, through narrative suppression of the modern in Chinese history, manages to establish a link between the *Shujing* and modern Chinese conceptions of race. In the process, modern racism (Euro-American and Chinese) becomes as old as Chinese history.

It is ironic that a "China-centered history," with its basic assumption about an inside/outside distinction, should come forth and achieve some measure of acceptance precisely at a time when such a distinction has become less tenuous than ever in the history of modern China.[30] It is also ironic that Chinese should be denied their modernity at a time when what is most striking about Chinese intellectual and cultural life is a fetishism of modernity.

The irony suggests that "China-centered history" may have more in common with the modernization narrative it rejects than meets the eye at first. The historicism of the latter extends the present to the past through a narrative strategy and rejects as traditional those aspects of the past that do not fit in with the present. The historicism of "China-centered history" seeks to make narrative the present in terms of criteria that reach back to the origins of Chinese history. In spite of some reference to "new periodizations," "China-centered history" has shown little sensitivity to structural contexts from which historical phenomena or concepts, old and new, derive their historical meaning, especially where the "modern" is concerned. In its very efforts to erase "modernity" from modern Chinese history, it also precludes the very historical possibility of a "Chinese modernity."

Indeed, contrary to Cohen, "China-centered history" seems to express above all an Orientalist nostalgia. Traces of such nostalgia are apparent in the self-indulgent sentimentalities of *Discovering History in China*. The Orientalist legacy is also apparent in the conception of history imbedded in the text, as well as the roles it assigns to Chinese and U.S. historians. China is once again set apart from the West, into a space where Western conceptions of history and society ought not to be permitted (as far as *humanly possible*). And, once again, U.S. historians are to show the way to Chinese historians in the writing of Chinese history, because the latter, having been tainted by modernity, have lost touch with their traditions. Cohen must be very satisfied now that the Chinese are once again asserting their kinship to the Yellow Emperor.

This Orientalism, however, is also a very contemporary, postrevolutionary Orientalism. The very transposition of the authority over the past of U.S. and Chinese historians reveals the tenuousness of the boundaries that divide China from the West that are so crucial to the argument for a "China-centered history." In his notion of "cultural China," Tu Wei-ming includes "sinified" Western intellectuals in the outer realms (the innermost being Chinese in China and diasporic China, in that order). The very distancing of China also brings it to our midst. An older Orientalism emphasized difference to relegate the Other to the past. The emphasis on difference presently seeks to bring the Other to the centers of global power and global ideology. Can we understand "China-centered history" without reference to the global conditions that make such motions possible; namely, loss of confidence in a "Western" modernity, and the space that makes possible for the reassertion of alternative pasts—which also read as alternative presents?

Postcolonial Encounters:
From *Modern China* to *Positions*

The modernizationist and the antimodernizationist paradigms may be viewed as postrevolutionary versions of older attitudes toward modern Chinese history. Genuinely new is the attitude represented by *Positions* magazine, which is informed by poststructuralist methodologies. What makes the *Positions* attitude interesting in this context is that its methodological presuppositions call not for a new paradigm but for the dissolution of paradigms.

It is instructive in enunciating the shift during the past two decades in attitudes concerning questions of modern China historiography, to set *Positions,* which began publication in 1993, against *Modern China,* which has been published for more than twenty years.[31] The comparison is relevant especially because *Positions* seeks to claim a radical legacy; its goal would appear to be to improve on, rather than to negate, the radical scholarship associated with *Modern China* and the *Bulletin of Concerned Asian Scholars.* Needless to say, both of these journals must be viewed against the backdrop of the *Journal of Asian Studies* and *China Quarterly,* which serve as reminders of a more constant landscape.

Modern China was the product of a new orientation to questions of the Chinese Revolution. While those who participated in its founding by no means shared a uniformed outlook, they were convinced nevertheless of the necessity of reinterpreting the revolution. The first item on the agenda was to take the revolution seriously as a *modern* historical event, rather than as a manifestation of some Chinese peculiarity, a Chinese escape from modernity represented by the West, or a foreign transplant. This entailed also taking seriously the claims of the revolution, of which three were particularly significant. First, that the revolution was not against modernity but against imperialism. Second, that the Marxism of the revolution was not merely a cover for some cultural peculiarity or dilemma but an authentic Third World Marxism that sought an alternative to capitalism. And third, that the revolution, rather than being merely a national revolution, was motivated by a genuine urge to resolve the class contradictions of a society that was distorted in its structure by the imposition of capitalist class formations on those of a premodern agrarian society. In all these respects, moreover, the Chinese Revolution was not historically peculiar but shared much in common structurally with other Third World societies.

It is fair to suggest that, methodologically, *Modern China* was most prominent for its anticulturalist positivist orientation. It was anticulturalist in two senses. The first sense was that of a revolt against the culture-based explanations of modern Chinese history that had hitherto dominated the field. An obvious reason for the latter was a long-standing Orientalist preoccupation with Chinese culture as a unique historical phenomenon. Another reason, however, was the culturalism imbedded in the modernization narrative. Though the modernization narrative had not been artic- ulated in the China field with the explicitness of its articulation in other Third World studies, its assumptions infused the field, reinforcing the Orientalist legacy. The second sense in which *Modern China* was anticulturalist derived from a partic- ular reading of Marxism that emphasized economism over questions of ideology and culture. This positivist reading of Marxism was encouraged by the dissatisfac- tion with the culturalist orientation of the field. On the positive side, it encouraged *Modern China* historians to ground their work in the material circumstances of Chi- nese history.

For more than two decades, *Modern China* has made an enormous impact on the field in its encouragement of social and economic history. The work produced by social and economic historians associated with the journal has reshaped our under- standing of modern Chinese history. Not the least of these historians' contribution has been to make use of historical scholarship in China, which has brought closer U.S. and Chinese historians' work. As historical scholarship has gotten more detailed in pursuit of the original questions raised by the journal, there has been also a move away from the political/ideological concerns that had led to its launching. Commendable as this is, it has led to some ossification of methodological orienta- tions, with the consequence that the journal has been immune to post-Marxist, poststructuralist methodologies. The journal, in other words, has been integrated into the profession.[32] Although social and economic history remain as its hallmarks, there is by now little that is unique about this orientation, and *Modern China* these days is barely distinguishable from the conservative scholarship that it once chal- lenged; it may even be asserted that the revolutionary paradigm that launched the journal has been integrated into the modernization narrative. Journal discussions over methodological issues have scrupulously stayed away from ideological and political issues, as well as questions concerning the China field as a professional undertaking, but instead have focused on empirical evaluation of competing para- digms—which contrasts sharply with the early days of the journal.[33]

Enter *Positions*. As with *Modern China, Positions* involves a diverse group of schol- ars, in this case scholars who at least theoretically are committed to notions of dif- ference and diversity (note the journal's name itself). Generalization is rendered more tenuous by the fact that the journal has been in existence for only a short time, and where it might be headed is anyone's guess. What it aspires to may be gleaned from formal statements and its contents so far. The very subtitle of the journal, *East Asia Cultures Critique,* distinguishes it readily from *Modern China,* which was, and is, subtitled *An International Quarterly of History and Social Science.* So do the titles for the first two special issues, *Colonial Modernity* and *Making Histories.* The journal is self-consciously poststructuralist.

In a review of "postwar China studies" in the inaugural issue of the journal, Tani Barlow, the editor, described her approach as a "modified postcolonial critique," which probably could serve as a fair description of the methodological stance of

Chapter 6

Positions. Having reviewed works in a modernization mode produced by the first generation of postwar historians and social scientists and the critique of imperialism that was characteristic of *Bulletin of Concerned Asian Scholars* and *Modern China* writers, Barlow writes:

> There are two reasons why in this article I turned to a modified postcolonial critique rather than back to the older focus on imperialism. One, reevaluating the economistic strain in imperialism studies of China involves questioning other categories in relation to, and in addition to, the socioeconomic. It also requires an end to the strict boundaries that have separated high, super, cultural, and ideological from low, sub, social, and economic. . . . That, I suggest, is best done with a focus on semicolonialism, including colonial discourses and scholarship. Two, I have noticed that whereas the earlier imperialism critique focused principally on economic determination, "the Harvard School," as is well known, is in fact characterized by the persistence with which it has argued cultural theses. A remediable weakness of progressive scholarship on China might be this refusal to contest the culture question. The antidote may be to seek answers to questions of ideological concern in representation, foundationalist critiques of various kinds, questions of subjectivity, interpenetration of realms, contextualization, and so on. The usefulness, particularly of deconstructive forms of postcolonial criticism, has figured into my focus on Cold War discourse, specifically when I ask where China appears in any specific discursive economy and under what terms.[34]

I have quoted Barlow at length here because the critique states both what *Positions* seeks to overcome and how it proposes to do so.[35]

There is little question that *Positions* answers a need in the field, and in aspiration at least, presents an important challenge to it. First, while there has been no lack of discussion and debate in the China field, most such discussion in recent years has focused on parochial questions, without addressing problems of a fundamental nature that pertain to the premises of the field as a whole; indeed, the discussions have served to disguise such problems by a scholastic empiricism. The call for theoretical debate issued by *Positions* is reminiscent of the earlier days of *Modern China*. The specific issue of the relationship between culture and political economy, moreover, is highly significant and resonates with broad concerns in a number of fields in our day.

Second, *Positions* seeks to address explicitly the concerns of new constituencies in the field and to explore the ways in which such concerns may bear upon general theoretical problems; while discussions of feminism, gay theory, ethnicity, and other issues may not be novel, what they imply in terms of political economy, class, and culture is a question that has not been confronted in the field.

Third is the journal's call for new epistemologies, which is especially evident in its contents. While the influence of epistemologies connected with postmodernism and poststructuralism have been felt already in the field, they too need to be addressed more explicitly in their concrete relevance to the China field. Especially important in this regard is the status of historical interpretation, history as discovery versus history as construction or representation. A field as unstable in interpretation as the field of modern China may hardly pretend that historiographical problems are merely empirical problems that depend for their resolution on the discovery of more "facts," without considering the relationship between interpretation and the discovery and construction of the "facts" themselves.

Finally, if I may insert a personal concern, *Positions* has come into existence at a time of crucial change not just in the historiography of modern China, but also more significantly at a time of radical change in Chinese society and the world at large; its own epistemological stance is tied in with these changes, which need to be considered explicitly in the field. It may be interesting to recall that *Modern China* came into existence in the atmosphere of anticolonialism that was emblematized by the Vietnam War and the Cultural Revolution in China; the publication of *Positions* coincides with a pervasive feeling that we have now entered the postcolonial era. This seems to be on the minds of those associated with the journal; its publication provides an occasion for addressing explicitly the relationship between the China field and a changing global situation.

Of the alternative approaches discussed in this chapter, *Positions* best exemplifies what I described above as "postrevolutionary" historiography, in both senses. It is postrevolutionary because it seeks to pursue questions raised in earlier historiography by the paradigm of revolution but that remain marginalized because of the domination of that historiography of economism. Methodologically, it seeks to overcome economism by a renewed emphasis on cultural criticism and thereby improve on earlier radical historiography.

Judging by appearances, *Positions* is also postrevolutionary in the second sense of "antirevolutionary." I acknowledge readily that the ascription to the journal of this latter attribute is somewhat speculative on my part and involves "guilt by association." The journal has been in existence for only a short while, and neither the editor nor others involved with it have provided us with a clear statement on this issue. This attribute I am deducing from statements and tacit orientations associating the journal with "postcolonial criticism." In the statement above, Barlow refers to her approach as a "modified postcolonial criticism." Since she does not offer an explanation of the "modifications," I will speak to questions raised by "postcolonial criticism."

So-called postcolonial criticism has in recent years become quite fashionable in Third World studies and cultural criticism in general. Its basic thrust is implicit in the term "postcolonial": With the end of colonialism, the categories of analysis of an earlier day have become irrelevant, and new approaches have become necessary that are free of the vocabulary of colonialism. What is not apparent from the name is that: (a) postcolonial criticism is deemed to be applicable not only to those societies that were former colonies but globally, and, (b) postcolonial criticism is extended back to the colonial period to replace an earlier vocabulary of exploitation, oppression, and so on, with a new vocabulary of contestations and more between colonialists and the colonized. Concrete in origin, postcolonialism criticism has acquired the status of an abstraction that guides analysis, present and past.

I have offered an elaborate critique of "postcolonial criticism" elsewhere and will merely summarize a few relevant points to demonstrate why postcolonial criticism is antirevolutionary:[36]

1. In globalizing the "postcolonial condition," postcolonialism suppresses the persistence of colonialism as well as the colonial structures that are the legacy of colonialism. Examples of the former are the continued colonization of indigenous peoples and of numerous ethnicities globally. Examples of the latter are to be found globally, in the economic, political, and cultural domination of the world by former colonial powers, now in collaboration with Third World elites. Extended to the past, postcolonialism erases not only the origins of this domination but also the struggles against such domination implicit in the categories of imperialism, Third World, and so on, which may no longer be relevant to analysis but have not lost their significance in understanding the historical origins of the present.

2. Postcolonial criticism, as with postmodernism, argues against metanarratives, or so-called foundational categories, ranging from imperialism, capitalism, and class, to Orientalism, Third World nationalism, and so forth, in favor of localized encounters and contestations imbedded in such terms as "politics of location" and "politics of identity." In other words, it opts for an extreme historicism against structural analysis. In this view, structures, and the categories that enunciate them, perpetuate suppression of the local, denying the subjectivity of the oppressed who have not been passive recipients of oppression but active creators of resistance, and new forms of "modernity." (I presume that this repudiation of "foundational" categories is what Barlow has in mind when, in her essay, she crosses out terms such as colonialism with a line. The effect is something reminiscent of "Wayne's World" in television's *Saturday Night Live:* Colonialism—*NOT!*)

The repudiation of structure has the effect of flattening the world by equalizing differences: first, differences in power in local encounters, which are not to be understood without reference to structural context; second, the equalization of differences, as if all differences had the same significance. This may be seen in the encompassing of class, gender, ethnic, and indigenous differences in the language of postcolonial criticism in the one catchall category of "subalternity." While it is important to be cognizant of the variety of oppressions in society, it is misleading to reduce them to an undifferentiated variety, both spatially and temporally. In this case, too, historicism leads to an erasure of historicity: of the fact, for example, that while a particular form of oppression, such as class or gender or ethnicity, may be present at all times, it may not carry the same significance. It is possible that one or the other comes to the fore at different times, depending on structural conditions. It is for the same reason that postcolonial criticism makes judgments of significance difficult if not impossible in politics, which is then reduced to regional politics, negating the possibility of analysis that can guide political action at a broad level. Postcolonial criticism, in other words, becomes complicit in the fragmentation of politics in its very efforts to redefine it.

3. Most important in this regard is the repudiation in postcolonial criticism of "capitalism" as a "foundational" category. Postcolonial criticism makes "Eurocentrism" rather than capitalism the main target of criticism, ignoring both the power of capital to shape the world and the ways in which Eurocentrism may be imbedded in capitalism itself. In the previous quotation from Barlow, this shift is apparent in the diversion of attention from political economy to "discursive economy," as if the discursive economy could be comprehended without reference to political economy. This shift, ironically, undermines the critique of Orientalism as well. With the globalization of capitalism, Eurocentric Orientalism has found a counterpart in the "self-Orientalization" of Third World societies, which assert their newfound power by the proclamations of "cultural nationalisms" of one kind or another. These, ironically, echo earlier Orientalist representations of these societies. Orientalism, rather than disappearing, has moved to the center of global ideology. A critique of Eurocentrism is no longer sufficient, under the circumstances, but must proceed to a critique of new forms of global hegemony, which are imbedded in new configurations of capitalism.

As noted above, contemporary capitalism at once homogenizes and fragments the globe, congratulating itself for its "localization" ("domestication") of the economy while concealing the centralizing forces at work in institutions of transnational capitalism. For postcolonial criticism to repudiate the "foundational" status of capitalism while celebrating "localization" is to become complicit in the power and the ideology of capital. I might note here in passing that the anti-Eurocentrism and antifoundationalism of postcolonial criticism may be a reason for the affinity that some *Positions* writers, including Barlow, have expressed for the antimodernizationist arguments of "China-centered history."

4. Finally, postcolonial criticism itself is ideological in expressing the newfound power of Third World intellectuals who have moved to the centers of power as part of a new transnational class. The repudiation of "foundational" categories such as capitalism and class also helps disguise the class origins of these new intellectuals, who are beneficiaries of contemporary capitalism.

I cite the pitfalls of postcolonial criticism for radical criticism not because they represent what *Positions* magazine has done, but because the journal so far has not shown an awareness of these problems in spite of its proclamations of affinity with postcolonial criticism. These are questions worth pondering for all of us. To the extent that they are not brought to the surface for discussion, a new historiography with radical pretensions may be vulnerable to complicity in the antirevolutionary orientation that in our day plagues so much radical criticism. The point here, I might add, is not to revive an older paradigm of revolution but to reinvent it.

Let me briefly recapitulate the methodological premises of the critique offered above of what I take to be the major orientations in China historiography presently. First is a critique of historicism, whether it is of the type associated with earlier narratives of modernization of revolution, the antimodernizationist argument of

"China-centered history," or the poststructuralist historicism of *Positions*. The first three suffer from the weakness of both narrative and conceptual teleology, imbedded in teleologies of revolution, modernization, nation, and so on, which erases alternative possibilities available in the past by marginalizing or erasing them.[37] The postmodernism implicit in *Positions* does represent a challenge to such teleologies. But this postmodernist historicism presents problems of its own by depriving the past and the present of all coherence and, in the process, disguising the importance of new forms of power. In each case, historicism leads, ironically, not to an affirmation but to a negation of historicity. The latter requires attention to structural contexts in the past (and the present), which endow both the legacies of the past and its phenomena with changing meanings. These structural contexts are not outside "history" but are products of human activity in making and remaking history, ranging in scope from the structures of daily life to structures of broad temporal and spatial scope, such as modes of production. In this perspective, history itself appears as a process of the ceaseless structuring and restructuring (or reinvention) of life. The attention to structure is also necessary to keep narrative teleologies from erasing alternative pasts.

Second, these alternative orientations to history all have claims upon the truth of the past, including that represented by the paradigm of revolution; in spite of efforts to erase it, revolution remains the central problem of Chinese history, and it is precisely on those grounds that all these orientations appear "postrevolutionary." To recognize these competing and contested truths, however, is to acknowledge that they are also all representations of the past. History as invention or construction is hardly novel for the historian, even though postmodernists these days claim it for themselves. It is also a liberating idea because the recognition of invention and construction rescues the past from narrative teleologies that pretend to the truth of the past even as they suppress aspects of the past that do not accord with their particular paradigmatic assumptions. It also brings to the foreground the ideology in history; invention draws our attention to the inventor and makes possible a critical historiography that goes beyond criticism based on empirical contestations. To say that the past is invented is not to deny reality to the past or to render history fictional. Invention does not imply invention out of thin air, but a rearrangement of past realities in new ways; think, if you like, of the invention of the steam engine. Invention is not arbitrary, in other words, as it might be in fictional representations of the past, but consists of the rearrangement of available data from new perspectives. There is a danger here of what has been described as "presentism." Without getting into the question of whether the present can ever be absent from historical work of even the most antiquarian kind, let me suggest here that it is better to be critically self-conscious about "presentism" than to pretend it does not exist. What the historian must strive for is a critical awareness of his or her conditions in the production of history as well as of the structural contexts in history that endow past events with contemporary meaning and significance—much as anthropologists in our day strive to be self-critical about their own methodologies while also learning to listen to their subjects, who have their own interpretations of the meaning of their existence.

Finally, it should be evident why I am opposed to establishing paradigms to guide inquiry into the field. In the work cited in this chapter, Feyerabend argues that the data the scientist generates depend on the theory that he or she utilizes; to express it in commonplace idiom, if we do not ask the questions, we do not get the answers.[38] Alternative paradigms enable us to see the alternative structures that in their contestation reveal the complexity of human activity and, therefore, of history. To bind history to a single paradigm is not merely to subject it to professional and social power, but also to exclude investigation that does not accord with the current paradigm—such as is happening today in the China field with the exclusion of the revolutionary paradigm. The dominance of a paradigm over others, enforced by professional organization and social ideology, exacts a heavy price not just intellectually but politically as well.

IS RADICAL HISTORY POSSIBLE?

If there is any validity to the argument above that in all its various manifestations, modern China historiography today is a postrevolutionary historiography? Is there any possibility of "reinventing revolution" and, with it, a radical historiography? Even more broadly, has history come to an end, so that there is no point to critical history any longer? I offer some consideration here of new possibilities for a radical history that is postrevolutionary without being antirevolutionary.

Alternative development

Regardless of whether it is modernizationist or revolutionary, modern China historiography has been dominated by a paradigm of capitalist development—in other words, judged against a model of capitalist development. From Mark Elvin's *The Pattern of China's Past* to Philip Huang's *The Peasant Family and Rural Development in the Yangzi Delta,* from liberal historiography in the United States to Marxist historiography in China, the guiding question has been why China failed to develop capitalism as did Europe. This is true even of work that, on the surface, challenges the conclusions of these works in the field. In *Sugar and Technology in China: Peasants, Technology and the World Market* (Cambridge, MA: Harvard University Asia Center, 1998), Sucheta Mazumdar offers a counter, a reverse-Brennerian argument that suggests that state power and peasant resistance combined to forestall a capitalist development in China.[39]

None of these works bothers to ask why China should have developed capitalism! Instead of historicizing capitalism as the product of a historical conjuncture in Europe, all available work endows it with an ahistorical universality. Mazumdar, who uncovers the technologies that were developed in China to promote sugar production as part of the domestic economy, fails to recognize such development as an alternative to capitalist technology, which was suppressed later by the incorporation of the Chinese within a global economy. Capitalist development, both in Europe and elsewhere, emerged victorious with the suppression of alternative modes of change. At a time when Eurocentrism has been challenged, it is remarkable that historians should still work with a question that universalizes, through the agency of capitalism, the pattern of European development. At a time when radical movements around the world have taken the form of local movements searching for alternatives to capitalist development in socially and ecologically sustainable technologies, it is incumbent on any radical historiography to uncover these suppressed paths of development.

Alternative modernities

A closely connected issue is that of modernity. Rather than reject modernity as Eurocentric, it is necessary for radical historiography to recognize modernity, with all its hegemonic assumptions, as a given of modern history and investigate seriously the various antimodernisms in the Third World, ranging from Mao Zedong to Gandhi, who for all their antimodernism sought to create alternative modernities. Modernity per se need not be rejected, as it is these days by both conservative self-Orientalizers and supposed radical postcolonialists, who would shift the sources of domination in the modern world from the political economy of capitalism to the discursive economy of the Enlightenment. Enlightenment narratives may be complicit in the hegemony of capitalism to the extent that they have provided capitalist domination with ideological legitimation. But they also raised radical questions about inherited inequalities and dominations of the past. All we need to do is to look around to see how the repudiation of Enlightenment ideals serves today the revival of everything from right-wing religious movements to the denial of gains in social and human rights for women. If we are to create alternative modernities that recognize subjectivity to non-European pasts that were suppressed by Enlightenment narratives, these are pasts nevertheless that have been worked over already by both capitalism and Enlightenment ideals.

Third World discourses

In modern China historiography, as in all Third World historiographies, the domination of Europe is apparent in what the European model of capitalist development offers as a frame of reference for native history. What has been suppressed in the process are the actual interactions and the discursive interactions that non-European societies provided to one another in the course of their struggles against European domination to create native modernities. Gandhi provided inspiration for Chinese intellectuals; Mao Zedong provided inspiration for national liberation struggles globally; the Chinese, Vietnamese, and Korean revolutions were part and parcel of the same process. The examples could be multiplied indefinitely. These Third World discourses sought not just to create alternatives to capitalist development but also native modernities that drew upon one another for inspiration. It is important to bring this past to the foreground once again at a time when local Third World struggles desperately need legitimation for the networks that seek to challenge global capital on its global terrain.

Diasporas

As noted above, the increasing prominence of diasporas (which include post-colonial intellectuals) has called into question teleologies informed by the nation-state as well as national cultures. While the diasporas (of laborers and women) may be viewed as products of global capitalism, they nevertheless also call into question the self-Orientalizations of nation-states that seek to contain the cultural dispersal implicit in the very phenomenon of the diaspora. Extended to the past, the diasporic insight calls into question the claim on history of the nation-state, which is another source of oppression and domination; for example, in the use of "cultural difference" as an argument for justifying the denial of basic rights by states to their citizens. The questions about the historicity of the nation-state and national culture raised by the phenomenon of diasporas represents nations as products of not progress but oppression and suppression as well, which in fact makes it possible to imagine the world in terms other than the nation.[40]

Community

One of these terms is that of the local community. An earlier nationalist historiography, much like modernizationist and revolutionary historiography, took the nation-state as its unit of analysis and associated national homogenization with progress.[41] A new radicalism, responding to conditions created by global capitalism, has focused on the local community as the location for struggles against domination by both capital and the state. These local struggles are empowered by new visions that take as their points of departure those that have been marginalized by both capitalist and socialist modernity, from peasant women to indigenous peoples, whose marginalization calls into question the assumptions of modernization and the productionist and consumptionist ideology that it promotes. The survival of the local community calls for new values (such as ties to the land and localized sustainable technologies) as well as new political alliances that may help in the struggle against domination and for survival.

Much of what was discussed in this chapter, from alternative development to alternative modernity to Third World discourses and even the localized cultures created by diasporas, focus attention on the community—community not as it has been inherited from the past, carrying on it the catalog of inherited oppressions, but community that has been worked over already by modern forces of liberation and the struggle against oppression. The history of these struggles must be brought to the foreground of historical work if the study of the past is to make a contribution to the struggles of the present.

NOTES

1. *Modern China* vol.17, no. 3 (July 1991); vol.19, no.1 (January 1993); vol.19, no. 2 (April 1992); and vol. 21, no. 1 (January 1995).

2. The developmental failure runs through much of the literature on China. For an example, important *because* it recognizes tremendous growth after 1949, see Philip C. C. Huang, *The Peasant Family and Rural Development in the Yangzi Delta, 1350–1988* (Stanford, CA: Stanford University Press, 1990). For civil society, see Mary B. Rankin, William H. Rowe, and David Strand. These authors have presented their views on civil society in a variety of works. Their views may be gleaned conveniently from their contributions to the symposium on civil society sponsored by *Modern China,* "'Public Sphere'/'Civil Society' in China?" *Modern China* 19, 2 (April 1993). The ethical degeneration idea was put forth most forcefully in Anne F. Thurston, *Enemies of the People* (New York: Alfred A. Knopf, 1987). For an account that combines themes of failure with those of ethical degeneration, see Edward Friedman, Paul Pickowicz, and Mark Selden, *Chinese Village, Socialist State* (New Haven, CT: Yale University Press, 1991).

3. I am referring here to Harrison E. Salisbury, *The New Emperors: China in the Era of Mao and Deng* (New York: Little, Brown, 1992); Nicholas Kristoff and Sheryl WuDunn, *China Wakes: The Struggle for the Soul of a Rising Power* (New York: Times Books, 1994); and the account by Mao's personal doctor, Li Zhisui, *The Private Life of Chairman Mao* (New York: Random House, 1992). Needless to say, the popularity of these books owes much to the marketing strategies of commercial publishers, which find in the titillation of the reading public the best way to sell books.

4. Gilbert Rozman, "Theories of Modernization and Theories of Revolution: China and Russia," in *Zhongguo xiandaihua lunwen ji* (Collection of Essays on the Modernization of China) (Taipei: Academia Sinica, 1991), 633–646; Marie-Claire Bergere, *The Golden Age of the Chinese Bourgeoisie* (London: Cambridge University Press, 1989).

5. James Sheridan, *China in Disintegration* (New York: Free Press, 1977).

6. I have discussed this at length in Arif Dirlik, "National Development and Social Revolution in Early Chinese Marxist Thought," *China Quarterly* 58 (April–June 1974), pp. 286–309.

7. For one analysis, see Xiangming Chen, "China's Growing Integration with the Asia-Pacific Economy," in Arif Dirlik (ed.), *What Is in a Rim? Critical Perspectives on the Pacific Region Idea* (Boulder, CO: Westview Press, 1993), pp. 89–119.

8. For the implications and transformations of "constructed" ethnicity, see, Pamela Crossley, "Thinking about Ethnicity in Early Modern China," *Late Imperial China* 11, 1 (June 1990), pp. 1–34; Dru Gladney, *Muslim Chinese: Ethnic Nationalism in the People's Republic* (Cambridge, MA: Harvard University Press, 1991), and his more recent "Representing Nationality in China: Refiguring Majority/Minority Identities," *Journal of Asian Studies* 53, 1 (February 1994) pp. 92–123. Emily Honig has offered an excellent treatment of the connection between localism and ethnicity in her *Creating Chinese Ethnicity: Subei People in Shanghai, 1850–1980* (New Haven, CT: Yale University Press, 1992).

9. Cho Hae-joang, *Reading Texts and Reading Everyday Lives in the Postcolonial Era 2: From One's Own Standing* (Seoul: Alternative Culture Pub., 1994, in Korean). I am grateful to the author for sharing this map with me.

10. For two extensive discussions, see the two special editions of *Daedalus* edited by Tu Wei-ming: *The Living Tree: The Changing Meaning of Being Chinese Today* (Spring 1991) and *China in Transformation* (Spring 1993).

11. For a more elaborate discussion, see Arif Dirlik, *After the Revolution: Waking to Global Capitalism* (Hanover, NH: University of New England Press for Wesleyan University Press, 1994).

12. Samuel P. Huntington, *Political Order in Changing Societies* (New Haven, CT: Yale University Press, 1972 [1968]). There is little need to belabor here the revolutionary impact on China of Euro-American capitalism and culture. Scholars have also pointed to the importance of the very effort to modernize the Chinese state as a source of destabilization and revolution. See Roxann Prazniak, "Weavers and Sorceresses of Chuansha: The Social Origins of Political Activism Among Rural Chinese Women," *Modern China* 12, 2 (April 1986), pp. 202–229, and "Tax Protest at Laiyang, Shandong, 1910: Commoner Organization versus the County Political Elite," *Modern China* 6, 1 (January 1980), pp. 41–71. See also Prasenjit Duara, *Culture, Power and the State: North China, 1900–1942* (Stanford, CA: Stanford University Press, 1988). While these two authors deal with comparable phenomena, their evaluations of what they analyze are paradigms apart (one premised on problems of class and gender, the other on their denial). Prazniak sees in peasant protests, provoked by the New Policy Reforms of the late Qing, an empowerment of the peasantry to voice its explanation. Duara sees in the Guomindang reforms of the 1930s a weakening of the cultural ties that had bound together the rural elite and the peasantry, which then made possible Communist infiltration; in other words, revolution by default, a la Huntington. While this argument is plausible on the surface, it ignores completely that "cultural ties" may have represented "cultural hegemony," and that the breakdown of the ties may have enabled the peasants to express themselves politically by responding to the Communists.

13. Dean Tipps, "Modernization Theory and the Study of National Societies: A Critical Perspective," *Comparative Studies in Society and History* 15, 2 (March 1973); Lloyd I. Rudolph and Susanne H. Rudolph, *The Modernity of Tradition: Political Development in India* (Chicago: University of Chicago Press, 1967). For "world-system analysis," see the many works by, among others, Paul Baran, Paul Sweezy, Immanuel Wallerstein, and Samir Amin.

14. Recall, for example, the controversy generated by Frances Moulder's *Japan, China and the Modern World Economy: Toward a Reinterpretation of East Asian Development, ca 1600 to ca 1918* (New York: Cambridge University Press, 1977), which was the first work to explicitly apply "world-system analysis" to China. It came under immediate attack from promoters of an older modernization theory, such as Albert Feuerwerker, Gilbert Rozman, and Marion Levy. The "Princeton School" was particularly enthusiastic about the defense of modernization and its culturalist premises. See Gilbert Rozman (ed.), *The Modernization of China* (New York: Free Press, 1981).

15. For an example, see Stewart R. Clegg and S. Gordon Redding (eds.), *Capitalism in Contrasting Cultures* (Berlin: Walter de Gruyter, 1990).

16. Samuel P. Huntington, "The Clash of Civilizations," *Foreign Affairs* 72, 3 (Summer 1993), pp. 22–49. In case this sounds like a crackpot idea, note that in November 1994, Huntington was the keynote speaker for a conference, organized by the U.S. Institute of Peace, titled, "Managing Chaos." Other speakers at the conference were television journalist Ted Koppel and Henry Kissinger, a former U.S. Secretary of State.

17. A good illustration of this is the recent article by Edward Friedman, "Reconstructing China's National Identity: A Southern Alternative to Mao-Era Anti-Imperialist Nationalism," *Journal of Asian Studies* 53, no.1 (February 1994), pp. 67–91. Friedman's poststructuralist vocabulary disguises the fact that he is still working with old notions of the nation. Rather than notice the fragmentation implicit in the "Southern Alternative," he uses the latter as a legitimation of capitalist against Maoist notions of the nation.

18. I might give as an example here Philip Huang's discussion of rural industrialization as the answer to "six centuries of involution" in Chinese agriculture. When anarchists, inspired by Kropotkin, first suggested rural industrialization in China by anarchists, it carried little weight, because it was a utopian idea that was concerned less with development than with social reorganization. When the Great Leap Forward sought to practice it, it was viewed as an expression of Mao's self-defeating utopianism. In the 1980s, when rural industrialization was put into practice, it was hailed as a major innovation in socialist development policy. Huang fails to note that the success of rural industrialization in the 1980s was also guaranteed by the fact that it was now tied in with global capitalism, rather than serving localized economies as originally conceived. See Huang, *The Peasant Family and Rural Development in the Yangzi Delta, 1350–1988*. For the anarchists and their possible influence on Mao, see Arif Dirlik, *Anarchism in the Chinese Revolution* (Berkeley: University of California Press, 1992). The global context of rural industrialization is examined in David Zweig, "Internationalising China's Countryside: The Political Economy of Exports from Rural Industry," *China Quarterly* 128 (December 1991), pp. 716–741.

19. For an extensive discussion, see Arif Dirlik, "Confucius in the Borderlands: Global Capitalism and the Reinvention of Confucianism," *boundary 2,* vol. 22, no. 3 (November 1995), pp. 158–183.

20. Paul A. Cohen, *Discovering History in China: American Historical Writing on the Recent Chinese Past* (New York: Columbia University Press, 1984).

21. Ibid., p. x.

22. Ibid., p. xii.

23. Ibid., pp. 186–187.

24. See, for example, ibid., p. 115.

25. Ibid., pp. 196–198.

26. Arif Dirlik, "Mirror to Revolution: Early Marxist Images of Chinese History," *Journal of Asian Studies* 33, 2 (February 1974), pp. 193–223, p. 223.

27. Ibid., p. 1.

28. John Schrecker, *The Chinese Revolution in Historical Perspective* (New York: Praeger, 1991).

29. Frank Dikotter, *The Discourse of Race in Modern China* (London: Hurst and Co., 1992). For debt to Cohen, see Frank Dikotter, "Racial Identities in China: Context and Meaning," *China Quarterly* 138 (June 1994), pp. 404–412, p. 409.

30. This inside/outside distinction also underlies the recent influential text by Jonathan Spence, *The Search for Modern China* (New York: W.W. Norton, 1990). Spence's book, however, is written in the modernization narrative, which adjudges China a failure against criteria of modernity. Whereas Cohen repudiates modernity, Spence reaffirms it to deny modernity to China.

31. That other important publication, *Bulletin of Concerned Asian Scholars,* I leave out of the discussion here because, in spite of the vanguard role it played in the field in introducing new concepts and attitudes, it has been less concerned with strictly historiographical issues.

32. To avoid misunderstanding, let me underline here that the point is not to criticize historians for detailed work or to enjoin them always to pursue "big" questions with paradigmatic consequences. Rather, the point is to draw attention to the criteria employed in the selection of problems, the manner in which problems are phrased, and the frameworks used in explanatory strategies. I do object, however, to the suppression of political problems and of the political implications of historical research—more accurately, to the representation of politically charged problems as mere problems of method or of empirical evidence.

33. Readers of the journal will be familiar with the discussions I have in mind here. One example is the discussion about "civil society." In spite of the highly ideological context for the revival of "civil society" in our day, the discussions in this special issue for the most part focused on the scholastic questions raised by "civil society," with hardly a word on its ideological implications and functions. For a critique, see Arif Dirlik, "Civil Society/Public Sphere in China," *Zhongguo shehui kexue jikan* (Chinese Social Sciences Quarterly), summer volume (August 15, 1993), pp. 10–17.

34. Tani E. Barlow, "Colonialism's Career in Postwar China Studies," *Positions* 1.1 (Spring 1993), pp. 224–267, p. 251.

35. I recognize that Barlow is not speaking for the journal here. Nevertheless, an editor's remarks are not to be taken lightly, even in the case of a "collective." And the publications in the journal so far disclose at least some shared attitudes on these questions.

36. Arif Dirlik, "The Postcolonial Aura: Third World Criticism in the Age of Global Capitalism," *Critical Inquiry* 20, 2 (Winter 1994), pp. 328–356.

37. By conceptual teleology, I am referring to those tendencies to "naturalize" and homogenize concepts such as class, gender, ethnicity, and so forth. The phenomena described by these concepts never appear in nonproblematic form but are overdetermined by circumstances as complex as the complexity of life. Class, for instance, is overdetermined by, among other things, locality, gender, ethnicity, and nationality. For individuals to "think in class ways," a class discourse must be constructed so as to endow it with a hegemonic status vis-à-vis other attributes of existence (This is what Mao Zedong described as a "primary contradiction."). For a recent work that recognizes such overdeterminedness of class, see Elizabeth J. Perry, *Shanghai on Strike: The Politics of Chinese Labor* (Stanford, CA: Stanford University Press, 1993).

Among works in the China field that have recognized the constructedness of class in the course of the revolution, see Chen Yung-fa, *Making Revolution: The Communist Movement in Eastern and Central China, 1937–1945* (Berkeley: University of California Press, 1986), and the study by Odoric Y. K. Wou, *Mobilizing the Masses: Building Revolution in Henan* (Stanford, CA: Stanford University Press, 1994). In this sense, the revolution in China may be seen as a contest between alternative revolutionary discourses. See Daniel Y. K. Kwan, *Marxist Intellectuals and the Chinese Labor Movement: A Study of Deng Zhongxia (1894–1933)* (Seattle: University of Washington Press, 1997) for a work that examines the discourses of laborers and Communist intellectuals as contradictory discourses. A positivist historicism, which searches for class (or of any other concept, for that matter) as an "objective" fact, misses the historicity of class and, therefore, declares it nonexistent, as it does most other phenomena that do not fit in with objectivist definitions of significance (what "really" happened!).

38. The obvious example of this, of course, is gender-based historiography of recent vintage. Examining modern Chinese history from gender perspective has elicited new answers and brought forth alternative constructions of modern China. See Christina K. Gilmartin, Gail Hershatter, Lisa Rofel, and Tyrene White (eds.), *Engendering China: Women, Culture and*

the State (Cambridge, MA: Harvard University Press, 1994). For a discussion that utilizes gender and ecological perspectives, see, Roxann Prazniak, "Mao and the Woman Question in an Age of Green Politics: Some Critical Reflections," in Arif Dirlik, Paul Healy, and Nick Knight (eds.), *Critical Perspectives on Mao Zedong Thought* (New York: Humanities Press, 1997).

39. In a private communication with the author, Philip Huang points out that his work is critical of the market-economy paradigm associated with capitalism, which is indeed the case (as it is the case also with Mazumdar's work). I am concerned here not with the particular form of the economy, but the developmentalism of the paradigm of capitalist development, which has also infused socialism as we have known it.

40. This questioning of the nation does not imply the erasure of nation and nationalism as a historical force, which Prasenjit Duara sets out to do in his recent *Rescuing History from the Nation: Questioning of Narratives of Modern China* (Chicago: University of Chicago Press, 1995). Presumably inspired by the Subaltern Studies historians in India, Duara seeks to draw attention to social and political phenomena that purportedly were hidden in a historiography informed by nationalism; the very fact that there is not much that is original in what he uncovers suggests that nationalism in his work appears merely as a straw target that enables a fashionable title (and a fashionable attack on "Enlightenment" narratives) but misses many of the most crucial problems thrown up by the relationship between place-based narratives and narratives fashioned by nationalism and/or globalism. It may not be surprising, therefore, that the work consistently brings in by the back door essentialist notions of the nation. A serious historiographical and political agenda requires a recognition that while nationalism is a historical construct, it is not for that reason any the less "real" as a historical force and phenomenon. It is only on the basis of such recognition of the historicity of the nation (or of the Enlightenment, or whatever) that we may be able to imagine political alternatives. Confusion of constructedness, inventedness (or "imaginedness"), and illusoriness are fairly common in contemporary social and political literature. In the case of nationalism, Benedict Anderson's influential work, *Imagined Communities,* rev. ed. (London: Verso, 1995) has played some part in encouraging such confusion, which is in many ways contrary to Anderson's own intention, as *Imagined Communities* argues for the durability of nationalism as a historical force in spite of its imaginedness; if Anderson is to bear responsibility for such unintended misreadings of his argument, it may be because of an overemphasis in the work on ideology.

41. For a discussion of the suppression of community by nationalist discourses (as well as discourses of civil society), see Partha Chatterjee, *The Nation and Its Fragments: Colonial and Postcolonial Histories* (Princeton, NJ: Princeton University Press, 1993).

7

Conflict and Connection: Rethinking Colonial African History

Frederick Cooper

This chapter is part of an effort to bring historiographies of Africa, Latin America, and Asia—with their particular scholarly traditions, insights, and blind spots—into relationship with each other, avoiding the assumption that interaction simply means borrowing from apparently more "developed" historiographies. South-South intellectual exchange is not new. The earliest attempts by African intellectuals to confront the issues of colonialism and racism, beginning in the nineteenth century, entailed contacts forged with Americans of African descent and later with anticolonial leaders from Asia and the Caribbean. Later still, the limitations of anticolonial ideologies and of nationalism were analyzed in Africa with the help of arguments originating with Latin American dependency theorists.

The Subaltern Studies Group has had a particularly empowering effect on the scholarship of once-colonized regions, for it has put the process of making history into the picture. While striving to recover the lives of people forgotten in narratives of global exploitation and national mobilization, this collective of historians has called into question the very narratives themselves, indeed, the source material, theoretical frameworks, and subject position of historians. The "subalternity of non-Western histories" as much as the subalternity of social groups within those histories has been uncovered. Those histories exist in the shadow of Europe not solely because of colonization's powerful intrusion into other continents but because Europe's self-perceived movement toward state-building, capitalist development, and modernity marked and still mark a vision of historical progress against which African, Asian, or Latin American history appears as "failure": of the "nation to come to its own," of the "bourgeoisie as well as of the working class to lead."[1]

In these pages, I will take advantage of the emphases in the essays of Gyan Prakash and Florencia Mallon to take a somewhat different tack. They have explained the contributions of Subaltern Studies to a wider historiography, and they bring out the important tension in its writings between efforts to recover the history and the agency of the subaltern and to analyze the discursive production of the subaltern, how colonial categories of knowledge flattened the multi-sided experiences of people in colonies into such a category. I want to explore the ways—with parallels and differences—in which historians of Africa have confronted the experience of colonial rule. To the African historian, the value of Indian historiography is not that our colleagues offer ready-made solutions to our problems but that all of us are engaged in different ways with closely related debates.[2] Both historiographies wrestle with— but do not quite escape—the dichotomous vision characteristic of colonial ideologies, originating in the opposition of civilized colonizer and primitive colonized. The risk is that in exploring the colonial binarism one reproduces it, either by new variations of the dichotomy (modern versus traditional) or by inversion (the destructive imperialist versus the sustaining community of the victims). The difficulty is to confront the power behind European expansion without assuming it was all-determining and to probe the clash of different forms of social organization without treating them as self-contained and autonomous. The binaries of colonizer/colonized, Western/non-Western, and domination/resistance begin as useful devices for opening up questions of power but end up constraining the search for precise ways in which power is deployed and the ways in which power is engaged, contested, deflected, and appropriated.

With Africa's independence, historians were strongly moved to find a domain that could be defined as both unambiguously African and resistant to imperialism. In the historiography of Subaltern Studies, the clarity of such categories is questioned, but they keep coming back in the very concept of the subaltern and in Ranajit Guha's insistence that one can examine the "autonomous" domain of the subaltern and reveal people acting "on their own."[3] Guha, like many African historians, wants his subalterns to have a rich and complex consciousness, to exercise autonomous agency, and yet to remain in the category of subaltern, and he wants colonialism to remain resolutely colonial, despite the contradictions of its modernizing projects and its insistence on maintaining boundaries, despite its interventionist power being rendered contingent by the actions of subalterns.[4] Colonial discourse, Subaltern Studies rightly points out, has tried to contain its oppositions— whether in the form of its "liberal" ideas of self-determination or the "irrational" actions of "primitive" people—within its own categories. How far colonial discourse could actually contain its challenges and tensions remains in question.

The Subaltern Studies Group has turned what could be yet another exercise in Western self-indulgence—endless critiques of modernity, of the universalizing pretensions of Western discourse—into something more valuable because it insists that the subject positions of colonized people that European teleologies obscure should not simply be allowed to dissolve. While profiting from the insights of Subaltern Studies to reexamine work in African colonial history, I also hope to push back the dualisms that are coming in the rear door in both historiographies. African historians' use of the concept of "resistance" is generally less subtle, less dialectic, less self-questioning than Indian historians' deployment of the idea of subaltern agency, yet both concepts risk flattening the complex lives of people living in colonies and underestimate the possibility that African or Indian action might actually alter the boundaries of subordination within a seemingly powerful colonial regime. The critique of modernity has its own dangers, as Dipesh Chakrabarty recognizes in warning that too simple a rejection could be "politically suicidal."[5] One can agree with Guha and his colleagues that Marxist master narratives of relentless capitalist advance are yet another form of Western teleology—as are nationalist metanarratives of the triumphal takeover of the nation-state—yet historians should not deprive themselves of the analytical tools necessary to study capitalism and its effects around the world—in all their complexity, contingency, and limitations. Nor should the recognition of the violence and oppression within the generalization of the nation-state model around the world blind us to the potential for violence and oppression that lies in other social formations. I am also trying to push capital and the state back in, making them the object of an analysis more nuanced and interactive than attacks on metanarrative and modernity.

There are reasons for different emphases in the historiographies of the two continents. Subaltern Studies emerged in the 1980s, nearly forty years after India's independence, as a critique of an established nationalist interpretation of history, as well as of "progressive" arguments, whether liberal or Marxist. Africa's independence movements are more recent, their histories only beginning to be written. Africans' and Africanists' disillusionment with the fruits of independence in the 1970s took the form of an emphasis on the external determinants of economic and social problems, and hence a look toward Latin American dependency theory. Most important of all have been the obstacles to the density of debate possible in India: the catastrophic economic situation Africa faced, particularly since the 1980s, and the harsh material conditions in which African scholars and educational and cultural institutions function.[6]

Different experiences give rise to different initial assumptions. The category of subaltern is an intuitively attractive point of departure for South Asianists, given the widely shared perception of social distinction in India as long-lasting, coercive, and sharply delineated, even when scholars put the bases of social distinction in question. Recent generations of African scholars have witnessed—and often been part of—a moment, perhaps not to be repeated, of considerable mobility and category jumping, reflecting the sudden expansion of education systems in the 1950s, the post–World War II export boom, the precipitous Africanization of the civil service, and the rapid development by African rulers of clientage networks and distributional politics. Whereas many scholars have been trying to pull apart and examine the idea of an essential "India," others have felt they had to put together "Africa" in the face of general perceptions of everlasting and immutable division. Subaltern Studies' critique of ways in which a nationalist state picks up the controlling project of a colonial state gives rise to sympathetic echoes among

Africans and Africanists—disillusioned with post-independence states—but also to a measure of skepticism about conceivable alternatives, given bitter experience, as in contemporary Somalia, with what "communities" can do to one another when a state loses its controlling capabilities in the age of automatic weapons.[7]

What follows is a consideration of African historiography, stressing the connections between the "resistance" model that was crucial to its development and the new scholarship on colonialism. Both concepts, I argue, should be further scrutinized. Politics in a colony should not be reduced to anticolonial politics or to nationalism: the "imagined communities" Africans saw were both smaller and larger than the nation, sometimes in creative tension with each other, sometimes in repressive antagonism.

The burst of colonial liberations that followed Ghana's independence in 1957 led Africanists to project backward the idea of the nation. The new states of Africa needed something around which diverse peoples could build a sense of commonality. Africa scholars, as one acute observer put it, acted like the "Committee of Concerned Scholars for a Free Africa."[8] The first generation of historians of Africa, seeking to differentiate themselves from imperial historians, were eager to find a truly African history.

African resistance to European conquest and colonization both ratified the integrity of pre-colonial polities and structures (themselves a major topic) and provided a link between them and the nationalist challenge to colonial rule. Resistance was the key plot element in a continuous narrative of African history. Terence Ranger argued specifically for a connection between "primary resistance movements" in the early days of colonization and "modern mass nationalism." Early resistance implied mobilization across a wider network of affiliation than kinship units or "tribes" provided, and this enlargement of scale created a basis for subsequent movements. In a detailed study of a revolt in Southern Rhodesia, Ranger pointed to the role of spirit mediums in mobilizing rebels across a large region and providing a coherent framework for the resistance.[9]

While analyses such as these attempted an Africa-centered perspective, they paradoxically centered European colonialism as the issue that really mattered in the twentieth century.[10] An apparently populist rhetoric concealed the privileging of African elites—in the 1960s as much as the 1890s—by virtue of their anticolonialism and downplayed tensions and inequalities within African societies. Sensitive to these historiographical issues, Ranger himself stepped away from the linearity of his earlier argument and advocated a more multivalent and nuanced approach to African political mobilization.[11] Nonetheless, studies within the resistance framework conclusively showed that colonial conquests and heavy-handed interventions into African life were vigorously challenged, that guerrilla warfare within decentralized polities was as important as the fielding of armies by African states, that women as well as men engaged in acts of resistance, and that individual action—moving away from the tax collector or labor recruiter, ignoring orders, speaking insolently, and criticizing the claims of missionaries, doctors, and educators—complemented collective actions.[12]

For the authors of the UNESCO history of Africa (a collective series intended to reflect the first generations of post-independence African and Africanist scholarship), the key issue of the early colonial era was the defense of sovereignty. Adu Boahen, the editor of the relevant volume, saw African societies in the late nineteenth century as dynamic, moving toward a form of modernity that retained sovereignty but selectively engaged with European commerce, religion, and education. The dynamism of African societies before colonization is no longer in question, but Boahen's conception grants Western modernity too much power—particularly in its emphasis on the strength of the state as a marker of political progress and a unit for social advancement—while it fails to address the contradictions stemming from specific social structures within Africa. Boahen has little to say about Africans who conquered other Africans or about the slaveowners in coastal Dahomey or Sahelian Sokoto or island Zanzibar who made other Africans bear the burden of expanding commerce. Sovereignty was not the only issue facing Africans, and the European invasions entered a long and complex process of state-building and oppression, of production and exploitation, as well as a history of small-scale producers and merchants for whom the overseas connection offered opportunities they did not want to give up and oppressions they wanted to contest.[13]

Here, I will break the linearity of the discussion of the historiography itself for a moment and point to another pioneering approach. In 1956, K. Onwuka Dike, generally regarded as the first African to become a professional African historian, authored *Trade and Politics in the Niger Delta,* seeking to make a decisive break with the imperial historians who had been his mentors and to write history from an African perspective. His book is less remarkable for the new sources it used than for the matter-of-fact way in which it analyzed interaction. Africans do not appear in this text as either resistors or collaborators in the face of European involvement in the Delta; Europeans, indeed, appear as actors in the universe of different actors within the region, all trying to work with the opportunities and constraints of overseas trade and regional political structure. Dike knew what the Delta traders could not—that the European traders' metropolitan connections would one day break the framework of interaction—but he nonetheless provided an account of African agency intersecting with European in a crucial moment of history.[14]

Resistance had a special power in the two decades after Dike's study appeared. Scholars and journalists wanting to make the world aware of anticolonial movements in Africa—Thomas Hodgkin and Basil Davidson the most knowledgeable among them—sought to show the complex roots of political mobilization, from Africa's own traditions of rule to memories of battles against foreign conquerors, to religious and labor movements that provided an experience of organization culminating in the development of nationalist political parties.[15] Dike's own project took on a nationalist bent as well: the "Ibadan" school emphasized the integrity of pre-colonial African societies, which sometimes appeared as precedents for independent

Africa. J. F. Ade Ajayi termed colonialism an "episode in African history," a break in the otherwise continuous exercise of African political agency.[16] What was most neglected was colonial rule itself: to my cohort in graduate school (1969–74), studying pre-colonial history or resistance constituted genuine African history, but bringing a similar specificity of inquiry to that which was being resisted risked having one's project labeled as a throwback to imperial history.

Questionings of the nationalist metanarrative came from two generations of African scholars. B. A. Ogot, the senior historian of Kenya, in an essay of 1972 on the "Loyalist crowd" in Mau Mau, pointed out that the violent conflicts of the 1950s could not be reduced to a simple morality play: both sides had their moral visions, their moral discourses. The "Loyalists" saw themselves as engaged in a defense of a way of life in which Christianity, education, and investment in small farms were the means to progress. Colonial policy could be contested within limits, but to the Loyalists the young rebels were violating Kikuyu traditions of respect for elders and threatening the community.[17] Some twenty years later and across the continent, Mamadou Diouf published a book that debunked Senegal's basic myth of resistance, the battle of Lat Dior and his Wolof kingdom against the French. Lat Dior, Diouf argued, was defending "the privileges of the ruling class and the traditional field in which it exercised its exploitation" as much as sovereignty. His study entailed a complex engagement with how power was mobilized and contested within Africa and the extent to which the long-term French presence first made the emergence of a Lat Dior possible and then rendered the continued existence of this sort of polity impossible.[18]

The metanarrative of nationalist victory—and many of the tales of "resistance"—have most often been told as stories of men, with a rather macho air to the narrating of confrontation. Women's history, to a significant extent, began by arguing that "women could do it, too" or by adding African patriarchy to the colonial object of resistance. As historians increasingly showed that economic and social activity was defined, contested, and redefined in terms of gender, the gendered nature of politics needed to be examined as well.[19] The contestation of gender roles within the Mau Mau movement is being explored by Cora Ann Presley, Luise White, and Tabitha Kanogo, while Timothy Scarnecchia shows the masculinzation of African politics in the 1950s in Harare. Housing regulations that effectively disallowed women access to residential space except through a man meant that women on their own were by definition outside the law, and they were driven into certain niches in the unofficial economy. For a time, such women worked with a male-led union-cum-political movement to challenge the way the state defined and constrained urban women. The movement failed; and, when nationalists later began to challenge the colonial state in other ways, their quest to balance respectability against the movement's need to recruit migrant male laborers meant that they, too, treated such women as dangerous and disruptive. Nationalism in the 1950s explicitly constructed itself in masculine—as much as class—terms, leaving aside its own more ambiguous history.[20]

Apartheid in South Africa affected women in particular ways: through male-only labor compounds, the policing of migration, the feminization of rural poverty, and a complex hierarchy of residential rights that divided black workers and families. Protest was thus also shaped by gender. Women led bus boycotts and demonstrations against the application of pass laws to women. A strong and sustained series of women's protest movements in the Herschel district of Cape Province reflected the circumstances of women in the context of increasing male out-migration, but the more formally organized Industrial and Commercial Workers' Union largely shunted women aside.[21]

The heroic narrative fell victim not only to wise elders and young scholars with new questions but also to continuing crises in Africa itself. African novelists were the first intellectuals to bring before a wide public inside and outside the African continent profound questions about the corruption within postcolonial governments and the extent to which external domination persisted.[22] Growing disillusionment made increasingly attractive the theories of "underdevelopment," which located the poverty and weakness of "peripheral" societies not in the colonial situation but in the more long-term process of domination within a capitalist world system. The debate that dependency theory unleashed had the beneficial effect of legitimizing among African intellectuals the notion that theoretical propositions were not mere impositions of Western models on a unique Africa but offered ways of understanding the predicament Africa shared with other parts of what had come to be called the "Third World." The direct link in bringing dependency theory to Africa from Latin America was Walter Rodney, a Guyanese of African descent, instrumental in founding the "Dar es Salaam" school of radical African history.[23] It may be that an engaged expatriate was better positioned than were Tanzanians to open the challenge to nationalist conventions, the tragic counterpart to this being Rodney's assassination after his return to Guyana and the detention, in their own country, of several Kenyan historians who had questioned reigning myths.

The issues opened by dependency theorists prompted an increasing interest in Marxist theory among Africanists and Africans in the 1970s and opened the possibility of a dialogue across the continents.[24] Ironically, dependency theory emphasized common subordination and gave little place to African or Latin American agency. Certain Marxist approaches assumed the dominance of capitalism, although a useful contribution of African history to Marxist theory would be to point to the limits capital encountered in trying to tame Africa's labor power.[25] More recently, poststructuralist theory has turned toward an examination of discourse and modes of representation—including the scholar's own—but often at the cost of surrendering the tools with which to undertake studies of global power and exploitation. For all the critique and countercritique among these approaches, there has been a certain facility with which historians outside the African continent have slid from one paradigm to another, post-Marxism and poststructuralism embodying this tendency in their very labels. To many American or European scholars, insisting that

Africa had a history—irrespective of what one said about it—was evidence of a progressive bent; African history was subaltern studies by default.[26]

The notable exception to this observation comes from the part of Africa that did not fit into the 1960s narrative of liberation from white rule, South Africa. My cohort of graduate students in the United States felt that the history of South Africa was not African enough.[27] South African expatriates contributed the most in the 1970s to the focus on that region, and as they did one of the sharpest theoretical divides opened up: a "liberal" view that stressed African initiative and Afro-European interaction stymied by the rigid racism of Afrikaners versus a "radical" paradigm that saw South African racism as itself a consequence of the way in which capitalism emerged in the late nineteenth and early twentieth century. Within the "radical" approach, one branch tended toward a structuralist conception of an unfolding logic of capital determining South African history, but another looked directly to the inspiration of European and American social historians to uncover the ways in which Africans carried out their struggles and forged community as well as class.[28] South African historians shared some of the "history from the bottom up" concerns with Subaltern Studies but generally not their conception of the subaltern's autonomy. Charles van Onselen has most sharply described the element of shared culture across racial divisions and antagonisms within poor farming communities, and likewise the efforts of diverse and changing groups of blacks and whites to make their way in the rough world of urbanizing Johannesburg.[29] The most interesting autonomist argument—independent of Subaltern Studies—comes from Keletso Atkins' analysis of a distinctly African work culture, although her point is that this work culture influenced and constrained the apparently dominant work culture of developing capitalism.[30] South African history in the 1970s and 1980s was thus distinguished by a focused debate—only occasionally engaging the historiography of the rest of Africa—over race, class, and capital. In the 1990s, poststructuralist questionings of the categories and narratives of Marxist history have been strongly resisted in South Africa by those who insist that here, at least, the lines of power and exploitation are clear.[31] This is a useful debate and another instance of the "irresolvable and fertile tensions" between different conceptions of history, theory, and political activism that Florencia Mallon stresses in her contribution to the *Forum*. It also opens opportunities for engagement with the issues being raised by Subaltern Studies.

Over the past several years, a new colonial history has emerged, in dialogue with anthropology and literary studies and ranging over many areas of the world.[32] Anthropologists questioned past and current modes of ethnographic inquiry, suggesting the need for a more contextual and historical examination of the apparatus that collected and classified knowledge of Africa or Asia.[33] Literary critics began to study the politics of representation and the process by which the assertion within European discourse of a sense of national or Continental identity depended on inscribing "otherness" on non-European populations.[34] Both scholarly traditions encouraged an examination of the categories and tropes through which the Africa of explorers, missionaries, settlers, scientists, doctors, and officials was symbolically ordered into the grid of "tribe" and "tradition." Historians explored how census defined or reified such categories as caste, how medicine defined susceptibility to disease in racial or cultural terms, how colonial architecture inscribed modernity onto the built environment, while appropriating a distilled traditionalism to its own purposes, and how missionaries sought to "colonize minds" by forging an individual capable of thinking about his or her personal salvation, separated from the collective ethos of the community.[35] The Subaltern Studies Group took the further step of asking whether categories of colonial knowledge set the terms in which oppositional movements could function and in which colonialism itself could be critiqued.[36]

This trend has opened up possibilities of seeing how deeply colonies were woven into what it meant to be European and how elusive—and difficult to police—was the boundary between colonizers and colonized.[37] It is nonetheless open to the danger of reading a generalized "coloniality" from particular texts, abstracting what went on in colonies from local contexts and contradictory and conflictual global processes.[38] Even as subtle and interactive an argument as Homi Bhabha's treatment of mimicry, in which the colonized person's acting as if "white but not quite" destabilizes the colonizer's view of the boundaries and control, relies on detaching the dyad of colonizer/colonized from anything either subject might be engaged in except their mutual confrontation.[39]

It is far from clear what Africans thought about the symbolic structure of colonial power or the identities being inscribed on them. The cultural edifice of the West could be taken apart brick by brick and parts of it used to shape quite different cultural visions.[40] Piecing together such processes is one of the most promising endeavors being undertaken by innovative scholars. A scholarly trend that began from the opposition of "self" and "other" has thus ended up confronting the artificiality of such dichotomies and the complex *bricolage* with which Africans in colonies put together practices and beliefs.[41]

The problem of recovering such histories while understanding how colonial documents construct their own versions of them has been the focus of thoughtful reflections by Ranajit Guha.[42] At first glance, these contributions may appear to the African historian more as sound practice than a methodological breakthrough. African historians cut their teeth in the 1960s on the assertion that colonial sources distorted history, and they saw the use of oral sources—as well as reading colonial documents against the grain—as putting themselves on the path to people's history. But Africa scholars put more emphasis on showing that Africans had a history than on asking how Africans' history-making was implicated in establishing or contesting power.[43] Guha and his colleagues, facing the rich but problematic corpus of Indian colonial documents, have provoked a useful discussion over the conceptual difficulties in the attempt to recover consciousness and memory outside of a literate elite—and the ultimate impossibility of true knowledge across the barriers of class and colonialism—while African historians have tried to see how far one could push with nondocumentary sources. There is room here for exchange across differing perspectives, although Gayatri Chakravorty Spivak's rhetorical question "Can the Subaltern Speak?" may tempt the historian struggling for his or her modest insights to ask in return, "Can the theorist listen?"[44]

Recognition of the much greater power of the Europeans in the colonial encounter does not negate the importance of African agency in determining the shape the encounter took. While the conquerors could concentrate military force to defeat African armies, "pacify" villages, or slaughter rebels, the routinization of power demanded alliances with local authority figures, be they lineage heads or recently defeated kings. A careful reading of colonial narratives suggests a certain pathos: the civilizing mission did not end up with the conversion of Africa to Christianity or the generalization of market relations throughout the continent, and colonial writing instead celebrated victories against "barbarous practices" and "mad mullahs." Colonial violence, in such a situation, became "acts of trespass," vivid and often brutal demonstrations distinguishable for what they could violate more than what they could transform.[45]

The economic geography of colonization is as uneven as the geography of power. Colonial powers established islands of cash crop production and mining surrounded by vast labor catchment areas in which coercion and, as time went on, lack of alternatives were necessary to extract laborers. To a significant extent, the wage labor force that capital could use—whatever the wishes of employers—was largely male and transitory, in large measure because Africans were seeking to incorporate periods of wage labor into their lives even as capital was trying to subordinate African economies.[46] It took the wealth and power of South Africa—where a racialized version of "primitive accumulation" took place through the relative density of white settlement, the impetus of gold mining after the 1880s, and the agency of the state—for labor power to be detached from its social roots. Even in South Africa, the struggle over how, where, and under what conditions Africans could actually be made to work never quite ended.[47] Elsewhere, some of the greatest success stories of colonial economies came about through African agency: the vast expansion of cocoa production in the Gold Coast at the turn of the century, Nigeria from the 1920s, and the Ivory Coast from the 1940s was the work of smallholders and did not depend on colonial initiatives. Cash cropping was neither a colonial imposition nor an unmediated African response to price incentives; it gave rise, in certain places, to accumulation without producing a bourgeoisie. This is the kind of history that Subaltern Studies scholars want to have told, a history that breaks out of the molds of European modernity and Afro-Asiatic stasis, yet these farmers' experience cannot easily be contained within a notion of subalternity.[48]

The juxtaposition of a disruptive but concentrated colonizing presence and a large and unevenly controlled "bush" had paradoxical consequences: fostering episodic exercises or collective punishment or direct coercion against unwilling workers or cultivators on whom the effects of routinized discipline had not been successfully projected;[49] making the boundaries of African communities more rigid and their "customary law" more categorical than in days before colonial "progress";[50] marginalizing educated and Christian Africans as the colonizing apparatus assumed control and established alliances with "traditional" leaders;[51] fostering commercial linkages that enabled Africans who adapted to them to acquire collective resources that later enabled them to resist pressures to enter wage labor;[52] expanding an ill-controlled urban economy that offered opportunities for casual laborers, itinerant hawkers, criminal entrepreneurs, and providers of service to a migrant, largely male African working class, thus creating alternatives (for women as well as men) to the roles into which colonial regimes wished to cast people;[53] and creating space for missionary-educated Africans to reject mission communities in favor of secular roles in a colonial bureaucracy or to transform Christian teaching into critiques of colonial rule.[54]

This is not just an argument about African "adaptation" or "resistance" to colonial initiatives. Rather, it is an argument that policy and ideology also reflected European adaptation (and resistance) to the initiatives of the colonized. This notion extends to the periodization of colonial history: Imperial conquerors began by thinking they could remake African society and rationalize the exploitation of the continent; by World War I, they were largely frustrated in such endeavors and began to make—through policies of "indirect rule" and "association"—their failures sound like a policy of conserving African society and culture; by the late 1930s, the imagined Africa of "tribes" was proving unable to contain the tensions unleased by the much more complex patterns of economic change; in the late 1930s and 1940s, Great Britain and France tried to re-seize the initiative through a program of economic and social development; African political parties, trade unions, and rural organizers turned the development initiative into a claim for social and political rights, effective enough for the abdication of power and responsibility to become increasingly attractive in London and Paris; most recently, the tendency of Western powers to write off Africa as a continent of disasters and bad government is a sign that the development framework still has not pushed Africans into the role of a quiet and productive junior partner in the world market.[55]

Ranajit Guha has characterized colonization as dominance without hegemony, a direct contradiction of the trends in metropoles to envelop the exercise of power under universal social practices and norms.[56] The claim of a colonial government to rule a distinct people denied the universality of market relations, revealed the limits to capitalism's progressive thrust, and led colonial regimes to seek legitimacy by hitching themselves to indigenous notions of authority and obedience. Nationalists, seeking to displace colonial rulers without undermining their own authority, continued to practice dominance without hegemony.

The distinction between capitalist universality and colonial particularism is a compelling one, but Guha does not get to the bottom of it. He misses the implications of the limits of coercion, and he underplays the dynamic possibilities stemming from the partial and contradictory hegemonic projects that colonial rulers attempted: the disputes within colonizing populations and metropolitan elites over different visions of colonial rule and the space that efforts to articulate hegemony opened up for contestation among the colonized. He implicitly draws a contrast between colonial dominance and metropolitan hegemony that the exclusions and violences of twentieth-century Europe belie. Guha's insight, however, offers an opportunity to explore the tensions of particularism and universality within colonies themselves and in a dynamic interconnection of colony and metropole. As I will argue below, the inability of colonial regimes to establish and maintain "dominance" amid the uneven effects of capitalism led them to deploy the "universalistic" conceptions of social engineering developed in Europe, only to find that their own hopes for the success of such technologies required giving up the beliefs about Africa on which a sense of "dominance" depended.[57]

The incompleteness of capitalist transformation in a colonial context has been a major theme of Subaltern Studies, but the tensions of colonialism in a capitalist context are equally important to analyze. Just as elusive are the conceptual categories with which scholars try to understand the movements that have challenged colonial and capitalist power in Africa, Asia, and Latin America.

At one level, the concept of resistance is generally accepted and unproblematic. In the clash of African and colonial armies, individual acts of disobedience or flight, and the elaboration of powerful arguments for liberation, colonial rule has been continually and severely challenged. But much of the resistance literature is written as if the "R" were capitalized. What is being resisted is not necessarily clear, and "colonialism" sometimes appears as a force whose nature and implications do not have to be unpacked. The concept of resistance can be expanded so broadly that it denies any other kind of life to the people doing the resisting. Significant as resistance might be, Resistance is a concept that may narrow our understanding of African history rather than expand it.

Scholars have their reasons for taking an expansive view. Little actions can add up to something big: desertion from labor contracts, petty acts of defiance of white officials or their African subalterns, illegal enterprises in colonial cities, alternative religious communities—all these may subvert a regime that proclaimed both its power and its righteousness, raise the confidence of people in the idea that colonial power can be countered, and forge a general spirit conducive to mobilization across a variety of social differences. The problem is to link the potential with the dynamics of a political process, and this problem requires careful analysis rather than teleology. It is facile to make causal generalizations across diverse circumstances, as Donald Crummey does in proclaiming, "Most popular violence is a response to state or ruling-class violence," and it is questionable to link all acts of assertion with a military metaphor, as James Scott does in terming them "weapons of the weak."[58]

Foucault saw resistance as a constitutive of power and power of resistance; he denied that there was a "single locus of great Refusal." He found "mobile and transitory points of resistance, producing cleavages in a society that shifts about, fracturing unities and effecting regroupings." Although "strategic codification" of those points can make for revolution, such a process cannot be assumed, and his stress was on the continual reconfiguration of both power and resistance.[59] In the current atmosphere of postcolonial pessimism, such an idea resonates: even the counterhegemonic discourse of the colonial era and the subversions of European notions of modernity become enmeshed in concepts—the nation-state most prominent among them—that redeploy ideas of surveillance, control, and development within post-independence politics, fracturing and producing unities and reconfiguring resistances. In such a light, Subaltern Studies scholars have scrutinized the reconfiguration of power-resistance at the moment of nationalist victory.[60]

The difficulty with the Foucauldian pairing of power and resistance lies in Foucault's treatment of power as "capillary," as diffused throughout society. However much surveillance, control, and the narrowing of the boundaries of political discourse were a part of Europe in its supposedly democratizing era, power in colonial societies was more arterial than capillary—concentrated spatially and socially, not very nourishing beyond such domains, and in need of a pump to push it from moment to moment and place to place.[61] This should be a theoretical rallying point for historians: they have the tools (and often the inclination) to analyze in specific situations how power is constituted, aggregated, contested, and limited, going beyond the poststructuralist tendency to find power diffused in "modernity," "the post-enlightenment era," or "Western discourse."

The resistance concept suffers from the diffuseness with which the object of resistance is analyzed, as well as from what Sherry Ortner calls "thinness." The dyad of resistor/oppressor is isolated from its context; struggle within the colonized population—over class, age, gender, or other inequalities—is "sanitized"; the texture of people's lives is lost; and complex strategies of coping, of seizing niches within changing economies, of multi-sided engagement with forces inside and outside the community, are narrowed into a single framework.[62]

Some of the best recent work in African history discards the categories of resistors and collaborators and starts with the question of how "rural people saw their circumstances, made their choices, and constructed their ideas about the larger society."[63] The relationship of gender issues and colonization, for example, emerges in a complex way from the studies of Elias Mandala and Elizabeth Schmidt. Before the conquest, women had once exercised considerable control over farming and the crops they produced, but the expanding slave trade made women vulnerable to kidnapping or to the control of their would-be protectors. Colonial rule—the decline of warfare and increased possibilities for cash cropping—for a time gave women space to reassert power within domestic economies, but the subsequent decline of village agriculture and the increasing importance of labor migration made women increasingly dependent on men's fortunes.[64] Luise White, meanwhile, has shown that women sometimes seized niches in the expanding and ill-organized urban economy, as prostitutes and landlords, providing cheap services to male migrant laborers. White's study points up the basic ambiguity in colonial relationships: her women were both subverting the cultural project of colonialism and subsidizing the economic one. Officials were indeed confused, in some contexts willing to let women furnish low-cost services, in others afraid that women's knowledge of urban society and their social networks were reproducing the wrong kind of African working class.[65]

The complexities of engagement and autonomy surface again and again. Karen Fields' analysis of Watchtower in Central Africa reveals a substantial refashioning of Christian doctrines in relation to the local power structure and labor migration. What made Watchtower subversive in official eyes was not that it encouraged active "resistance" but that it defined a moral community in which the structures, notably chieftaincy, painfully elaborated by the colonial regime became irrelevant.[66] Did such processes contribute in the long run—as the secular Africanists of the 1960s thought they would—to a coming together of diverse strands of African thought and practice that rejected colonial rule in its entirety? Or did such movements go off in their own direction, as likely to clash with secular nationalism as to assist their assault on the colonial state?

I am arguing here for the complexity of engagement of Africans with imported institutions and constructs, as opposed to James Scott's emphasis on a "hidden transcript" among colonized people that develops among them only to burst forth into a "public transcript" in moments of confrontation.[67] My approach also differs from Ranajit Guha's quest to explore the "autonomous" domain of the subaltern, although the complex and varied practice of historians in the Subaltern Studies collective, more so than the manifestos, is filled with stories of engagement.[68]

In discussing labor, as Dipesh Chakrabarty points out, the historian can usefully invoke general theories about "abstract labor," a set of relationships characteristic of capitalism, while preserving a notion of "real labor," located in his case in the systems of authority and clientage of Bengali villages and the power structure of colonial India.[69] In my own research on Africa in the era of decolonization, I examine both the tensions between African labor movements whose demands are shared around the capitalist world—wages, family welfare, security, and working conditions—and whose rhetoric invoked the universality of wage labor through a demand for equal pay for equal work, and a political movement focusing on self-determination for all Africans.[70] Ironically, the wave of strikes and general strikes in French and British Africa from the mid-1930s into the 1950s drew on the integration of workers into a wider population—which provided food to sustain strikers and at times brought about generalized urban mobilization—yet the workers' demands distanced them from that population.

Colonial regimes sought to regain the initiative through "stabilization," to form the poorly differentiated, ill-paid population that moved in and out of urban jobs into a compact body of men attached to their employment. They wanted employers to pay workers enough to bring families to the city so that the new generation of workers would be properly socialized to industrial life and separated from the perceived backwardness of village Africa. The dynamic of the situation lay in the fact that trade unions were able to capitalize on this yearning for predictability, order, and productivity—on officials' hope that Western models of the workplace and industrial relations might actually function in Africa—to pose their demands in ways officials found difficult to reject out of hand. Unions seized the developmentalist rhetoric of postwar imperialism and turned it into claims to entitlements, even as officials began to concede that a unionized work force might aid stabilization.[71]

By the mid-1950s, colonial regimes feared that their development initiatives were being undermined by rising labor costs, and they began to pull back from their own universalizing stance. They realized that conceding African politicians a modest measure of power in colonial governments would force them to weigh the cost of labor against the territorial budget. A national reference point now seemed less threatening economically than a universalistic one. This time, colonial officials guessed right, for nationalist leaders, granted limited territorial authority, quickly set about disciplining African labor movements in the name of a single-minded focus on a national unity defined by the political party.

One can read the actions of labor movements in French and British Africa as one example among many of the African militance or as an instance of the universal struggle of the working class or as the successful cooptation of an unquiet section of the African population into a set of structures and normalizing practices derived from Europe. All three readings have some truth, but the important point is their dynamic relationship: labor movements both brought material benefits to a specific class of people and opened new possibilities for other sorts of actions, which themselves might have mobilizing or normalizing consequences. In this period, labor had a window of opportunity it lacked before and lost afterward, facing a colonial regime invested in a tenuous development initiative and fearing the mobilization of an unpredictable mass. The tension between the demands of labor and efforts to forge unity against the colonial state was often a creative one—except in the too-common instance in which party elites fearful of organized challenges and insistent on the supremacy of the national struggle moved to deny the tension and suppress such movements.

Rural mobilization, which was sometimes led by "organic intellectuals" emerging from a peasant milieu, also developed in alliance and tension with movements led by Western-educated people from towns and constituted a challenge to the tyranny of colonial agricultural officers with their ideas of scientific agriculture. Rural political discourse sometimes focused on the integrity and health of the local community, and it also deployed the transcendent languages of self-determination, Christianity, or Garveyism. But, as Norma Kriger has shown, the connections of cultivators with the commercial economy and the state were so varied and complex that "polarizing society along racial lines" was difficult for radical movements to accomplish.[72]

Whether nationalist movements by themselves were strong enough to overthrow colonial rule is unclear, but a variety of social movements from labor unions to anticonservation movements disrupted the economic project of post-

war colonialism while discrediting its hegemonic project. Unable to get the
Africa they wanted, European powers began to think more seriously about the
Africa they had. Empire became vulnerable to another of bourgeois Europe's
contradictory tendencies: the calculation of economic interest. By the mid-1950s,
France and Great Britain were adding up the costs and benefits of colonial rule
more carefully than ever before and coming up with negative numbers.[73]

To the extent—never complete—that issue-specific or localized movements
came together in the 1940s and 1950s, the threads also came apart, leaving the
unsolved problems of the colonial era to new governments and a tenuously constituted political arena. It is to the problem of framing the national question in relation to other political questions that I now turn.

From the cauldron of politics in the 1950s and 1960s, nation-states emerged across
the African continent. Benedict Anderson's conception of the nation as an imagined community should be set against two related notions: the nation was not the
only unit that people imagined,[74] and the predominance of the nation-state in post-
1960 Africa resulted not from the exclusive focus of African imaginations on the
nation but from the fact that the nation was imaginable to colonial rulers as well.[75]
Pan-Africanism—embracing the diaspora as well as the continent—had once been
the focus of imagination more than the units that eventually became states, but pan-
Africanist possibilities were written out of the decolonization bargains.[76] Regional
federation, though once a basis of French administration and of the mobilization of
trade unions and political parties, fell victim to a French program of "territorialization" and to the interests in territorial institutions that the partial devolution of
power to individual colonies gave African politicians.[77] At the same time, linguistic and ethnic groups were denied a legitimate place in politics—which did not prevent them from becoming even more salient and more sharply demarcated in postcolonial politics—and the menace of "tribalism" was used by governing elites to
try to eliminate many sorts of subnational politics.[78] In the confrontation of the
1950s, colonial states used violence to exclude certain options, for example, the
explicit leftism and the premature (in official eyes) claims to independence of the
Union des Populations du Camaroun or the antimodern radicalism of Mau Mau
rebels in Kenya.[79] Imperial bureaucrats, however, gave up aspects of their own
imaginings: the idea that social and economic change could be directly controlled
by those who claimed already to have arrived was lost in the struggles over decolonization.[80] Where the imagination of anticolonial intellectuals in Africa and imperial bureaucrats overlapped was in the formal apparatus of the nation-state, the institutions and symbols contained within territorial borders.[81]

Pan-Africanism actually predated nationalism—defined, as it should be, as a
movement to claim the nation-state.[82] Leading intellectuals, notably Léopold Senghor, navigated the perspectives of Pan-Africanism, nationalism, and a desire for
social and economic reform in complex ways: Senghor's "négritude" embraced
essentialist notions of African culture yet inverted the valuation placed on them,

erasing difference and eliminating conflict within an idealized Africa. Senghor was just as brilliant at analyzing and working through the specific social structures of his own Senegal: a Christian politician with a political machine based on Muslim brotherhoods, a poet who expressed his ideas of Africa through the French language, a man who defended Africa from a seat in the French legislature, a romantic defender of African village life who after independence sought to use trade and aid to transform an African nation. Living these complexities entailed pain and difficulty, but there is no indication that Senghor—or the many others navigating similar currents—experienced them as personally destabilizing, as intellectually contradictory, or as threatening to his sense of cultural integrity: *in between* is as much a place to be at home as any other.[83] The implications for the historian are crucial: we must analyze the culture of politics and the politics of culture by constantly shifting the scale of analysis from the most spatially specific (the politics of the clan or the village) to the most spatially diffuse (transatlantic racial politics) and examine the originality and power of political thought by what it appropriated and transformed from its entire range of influences and connections.[84]

The triumph of nationalist movements appears less as a linear progression than as a conjuncture, and the success of African political parties less a question of a singular mobilization in the name of the nation than of coalition building, the forging of clientage networks, and machine politics. For a time, nationalist parties made the colonial state appear to be the central obstacle facing diverse sorts of social movements, from labor to anti-conservation to regional movements. Coalition politics may not have been the stuff of revolutionary drama, but it was often conducted with enthusiasm and idealism. The give-and-take of this era forced—and allowed—colonial governments to make a necessary imaginative leap themselves. They came to envision a world that they no longer ruled but that they thought could function along principles they understood: through state institutions, by Western-educated elites, in the interest of progress and modernity, through integration with global markets and international organizations. British archives, notably, disclose that top echelons of government wanted to believe all this but were not quite convinced. A non-hostile postcolonial relationship was the best they thought they could achieve.[85] In the process, they could eliminate some enemies, but in other cases the one-time Apostles of Disorder—Kwame Nkrumah, Jomo Kenyatta, Nnamdi Azikiwe—were remade in the colonial imagination into the Men of Moderation and Modernity.[86]

Some of the best recent studies of post-World War II politics focus not on the parties that took over the state but on Asante nationalism in the Gold Coast (thrust aside by Nkrumah's quest for a unitary Ghana), on the guerrilla movement of the Cameroon, which the French successfully marginalized and destroyed, on the rural people who were caught in the middle of guerrilla-government warfare in Zimbabwe, and on the squatters who fought the hardest, suffered the most, and won the least in the violent decolonization of Kenya.[87] The nationalist parties paid a price for their conjunctural coalitions: the social struggles they tried to attach to their cause remained unresolved. As Aristide Zolberg first showed in 1966, the public's nationalist sentiment was actually quite thin. Attempts at building national institutions were inevitably read as building up particularistic interests: for the leader's tribe, for his class, for his clientele, for himself. New states, taking on a transformative project at which European powers had failed, were politically fragile and ideologically brittle, their insistence on unity for the nation and development denying legitimacy to the social movements out of which political mobilization had often been achieved.[88]

The idea of the nation, as Benedict Anderson stressed, emerged in a particular historical context, when the circuits along which creole elites (starting in Latin America) moved and built their careers began to exclude the metropole and focus on the colonial capital and when print capitalism provided a medium to establish a bounded identity.[89] Europe learned to imagine the nation from the tensions that emerged within its old empires and passed the imaginative possibility along to its new colonial conquests. Partha Chatterjee reluctantly grants Anderson a point: the kind of politics that eventually took over colonial states was this nation-centered one, focused on the European-defined boundaries and institutions, on notions of progress shaped by capitalism and European social thought. The idea of "reason" through which nationalists critiqued colonialism arrived in the colonies wed to capitalism and colonialism. In making claims on colonial powers, nationalists became caught up in the colonial regimes' categories; nationalism was a "derivative discourse." Chatterjee finds possibilities for "a 'modern' national culture that is nevertheless not Western" but locates them in a spiritual domain set outside economy and statecraft.[90] The Indian elite, drawing its power both from notions of caste and communalism rigidified by British rule and from its immersion in colonial commerce, was willing neither to undertake a drastic assault on the Indian past nor to repudiate those elements of the colonial present from which it benefited. Chatterjee, following Antonio Gramsci, identifies elite nationalism as a "war of position," an effort to change society bit by bit, rather than a more radical "war of movement." At some moments, more radical appeals—notably those of Mohandas Gandhi himself—were necessary to widen the mobilization of the Indian National Congress; but, as victory came into sight, the Congress leadership's immersion in the economic, political, and ideological structures of the Indian state marginalized alternative visions. The institutions of state and the goal of state-directed development were only a part of Indian politics in the twentieth century, but they were the politics that triumphed.[91]

Both Anderson and Chatterjee do more than take the nation and nationalism from the realm of "natural" sentiment to social construct;[92] they do so in a way grounded in material conditions and aspirations of certain social groups, in the life trajectories of those who imagined the nation, in the networks of intellectuals and political leaders, in the ways in which ideas were circulated. The "state" should be examined with the same care as the "nation"—its institutions and rhetorics carefully scrutinized.[93] One can agree up to a point with Anthony D. Smith that particular qualities of the colonial state—"gubernatorial, territorial, bureaucratic, paternalist-educational, caste-like"—were carried over to postcolonial states, yet African rulers gave their own meanings to institutions they took over, adapting them to patrimonial social structures and complex modes of representing power.[94]

To historicize the nation-state is not, however, to postulate that it is Africa's "curse," as Basil Davidson called it. One should not assume the innocence or autonomy of community or "civil society" any more than that of the nation, and the articulation between state and social units within and beyond it is where analysis should focus. The "national order of things" should neither be taken as natural nor dismissed as an artificial imposition on Africa. State and nation need to be examined in relation to diasporic communities, to the migratory circuits around which many people organize their lives, to the structures and rules—from market transactions to factory discipline—that also cross borders, and to the cleavages that exist within borders and at times both destroy and remake the nation-state.[95]

In concluding this discussion, I turn to a view of colonialism and resistance that in the recent past would have been a likely starting point: Frantz Fanon. The West Indian psychiatrist and intellectual who devoted much of his life to Algeria and was read as a voice of the "African Revolution" epitomizes the anti-imperialist who crosses borders. His view of violence negating the psychological power of colonialism captured the imagination of other African intellectuals and, above all, those in the West who did not have to face the consequences of that violence.[96]

Fanon was no nationalist. For him, nationalism was a bourgeois ideology, espoused by those who wanted to step into the colonial structure rather than turn that structure upside down. Nor was Fanon a racialist: he criticized "négritude" and saw no solace in the sharing of a mythic black identity, opposing a universalistic notion of liberation to arguments about authenticity of cultural autonomy. Fanon's future came out of the struggle itself: "'The last shall be first and the first last.' Decolonisation is the putting into practice of this sentence."[97]

Yet Fanon was also denying colonized people any history but that of oppression, an ambiguity to the ways they might confront and appropriate the intrusions of colonizers. Instead, he provided a sociological determinism: the petty bourgeoisie was absorbed in mimicking the culture of the colonizer and was best understood in terms of psychopathology;[98] the working class had become a labor aristocracy intent only on capturing the privileges of white workers; the peasantry and the lumpenproletariat, by contrast, were the true liberationists, the last who would become first. The categories were actually colonial ones, and the irony of Fanon's fervent argument was that it allowed—by its inversionary logic—France to define the present and future of people in colonies.[99]

Fanon's reduction of ideology and political strategy to traits of social groups in effect created purge categories: the organized worker or the petty bourgeois, like the kulak of the Stalinist Soviet Union, was a traitor by definition. And the singularity with which the "anticolonial" eclipsed all other notions of affiliation or common interest implied postcolonial uniformity as much as anticolonial unity.

Some African leaders were saying exactly that. Sékou Touré, one of Africa's most notable radical nationalists, himself once a trade unionist, spoke on the eve of his assuming power in Guinea of the new imperatives of African rule. Trade unions were "a tool" that should be changed when it got dull; striking against the "organisms of colonialism" had been a legitimate action, but a strike "directed against an African Government" was now "historically unthinkable," and the labor movement was "obligated to reconvert itself to remain in the same line of emancipation" as the government.[100] Sékou Touré was to practice what he preached by destroying the autonomy of the trade union movement and jailing much of its leadership. Other once-autonomous, once-activist organizations were similarly destroyed, coopted, or marginalized in many African countries.[101] There were, of course, complex questions to be faced about the role of unions, of regionally or ethnically based associations, of representatives of farmers, traders, and other economic interests in postcolonial polities, as well as questions of allocating more resources to groups that had fared well or badly under colonial rule. But Sékou Touré was not issuing an invitation to a debate. Nor were his fellow leaders who made the national ideal compulsory, via such devices as one-party states and such ideological constructs as Mobutu's *authenticité* or Kenyatta's *harambee* (pulling together).[102] The last were not declared to be first. The others deserved to be last.

This is not to deny Fanon's critique of the self-serving nationalists of his day or the appeal of his call for a liberation that overrode national or racial chauvinisms. The issue is one of facing consequences. The casting out of all but the True Anticolonialist from the political arena and the reduction of entire categories of people to class enemies gave an exhilarating legitimacy to state projects, which were often deflected into less liberationist goals than Fanon had in mind. Enthusiasms for projects of state-building, modernization, and development, in the name of the market or of socialism or of good governance, have consequences, too. Those who find in notions of "community" or "new social movements" a welcome antidote to one sort of oppression need to worry about the other forms of oppression that lie within them. For the historian, searching for those historical actors who found the true path is a less fruitful task than studying different paths into engagement with colonization as well as the tensions between different sorts of liberations, between local mobilization and state institutions, between cultural assertion and cultural interaction.

For the historian who seeks to learn what can be learned about the lives that African workers or market women lived day by day, the Manichean world of Frantz Fanon is no more revealing than a colonial bureaucrat's insistence that such people stood at the divide between African backwardness and Western modernity or a nationalist's dichotomy between an authentic community and an imposed westernization.[103] The Guinean port worker was not just seeking European wages or fighting colonialism: he may also have used his job for a colonial firm to seek autonomy from his father, just as his wife may well have been acting within the urban commercial sector to attain a measure of autonomy from him. As a trade unionist, he drew on organizational forms and institutional legitimacy from the French model of industrial relations, but union and political activities also drew on and contributed to webs of affiliation, languages of solidarity, and a range of cultural institutions that colonial officials did not understand and could not adequately monitor. The worker and the market seller were remaking institutions and their meanings even as they used them.

The concept of subalternity also does not categorize the lived experience of such people, but Subaltern Studies historians are not saying that it should. Their emphasis is on the tension between such experiences and the historical process that generates the categories of knowledge themselves. The tension defines a valuable entry point for probing colonial experiences and an essential reminder of the scholar's inability to escape the implications of the material and cultural power that Europe exercised overseas. Yet, as we look ever more deeply into the contested spaces of colonial politics, we would do well to look beyond the notion of subalternity—and conceptions of colonialism that assume its ability to coerce, coopt, and categorize challenges into its own structure of power and ideology—in order to pry apart further the ways in which power was constituted and contested. The violence of colonizers was no less violent for the narrowness of its range and the limits of its transformative efficacy, and the totalizing arrogance of modernizing ideologies is not diminished by the fact that Africans often disassembled them and created something else. But if "subalterns" are to be seen as vital parts of history, the possibility, at least, that the very meanings of domination and subalternity could be undermined should be kept open. And if, at the same time, we are to follow the call of Chatterjee and Chakrabarty to "provincialize" European history—to subject its universalizing claims to historical examination rather than use them as measures of other people's histories—we should move beyond treating modernity, liberalism, citizenship, or bourgeois equality as if they were fixed and self-contained doctrines unaffected by the appropriations and reformulations given to them by processes of political mobilization in Asia, Africa, or Europe itself.[104]

Nationalism, meanwhile, can be explored in tension with a range of social movements, and, as with the colonization process, the ability of nationalist parties to subsume other sorts of mobilizations under its roof should be seen as contingent and partial. The forms of power in Africa after decolonziation—the institutions through which it is exercised and the idioms in which it is represented—reflect not so much the all-consuming thrust of the national order of things but the fragilities, the compromises, and the violences of insecure leaders that emerged in the process of ending colonial rule.

In Africa, the encounters of the past are very much part of the present. Africa still faces the problems of building networks and institutions capable of permitting wide dialogue and common action among people with diverse pasts, of struggling against and engaging with the structures of power in the world today. Africa's crisis derives from a complex history that demands a complex analysis: a simultaneous awareness of how colonial regimes exercised power and the limits of that power, an appreciation of the intensity with which that power was confronted and the diversity of futures that people sought for themselves, an understanding of how and why some of those futures were excluded from the realm of the politically feasible, and an openness to possibilities for the future that can be imagined today.

NOTES

I am grateful for the criticisms and advice of Shiva Balaghi, Keith Breckenridge, Jane Burbank, Catherine Burns, David William Cohen, Fernando Coronil, Mamadou Diouf, Nicholas B. Dirks, Prasenjit Duara, Dorothy Hodgson, Florencia E. Mallon, Mohamed Mbodj, Gyan Prakash, Timothy Scarnecchia, Julie Skurskie, John Soluri, Ann Stoler, Kerry Ward, and Luise White.

1. Dipesh Chakrabarty, "Postcoloniality and the Artifice of History: Who Speaks for 'Indian' Pasts?" *Representations,* 37 (1992): 19; Ranajit Guha, "On Some Aspects of the Historiography of Colonial India," in Ranajit Guha and Gayatri Chakravorty Spivak, eds., *Selected Subaltern Studies* (New York, 1988), 43.

2. An example of useful debate is that between Gyan Prakash—arguing for an "antifoundationalist" history of the Third World—and Rosalind O'Hanlon and David Washbrook—arguing that such an approach disabled the historian from analyzing the global process of capitalist development. Their debate is notable not only for the intelligence and civility with which it was carried out but for the fact that both sides have a point. Gyan Prakash, "Writing Post-Orientalist Histories of the Third World: Perspectives from Indian Historiography," Rosalind O'Hanlon and David Washbrook, "After Orientalism: Culture, Criticism, and Politics in the Third World," Gyan Prakash, "Can the 'Subaltern' Ride? A Reply to O'Hanlon and Washbrook," *Comparative Studies in Society and History,* 32 (1990): 383–408; 34 (1992): 141–67, 168–84.

3. Guha, "On Some Aspects," 39, 40. Guha admits that elite and subaltern worlds were not isolated from each other but insists that they represent "dichotomies," p. 42. In practice, he complicates the dichotomy, and as Gyan Prakash points out in his essay in this issue, other Subaltern Studies historians, including Gyandera Pandey and Shahid Amin, have complicated it further with subtle analyses of the relationship of elite and peasant movements, of local and national politics. See also the critical essay by Rosalind O'Hanlon, "Recovering the Subject: *Subaltern Studies* and Histories of Resistance in Colonial South Asia," *Modern Asian Studies,* 22 (1988): 189–224.

4. Gayatri Chakravorty Spivak, "Subaltern Studies: Deconstructing Historiography," in Guha and Spivak, *Selected Subaltern Studies,* 15, questions the subject position into which the category of "subaltern" drives colonized peoples but accepts that such a concept nonetheless represents a "strategic" essentialism—a useful device to open up a politically vital question. The question is whether the essentialism might outlive the strategy.

5. Chakrabarty, "Postcoloniality and the Artifice of History," 23.

6. In the decade after independence, Africa-based historians and social scientists made a strong effort to found journals and hold congresses. Their drive has been impossible to sustain. Besides Africa's size and linguistic diversity, the economic crisis of the 1980s has had disastrous consequences for universities and other institutions (the Dakar-based consortium, CODESRIA, being the most notable effort to reverse this trend) and has led to considerable intellectual out-migration. Conditions worsened just when a younger generation of schol-

ars, some of them trained in Africa itself, were injecting new ideas and questions into schol-arship. The recent "structural adjustment programs" imposed on Africa by outside lending institutions—forcing governments to cut services—do not consider that a vibrant and criti-cal intellectual life helps to distinguish a creative society from one incapable of adjusting its structures. Differential access to the resources for research, publishing, and scholarly inter-change is probably the single most important way in which scholars based in Africa are dis-tinguished from those in the United States or Europe.

7. Although Subaltern Studies is increasingly mentioned by Africanists, the only sus-tained effort I know of both to use and critique this body of literature is Terence Ranger, "Subaltern Studies and 'Social History,'" *Southern African Review of Books* (February–May 1990): 8–10; and Terence Ranger, "Power, Religion and Community: The Matobo Case," in Partha Chatterjee and Gyanendra Pandy, eds., *Subaltern Studies VII* (Delhi, 1993), 221–46.

8. John Lonsdale, "States and Social Processes in Africa: A Historiographical Survey," *African Studies Review*, 24 no. 2/3 (1981): 143.

9. Terence Ranger, "Connexions between 'Primary Resistance' Movements and Mod-ern Mass Nationalism in East and Central Africa," *Journal of African History*, 9 (1968): 437–53, 631–41; Ranger, *Revolt in Southern Rhodesia, 1896–7* (London, 1967). Similarly, John Iliffe showed that a major rebellion in German East Africa followed lines of religious cults across ethnic boundaries. The revolt—though brutally repressed—caused Germany to alter its colonial policy. "The Organization of Maji Maji Rebellion," *Journal of African History*, 8 (1967): 485–512. In a more recent context, David Lan found spirit mediums mobilizing peasants in the guerrilla war against the white regime in Rhodesia in the 1970s. Lan, *Guns and Rain: Guerrillas and Spirit Mediums in Zimbabwe* (Berkeley, Calif., 1985).

10. Specific questions have been raised as well, mainly about the importance of spirit mediums in the Southern Rhodesian revolt and the extent to which the revolt's organiza-tion went beyond the pre-colonial Shona polity. David Beach, "'Chimurenga': The Shona Rising of 1896–97," *Journal of African History*, 20 (1979): 395–420; Julian Cobbing, "The Absent Priesthood: Another Look at the Rhodesian Risings of 1896–1897," *Journal of African History*, 18 (1977): 61–84.

11. Terence Ranger, "Religious Movements and Politics in Sub-Saharan Africa," *African Studies Review*, 29 (1986): 1–69. For a comprehensive review of recent literature on the rural dimension of these issues, see Allen Isaacman, "Peasants and Rural Social Protest in Africa," in Frederick Cooper, Allen Isaacman, Florencia Mallon, William Roseberry, and Steve J. Stern, *Confronting Historical Paradigms: Peasants, Labor, and the Capitalist World System in Africa and Latin America* (Madison, Wis., 1993).

12. See, for example, Allen F. Isaacman, *The Tradition of Resistance in Mozambique: Anti-Colonial Activity in the Zembesi Valley, 1850–1921* (Berkeley, Calif., 1976); Timothy C. Weiskel, *French Colonial Rule and the Baule Peoples: Resistance and Collaboration, 1889–1911* (London, 1980); Yves Person, *Samori: Une révolution dyula*, 3 vols. (Dakar, 1968–75). The resistance model is alive and well in such studies as John Lamphear, *The Scattering Time: Turkana Responses to Colonial Rule* (Oxford, 1992); and Les Switzer, *Power and Resistance in an African Society: The Ciskei Xhosa and the Making of South Africa* (Madison, Wis., 1993). There is something in the choice of the word "resistance"—as opposed to alternatives such as "liberation" or "emancipation"—that fits the mood of many Western leftists: identifica-tion with the heroic but vain defense of community against intrusion. Jan Nederveen Pieterse, "Emancipations, Modern and Postmodern," *Development and Change*, 23 (1992): 5–41.

13. A. Adu Boahen, "Africa and the Colonial Challenge," in A. Adu Boahen, ed., *Africa under Colonial Domination, 1880–1935* (Berkeley, Calif., 1985), 1–18. The seven chapters that follow contain "African initiatives and resistance" in their titles. For a fuller exposition of Boahen's views, see A. Adu Boahen, *African Perspectives on Colonialism* (Baltimore, Md., 1987). For an interpretation of the same era that stresses the cleavages within Africa, see John Lonsdale, "The European Scramble and Conquest in African History," in Roland Oliver and G. N. Sanderson, eds., *Cambridge History of Africa,* Volume 6: *From 1870 to 1905* (Cambridge, 1985), 680–766.

14. K. Onwuka Dike, *Trade and Politics in the Niger Delta 1830–1885: An Introduction to the Economic and Political History of Nigeria* (Oxford, 1956). Dike did mention the importance of oral sources, but they informed his interpretations rather than provided evidence to be cited. In its time, the book derived much of its legitimacy from its scrupulous use of conventional archival material. The francophone African equivalent of Dike's book, also keeping its distance from nationalist historiography and focusing on Afro-European interaction, is Abdoulaye Ly, *La compagnie du Sénégal* (Paris, 1958).

15. Thomas Hodgkin, *Nationalism in Colonial Africa* (London, 1956); Basil Davidson, *The Liberation of Guinea: Aspects of an African Revolution* (Hammondsworth, 1969); Davidson, *In the Eye of the Storm: Angola's People* (Hammondsworth, 1972); Davidson, "African Peasants and Revolution," *Journal of Peasant Studies,* 1 (1974): 269–91.

16. J. F. Ade Ajayi, "The Continuity of African Institutions under Colonialism," in Terrence O. Ranger, ed., *Emerging Themes in African History* (London, 1968), 189–200. The francophone equivalent is "colonial parenthesis." See Marc H. Piault, ed., *La colonisation: Rupture ou parenthèse?* (Paris, 1987).

17. B. A. Ogot, "Revolt of the Elders: An Anatomy of the Loyalist Crowd in the Mau Mau Uprising," in B. A. Ogot, ed., *Hadith 4* (Nairobi, 1972), 134–48. The moral complexity of Mau Mau was also addressed in the early novels of Ngugi wa Thiong'o, particularly *A Grain of Wheat* (London, 1967). Some of the issues of Kikuyu discourse first raised by Ogot have been pursued in a stimulating fashion by Bruce Berman and John Lonsdale, *Unhappy Valley: Conflict in Kenya and Africa,* Book 2: *Violence and Ethnicity* (London, 1992).

18. Mamadou Diouf, *Le Kajoor aux XIXe siècle: Pouvoir ceddo et conquête coloniale* (Paris, 1990), 283. Diouf's efforts got him into a confrontation with Lat Dior's descendants, in which Diouf stood his ground. Martin Klein, "The Development of Senegalese Historigraphy," in Bogumil Jewsiewicki and David Newbury, eds., *African Historiographies: What History for Which Africa?* (Beverly Hills, Calif., 1986), 222–23. One should also note the more sweeping attacks on nationalist historiographies (as practiced by African and non-African scholars alike), in Arnold J. Temu and Bonaventure Swai, *Historians and Africanist History: A Critique* (London, 1981).

19. On the evolution and accomplishments of the field, see Nancy Rose Hunt, "Placing African Women's History and Locating Gender," *Signs,* 14 (1989): 359–79; and Susan Geiger, "Women and African Nationalism," *Journal of Women's History,* 2 (1990): 227–44.

20. Luise White, "Separating the Men from the Boys: Construction of Gender, Sexuality, and Terrorism in Central Kenya, 1939–1959," *International Journal of African Historical Studies,* 23 (1990): 1–27; Cora Ann Presley, *Kikuyu Women, the Mau Mau Rebellion, and Social Change in Kenya* (Boulder, Colo., 1992); and Tabitha Kanogo, *Crossing Boundaries: African Women's Experience in Colonial Kenya,* forthcoming; Timothy Scarnecchia, "The Politics of Gender and Class in the Creation of African Communities, Salisbury, Rhodesia, 1937–1957" (Ph.D. dissertation, University of Michigan, 1993). Norma J. Kriger writes of gen-

der—as well as age—cleavages in *Zimbabwe's Guerrilla War: Peasant Voices* (Cambridge, 1992).

21. Julia Wells, "We Have Done with Pleading: The Women's 1913 Anti-Pass Campaign," *History Workshop Topic Series 3* (Johannesburg, 1991); Cherryl Walker, *Women and Resistance in South Africa* (London, 1982); William Beinart, "*Amafelandawonye* (the Die-Hards): Popular Protest and Women's Movements in Herschel District in the 1920s," in William Beinart and Colin Bundy, *Hidden Struggles in Rural South Africa: Politics and Popular Movements in the Transkei and Eastern Cape, 1890–1930* (Berkeley, Calif., 1987), 222–69; Helen Bradford, *A Taste of Freedom: The ICU in Rural South Africa, 1924–1930* (New Haven, Conn., 1987); Belinda Bozzoli, *Women in Phokeng: Consciousness, Life Strategy, and Migrancy in South Africa, 1900–1983* (Portsmouth, N.H., 1991).

22. See above all the depiction of the highs and lows of Ghana's independence in Ayi Kwei Armah, *The Beautyful Ones Are Not Yet Born: A Novel* (Boston, 1968). One can also contrast Chinua Achebe's novel of European conquest, *Things Fall Apart* (New York, 1959), with his sarcastic novel of post-independence moral decay, *Man of the People* (New York, 1966), but Achebe's work is much more complex than a romanticization of pre-conquest Africa, and indeed both novels portray masculine power in telling ways.

23. Walter Rodney, *How Europe Underdeveloped Africa* (London, 1972).

24. Florencia Mallon, "Dialogues among the Fragments: Retrospect and Prospect," in Cooper, *et al., Confronting Historical Paradigms,* 371–404.

25. The power of the capitalist world system has not so much been its capacity to call into being new structures that maximize the extraction of commodities or surplus value as its global flexibility in finding alternatives to areas it could not rigorously exploit and, ideologically, to marginalize and demean the people it could not incorporate. This theme is explored in Frederick Cooper, "Africa and the World Economy," in Cooper, *et al., Confronting Historical Paradigms,* 84–204.

26. The ethical conundrums of radical scholarship have been probed in Bogumil Jewsiewicki, "African Historical Studies: Academic Knowledge as 'Usable Past' and Radical Scholarship," *African Studies Review,* 32, no. 3 (1989): 1–76.

27. My former adviser remembers student fashions at the time much the same way. Leonard M. Thompson, "The Study of South African History in the United States," *International Journal of African Historical Studies,* 25 (1992): 27–28.

28. The relevant literature here is now vast. The battle lines were first drawn in reviews of the pioneering "liberal" text, Monica Wilson and Leonard Thompson, eds., *The Oxford History of South Africa,* 2 vols. (New York, 1969–71). Early structuralist arguments are Frederick A. Johnstone, *Class, Race and Gold* (London, 1976); and Harold Wolpe, "Capitalism and Cheap Labour Power in South Africa: From Segregation to Apartheid," *Economy and Society,* 1 (1972): 425–56; whereas the social history school may be seen in Charles van Onselen, *Studies in the Social and Economic History of the Witwatersrand, 1886–1914,* 2 vols. (London, 1982).

29. Charles van Onselen, "Race and Class in the South African Countryside: Cultural Osmosis and Social Relations in the Sharecropping Economy of the South-Western Transvaal, 1900–1950," *AHR,* 95 (February 1990): 99–123; and *Studies.* For another complicated history of how ties of class and gender sometimes crossed racial frontiers—and sometimes did not—see Iris Berger, *Threads of Solidarity: Women in South African Industry, 1900–1980* (Bloomington, Ind., 1992). On the complexities of politics, see Shula Marks, *The Ambiguities of Dependence in South Africa: Class, Nationalism, and the State in Twentieth-Century Natal* (Baltimore, Md., 1986).

30. Keletso E. Atkins, *The Moon Is Dead! Give Us Our Money!: The Cultural Origins of an African Work Ethic, Natal, South Africa, 1843–1900* (Portsmouth, N.H., 1993).

31. I witnessed the debate at the June 1993 symposium of the Johannesburg History Workshop, whose title, "Work, Class, and Culture," specifies the categories in contention. For a history influenced by poststructuralism, see Clifton Crais, *White Supremacy and Black Resistance in Pre-Industrial South Africa: The Making of the Colonial Order in the Eastern Cape, 1770–1865* (Cambridge, 1992).

32. See Frederick Cooper and Ann Stoler, "Tensions of Empire: Colonial Control and Visions of Rule," *American Ethnologist,* 16 (1989): 609–21, and the essays that follow; and Nicholas B. Dirks, ed., *Colonialism and Culture* (Ann Arbor, Mich., 1992).

33. Talal Asad, ed., *Anthropology and the Colonial Encounter* (London, 1973); James Clifford and George E. Marcus, eds., *Writing Culture: The Poetics and Politics of Ethnography* (Berkeley, Calif., 1986); George W. Stocking, Jr., *Colonial Situations: Essays on the Contextualization of Ethnographic Knowledge* (Madison, Wis., 1991).

34. The pioneering text is Edward W. Said, *Orientalism* (New York, 1978); and a more recent example is Mary Louise Pratt, *Imperial Eyes: Travel Writing and Transculturation* (London, 1992).

35. Bernard S. Cohn, "The Census, Social Structure and Objectification in South Asia," in Cohn, *An Anthropologist among the Historians and Other Essays* (Delhi, 1987), 224–54; Randall M. Packard, "The 'Healthy Reserve' and the 'Dressed Native': Discourses on Black Health and the Language of Legitimation in South Africa," *American Ethnologist,* 16 (1989): 686–703; Megan Vaughan, *Curing Their Ills: Colonial Power and African Illness* (Cambridge, 1991): David Arnold, *Colonizing the Body: State Medicine and Epidemic Disease in Nineteenth-Century India* (Berkeley, Calif., 1993): Jean Comaroff and John Comaroff, *Of Revelation and Revolution,* Volume 1: *Christianity, Colonialism, and Consciousness in South Africa* (Chicago, 1991): T. O. Beidelman, *Colonial Evangelism: A Socio-Historical Study of an East African Mission at the Grassroots* (Bloomington, Ind., 1982); Gwendolyn Wright, *The Politics of Design in French Colonial Urbanism* (Chicago, 1991).

36. Ranajit Guha, "The Prose of Counter-Insurgency," and Dipesh Chakrabarty, "Conditions for Knowledge of Working-Class Conditions: Employers, Government and the Jute Workers of Calcutta, 1890–1940," in Guha and Spivak, *Selected Subaltern Studies,* 45–84, 179–232. See also Partha Chatterjee, *Nationalist Thought and the Colonial World: A Derivative Discourse?* (London, 1986).

37. Ann Stoler, "Sexual Affronts and Racial Frontiers: European Identities and the Cultural Politics of Exclusion in Southeast Asia," *Comparative Studies in Society and History,* 34 (1992): 514–51.

38. Literary scholars, among whom the terms postcolonial moment, postcolonial discourse, postcolonialism, and postcoloniality arose, are not unaware of the problems with them, as one can see in the papers, "On 'Post-Colonial Discourse,'" edited by Tejumola Olaniyan and published in *Calaloo,* 16 (1993): 743–1033, or the telling critique of Anne McClintock, "The Angel of Progress: Pitfalls of the Term 'Post-Colonialism,'" *Social Text,* 31–32 (1990): 84–98. How "post" the "postcolonial" world is, is one question: another is whether the histories of all parts of the world that experienced colonial rule can be reduced to that one essence. The adjective "colonial," minus "isms" or "itys," has the virtue of being a native category, a term by which Europeans described what they were about. It described a project that was simultaneously incorporative and differentiating: the extension of power to areas whose people were regarded as distinct in such a manner that distinction was repro-

duced. The "ism" makes "colonial" an explicitly political issue, and in the twentieth century "colonialism" was most often used by critics to demarcate a set of ideologies and practices they wanted to remove from the body politic; the word has the value and the inadequacies of most polemicizing terms. What the "ity" gives in return for its homogenizing and essentializing quality is not so clear.

39. Homi Bhabha, "Of Mimicry and Man: The Ambivalence of Colonial Discourse," *October*, 3–4 (1985): 125–33.

40. The growth of messianic Christian cults, with the message of missionaries turned upside down, is only one example of this process. When Jean-Pierre Chrétien uses the words "mutations," "adaptations," "reinterpretations," "reconstructions," "crystallizations," and "inventions" to describe the dynamics of African religions and their interactions with Christianity and Islam, he at least makes clear that there is a complex problem of analysis here. Chrétien, "Introduction," *L'invention religieuse en Afrique: Histoire et religion en Afrique noire* (Paris, 1993), 9. See also Achille Mbembe, *Afriques indociles: Christianisme, pouvoir et état en société postcoloniale* (Paris, 1988).

41. Achille Mbembe, "Domaines de la nuit et autorité onirique dans les maquis du Sud-Cameroun (1955–1958)," *Journal of African History*, 32 (1991): 89–122; Luise White, "Cars Out of Place: Vampires, Technology, and Labor in East and Central Africa," *Representations*, 43 (1993): 27–50; David William Cohen and E. S. Atieno-Odhiambo, *Burying SM: The Politics of Knowledge and the Sociology of Power in Africa* (Portsmouth, N.H., 1992); Leory Vail and Landeg White, "Forms of Resistance: Songs and Perceptions of Power in Colonial Mozambique," *AHR*, 88 (October 1983): 883–919. One can also learn a great deal from older anthropological literatures on witchcraft eradication movements, possession cults, and religious movements, as well as from philosophy, literary studies, and intellectual history, including Kwame Anthony Appiah, *In My Father's House: Africa in the Philosophy of Culture* (New York, 1992); V. Y. Mudimbe, *The Invention of Africa: Gnosis, Philosophy, and the Order of Knowledge* (Bloomington, Ind., 1988); Christopher L. Miller, *Theories of Africans: Francophone Literature and Anthropology in Africa* (Chicago, 1990). The concept of *bricolage* was deployed effectively in Jean Comaroff, *Body of Power, Spirit of Resistance: The Culture and History of a South African People* (Chicago, 1985), although within a resistance framework that is less persuasive.

42. Guha, "Prose of Counter-Insurgency."

43. Such questions as what made narratives credible, what was remembered and what forgotten, how written and oral texts derived authority from each other have been receiving increasing attention. The starting point for rigorous analysis of African oral sources was Jan Vansina, *Oral Tradition: A Study in Historical Methodology*, H. M. Wright, trans. (Chicago, 1965); and an important example of analyzing the implications of the production of history is David William Cohen, *The Combing of History* (Chicago, 1994).

44. Gayatri Chakravorty Spivak, "Can the Subaltern Speak?" in Cary Nelson and Lawrence Grossberg, eds., *Marxism and the Interpretation of Culture* (Urbana, Ill., 1988), 271–313; Benita Parry, "Problems in Current Theories of Colonial Discourse," *Oxford Literary Review*, 9 (1987): 27–58. Fernando Coronil argues that Spivak pushes the subaltern "outside the realm of political exchange," beyond relationships, and he posits instead that "subalternity is a relational and relative concept." Coronil, "Listening to the Subaltern: The Poetics of Neocolonial States," *Poetics Today*, 15 (1994). Likewise, Mallon, in this issue, wants to restore plural voices and multiple subject positions to the subaltern. All these scholars want to compliate and enrich their subalterns but still keep them subaltern.

45. I am following the insightful argument of David Edwards, "Mad Mullahs and English-men: Discourse in the Colonial Encounter," *Comparative Studies in Society and History,* 31 (1989): 649–70. The colonial assault on "barbarous practices: has been most fully explored in the case of slavery, where colonial regimes focused on the symbol of African backwardness and often shrank before the complexities of what slavery actually meant in its context. See Richard Roberts and Suzanne Miers, eds., *The End of Slavery in Africa* (Madison, Wis., 1988); Freder-ick Cooper, *From Slaves to Squatters: Plantation Labor and Agriculture in Zanzibar and Coastal Kenya, 1890–1925* (New Haven, Conn., 1980); and Paul E. Lovejoy and Jan S. Hogendorn, *Slow Death for Slavery: The Course of Abolition in Northern Nigeria, 1897–1936* (Cambridge, 1993). Gyan Prakash shows how a British government effort to focus narrowly on slavery in India avoided more difficult questions of how inequality and exploitation were constituted; Prakash, *Bonded Histories: Geneologies of Labor Servitude in Colonial India* (Cambridge, 1990).

46. The gender implications of this are discussed with particular effectiveness in Elias Mandala, *Work and Control in a Peasant Economy: A History of the Lower Tchiri Valley in Malawi, 1859–1960* (Madison, Wis., 1990); and Elizabeth Schmidt, *Peasants, Traders, and Wives: Shona Women in the History of Zimbabwe, 1870–1939* (Portsmouth, N.H., 1992).

47. Atkins, *Moon Is Dead!;* William Beinart, *The Political Economy of Pondoland, 1860–1930* (Cambridge, 1982); William H. Worger, *South Africa's City of Diamonds: Mine Work-ers and Monopoly Capitalism in Kimberley, 1867–1895* (New Haven, Conn., 1987).

48. Some scholars have tried to preserve monolithic views of a colonial economy or peripheral capitalism by confining these experiences to categories such as "coerced cash crop producers" (which is simply wrong) or "disguised proletarians" (which devoids the concept of proletarian of any meaning). See critical surveys in Cooper, "Africa and the World Econ-omy"; Isaacman, "Peasants and Rural Social Protest in Africa." David Ludden argues that in India, capitalism also had a varied impact, and examples of mobility and accumulation among relatively poor or middling cultivators need to be set alongside sharply exploitative systems of labor and tenancy, a process he believes makes the category of subaltern overly rigid. Lud-den, "Subalterns and Others, or Competing Colonial Histories of Agrarian India," paper for Workshop on "Historicizing Development," Emory University, December 10–12, 1993.

49. Colonial violence—the most obvious feature of colonial rule—is inadequately stud-ied, largely because anticolonial intellectuals portrayed it as ubiquitous while apologists saw it as incidental, whereas it was above all *located* and often all the more brutal for its limita-tions. See William Beinart, "Political and Collective Violence in Southern African Histori-ography," *Journal of Southern African Studies,* 18 (1992): 453–86.

50. Martin Chanock, *Law, Custom, and Social Order: The Colonial Experience in Malawi and Zambia* (Cambridge, 1985); Kristin Mann and Richard Roberts, eds., *Law in Colonial Africa* (Portsmouth, N.H., 1991); Terence Ranger, "The Invention of Tradition in Colonial Africa," in Eric Hobsbawm and Terence Ranger, eds., *The Invention of Tradition* (Cambridge, 1983), 211–62.

51. Two pioneering studies are J. F. A. Ajayi, *Christian Missions in Nigeria, 1841–1891: The Making of a New Elite* (Evanston, Ill., 1965); and Margaret Priestley, *West African Trade and Coast Society: A Family Study* (London, 1969).

52. For a bibliography on labor history, see Bill Freund, *The African Worker* (Cambridge, 1988).

53. Luise White, *The Comforts of Home: Prostitution in Colonial Nairobi* (Chicago, 1990); Claire Robertson, *Sharing the Same Bowl?: A Socioeconomic History of Women and Class in Accra, Ghana* (Bloomington, Ind., 1984).

54. Beidelman, *Colonial Evangelism;* Comaroff and Comaroff, *Of Revelation and Revolution.*

55. The early periodization of colonial policy given here emerges in the case of British and French West Africa as described by Anne Phillips, *The Enigma of Colonialism: British Policy in West Africa* (London, 1989); and Alice Conklin, "A Mission to Civilize: Ideology and Imperialism in French West Africa 1895–1930" (Ph.D. dissertation, Princeton University, 1989); while I have argued along these lines for East Africa in *From Slaves to Squatters;* and *On the African Waterfront: Urban Disorder and the Transformation of Work in Colonial Mombasa* (New Haven, Conn., 1987); and in current research on the colonial development initiative.

56. Ranajit Guha, "Dominance without Hegemony and Its Historigraphy," in Ranajit Guha, ed., *Subaltern Studies VI: Writings on South Asian History and Society* (Delhi, 1989), 210–309. For a quite different perspective on the contradictions of imperialism in a bourgeois world, see Bernard Semmel, *The Liberal Ideal and the Demons of Empire: Theories of Imperialism from Adam Smith to Lenin* (Baltimore, Md., 1993).

57. Similarly, the failure of French efforts to contain colonial challenges in the 1940s by extending to colonial subjects a form of citizenship in Greater France eventually led—as many of those ex-citizens migrated from colony to metropole—to pressures that threaten the definition of citizenship in France itself and the universalistic logic of French political ideology. Rogers Brubaker, *Citizenship and Nationhood in France and Germany* (Cambridge, Mass., 1992). For the case that the structure of power and the forms of exclusions in modern metropolitan societies were shaped in relation to colonization, see Ann Stoler, *Race and the Education of Desire: A Colonial Reading of Foucault's History of Sexuality* (Durham, N.C., forthcoming).

58. Donald Crummey, "Introduction: 'The Great Beast,'" in Crummey, ed., *Banditry, Rebellion, and Social Protest in Africa* (London, 1986), 1; James C. Scott, *Weapons of the Weak: Everyday Forms of Peasant Resistance* (New Haven, Conn., 1985). Crummey tries to get beyond the assimilation of popular violence to anticolonial resistance by arguing that precolonial regimes were resisted too, but he ends up treating in this context "the agent of oppression" (p. 21) in an even more abstract manner than was colonialism when seen as the object of African resistance.

59. Michel Foucault, *The History of Sexuality,* Volume 1: *An Introduction,* Robert Hurley, trans. (New York, 1978), 95–96.

60. Chatterjee, *Nationalist Thought and the Colonial World;* Douglas Haynes and Gyan Prakash, "Introduction: The Entanglement of Power and Resistance," in Haynes and Prakash, eds., *Contesting Power: Resistance and Everyday Social Relations in South Asia* (Berkeley, Calif., 1991), 1–22.

61. Megan Vaughan points out that surveillance and control in metropolitan societies addressed the individual, whereas colonial power tended to address collectivities. Her latter point has some validity (less in relation to the developmentalism of the 1940s than the control mechanisms of "indirect rule" in the 1920s and 1930s), but the Euro-African dichotomy is too stark. Vaughan, *Curing Their Ills,* 8–12. Even after formal decolonization, global power remains arterial—even aortic—rather than capillary, given the immense power of the World Bank and the International Monetary Fund over decision making by African states.

62. Sherry Ortner, "Resistance: Some Theoretical Problems in Anthropological History and Historical Anthropology," in Terrence McDonald, ed., *The Historic Turn in the Human Sciences* (Ann Arbor, Mich., forthcoming).

63. Beinart and Bundy, *Hidden Struggles in Rural South Africa,* 31.

64. Mandala, *Work and Control:* Schmidt, *Peasants, Traders, and Wives.*

65. White, *Comforts of Home.*

66. Karen E. Fields, *Revival and Rebellion in Colonial Central Africa* (Princeton, N.J., 1985).

67. James C. Scott, *Domination and the Arts of Resistance: Hidden Transcripts* (New Haven, Conn., 1990). Scott is vague in specifying the domain to which his arguments apply, eliding slavery and colonialism and taking examples from a wide array of cases as if the particular structures of power in each were of little consequence.

68. Subaltern Studies historians have, for example, studied communalism as a colonial category of description, as a nationalist category to be used as a foil against the Indian nation, and as a shifting, manipulated, and contested category of popular action; wage labor appears as a universal construct and as particular lived experience; and Gandhi is shown to imply very different meanings within the Indian National Congress and local contexts. Gyanendra Pandey, *The Construction of Communalism in Colonial North India* (Delhi, 1990); Dipesh Chakrabarty, *Rethinking Working-Class History: Bengal, 1890–1940* (Princeton, N.J., 1989); Shahid Amin, "Gandhi as Mahatma," in Guha and Spivak, *Selected Subaltern Studies,* 288–350. See also the discussion of these issues in O'Hanlon, "Recovering the Subject."

69. Dipesh Chakrabarty, "Marx after Marxism: History, Subalternity and Difference," *Meanjin,* 52 (1993): 421–34; and Chakrabarty, *Rethinking Working-Class History.*

70. Labor was a numerically small category but an extremely influential one, because the very narrowness of colonial commercial, mining, and industrial channels meant that a small group—in a position to use face-to-face relations to organize—could disrupt the entire import-export economy; in the post–World War II era, rising prices for African commodities and the colonial development initiative (combined with inflationary pressures on workers) shaped a favorable conjuncture for labor activism. This section is based on Frederick Cooper, *Decolonization and African Society: The Labor Question in French and British Africa,* forthcoming.

71. The leaders of African political parties were not necessarily sympathetic to strikers or labor movements. In the strike that contributed most to the myth of labor as the spearhead of nationalism—the great French West African railway strike of 1947–1948—the region's leading politicans were notably diffident about taking up the workers' cause, and some of them worked to betray it. Workers' demands for equality within the French labor system had an ambiguous relationship to anticolonial politics. The myth is most clearly developed in the novel of Sembene Ousmane, *God's Bits of Wood,* Francis Price, trans. (London, 1962).

72. Beinart and Bundy, *Hidden Struggles,* esp. 31–37; Steven Feierman, *Peasant Intellectuals: Anthropology and History in Tanzania* (Madison, Wis., 1990); Richard Grove, "Colonial Conservation, Ecological Hegemony and Popular Resistance: Towards a Global Synthesis," in John M. MacKenzie, ed., *Imperialism and the Natural World* (Manchester, 1990); Kriger, *Zimbabwe's Guerrilla War,* 157. Kriger is critical of the view that a particular kind of politics flowed from the very existence of a peasantry, as argued in Terence Ranger, *Peasant Consciousness and Guerrilla War in Zimbabwe* (Berkeley, Calif., 1985).

73. The most persuasive account so far of the calculations that ended a colonial empire is Jacques Marseille, *Empire colonial et capitalisme français: Histoire d'un divorce* (Paris, 1984), but his resolutely metropolitan focus does not allow him to explain the factors within colonies that raised the costs and diminished the benefits. In the British case, see Prime Minister Macmillan's call for an explicit cost-benefit analysis of each colony, in Prime Minister's Minute, January 28, 1957, CAB 134/155, Public Record Office, London. Portugal, economically weaker, fell back on its empire and sought to extract more from it, exacerbating conflict even as the international climate turned Portugal from a laggard but acceptable colonial partner to a pariah. Settler colonists fought even longer.

74. A notorious instance of scholarly hubris is Fredric Jameson's insistence that the literature of Third World people—oppressed as they were by imperialism—was supposed to consist of "national allegories." He was duly rebuked for the presumption of his telling oppressed people that they could only write about their oppression and could only feel themselves oppressed in national terms. Fredric Jameson, "Third World Literature in the Era of Multinational Capitalism," *Social Text,* 15 (1986): 65–88, 69 quoted: Aijaz Ahmad, "Jameson's Rhetoric of Otherness and the 'National Allegory,'" *Social Text,* 17 (1987): 3–25.

75. Benedict Anderson, *Imagined Communities: Reflections on the Origin and Spread of Nationalism,* rev. edn. (London, 1991).

76. J. Ayodele Langley, *Pan-Africanism and Nationalism in West Africa, 1900–1945: A Study in Ideology and Social Classes* (Oxford, 1973). An intriguing but vain attempt by a leading intellectual at the moment of independence to turn an argument about the historical unity of Africa into a case for continent-wide federal system is Cheikh Anta Diop, *Les fondements culturels, techniques et industriels d'un futur état fédéral d'Afrique noire* (Paris, 1960). The concept of "Africa" itself is a tricky one, and as Kwame Anthony Appiah argues, seeing Africa as an entity risked engaging in the kind of racial essentializing that leaders such as W. E. B. Du Bois were intent on combating. He insists that "Africa" should be defined not by some kind of racial or cultural authenticity but by looking at the history of struggle itself: how slavery and colonization defined Africans and how Africans turned this imposed definition into something positive. Appiah, *In My Father's House.* See also Mudimbe, *Invention of Africa,* and, for an Indian parallel, Sudipta Kaviraj, "The Imaginary Institution of India," in Chatterjee and Pandey, *Subaltern Studies VIII,* 1–39.

77. Territorialization was more than a divide-and-rule strategy aimed at African political movements. It was also an attempt to break away from the notion, much invoked by African unions, that government wages and benefits throughout Greater France should be equalized across the races. By giving African politicians authority over the budgets at the territorial level, the policy made government wage policy beholden to the territorial taxpayer. Territorialization in 1956 had powerful incentives attached to it—a genuine devolution of power to elected officials within each colony. Although some officials tried to revive federation, each had to look first to his own electoral base—and the wealthiest territory, the Ivory Coast, stood to gain the most by keeping its resources within its borders. Federation became politically impossible to revive. William J. Foltz, *From French West Africa to the Mali Federation* (New Haven, Conn., 1965). A post-independence attempt to build federation in former British East Africa also failed. Joseph S. Nye, Jr., *Pan-Africanism and East African Integration* (Cambridge, Mass., 1965).

78. Pandey's study, *The Construction of Communalism in Colonial North India,* has echoes in colonial and postcolonial Africa: nationalists took over from colonial officials the idea that religious and communal movements were "irrational" and legitimized only "the mass of the people mobilized into a new national community" (p. 254). Some of the same rhetoric was also used to delegitimize movements, including labor, that were secular and "modern" yet limited to particular segments of the national community.

79. Richard A. Joseph, *Radical Nationalism in Cameroun: Social Origins of the U.P.C. Rebellion* (Oxford, 1977); Achille Mbembe, *La naissance du maquis dans le Sud-Cameroun: Histoires d'indisciplines (1920–1960)* (Paris, 1993); Berman and Lonsdale, *Unhappy Valley.*

80. I do not accept the argument made by Ronald Robinson and others that in the British case, a clear plan to devolve power was developed prior to the rise of nationalist movements and that these movements—the consequence rather than the cause of British policy—did no

more than speed up a previously conceived policy. This "Whig" interpretation, as John Darwin calls it, misses the extent to which urban and rural movements—not specifically nationalist—destabilized colonial regimes' sense of control, pushed them to emphasize their own developmentalist objectives while trying to play down what was "colonial" about colonial authority, and later helped to reveal that the developmental initiatives would themselves generate conflict more than alleviate it. Ronald Robinson, "Andrew Cohen and the Transfer of Power in Tropical Africa, 1940–1951," in W. H. Morris-Jones and Georges Fischer, eds., *Decolonisation and After: The British and French Experience* (London, 1980), 50–72; John Darwin, "British Decolonization since 1945: A Pattern or a Puzzle?" *Journal of Imperial and Commonwealth Studies,* 12 (1984): 187–209.

81. Dipesh Chakrabarty argues that "what European imperialism and third-world nationalisms have achieved together" is "universalization of the nation-state as the most desirable form of political community." Chakrabarty, "Postcoloniality and the Artifice of History," 19. Some argue that, given the internal weakness of Third World states, it is their insertion into international relations that preserves them. Robert H. Jackson, *Quasi-States: Sovereignty, International Relations, and the Third World* (Cambridge, 1990).

82. Such definitions have been controversial for decades, since James Coleman insisted on limiting "nationalist" to movements specifically directed at assuming power within a nation-state. Thomas Hodgkin wanted nationalism to include all anticolonial protests and ideologies. Hodgkin's notion is really a definition of political action and barely allows a political movement in a colony to be anything but nationalist. The words mean more if nationalism is viewed as only one of many possibilities for politics. James S. Coleman, "Nationalism in Tropical Africa," *American Political Science Review,* 48 (1954): 404–26; Hodgkin, *Nationalism,* 23.

83. Janet G. Vaillant, *Black, French, and African: A Life of Léopold Sédar Senghor* (Cambridge, Mass., 1990); Appiah, *In My Father's House;* Mudimbe, *Invention of Africa;* Miller, *Theories of Africans.*

84. On this last point, see Edward Said's impassioned defense of colonial and ex-colonial intellectuals' engagement with European literature and culture as well as his critique of nationalist thought; Said, *Culture and Imperialism* (New York, 1993).

85. Note by the Secretaries, "Future Constitutional Development in the Colonies," May 30, 1957, CP (O) 5, CAB 134/1551, Memorandum by the Secretary of State, "Nigeria," C 57 (120), May 14, 1957, CAB 129/87, Memorandum by the Secretary of State, "Future Policy in East Africa," CPC (59) 2, April 10, 1959, CAB 134/1558, Public Record Office.

86. Joseph, *Radical Nationalism:* Mbembe, *Naissance du maquis.* Such remaking of political figures is not unique to Africa: Yasser Arafat seems to be the latest beneficiary.

87. Jean Marie Allman, *The Quills of Porcupine: Asante Nationalism in an Emergent Ghana* (Madison, Wis., 1993); Mbembe, *Naissance du maquis;* Kriger, *Zimbabwe's Guerrilla War;* Tabitha M. Kanogo, *Squatters and the Roots of Mau Mau, 1905–63* (London, 1987).

88. Aristide Zolberg, *Creating Political Order: The Party-States of West Africa* (Chicago, 1966).

89. There is a problem in Anderson's argument about creole nationalism that is related to the issue raised here: the claim of elites to transcend social divisions. As Julie Skurskie argues, the politics of the creole elite were not so much inclusive—trying to cut across, coopt, and minimalize conflict in the name of the nation—as exclusive, violently defining racial and cultural groups out of the nation. Skurskie, "The Ambiguities of Authenticity in Latin America: *Dona Barbara* and the Construction of National Identity," *Poetics Today,* 15 (1994).

90. Chatterjee, *Nationalist Thought and the Colonial World:* Partha Chatterjee, *The Nation and Its Fragments: Colonial and Postcolonial Histories* (Princeton, N.J., 1993), 6. Chatterjee is only opening the door on what is likely to be a long and useful debate over the interrelation of economic/political and domestic/spiritual domains. See also Karen Tranberg Hansen, ed., *African Encounters with Domesticity* (New Brunswick, N.J., 1992); and Dipesh Chakrabarty, "The Difference-Deferral of (a) Colonial Modernity: Public Debates on Domesticity in British Bengal," *History Workshop,* 36 (1993): 1–34.

91. See also David Ludden, "The Development Regime in India," in Dirks, *Culture and Colonialism,* 247–88.

92. The construction argument is often made. See, for example, Homi K. Bhabha, ed., *Nation and Narration* (London, 1990).

93. One subject into which this kind of inquiry has begun is health. A Subaltern Studies historian (Arnold, *Colonizing the Body*) has done a pioneering study on India, and state and health have been studied perceptively by Vaughan, *Curing Their Ills,* and Packard, "'Healthy Reserve' and the 'Dressed Native.'"

94. Anthony D. Smith, *State and Nation in the Third World: The Western State and African Nationalism* (Brighton, 1983), 56. As in my study of labor, one can examine in many domains how institutions (trade unions, industrial relations boards) of specifically European origin— but discussed by officials as if universal—were used by Africans in particular ways, while they, too, made claims to universality to serve their ends. On modes of exercising and representing power in Africa, see Jean-François Bayart, *L'état en Afrique: La politique du ventre* (Paris, 1989); and the controversy unleashed in *Public Culture,* 5, no. 1 (1992), by an article by Achille Mbembe, "The Banality of Power and the Aesthetics of Vulgarity in the Postcolony," *Public Culture,* 4, no. 2 (1992): 1–30.

95. Basil Davidson, *The Black Man's Burden: Africa and the Curse of the Nation-State* (New York, 1993); Pieter Boele van Hensbroek, "Cursing the Nation-State," *Transition,* 61 (1993): 114–21; Liisa Malkki, "National Geographic: The Rooting of Peoples and the Territorialization of National Identity among Scholars and Refugees," *Cultural Anthropology,* 7 (1992): 24–44; Akhil Gupta, "The Song of the Nonaligned World: Transnational Identities and the Reinscription of Space in Late Capitalism," *ibid.,* 63–79.

96. Recent entries on Fanon—commenting on the other entries—are Cedric Robinson, "The Appropriation of Frantz Fanon," *Race and Class,* 15 (1993): 79–91; Henry Louis Gates, Jr., "Critical Fanonism," *Critical Inquiry,* 17 (1991): 457–70; and a particularly critical discussion in Miller, *Theories of Africans,* 45–62.

97. Frantz Fanon, *The Wretched of the Earth,* Constance Farrington, trans. (New York, 1966), 30. See also Frantz Fanon, *Black Skin, White Masks,* Charles Lam Markmann, trans. (New York, 1967), 226–29. Said, *Imperialism and Culture,* 267–70, finds Fanon a useful ally in his critique of nationalism. Fanon did not seek to build a "true Algeria" embodying some national essence but rather a society emancipated of its colonial oppression. Yet, in his own way, Fanon isolates the "true anticolonialist" from history and experience, turning impure categories into criteria for exclusion from the liberation project. I use the word "true" in the ironic sense applied to the other side of the colonial divide by Herman Lebovics, *True France: The Wars over Cultural Identity, 1900–1945* (Ithaca, N.Y., 1992).

98. Fanon's psychologizing of the colonial situation—and other versions of this enterprise—strike me as deeply flawed, a too-easy transposition of issues of state sovereignty to personal autonomy, abstracted from the multidimensional contexts in which personalities are actually shaped. A more recent and sophisticated attempt to address issues of personality and

Chapter 7

colonization, not wholly convincing is Ashis Nandy, *The Intimate Enemy: Loss and Recovery of Self under Colonialism* (Delhi, 1983). There were colonialist versions of the psychologizing argument, too, eliding individual and collective psychologies, claiming that Africans were unable to stand up to the pressures of modernization or move between different social universes. The most notorious instance is J. C. Carothers, *The Psychology of Mau Mau* (Nairobi, 1954).

99. "The colonial world is a Manichean world," wrote Fanon (*Wretched,* 33) apparently not realizing how much deeper he was in that world than the people about whom and in whose cause he wrote.

100. Exposé de M. lé Vice Président Sékou Touré à l'occasion de la conférence du 2 février 1958 avec les résponsables syndicaux et délégués du personnel RDA, "Le RDA et l'action syndicale dans la nouvelle situation politiques des T.O.M.," PDG (9)/dossier 7, Centre de Recherche et de Documentation Africaine, Paris. His minister of labor, Camara Bengaly, insisted that unions must become "the precious collaborators" of an African government and abandon their sectional claims: "Any conception of trade unionism contrary to this orientation must be discarded, and courageously fought in order to be eliminated definitively." Speech in name of Council of Government of Guinea to Congrès Constutatif de l'UGTAN, Conakry, May 23–25, 1958, sous-dossier UGTAN, K 421 (1965), Archives du Sénégal.

101. A Guinean intellectual's conclusion on Sékou Touré is well expressed in the title of his book: Ibrahima Baba Kaké, *Sékou Touré: Le héros et le tyran* (Paris, 1987). See also Claude Rivière, "Lutte ouvrière et phenomène syndical en Guinée," *Cultures et Développement,* 7 (1975): 53–83.

102. One should not assume that postcolonial African states were uniformly authoritarian or that an authoritarian state could not in many ways be a weak state. For one of the first critiques of the brittleness of African regimes and the ideological moves by which contestation was delegitimized, see Zolberg, *Creating Political Order.* My argument parallels Chatterjee's view of the "plural development of social identities" emerging from struggles with the colonial state "that were violently disrupted by the political history of the postcolonial state seeking to replicate the modular forms of the modern nation-state." Chatterjee, *Nation and Its Fragments,* 156.

103. On the dualism of late colonial conceptions of society, see Cooper, *Decolonization and African Society.*

104. Chatterjee, *Nation and Its Fragments,* 237–38; Chakrabarty, "Postcoloniality and the Artifice of History," 20. The "provincializing" argument is a very good one, but it implies a detailed and nuanced engagement with the vagaries of European history. The argument is weakened when it slips into blanket dismissals of liberalism or assumptions that bourgeois equality is an unchanging construct. See Chakrabarty, 20–21; Chatterjee, 198.

8

The Promise and Dilemma of Subaltern Studies: Perspectives from Latin American History

Florencia E. Mallon

This is not an easy time for scholars who work on Latin America. Over the past five years or so, many of our most important and inspirational historical narratives have come undone. The Cuban Revolution is dying a slow death after the collapse of the Soviet Union, dragged down by the morass of global capitalism, the internal erosion of social gains, and a leadership grown old in the holding of centralized power. The Sandinistas lost control of the state in 1990 and face the future internally divided, needing to make broad coalitions if they are to regain a place in the executive branch. (Where is their stunning political majority of 1979–1981?) In Chile, the post-Pinochet Christian Democrats have hailed the dictatorship's radical privatization and free market reforms as "modernization," tarnishing the memory of Chilean aspirations for social justice under Salvador Allende and the Chilean statist model of economic development that emerged from the first "popular unity" government of the late 1930s. In Peru, Sendero Luminoso has confused and confounded those of us accustomed to supporting people's struggles, first by killing an astounding number of people they were supposedly struggling for, then because their "maximum leader" reached an agreement with an authoritarian, free market–oriented president after only a few weeks in captivity.

One could go on and on. But the main question, simply put, is, what is a progressive scholar to do? If we continue to commit to emancipatory, bottom-up analysis and yet can no longer simply ride one of our various Marxist or Marxian horses into the sunset, what are the alternatives? Are there other horses to ride, or must we eschew the enterprise entirely?

It is in this context that, for a few of us, the Subaltern Studies Group—organized around their series of collected essays, occasional conferences, and additional monographic publications on India and colonialism—has provided inspiration. A handful of Latin Americanists, from a variety of disciplinary backgrounds, are beginning to pepper their citations with references to the series and perhaps more often to some of its individual luminaries, such as Ranajit Guha, Partha Chatterjee, or Gayatri Chakravorty Spivak.[1] Latin Americanists, often Eurocentric in our borrowing from other historical or theoretical traditions, have in this instance taken as a model a school born and bred in another part of the so-called Third World. What is afoot?[2]

One partial explanation might lie in the nature of the intellectual and political crisis we presently face. It is precisely the models earlier imported from Europe—Marxisms, a belief in progress and modernity, a commitment to revolution as forward-looking, linear, developmentalist transformation—that are now in doubt. Many of us have thus been reluctant simply to pick up the most recent Eurocentric remedy to earlier Eurocentric ills and have hesitated before embracing the trends offered by postmodernism or poststructuralism. Some Latin American intellectuals, for example, have questioned the applicability of postmodernism to an area of the world not yet modern—at least not in the European or U.S. sense of the word. Others have doubted the ability of postmodernism to facilitate political engagement and commitment. And, in reading the work of those who have embraced the postmodern turn, some of us have been surprised by ahistorical claims that this approach has created a "new sense of modernity as paradoxical and contradictory" or that "[n]ew, 'horizontal' relations between intellectuals and both new and traditional social movements are emerging with the redefinition of political agency suggested by postmodernist perspectives."[3]

So doesn't Subaltern Studies offer us the perfect compromise? Formulated by a group of intellectuals based in the "Third World," anticolonial and politically radical yet conversant with the latest in textual analysis and postmodern methods: what more could a cautious, progressive scholar hope for? It is in this context that I reflect on the relevance of Subaltern Studies for the case of Latin America.

I begin by providing some background on and analysis of the Subaltern Studies Group as a whole, situating its project and its internal tensions and contradictions in the Gramscian tradition the group claimed at its inception. Next, I discuss how Subaltern approaches have been received and consumed so far in the Latin American literature, providing as well the historical, political, and historiographical context that might help us to extend and enrich the future application of Subaltern methods to the Latin Americans case. Finally, I use my reflections from Latin America to rethink the internal conflicts of Subaltern Studies as such, offering some suggestions for future work and dialogue that might contribute to extending the applicability of the project beyond its present reach.

These three goals, taken together, constitute the essence of non-hierarchical cross-regional dialogue, where neither of the two cases is taken as the paradigm against which the other is pronounced inadequate. Such an approach is a welcome corrective to the many instances in which European theories had been placed next to Third World cases and the latter have been found wanting. The Subaltern project itself has been involved, to some extent, in this kind of dialogue, especially in its attempts to extend and rethink, from the perspective of the colonial and postcolonial world, the messages of Antonio Gramsci, Jacques Derrida, and Michel Foucault. In Latin America, too, scholars have participated in more effective forms of mutual dialogue, especially on issues such as economic dependency, liberation theology, and indigenous movements. But it bears repeating that non-hierarchical cross-regional dialogue is not the application of a concept, part and parcel, without contextualization, to another area. Nor can it be framed in the assumption that one side of the exchange has little to learn from the other. It is my hope that these kinds of dialogues and exchanges, perhaps not accidentally among so-called Third World regions, we can find the seeds for a method of post-orientalist comparison.[4]

In the preface to the first volume of Subaltern Studies, dated in Canberra in August 1981, Ranajit Guha defined the subaltern very broadly as anyone who is subordinated "in terms of class, caste, age, gender and office or in any other way." He declared all aspects of subaltern life—historical, social, cultural, political, or economic—to be relevant to the Subaltern Studies Group's efforts to recover subaltern contributions to Indian history. He further stated that, because subordination is a two-way relationship involving both dominated and dominant, elite groups would also receive consideration in the work of the Subaltern Studies scholars. In a disclaimer tucked away among the various purposes that have constituted the group project as a whole, he firmly set its Gramscian genealogy: "It will be idle of us, of course, to hope that the range of contributions to this series may even remotely match the six-point project envisaged by Antonio Gramsci in his 'Notes on Italian History.'"[5]

It seems worthwhile to reflect briefly on Guha's choice in citing "Notes on Italian History." Gramsci's six-point project for the study of the subaltern was ambitious, indeed. He devoted only one point to research on "the objective formation of the subaltern social groups" in the economic transformations of a particular society and "their origins in pre-existing social groups, whose mentality, ideology and aims they conserve for a time." The five remaining points address the political formation of both dominant and subaltern social forces, which he saw as mutually interdependent. Gramsci asserted that subaltern groups attempt to influence "dominant political formations" from the start and that this critical engagement was crucial to the transformation of both dominant and subaltern political organizations. In response to pressure from below, dominant groups attempt to enlist the cooperation of subalterns through the formation of new reformist political parties. At the same time, when subalterns struggle politically to create their own increasingly autonomous organizations, they do so in dialogue with, and struggle against, dominant political forms.[6] This was precisely the purpose of the Subaltern Studies Group's proposed revision of Indian history: to demonstrate how, in the political transformations occurring in colonial and postcolonial Indian society, subalterns not only developed their own strategies of resistance but actually helped define and refine elite options.

But there was more to Guha's choice. "Notes on Italian History" is one of Gramsci's most detailed and historically dynamic writings, in which he pondered the question of why Italy did not develop into a strong nation-state in the nineteenth century, a question linked in his mind to the rise of fascism in the twentieth century. The constant shadow presence in his analysis, against which he defined the Italian "passive revolution" that led to state formation without the effective creation of a nation, is the French Revolution of 1789, and the Jacobin party as the political mediator channeling popular energy into an alliance with the bourgeoisie. Italy, as "not-France," does not have an active, transformative bourgeois revolution and thus emerges as a weak nation, in which dominant social groups "have the function of 'domination' without that of 'leadership': dictatorship without hegemony."[7] This is also the central problematic that Guha defines in the first volume of Subaltern Studies:

> It is the study of this *historic failure of the nation to come to its own*, a failure due to the inadequacy of the bourgeoisie as well as of the working class to lead it into a decisive victory over colonialism and a bourgeois-democratic revolution of either the classic nineteenth-century type under the hegemony of the bourgeoisie or a more modern type under the hegemony of workers and peasants, that is, a "new democracy"—*it is the study of this failure which constitutes the central problematic of the historiography of colonial India.*[8]

The compelling parallels between India and Italy, both "not-France," are bounded by the existence of colonialism. The "historic failure of the nation to come to its own," "the inadequacy of the bourgeoisie as well as of the working class," these, according to Guha, are "the central problematic of the historiography of colonial India." Not simply pre-capitalist or underdeveloped India but colonial India. This put a particular spin on the concept of subalternity and on the role of peasants in subaltern politics. In the case of a European "not-France," Gramsci had envisioned the need for a broad class alliance that, by uniting workers and peasants, would radicalize both groups and make them, along with their organic intellectuals, the leaders of a social revolution. But in the case of a colonial "not-France," the obstacles to overcome were even steeper. A smaller working class was even more isolated from a larger peasantry, and questions of social justice were inextricably intertwined with issues of national self-determination. Since nationalist elites had often benefited from the social arrangements reproduced under colonialism, subaltern movements and political visions had to attain an even larger and more militant presence in nationalist coalitions if the nation was ever to come into its own. Given the smaller size of the proletariat, peasants and rural communities had to take the lead in the forging of an Indian people-nation.[9]

As is the case in Gramsci's work, then, the Subaltern Studies commitment to the recovery of subaltern politics, culture, and traditions of resistance is not simply empirical but also political. Gramsci hoped to discover, in an understanding of subaltern practices and histories, a potential for building the Jacobin party of the left: the hegemonic party that truly led, rather than simply dominated, by channeling, understanding, and incorporating popular energies and beliefs. The Subaltern Studies Group also leaves open the possibility for a future reconstruction of an emancipatory and hegemonic postcolonial political order: if subaltern traditions and practices are better understood, they can still serve as the basis for building alternative political communities that will truly liberate "the people."

In fact, as Guha himself laid out in "The Prose of Counter-Insurgency," the Subaltern Studies Group was united first and foremost in its critique of neocolonialist, nationalist, *and* traditional Marxist approaches to the study of "the people." What unified these historiographies, according to Guha, was their inability to see and hear subaltern insurgents as they really were. "Blinded by the glare of a perfect and immaculate consciousness," Guha concluded, historians of all political persuasions had yet to investigate subaltern politics in all its contradictory complexity.[10] Because all schools of Indian historiography were complicit in their failure to investigate the potential countertraditions in Indian popular politics, the potential for constructing a Gramscian Jacobin party of the left in India was close to zero. Indeed, according to C. A. Bayly, during the decade preceding the founding of Subaltern Studies,

> Indian intellectuals found comfort, amidst all the signs of embourgeoisement, in the Maoist violence of the Naxalites. Later in the 1970s many who were not on the pro-Chinese left sniffed danger in the hegemonic ideology of the Indian National Congress, elevating "national unity" into an icon which could keep it permanently in power (the subaltern group, it must be remembered, came together not long after Mrs. Gandhi's Emergency). There was concern that, in official discourse, tribal resistance movements, poor peasant protest and working class rising could be bundled into the category of archaic disturbance, communialism, or "Naxalism." The ease with which many elements of the old left, particularly in Bengal, compromised with the authoritarian claims of the Congress, and the way in which their orthodox Marxist-Leninist theorists were able to accommodate this to economistic developmental theories of class-struggle set alarm bells ringing.[11]

Beyond all this complicity with official nationalist narratives, there was also the Gramscian critique of orthodox Marxist activists and intellectuals who continued to believe their politics was the direct translation of class—defined as position in or relation to the means of production—to the arenas of political action and consciousness. The necessity of such a critique was demonstrated by some of the answers appearing in Indian academic journals. "[T]here is a strong anti-Marxist bias in some of the essays collected in the two volumes," wrote Girish Mishra in 1983. After quoting extensively from Lenin for over two of the five pages in his review, Mishra suggested that Subaltern Studies scholars idealized the spontaneity of popular mobilization, when in fact it was "wrong to say that the workers or peas-

ants start having a clear understanding of politics after one or two rounds of agita-
tion. They need to be organized and trained." Instead, Mishra proposed, "It will
be better and more fruitful if the researchers into popular movements concentrate
more on their internal weaknesses and limitations of perspectives and outlook than
on finding a scapegoat in the form of some leader or the other of the Indian
National Congress betraying them." This was true, according to Mishra, because
the "hackneyed" accusations of betrayal did not hold up to close class analysis. If
the Indian National Congress was the party of the bourgeoisie and of the petty
bourgeoisie, then it was interested in increasing agricultural production. Of necessity, therefore, the Indian National Congress would ally with all antifeudal forces
and could not possibly betray the peasants.[12]

It was in the light of such a deductive analysis of politics that the need for a Subaltern Studies approach made the most sense. A hegemonic alternative for the future
needed to be built with what already existed. Activists and intellectuals concerned
with building an alternative needed to *know,* through investigation, what traditions
they had to work with. They could not deduce them simply through the application of Marxist categories. "Every trace of independent initiative on the part of subaltern groups should therefore be of incalculable value for the integral historian,"
Gramsci wrote. "Consequently, this kind of history can only be dealt with mono-
graphically, and each monograph requires an immense quantity of material which
is often hard to collect."[13]

Herein lies the deepest, most irresolvable, and also the most fertile tension in the
Subaltern Studies project. The recovery of subaltern practices, beliefs, and actions
necessitated the use of new documents but especially of new methods for reading
old documents. This laborious and methodologically complex task led many members of the group increasingly into semiotics, literary criticism, and many forms of
textual analysis. Yet, by encouraging the deconstruction of texts along lines of
power and hierarchy and by decentering all subjects that emerged in the documents, these techniques have ultimately questioned two assumptions central to the
group's political purpose: that subaltern practices had some autonomy from elite
culture and that subaltern politics had a unity and solidarity of its own.[14]

By January 1986, when the second Subaltern Studies conference was held in Calcutta, this tension came out into the open. As summarized by David Hardiman, himself a contributor to the project from its inception, the school was "standing at something of a crossroads. . . . One road leads towards greater concentration on textual
analysis and a stress on the relativity of all knowledge; another towards the study of
subaltern consciousness and action so as to forward the struggle for a socialist society." As reported by Hardiman, both positions received well-argued support. The
proponents of textual analysis emphasized the value of the group's deconstruction of
existing theories and pointed out the inevitable relativism of such an endeavor; Guha
himself stressed that the school was "born under a sign of negation—'negation' is
inscribed on the subaltern banner." The proponents of a more openly political purpose, however, emphasized the constructive rather than deconstructive aspects of

the school's original purpose, the need to focus on politics and on the interactions of elites and subalterns over time. If, indeed, the Subaltern School sought to "make the subaltern classes the subjects of their own history," some scholars argued, deconstruction was of necessity a tool rather than a goal. Guha also supported the need for an ultimately political purpose, and he suggested that this division might be a strength rather than a weakness. Hardiman, however, concluded his report by suggesting that this division could very well prove difficult to overcome in the long run, especially since "the debate during the conference served more to reveal these differences rather than to work towards their resolution."[15]

Can these differences be resolved? Is resolution in one direction or the other even the most desirable goal? I think not. In an essay published in 1985, Gayatri Spivak reflected on the productive aspects of these contradictions. By insisting that subalterns possessed positive human agency and could be thinking and autonomous historical subjects, she argued, the Subaltern Studies school was placing itself in a subaltern position within historiography. Yet the very act of doing so, Spivak insisted, could be "reinscribed as a strategy for our times." Subaltern identities and consciousness will always remain slightly out of reach, resisting attempts to fit them into a linear narrative. But historians must persist in their efforts at recovering subaltern subjectivity, even though they know it is an ultimately impossible task. "It is a hard lesson to learn," Spivak concluded. "[B]ut not to learn it is merely to nominate elegant solutions to be correct theoretical practice." By continuing to explore the politically positive, liberating potential of subaltern histories, then, by marshaling semiotics and postmodern techniques for emancipatory purposes that they can never entirely meet, by persisting in these apparently impossible attempts at combination, the Subaltern Studies Group can continue to make its greatest and broadest contribution.[16]

Obviously, the authors in this group are not the only ones involved in such a project. And, as Hardiman's report and much of the work in the seven Subaltern Studies volumes I have seen makes clear, not all scholars associated with the group agree on what has been accomplished or what the best strategy for the future might be. Further, as is evident from the different emphases presented here and in Gyan Prakash's essay that is also a part of this *AHR Forum,* the same theorists and the same contradictions can be interpreted as leading to quite distinct prescriptions for the future. But in having developed, over more than a decade, a commitment to the attempted combination of postmodern method and radical politics, the Subaltern Studies Group has provided scholars who have similar concerns, especially in other parts of the "Third World," with an important model to discuss. And it is along these lines of discussion and debate that Subaltern methods have begun to be invoked and debated in Latin America.

To my knowledge, the first major public invocation of the Subaltern Studies Group among Latin Americanists occurred in the pages of the 1990 *Latin American Research Review.* In an influential review article on Latin American banditry, Gilbert Joseph

suggested that the project and methods provided by Ranajit Guha in volumes I and
II of Subaltern Studies might help the field move beyond a sterile debate over
whether bandits were socially motivated or simply complicit with the existing
order. In an attempt to move the field back toward subaltern agency, Joseph used
Guha's insights in "The Prose of Counter-Insurgency"—as well as the work of
James Scott and others on "everyday forms of peasant resistance"—to underscore
the problems of relying on documents provided by state agencies oriented toward
social control when assessing the motives and behavior of bandits and their sup-
porters. As an alternative, which he hoped would help recover as well as recast the
insights in E. J. Hobsbawm's original formulations, Joseph proposed a more flexible and multi-layered approach to rural unrest and protest that took into account
the interactions among many forms of resistance and put bandit studies firmly back
in the field of agrarian studies. He also suggested that historians take more seriously
the power relations that underwrote all the documents on which they based their
claims.[17]

Joseph struck a nerve, especially in Richard Slatta, who edited the volume on
Latin American bandits extensively discussed in the original review essay. Slatta had
a particularly sharp barb ready for anything that smacked of "Foucaultism or other
strains of poststructuralism. Serious philosophical differences divide the practitioners," he wrote. "The cacophony of conflicting discourses and competing projects
often is too abstract, rarified, and sectarian to help working historians. . . . Philosophers are still working on what Foucault means by *dispositif* and other concepts.
How, then, can practicing historians employ his ideas with any confidence?" In the
footnote to this statement, he also summarily disposed of Gramsci: "Similar problems face historians taking up Gramscian *hegemony*. The term suffers confusing 'slippage' at the hands of the master and his disciples."[18]

So Joseph's effort to link questions of textual analysis, subaltern agency, and
recent advances in agrarian history to the history of banditry received a slap on the
wrist from a "working historian" who found all the theories associated with Foucault and Gramsci to be too confusing and half-baked. In order to dismiss methodological criticisms associated with an overreliance on typology, an underemphasis
on social analysis, and an uncritical use of official records, Slatta invoked the twin
ghosts of poststructuralist and Gramscian slippage. Although the celebration of the
linguistic turn was never Joseph's purpose in the first place, it is interesting to note
that his attempt to use the dual purposes of Subaltern Studies to overcome a dead
end in Latin American bandit studies was answered by an attempt to collapse both
purposes into a morass of postmodern confusion.[19]

Not long after the debate on banditry, the Subaltern Studies Group was once
again invoked in the pages of the *Latin American Research Review*. In a review essay
on colonial and postcolonial discourse, Patricia Seed stated that, in the historical
field, "members of the subaltern studies movement have been the leaders of the
postcolonial discourse movement." Although Joseph's original article on banditry
had appeared in the same journal a year before, Seed did not demonstrate an aware-

ness of it, or of other recent discussions on politics, ethnicity, and the state that had begun to appear in various subfields of Latin American history. In works that spanned the geographical and temporal spectrum from the early colonial period to the twentieth century, historians had begun to show that all subaltern communities were internally differentiated and conflictual and that subalterns forged political unity or consensus in painfully contingent ways. Some scholars had also uncovered the multiple ways in which oppressed peoples had engaged and used state institutions and the law, demonstrating that the same strategy increased people's room to move and made impossible a frontal assault on the existing balance of power. Authors actively questioned more linear or top-down renditions of major transitions, such as the conquest, the abolition of slavery, or the Nicaraguan Revolution, engaging in dynamic debate with other historians over the importance of subaltern political struggles in these transitions. It was only by ignoring this literature that Seed was able to conclude that "historians have been relatively reluctant to consider any form of reflexivity or reflexive self-critique of their practices."[20]

Seed shared with Richard Slatta an impatience for what can be loosely termed resistance studies.

> [A]nthropologists' and historians' versions of what happened were usually tales of either heroic resistance in which natives dramatically defended their homelands or accounts of manipulative accommodation in which colonial goals were maneuvered to serve the interests of the native community or some combination of the two story lines. In the late 1980s, these tales of resistance and accommodation were being perceived increasingly as mechanical, homogenizing, and inadequate versions of the encounters between the colonizers and the colonized.

In contrast to Slatta, however, who warned against postmodern slippage, Seed saw poststructuralism as the answer. "As narratives of resistance and accommodation were losing credibility," she wrote, "a major new intellectual movement was emerging in association with thinkers loosely grouped as poststructuralists." But she also agreed with Slatta when she linked poststructuralism, the linguistic turn, and postcolonial discourse studies directly to Subaltern Studies, once again collapsing the linguistic and textual analysis methods of the school into their more political goals and purposes, neatly covering over their Gramscian genealogy.[21]

In a sense, it could not have been otherwise for her. Openly to discuss the Gramscian project of Subaltern Studies would have led back into a part of the resistance studies literature Seed had summarily dismissed. It would have necessitated a more careful reading and analysis of the last generation of historical studies on subaltern practices, culture, politics, and resistance in Latin America.[22] It would have made the panacea of the linguistic turn seems less complete and therefore less attractive. And it would have led back into the deep creative tension centrally present in the Subaltern Studies Group itself.

Here we encounter, to my mind, the gravest problem with the kind of conceptual and methodological borrowing that the application of Subaltern Studies to other parts of the world entails. In the process of the dialogue itself, either or both sides can be flattened out, simplified, misrepresented. If this occurs, the nuances, internal tensions, and contradictions—in short, the very stuff of which meaningful academic discussion is made—are pushed aside in favor of defining *the* correct way. Once this has been done, it is no longer necessary to understand what has gone before, since it has become entirely irrelevant.

Latin Americanists who rediscovered Marxism and its many varieties in the 1960s and 1970s also tended to fall into this methodological trap. Dismissing earlier traditions and works as irrelevant and passé, we often missed important clues concerning the explanatory power of ethnicity, race, family, ecology, and demography because our newly discovered theoretical correctness told us that it all came down to class and mode of production.[23] Besides, what better way to circumvent entire literatures, often prohibitive in size and overwhelming in detail and complexity, than by lumping them into categories that were no longer theoretically current?

Especially in today's academic world, with its notorious overproduction, such techniques of dismissal are especially attractive. They make it possible for scholars such as Patricia Seed to pretend that a single approach to an issue such as resistance and accommodation—in the African, Asian, and Latin American fields, for the colonial and postcolonial periods—dooms the entire project and makes it irrelevant. "Such tales of 'adaptation and response,'" Seed concluded in her response to a query by Rolena Adorno,

> relying on notions of oppositional identity as untouched, authentic, and unproblematically created, coincided well with the narratives that were being produced by the leaders of emergent postcolonial states as well as by those opposing the largely economic domination and occasional direct political domination of the United States in Central and South America. Often producing a political redemptive narrative based on liberation from an evil oppressor, such tales found congenial readerships not simply in Latin America but throughout current and former colonial worlds.

To back up these broad generalizations, Seed cited only James Scott's work on Indonesia and a single introductory work on Latin American popular culture.[24]

One is left to wonder, for example, how it is possible to lump together questions of economic dependency with issues of nationalist redemption throughout the Third World. True, in the Latin American region, where political independence had been gained long before, questions of economic dependency were central to newly developmentalist policy makers interested in limiting the economic influence of the United States after World War II. In Africa, by contrast—as Frederick Cooper makes abundantly clear in his chapter in this volume—the dependency literature was used to counteract celebratory nationalisms and to question the value of redemptive political liberation. The interconnections between national liberation and economic autonomy or development, moreover, varied greatly from socialist to nonsocialist states, no matter what part of the Third World they inhabited.[25]

Turning back to Latin America, the existing historiography simply does not fit Seed's generalization. As Adorno has pointed out for the colonial Andes, issues of complicity, adaptation, collaboration, and resistance have been systematically articulated in complex ways by historians since the early to mid-1980s. Even in the early 1970s, with Karen Spalding's groundbreaking articles on Andean ethnic leaders (*kurakas*) as both protective of their communities and complicit with the colonial power structure, "oppositional identity" could no longer be seen as "untouched, authentic, and unproblematically created." Work on agrarian history and rural rebellions in Mexico, whether for the colonial period, the nineteenth century, or the Mexican Revolution of 1910, has also taken on questions of political mediation and complex, cross-cutting alliances that muddled questions of resistance and complicity, and has done so since the early 1980s. Finally, historians of slavery and the African diaspora have picked up on cues from historically minded anthropologists such as Sidney Mintz or Richard Price, producing multifaceted analyses of enslaved people's confrontations with and resistant adaptations to planter classes and state structures. These studies were not "political[ly] redemptive narrative[s] based on liberation from an evil oppressor." Instead, many explored the minute contradictions in power relations and in the alliances formed among the oppressed, tracing the various and sometimes internally conflictual strategies for coping developed by subaltern peoples.[26]

Although an in-depth treatment of all the available literature is beyond the scope and focus of this essay, let me cite a series of local confrontations with cases, people, and sources that challenged historians of Latin America, since the early 1980s, to begin struggling with many of the same issues that led, in India, to the founding of the Subaltern Studies school. Was there an alternative to deducing subaltern consciousness from theoretical categories? Was it possible to forge a politically committed intellectual project that respected the political cultures and political debates existing among subaltern groups? What could appropriately take the place of existing political and academic paradigms? In addition to the authors and studies already discussed above, Alberto Flores Galindo confronted the challenge of Sendero Luminoso in Peru by arguing for the centrality of Andean utopian thought to all emancipatory political projects. In Mexico, students of ethnic politics and indigenous communities told a very different history from that represented in the national or regional stories of revolutionary and postrevolutionary politics. In Argentina, Daniel James investigated Peronism from below and from the shop floor, and he found a very different phenomenon from the national-level histories of Juan Perón, whether laudatory or not. In these and other cases, analysts sought new ways to make sense of the multi-layered and contradictory nature of subaltern polities, cultures, and struggles. Whether or not they had discovered the postmodern turn, a confrontation with their work and its contradictions must be a crucial part of our attempt to move Latin American history forward self-reflexively.[27] Shortly after the

dust settled on the colonial and postcolonial discourse debate, the "Founding Statement" of the Latin American Subaltern Studies Group appeared in the special issue
of *boundary* 2 devoted to postmodernism in Latin America. Composed of fifteen
members—one historian, two anthropologists, and the rest literary critics—the group
began by citing Guha's familiar foundational pieces in volumes I and II of Subaltern
Studies in approvingly postmodern terms. Guha's original complex arguments, which
involved methodological as well as political calls to action, were summarized by the
group as a project for reading existing South Asian historiography "'in reverse' to
recover the cultural and political specificity of peasant insurrections." This project was
then defined as involving two techniques: "identifying the logic of the distortions in
the representation of the subaltern in official or elite culture; and uncovering the social
semiotics of the strategies and cultural practices of peasant insurgencies themselves."[28]
Once again, it seemed that Subaltern Studies was being reduced to half of its complexity: the methods and techniques of postmodernism.

But the Latin American Subaltern Studies Group went further and approached
Gilbert Joseph's earlier efforts to (re)prioritize subaltern agency. Among their
"founding concepts and strategies," the group included the need to call the nation
into question as a concept and as a boundary. Not only had recent world events
increasingly called the nation into question, they argued, but the nation itself was
an elite creation what "has obscured, *from the start,* the presence and reality of subaltern social subjects in Latin American history." In addition, wrote the group, the
subaltern was a "mutating, migrating subject" whose identity was varied and situ-
ational. It was necessary, therefore, to move beyond the privileging of particular
subaltern groups—workers, peasants, men—"to access the vast (and mobile) array
of the masses."[29]

So far so good, but what strategies and methods did the group propose in order
to bring their project to fruition? Here, the picture got a little sketchy. "To represent subalternity in Latin America, in whatever form it takes wherever it appears
. . . requires us to explore the margins of the state." "[R]etaining a focus on the
intelligentsia and on its characteristic intellectual practices—centered on the cultivation of writing, science, and the like—leaves us in the space of historiographic
prejudice and 'not-seeing' that Guha identified in his studies of peasant insurgency." "Not to acknowledge the contribution of the people to their own history
manifests the poverty of historiography and points to crucial reasons for the failures
of national programs of 'popular' entitlement."[30] How do we get beyond statements of intent, beyond programmatic calls to action? We need the complexity on
both sides of the dialogue—in Subaltern Studies itself and in the fields of Latin
American history, politics, and anthropology.

It is perhaps not surprising, in this context, that Patricia Seed, the only historian
in the group, has specialized in colonial Mexico and colonial studies, while both
anthropologists are Central American specialists—Carol Smith on Guatemala and
Roger Lancaster on Nicaragua. The rest of the group's members are spread more
widely across the region—including people who work on the Andes, the Carib-

bean, and the southern cone[31]—and they confront the challenge of Subaltern Studies from literary criticism and textual analysis. This preferred method comes out clearly in the founding statement, in which, aside from the early citations to Guha and one later reference to Carlos Vilas's book on revolutionary Nicaragua, almost all the specificity of the essay revolves around artistic and literary movements.[32] No wonder there is a "poverty of historiography"! This is true not only on the Latin American side but also on the Subaltern Studies side. As a result, the transparency, the innovation, and the simplicity of the project are all overrepresented.

Missing, on both sides of the dialogue, is a sense of what happens once the attempt to "access the vast (and mobile) array of the masses" is under way. What sources provide such access? Through what particular analytic methods? If we wish to place the new information into a narrative structure, how do we decide which one to choose? These questions have both technical and political answers; and, sometimes, as the experience of the original Subaltern group has shown, there is a strong tension between technique and politics. If we wish to get beyond "the cultivation of writing, science, and the like," we may well find that we are squarely back in the terrain of the "resistance studies" and ethnographic practitioners so roundly castigated by postmodern critiques.

One alternative, practiced by most of the members of the Latin American Subaltern Studies Group and quite a few of the Indian Subaltern scholars, is to read existing documents "against the grain." This technique can provide useful and fascinating alternative interpretations of elite projects, tantalizing bits of evidence about the subversive presence of subaltern voices, new and gendered readings of classic texts, or visions of the counter-identities being elaborated by "peripheral" or "minority" intellectuals. Some Latin Americanist anthropologists, also inspired by this method, have moved away from field work and toward the analysis of travel writings, photographs, and the practices or writings of other anthropologists.[33] But, beyond a certain point, one must admit that, with this method, access to most subalterns—after all, the word is Gramscian to its very roots—remains elusive.

Do we continue down the road of seeking access to subaltern voices, and, if so, how? It is hard to return to the archive or the field after engaging in a postmodern critique of the transparency of the enterprise. If we are no longer looking for "truth" as irrefutable, clearly knowable information, what are we looking for? I believe we are looking to maintain the irresolvable tension that is at the center of the Subaltern Studies project: the tension between technique and political commitment, between a more narrowly postmodern literary interest in documents as "constructed texts" and the historian's disciplinary interest in reading documents as "windows," however foggy and imperfect, on people's lives. If we privilege textual criticism as technique, and declare this the answer to the quandaries we face in our intellectual work, we start down the road to what Hernán Vidal has called "technocratic literary criticism: the presumption that when a new analytic and interpretive approach is being introduced, the accumulation of similar efforts in the past is left superseded and nullified."[34] Yet if we privilege documents as repositories of information, forgetting or ignoring them as constructed texts, we return to the deduction of consciousness, culture, and socio-political practice from abstract, sometimes implicit categories that often masquerades as "objective history." Consequently, we are left with the tension, an irresolvable and fertile tension, that can continue to inspire and energize our work.

In an article in 1985 on the methods and problems of archival work, Gayatri Spivak commented on this tension and the need to maintain it. A literary critic by training, someone steeped in the writings of Jacques Derrida, among others, Spivak expressed her dismay at historians who had begun to privilege literary criticism. Although conscious of the limitations involved in any effort to retrieve the voice or identity of women and other subalterns through records constructed by patriarchal and colonial forces, Spivak had nevertheless become involved in tracing, through archival sources, the life of the Rani of Sirmur, an Indian woman of privileged status. Her experience had led her consciously to inhabit the contradiction: she wanted to touch the Rani's picture yet rejected any retrieval of the Rani as empirical information. In the resulting study, she admitted, theoretical colleagues would find "too much concern with 'historical realism' and too little with 'theory,'" while "custodians of Critical Thought" would find "the linguistic nihilism associated with deconstruction." But, in the end, suggested Spivak, there was no other way.[35]

Like Spivak, I, too, want to touch the pictures of the historical subjects I struggle to retrieve; yet, I, too, know that "there is no 'real Rani' to be found."[36] This is precisely the point. The contradictory attempt to "know" the past, to become acquainted with the human beings who made it, leads us through archival sources that refuse to yield clear pictures. But because the archives provide unique clues abut power relations, and about the human, moral, and philosophical quandaries faced by the people who produced them and by the people whose shadows inhabit them, we cannot afford to do without them. In my experience, it is the process itself that keeps us honest: getting one's hands dirty in the archival dust, one's shoes encrusted in the mud of field work; confronting the surprises, ambivalences, and unfair choices of daily life, both our own and those of our "subjects." However poignantly our search is conditioned by the understanding that we will never know for sure, occasionally, just for a moment, someone comes out of the shadows and walks next to us. When, in a flash of interactive dialogue, something is revealed; when, for a brief span, the curtain parts, and I am allowed a partial view of protagonists' motivations and internal conflicts—for me, those are the moments that make the quest worthwhile.

The archive and the field are constructed arenas in which power struggles—including those generated by our presence—help define and obscure the sources and information to which we have access. The nuance and variation in those power struggles are themselves unique forms of information. We experience and learn from them in contentious documents such as judicial records, military or local municipal archives; in the confrontation between different kinds of sources, both written and oral; in the debates we have with others, be they local intellectuals, historical figures, or political authorities; in the local conflicts we may observe, whether in present-day human relations or in the documents themselves. The contentiousness of these arenas provides us with clues we do not get from the analysis of published works alone, even though both kinds of sources are constructed texts. The processes of production and preservation of archival versus published sources are distinct. The social relations that accompany the reading of one or the other are also different. Understanding these differences, and confronting their consequences, forces us continually to rethink our assumptions.

Before I am accused of sneaking empiricism in through the back door, let me reemphasize that reclaiming the centrality of the archive and the field can no longer be done in isolation from textual analysis or literary sources. The existence of published primary sources and manuscript literary sources makes it impossible to establish an always clear dividing line between the two in any case. What I object to is the privileging of textual analysis and literary sources to the exclusion of archival sources and field work, as well as the tendency to assume that, because both are constructed texts, they can be substituted for each other. From a Subaltern Studies perspective, Inga Clendinnen's excellent monograph on the early post-conquest Yucatán, based entirely on published archival sources, makes especially clear the limitations of relying only on published documents.

Clendinnen's highly original analysis of the confrontation between the Maya and the Franciscan missionaries in sixteenth-century Yucatán offers us an extremely variegated and sophisticated reading of early colonial missionary documents and of the written sources left by Maya literati. She uses these materials to probe the political, religious, cultural, and moral implications of the crisis that ensued when, in 1562, Franciscan missionaries on the Yucatán peninsula discovered "idolatry" and human sacrifice continuing among "their" Indians. Clendinnen reads the texts provocatively to suggest that the Maya's enduring, culturally constructed need to gain access to "high knowledge" as a strategy for ensuring the continuity and safety of life encouraged the "blasphemous" use of only partially understood Christian symbols in Maya rituals of human sacrifice. The Franciscans interpreted this use as conscious, sarcastic betrayal and, cut to the very quick of their abnegated paternalism, reacted with violent physical rage.

On the basis of published archival and literary sources alone, therefore, Clendinnen provides us with an original interior reading of both the Spanish and Maya, dominant and subaltern, sides of the colonial encounter in the Yucatán. Given the nature of her sources, however, the balance in detail and interior complexity is of necessity skewed toward the dominant Spanish side. The section of the book dealing with the missionaries is twice as long as the section dealing with the Indians. Although the internal conflicts and dissensions among the missionaries are discussed in depth, the Maya are represented through their intellectuals and spokesmen as a seamless whole, with little sense offered of whether internal disagreements animated their strategies or responses in the face of conversion and exploitation.[37]

In some cases, of course, access to the complexity and dissension present within subaltern communities is impossible. Yet the fractures of presentation and preservation in the archive and field can provide, in ways that published collections cannot, potential openings for getting inside. That these openings may take us in uncomfortable new directions is clear from some of the work of the original Subaltern Studies Group. When Ranajit Guha published "Chandra's Death," for example, I read it first as a powerful answer to the criticisms advanced by some scholars that Subaltern Studies was not dealing well with gender or caste issues. Chandra, a Bagdi widow who got pregnant while living in the house of her dead husband's family, faced the choice between permanent exile and termination of a pregnancy deemed illegitimate in *samaj* law. Magaram, her lover, delivered the ultimatum to Chandra's female kin: either abortion or *bhek,* the forced removal from caste relations. With the help of the female kin, "an abortion demanded by a man speaking for all of the local patriarchy" is set up; yet, ultimately, the potion obtained from a local healer kills Chandra as well as the fetus.[38]

In his conclusion, Guha reflected on the implications of this experience for the women of Chandra's kin network. "It is this knowledge of man's bad faith which makes woman wiser about the limits of a solidarity that pretends to be neutral to gender," he wrote. "The rounded, unitary world of kinship can never be the same for her again. 'Soiled and humiliated' she has recourse to an *alternative solidarity*—a solidarity of women. Not an 'open revolt' armed with trumpet and banner, it is still a visible and loud enough protest in a society where initiative and voice is given to man alone." Nevertheless, as Guha stated in his final sentence, women's solidarity was both strong and limited. Limited, because "[t]hey could not defy the authority of the samaj to the extent of enabling a widow with a child born out of wedlock to live honourably in the local society." Strong, because they surrounded Chandra with the support she needed in order not to submit to *bhek,* in order to go through the abortion as "the only means available for them to defeat the truly cock-eyed morality which made the mother alone culpable for an illicit childbirth, threw her out of society and allowed the father to go scot-free."[39]

After empathetically recounting the incident and mourning the lack of additional alternatives for Bengali women, however, Guha took the discussion no further. One possible line of further reflection is provided by Upendra Baxi in a discussion of the role of the law in Subaltern Studies. What if Chandra's female kin had chosen to kill Chandra's lover instead? Not only would they have fallen afoul of *samaj* law, Baxi contends, they would also have been forced to deal directly with colonial law. Another kind of choice emerges: surveillance, discipline, punishment, yes, but by the community or by the colonial state? Does either provide any liberation for women?[40]

The question of whether colonial law—with its debates on *sati,* female infanticide, and the like—might have provided alternative spaces for women is an old and contentious one. As Lata Mani has recently pointed out, colonial debates on the status and welfare of women were never about women's rights but about which legal or patriarchal entity was to exercise authority over women. Analogous conflicts erupted in many parts of the colonial world: debates over veiling in the Islamic world, over female genital surgeries in parts of East and West Africa. In most of these cases, neither side was interested in greater equality or autonomy for women. To the contrary, as Mani contends in the case of *sati*: women were the "ground" rather than the subject of a debate over ethnic/religious authority and customary versus colonial law.[41]

Ultimately, the message seems to be that neither native/subaltern legal practices nor colonial legal practices were in and of themselves liberating to women. In a sense, women could only choose between systems of hierarchy, colonial or ethnic/communal. Occasionally, depending on the specific historical situation, the changes brought about by colonial rule gave some women greater access to education or other privileges or opened up new social or economic opportunities through the market or in urban centers. Sometimes, the fissure between systems of rule allowed some personal autonomy for women. But, in many cases, colonialism simply added a new and invasive kind of domination to the old, increasing the protective value of communal, ethnic, and kinship networks that were themselves organized around patriarchal principles.[42]

When reintegrated into broad questions of colonialism and resistance, a gendered analysis that begins at the local level puts subaltern choices and alternative practices in a sobering new light. "Every trace of the independent initiative on the part of subaltern groups should . . . be of incalculable value for the integral historian," Gramsci wrote.[43] Yet, as Guha's essay demonstrates, when those traces of independent initiative are systematically investigated and local power relations are taken into account, the solidarity and unity of the subaltern presence—of subaltern culture and thus of subaltern resistance—begins to come apart in our hands. If there is no subaltern unity, if half of the subaltern community is oppressed and silenced by the other half, if anticolonial heroism has as a subtext the partial coercion of subaltern women, what happens to our Gramscian quest?

The question of complicity, hierarchy, and surveillance within subaltern communities and subaltern cultures is a thorny one indeed, one that cries out for nuanced and sympathetic treatment. On one side, raising this question makes clear that no subaltern identity can be pure and transparent; most subalterns were both dominated and dominating subjects, depending on the circumstances or location in which we encounter them. A leader of a movement can become a collaborator or go home and beat up a wife or children; a collaborator can use power to protect a subaltern community or individual; or, as happened repeatedly in anticolonial rebellions, individuals who had profited personally from the power structure reneged on their earlier complicity and led major upheavals. On the other side, complicity or hierarchy does not make impossible, in any larger sense, the occasional, partial, contingent achievement of a measure of unity, collaboration, even solidarity. These ever-shifting lines of alliance or confrontation, then, are not deduced from specific, already existing subaltern identities or subject positions. They are constructed historically and politically, in struggle and in discourse.

To see both sides at the same time, to mark the heroism and the treachery, is most certainly a challenge. Baxi suggests that it can also be liberating, not only to subaltern subjects themselves but also to the scholars who follow their trails through the labyrinth of surviving documentation. Expanding on an essay by Shahid Amin that treats the figure of the "Approver"— "a rebel who has shifted his locus within the event from protagonist of rebellion to agent of counterinsurgency"[44]—Baxi imagines what Shikari, Amin's "Approver," might have said in response to Amin's definition of him. "I accept your condemnation of me," the imagined Shikari says. But, at the same time, Shikari points out that his testimony served to increase the number of acquittals and lower the number of death sentences. Of course his actions made him "an 'instrument' of colonial justice," Baxi's Shikari admits. "But surely you can read my act of reneging as an act of service to most of my ex-comrades as well, some of whom have just before their natural death, secured pensions as 'freedom fighters' despite the longevity, as you put it, of the imputation of criminality."[45] Reassuming an academic voice, Baxi argues that reneging did not make Shikari "any the less subaltern." And doesn't the project of Subaltern Studies involve rescuing "all subalterns from the categorization of criminal law"? If all the participants in the colonial legal system became, in a sense, its victims, must the subaltern historian also become one? "Would it be too much to ask of the subalternist historian," Baxi concludes, "that while she shows to the rest of the world how Shikari was a victim of the colonial law, she too, like sister Chandra, may be redeemed by *Subaltern Studies,* if not wholly, to some degree?"[46]

It is not clear, however, what this redemption would entail. Would subalternist historians be redeemed from their blindness in ascribing to subaltern subjects the identities already given them by the dominant power structure? Would subalternist historians be redeemed "to some degree" if they accepted the version of events and the discourse of morality constructed by one faction within subaltern society? Would complete redemption be the ability to question all constructed versions and to empathize with all subaltern groups, collaborationist, oppressive, or not? Finally, who gets to answer the question, "Are we *there* yet?"

One way out of this dilemma, which seems to be reflected in Guha's most recent work in Subaltern Studies, is to avoid it entirely by abandoning the local level and reclaiming more general and abstract ground. At the level of the whole social formation, where the main contradiction is still between colonialism and resistance, or collaborationist elites and "the people," it is still possible to gloss over hierarchies internal to the subaltern community. The discussion can remain at the level of the failure of capitalism or of liberalism in colonial formations, or at the level of the failure of a dependent nationalist elite truly to mobilize the masses. Hegemony, as a general and seamless concept, survives intact in this context: Guha defines it as "*a condition of Dominance (D), such that, in the organic composition of the latter, Persuasion (P) outweighs Coercion (C).*"[47] The promise of hegemony, tied in Gramsci's writings to the promise of the Jacobin party truly leading rather than dominating the masses, can remain pure, for it has yet to be attained. Indian nationalists sold out the masses, dominating rather than leading them, disciplining rather than mobilizing them.

In Guha's more recent essays, India (re)joins—along with Italy and Germany—the ranks of "not-France." Guha quotes approvingly Marx's analysis of the French Revolution: "The French bourgeoisie of 1789 never left its allies, the peasants, in the lurch. It knew that the abolition of feudalism in the countryside and the creation of a free, landowning peasant class was the basis of its rule." This is in direct contrast to the Indian bourgeoise, which sold out the masses "in its bid for hegemonic dominance." In so doing, Guha concludes, the Indian bourgeoisie "never arrived."[48]

An alternative answer to the challenge of local analysis lies in the deconstruction of subaltern cultures and communities and their rearticulation, as factionalized and complex wholes, to questions of regional, national, and international power relations. As I have recently argued, this alternative method does not make the concept of hegemony irrelevant or passé. Rather, it makes it more flexible and multilayered. In this context, hegemony is not only the greater presence of persuasion over domination in national-level political systems, it is also a similar balance in local and regional political relations. How particular societies constructed hegemonic political systems becomes less a question of the bourgeoisie, the proletariat, or an organic political party. It becomes instead a historical question, to be answered through the kind of complex and never definitive confrontation with sources that a combination of Gramsci and Foucault makes necessary.[49]

It is perhaps not surprising that, in Latin America, the first efforts to engage in this new kind of Gramsci/Foucault combination, inspired openly by the work of the original Subaltern Studies Group, has occurred for the case of modern Mexico. From the standpoint of critical intellectuals, the Mexican case shares a number of similarities with India. A twentieth-century upheaval overthrew the old order in both cases, creating a new balance of power in which the party that led the upheaval rendered itself as *the* representative of the masses. Attempts by new generations of intellectuals to question the status quo floundered on the combined obstacles of an orthodox left and a still powerful official party. Local level, empirical analysis inspired by linguistic and textual techniques led to a questioning of revolutionary myths and to the beginnings of a deconstruction of local and subaltern cultures.

A recent and especially relevant effort in this regard is the collection of essays edited by Gilbert Joseph and Daniel Nugent titled *Everyday Forms of State Formation*. The product of a conference on twentieth-century Mexico that brought Mexicanists and nonspecialists together to debate questions of the state, popular culture and popular resistance, hegemony, and cultural revolution, the volume examines the dynamic intersection between popular cultures and state formation, tracing the multiple interactions between national power holders and internally conflictual popular cultures and communities. Different voices speak in the pages of the text, but they carry on a spirited conversation and debate with each other. Several cite directly from Subaltern Studies or from Gramsci; some debate the usefulness of the term hegemony, and most, at the very least, question its solidity and longevity. In the empirical essays, authors delve deeply into case studies and establish dialogues between critical theory and the information they have gathered. All the articles, whether theoretical, empirical, or both, question the transparency of domination and of resistance to it.[50]

The combination of Gramsci and Foucault, as practiced by the original Subaltern Studies Group and some historians of Latin America, does not provide a single, utopian, and technocratic answer to the quandries we scholars face in the present. As the work of Subaltern Studies scholars and others makes clear, it is easy to privilege one tradition over the other and retire from the challenge of the contradiction between the two. The theoretical and methodological contradiction between Gramscian hegemonic politics and Foucauldian regimes of decentered power is great and can sometimes make research and analysis close to impossible. Moreover, as South Asianist scholars Rosalind O'Hanlon and David Washbrook argued in their recent exchange with historian Gyan Prakash, "It is simply very difficult to combine arguments concerning fundamental rights and possibilities for emancipation with a postmodernist refusal of any kind of unitary or systematizing perspective as to what these rights might be or what emancipation is from or into." But, as Prakash emphasizes in his answer, the difficulty of this combination does not justify a mandate to choose between the two sides. Picking up on O'Hanlon and Washbrook's conclusion that he is trying "to ride two horses at once" and that one of the two—I assume the class analysis, Marxist one—"may not be a horse that brooks inconstant riders," Prakash extends the metaphor to exclaim, "As for me, I say, *let us hang on to two horses, inconstantly.*"[51]

An exploration of the contradictions, tensions, and internal conflicts within the Subaltern project leads me one step further, partially into self-reflection. When traveling the territory between Foucault and Gramsci, I have been personally unable to ride the horse provided by Jacques Derrida. To be fair, much of the more militantly textual and postcolonial influence in Subaltern Studies—whether on the Spivak-associated wing of the original school or among the more literarily inclined of the Latin American group—leans in what seems to me to be a Derrida-influenced direction. Spivak herself makes clear, in the works I have cited in this essay, that a Derrida-derived focus on language and textual construction is not sufficient. But the tendency among many practitioners of the Derrida side with Subaltern approaches is to transform the category of the subaltern into what Prakash calls, in this essay, "less of a sociological category and more of a discursive effect."

Such a turn in the Subaltern literature—as both Prakash and I argue, in differing ways—is especially friendly to concepts such as postcolonial criticism. However, it is only one of four possible directions in which the original tension in the Subaltern Studies school could lead. The other three are: maintaining the tension no matter what but relying more on Foucault-inspired emphases on regimes of power and less on Derrida-derived methods of textual and linguistic deconstruction; moving back more exclusively toward Gramsci, which I think Guha's last essays suggest, but with the cost of losing part of the critical postmodern edge in the understanding of historical metanarrative; and an attempt to use discursive/textual/linguistic analytical techniques to analyze subaltern practices/debates/discourses themselves—insofar as we can have partial and foggy access to them—as contested and constructed arenas of struggle over power. I hope that one of the benefits and contributions of this collection of essays will be to demonstrate how all four directions exist in dynamic relationship and tension with each other and how they can be further developed through "South-South" dialogues.

The final option I mentioned, which in my mind is the most potentially productive, would combine the Derrida and Foucault sides of postmodern criticism and use them in the service of a Gramscian project. Yet perhaps it is also the most dangerous and improbable option, one that O'Hanlon and Washbrook might liken not to "riding two horses at once" but to the physically impossible stunt of riding several steeds at all times! But if we are willing to learn from the struggles of scholars who have gone before, I think we must admit that riding many horses may be the only way to negotiate the pitfalls of a postmodern and politically committed intellectual project. Indeed, in the present state of the world, subalterns in Latin America and elsewhere—as well as the scholars who research them, accompany them, learn from them, and argue with them—must of necessity become stunt riders. Otherwise, we do not ride at all.

NOTES

I wish to thank my co-participants in the *Forum,* Frederick Cooper and Gyan Prakash, who shared early drafts of their essays and helped me improve mine through dialogue with theirs. Steve J. Stern read several versions of the essay and, as usual, offered insightful criticism and collegial support.

1. As I will discuss in more detail below, the theoretical positions of the different scholars associated with Subaltern Studies—as well as the uses to which their work is being put among Latin Americanists—are conflictual and contradictory and have changed over time. Although I will analyze many of the Latin Americanist scholars citing Subaltern Studies more extensively below, the main authors I am referring to here are: Gilbert Joseph, "On the Trail of Latin American Bandits: A Reexamination of Peasant Resistance," *Latin American Research Review* (hereafter, *LARR*), 25 (1990): 7–53; Patricia Seed, "Colonial and Postcolonial Discourse," *LARR,* 26 (1991): 181–200; Latin American Subaltern Studies Group, "Founding Statement," *boundary 2,* 20 (Fall 1993), special issue on the Postmodern Debate in Latin America, 110–21; Florencia E. Mallon, "Dialogues among the Fragments: Retrospect and Prospect," in Frederick Cooper, Allen F. Isaacman, Florencia E. Mallon, William Roseberry, and Steve J. Stern, *Confronting Historical Paradigms: Peasants, Labor, and the Capitalist World System in Africa and Latin America* (Madison, Wis., 1993), 371–401; Mallon, *Peasant and Nation: The Making of Postcolonial Mexico and Peru* (Berkeley, Calif., 1994); Gilbert M. Joseph and Daniel Nugent, eds., *Everyday Forms of State Formation: Revolution and the Negotiation of*

Rule in Modern Mexico (Durham, N.C., 1994); Fernando Coronil, "Listening to the Subaltern: The Poetics of Neocolonial States," forthcoming, *Poetics Today,* 15 (1994); Julie Skurski
and Fernando Coronil, "Country and City in a Postcolonial Landscape: Double Discourse
and the Geo-Politics of Truth in Latin America," in *Views beyond the Border Country: Raymond Williams and Cultural Politics,* Dennis L. Dworkin and Leslie G. Roman, eds. (New
York, 1993), 231–59; Skurski and Coronil, "Dismembering and Remembering the Nation:
The Semantics of Political Violence in Venezuela," *Comparative Studies in Society and History,*
33 (April 1991): 288–337; Joanne Rappaport, "Fictive Foundations: National Romances
and Subaltern Ethnicity in Latin America, *History Workshop Journal,* 34 (Autumn 1992):
119–31.

    2. This is not to say that "South-South" dialogue has not occurred before. Examples
include the work of James C. Scott on Southeast Asia, especially *The Moral Economy of the
Peasant: Rebellion and Subsistence in Southeast Asia* (New Haven, Conn., 1976); and *Weapons
of the Weak: Everyday Forms of Peasant Resistance* (New Haven, 1985), and the field of peasant studies of which it formed a part; the field of slavery and African diaspora studies, which
has connected the histories and cultures of Afro-America to African and especially West
African cultures and histories; and the various literatures debating concepts such as dependency, world systems, and articulation of modes of production. Other examples of such
"South-South" dialogue are discussed and modeled in *Confronting Historical Paradigms.* But
the main point continues to be that Latin American history, as a field, has tended to connect
more readily to historical and theoretical traditions based in Europe. In this sense, of course,
it is quite similar to other historical fields, including those based in Europe or the United
States, which are indeed a great deal less conversant across the "South-North" divide than
are scholars who work on so-called Third World areas.

    3. The various sources for hesitancy in using poststructuralism and postmodernism in
Latin America are summarized by John Beverley and José Oviedo in their "Introduction,"
boundary 2, special issue on the Postmodernism Debate in Latin America, 1–17, quotations
on 7 and 7–8, respectively. With regard to the second quotation, it is especially interesting
to note that, directly following Beverley and Oviedo point out that Xavier Albó, a contributor to the issue, models these "new" relationships in his work with the Aymara people,
which, among other things, involves "writing radio soap opera scripts in Aymara *for* them"
(emphasis added). See also, in the same issue, Martín Hopenhayn, "Postmodernism and
Neoliberalism in Latin America," 93–109; Aníbal Quijano, "Modernity, Identity, and
Utopia in Latin America," 140–155; Hernán Vidal, "Postmodernism, Postleftism, Neo-
Avant-Gardism: The Case of Chile's *Revista de Crítica Cultural,*" 203–27.

    Pointed reflections around the limitations of "post" perspectives, whether postmodernism
or postcolonialism, can be found in Mallon, "Dialogues among the Fragments"; Kwame
Anthony Appiah, "Is the Post- in Poststructuralism the Post- in Post-Colonial?" *Critical
Inquiry,* 17 (Winter 1991): 336–57; Fernando Coronil, "Can Postcoloniality Be Decolonized?
Imperial Banality and Postcolonial Power," *Public Culture: Bulletin of the Project for Transnational Cultural Studies,* 5 (Fall 1992): 89–108; Jorge Klor de Alva, "Colonialism and Post Colonialism as (Latin) American Mirages," *Colonial Latin American Review,* 1 (1992): 3–23. For a
further discussion of postcolonial as applied to Latin America, see below, this essay.

    4. For a discussion of post-orientalist history, see Gyan Prakash, "Writing Post-Orien-
talist Histories of the Third World: Perspectives from Indian Historiography," *Comparative
Studies in Society and History,* 32 (1990): 383–408; Rosalind O'Hanlon and David Washbrook, "After Orientalism: Culture, Criticism, and Politics in the Third World, *CSSH,* 34

(1992): 141–67; Prakash, "Can the 'Subaltern' Ride? A Reply to O'Hanlon and Wash-brook," *CSSH,* 34 (1992): 168–84. The original inspiration here belongs to Edward Said, *Orientalism* (New York, 1978).

5. Ranajit Guha, "Preface," *Subaltern Studies I,* as reprinted in *Selected Subaltern Studies,* Ranajit Guha and Gayatri Chakravorty Spivak, eds. (New York, 1988), 35–36; quotations on 35.

6. Antonio Gramsci, "Notes on Italian History," in *Selections from the Prison Notebooks,* Quintin Hoare and Geoffrey Nowell Smith, ed. and trans. (New York, 1971), 44–120. The six-point research project appears on 52.

7. Gramsci, "Notes on Italian History," esp. 55–106; quotation on 106. I am grateful for discussions with William Roseberry on the question of Gramsci and "Notes on Italian History," as well as on hegemony more broadly, that helped to focus and inspire my analysis. For a summary of Roseberry's views, see William Roseberry, "Hegemony and the Language of Contention," in Joseph and Nugent, *Everyday Forms of State Formation,* 355–66.

8. Ranajit Guha, "On Some Aspects of the Historiography of Colonial India," in *Subaltern Studies I,* reprinted in *Selected Subaltern Studies,* 37–44; quotation on 43, emphasis in the original.

9. On the ways in which the Indian case helped modify and expand Gramscian understandings of subalternity and peasant politics, see especially David Arnold, "Gramsci and Peasant Subalternity in India," *Journal of Peasant Studies* 11 (July 1984): 155–77.

10. Ranajit Guha, "The Prose of Counter-Insurgency," in *Subaltern Studies II,* reprinted in *Selected Subaltern Studies,* 45–86; quotation on 84.

11. C. A. Bayly, "Rallying around the Subaltern," *Journal of Peasant Studies,* 16 (October 1988): 110–20, quotation on 112–13.

12. Girish Mishra, "Elite-People Dichotomy: An Exaggerated View," *Indian Historical Review,* 10 (July 1983–January 1984): 133–38; quotations on 133, 135. For other critiques that began from Marxism, see Javeed Alam, "Peasantry, Politics and Historiography: Critique of New Trend in Relation to Marxism," *Social Scientist,* 11 (February 1983): 43–54; Sangeeta Singh, *et al.,* "Subaltern Studies II: A Review Article," *Social Scientist* 12 (October 1984): 3–41; Bayly, "Rallying around the Subaltern."

13. Gramsci, "Notes on Italian History," 55.

14. The tension of influences on the Subaltern Studies Group, which combined—in addition to Gramsci—Michel Foucault and Roland Barthes, structuralist anthropology, Russian structuralist literary criticism, and Althusserian Marxism, was pointed out relatively early by Gayatri Chakravorty Spivak in "Subaltern Studies: Deconstructing Historiography," *Subaltern Studies IV* (Delhi, 1985), rev. version printed in *Selected Subaltern Studies,* 3–32. Another important discussion around questions of the unitary subject in Subaltern Studies appeared in Rosalind O'Hanlon, "Recovering the Subject: *Subaltern Studies* and Histories of Resistance in Colonial South Asia," *Modern Asian Studies,* 22 (1988): 189–224.

15. David Hardiman, "'Subaltern Studies' at Crossroads," *Economic and Political Weekly* (February 15, 1986); 288–90; quotations on 290.

16. Spivak, "Subaltern Studies: Deconstructing Historiography," reprinted in *Selected Subaltern Studies;* quotation on 16. For a similar point, see Prakash, "Can the 'Subaltern' Ride?"

17. Joseph, "On the Trail of Latin American Bandits," 7–53.

18. Richard W. Slatta, "Bandits and Rural Social History: A Comment on Joseph," *LARR,* 26 (1991): 145–51; quotations on 150 and 150 n. 19.

19. Joseph clarifies his position on the linguistic turn and reemphasizes his desire to reconnect bandit studies to agrarian history more generally in "'Resocializing' Latin American Banditry: A Reply," *LARR*, 26 (1991): 161–74.

20. Patricia Seed, "Colonial and Postcolonial Discourse," *LARR*, 26 (1991): 181–200; quotations on 193, 200. Some of the new reflections within Latin American history are the following. On the construction of the colonial state: Karen Spalding, *Huarochirí: An Andean Society under Inca and Spanish Rule* (Stanford, Calif., 1984); and Steve J. Stern, *Peru's Indian Peoples and the Challenge of Spanish Conquest: Huamanga to 1640*, 2d edn. (Madison, Wis., 1993). On the nature of slave emancipation and the role of African Americans in the formation of political culture: Walter Rodney, *A History of the Guyanese Working People, 1881–1905* (Baltimore, Md., 1981); and Rebecca J. Scott, *Slave Emancipation in Cuba: The Transition to Free Labor, 1860–1899* (Princeton, N.J., 1985). On the nature of Nicaraguan politics and the 1979 revolution: Jeffrey L. Gould, *To Lead as Equals: Rural Protest and Political Consciousness in Chinandega, Nicaragua, 1912–1979* (Chapel Hill, N.C., 1990). Other attempts to innovate in the understanding of rural and subaltern politics include: Catherine Legrand, *Frontier Expansion and Peasant Protest in Colombia, 1850–1936* (Albuquerque, N. Mex., 1986); Florencia E. Mallon, "Peasants and State Formation in Nineteenth-Century Mexico: Morelos, 1848–1858," *Political Power and Social Theory*, 7 (1988): 1–54; and Steve J. Stern, ed., *Resistance, Rebellion and Consciousness in the Andean Peasant World: 18th to 20th Centuries* (Madison, 1987).

21. Seed, "Colonial and Postcolonial Discourse," esp. 182–83, 192–93; quotations on 182.

22. Rolena Adorno pointed to this superficiality for the case of the Andean colonial literature in her response to Seed. See Adorno, "Reconsidering Colonial Discourse for Sixteenth- and Seventeenth-Century Spanish America," *LARR*, 28 (1993): 135–45, esp. 136–37. Similar arguments could be made in the cases of the nineteenth and twentieth-century Andes, Mexico, Brazil, and Cuba. Some initial references, in addition to *Radical History Review*, 27, the issue on colonialism and resistance (1983), can be found herein, notes 20 and 26. See also below for a systematic examination of a few of the sources in this literature.

23. For critiques, see Mallon, "Dialogues among the Fragments"; and William Roseberry, "Beyond the Agrarian Question in Latin America," in *Confronting Historical Paradigms*, 318–68.

24. Patricia Seed, "More Colonial and Postcolonial Discourses," *LARR*, 26 (1993): 146–52; quotation and footnote on 149. This level of broad and lightly substantiated generalization is not, however, typical of all Seed's work on colonialism. See "Taking Possession and Reading Texts: Establishing the Authority of Overseas Empires," *William and Mary Quarterly*, 49 (April 1992): 183–209, where she does a fine-grained comparative analysis of early Spanish and British colonialism in the Americas.

25. Similar problems occur with the too facile use of such terms as postcolonial without proper context or historical framing. See Coronil, "Can Postcoloniality Be Decolonized?"; and Klor de Alva, "Colonialism and Post Colonialism," for critiques.

26. Karen Spalding, "*Kurakas* and Commerce: A Chapter in the Evolution of Andean Society," *Hispanic American Historical Review*, 53 (November 1973): 581–99; Spalding, "Social Climbers: Changing Patterns of Mobility among the Indians of Colonial Peru," *Hispanic American Historical Review*, 50 (November 1970): 645–64. On the Andes, see also, in addition to the sources listed in note 19, Brooke Larson, *Colonialism and Agrarian Transformation in Bolivia: Cochabamba, 1550–1900* (Princeton, N.J., 1988); Forencia E. Mallon, *The*

Defense of Community in Peru's Central Highlands: Peasant Struggle and Capitalist Transition, 1860–1940 (Princeton, 1983); Stern, *Peru's Indian Peoples and the Challenge of Spanish Conquest.* On Mexico, see, for example, David A. Brading, ed., *Caudillo and Peasant in the Mexican Revolution* (Cambridge, 1980); Marcello Carmagnani, "Local Governments and Ethnic Governments in Oaxaca," in Karen Spalding, ed., *Essays in the Political, Economic, and Social History of Colonial Latin America* (Newark, Del., 1982), 107–24; Carmagnani, *El regreso de los dioses: El proceso de reconstitución de la identidad étnica en Oaxaca, siglos XVII y XVIII* (Mexico City, 1988); Nancy M. Farriss, *Maya Society under Colonial Rule: The Collective Enterprise of Survival* (Princeton, 1984); Antonio García de León, *Resistencia y utopía,* 2 vols. (Mexico City, 1985); Gilbert M. Joseph, *Revolution from Without: Yucatán, Mexico, and the United States, 1880–1924,* rev. edn. (Durham, N.C., 1988); Friedrich Katz, ed., *Riot, Rebellion, and Revolution: Rural Social Conflict in Mexico* (Princeton, 1988); Mallon, "Peasants and State Formation"; Cheryl English Martin, "Haciendas and Villages in Late Colonial Morelos," *Hispanic American Historical Review,* 62 (February 1982): 19–48; Ilene V. O'Malley, *The Myth of the Revolution: Hero Cults and the Institutionalization of the Mexican State, 1920–1940* (Westport, Conn., 1986).

On slavery and African diaspora studies, see C. L. R. James, *The Black Jacobins: Toussaint L'Ouverture and the San Domingo Revolution,* 2d edn., rev. (New York, 1963); Verena Martínez-Alier, *Marriage, Class and Colour in Nineteenth-Century Cuba: A Study of Racial Attitudes and Sexual Values in a Slave Society,* 2d edn. (New York, 1989); Sidney W. Mintz and Richard Price, *An Anthropological Approach to the Afro-American Past: A Caribbean Perspective* (Philadelphia, 1976); Richard Price, *First-time: The Historical Vision of an Afro-American People* (Baltimore, Md., 1983); Walter Rodney, *A History of the Guyanese Working People, 1881–1905* (Baltimore, 1981); Stanley J. Stein, *Vassouras: A Brazilian Coffee County, 1850–1900,* 2d edn. (Princeton, 1985).

27. Alberto Flores Galindo, *Buscando un inca: Identidad y utopía en los Andes* (Havana, 1986); Carmagnani, "Local Governments and Ethnic Goverments"; and *El regreso de los dioses*: García de León, *Resistencia y utopía*; Daniel James, *Resistance and Integration: Peronism and the Argentine Working Class, 1946–1976* (Cambridge, 1988).

28. "Founding Statement," 110–21; discussions of Guha on 110–11, quotations on 111. The founding members, listed on page 237 of the issue, were: Robert Carr, Ileana Rodríguez, Patricia Seed, Javier Sanjinés, John Beverley, José Mazzotti, José Rabasa, Roger Lancaster, Robert Conn, Julio Ramos, María Milagros López, Carol Smith, Clara Lomas, Norma Alarcón, and Monica Szurmuk.

29. "Founding Statement," 117–21; quotations on 118, 121.

30. "Founding Statement," quotations on 119, 120, 119.

31. Of the fifteen members of the group, I was able to identify the disciplines of, and find works by, twelve of them. Of these twelve, nine were literary critics. In addition to her work as one of the forces in Chicana feminism and literary criticism, Norma Alarcón produced a dissertation in 1983 titled "Rosario Castellanos' Feminist Poetics: Against the Sacrificial Contract," and a later book on Castellanos, who is today considered one of Mexico's premier twentieth-century feminist writers. John Beverley co-edited the special issue of *boundary 2* and has also published on Spanish and Latin American literature more broadly, including two books dealing with Central America. A literary critic of Caribbean origin, Robert Carr is working on a book on black nationalism and has published an article dealing with testimonial literature and transnational feminisms that focuses on the testimony of Guatemalan activist Rigoberta Menchú. Roger Lancaster is an anthropologist who has pub-

lished two books based on oral history in Nicaragua; he is also known for groundbreaking work on gender, sexuality, and sexual orientation in contemporary Nicaragua. Clara Lomas is the author of a 1985 dissertation on three novels by Peruvian novelist Mario Vargas Llosa. José Rabasa has published on early colonial Latin American literature and on issues of conquest and mapping. Julio Ramos's speciality is nineteenth-century literature, especially the work of José Martí, around whom he organized his 1989 book *Desencuentros de la modernidad en América Latina*; he has also published on literature concerning "the other," both for Argentina and Cuba. An active force in the University of Minnesota's Ideologies and Literature group, Ileana Rodríguez co-edited a 1983 conference volume called *Process of Unity in Caribbean Society* and has also published on Nicaragua. Javier Sanjinés works on Bolivian literature, especially on the effect of the 1952 revolution on Bolivian fiction. In addition to her work already discussed extensively in this essay, Patricia Seed is the author of several articles on class and race in colonial Mexico and of a book concerning marriage choices and the Catholic church. Carol Smith's anthropological work on Guatemala has included important rethinking of the relationship between indigenous peoples and the national state. Monica Szurmuk is the author of articles on Rosario Castellanos and Reina Roffe.

32. "Founding Statement."

33. See, for example, Deborah Poole, "A One-Eyed Gaze: Gender in 19th Century Illustration of Peru," *Dialectical Anthropology*, 13 (1988): 333–64; and "Figueroa Aznar and the Cusco *Indigenistas*: Photography and Modernism in Early Twentieth Century Peru," *Representations*, 38 (Spring 1992): 39–75; Paul Sullivan, *Unfinished Conversations: Mayas and Foreigners between Two Wars* (New York, 1989).

34. Hernán Vidal, "The Concept of Colonial and Postcolonial Discourse: A Perspective from Literary Criticism," *LARR*, 26 (1993): 113–19; quotation on 117.

35. Gayatri Chakravorty Spivak, "The Rani of Sirmur: An Essay in Reading the Archives," *History and Theory*, 24 (1985): 247–72, see esp. 249, 271–72.

36. Spivak, "Rani of Sirmur," 271.

37. Inga Clendinnen, *Ambivalent Conquests: Maya and Spaniard in Yucatán, 1517–1570* (Cambridge, 1987).

38. Ranajit Guha, "Chandra's Death," *Subaltern Studies V* (Delhi, 1986), 135–65; quotation on 163.

39. Guha, "Chandra's Death," quotations on 165, 161.

40. Upendra Baxi, "'The State's Emissary': The Place of Law in Subaltern Studies," *Subaltern Studies VII*, Partha Chatterjee and Gyanendra Pandey, eds. (Delhi, 1992), 247–64; esp. 256.

41. Lata Mani, "Contentious Traditions: The Debate on *Sati* in Colonial India," in Kumkum Sangari and Sudesh Vaid, eds., *Recasting Women: Essays in Indian Colonial History* (New Brunswick, N.J., 1990), 88–126. On the veil, see Leila Ahmed, *Women and Gender in Islam: Historical Roots of a Modern Debate* (New Haven, Conn., 1992). On female genital surgeries, see Stanlie James, "Shades of Othering: Reflections on Female Circumcision/Genital Mutilation," unpublished manuscript, 1994; Olayinka Koso-Thomas, *Circumcision of Women: A Strategy for Eradication* (London, 1985); Hanny Lightfoot-Klein, *Prisoners of Ritual: An Odyssey into Female Genital Circumcision in Africa* (New York, 1989); Alison T. Slack, "Female Circumcision: A Critical Appraisal," *Human Rights Quarterly*, 19 (1988); Robin Cerny Smith, "Female Circumcision: Bringing Women's Perspectives into the International Debate," *Southern California Law Review*, 65 (July 1992): 2449–504; Alice Walker and Pratibha Parmar, *Warrior Marks: Female Genital Mutilation and the Sexual Blinding of Women* (New York, 1993).

42. For examples of the complexities of the situation for higher status women, see the following essays in Sangari and Vaid, *Recasting Women:* Uma Chakravarti, "Whatever Happened to the Vedic *Dasi?* Orientalism, Nationalism and a Script for the Past," 27–87; Sumanta Banerjee, "Marginalization of Women's Popular Culture in Nineteenth Century Bengal," 127–79; Vir Bharat Talwar, "Feminist Consciousness in Women's Journals in Hindi: 1910–1920," 204–32; Susie Tharu, "Tracing Savitri's Pedigree: Victorian Racism and the Image of Women in Indo-Anglian Literature," 254–68. On questions of choice between hierarchies, and how this affects nationalist movements, see Partha Chatterjee, "The Nationalist Resolution of the Women's Question," *Recasting Women,* 233–53; and, in Andrew Parker, Mary Russo, Doris Sommer, and Patricia Yaeger, eds., *Nationalisms and Sexualities* (New York, 1992): Rhonda Cobham, "Misgendering the Nation: African Nationalist Fictions and Nuruddin Farah's *Maps,*" 42–59; Ketu H, Katrak, "Indian Nationalism, Gandhian 'Satyagraha,' and Represenations of Female Sexuality," 395–406; R. Radhakrishnan, "Nationalism, Gender, and the Narrative of Identity," 77–95.

43. Gramsci, "Notes on Italian History," 55.

44. Shahid Amin, "Approver's Testimony, Judicial Discourse: The Case of Chauri Chaura," *Subaltern Studies V* (Delhi, 1987), 166–202; quotation defining the Approver on 168.

45. Baxi, "'The State's Emissary,'" 247–64; quotations on 263.

46. Baxi, "'The State's Emissary,'" 264.

47. Ranajit Guha, "Dominance without Hegemony and Its Historiography," *Subaltern Studies VI* (Delhi, 1989), 210–309, quotation, 231; Guha, "Discipline and Mobilize," *Subaltern Studies VII,* 69–120.

48. Guha, "Dominance without Hegemony," 227; Guha, "Discipline and Mobilize," 119–20. Of course, the increasing certainty in French historical literature that the French bourgeoisie never arrived either—indeed, that "arriving" was and is itself an increasingly problematic concept—conveniently gets left out. This allows for a seamless reconstruction of the attraction of the original national-revolutionary project at a time when the project as a whole has been subject to growing criticism in literatures throughout the world.

49. Mallon, *Peasant and Nation.*

50. See, for example, Marjorie Becker, "Torching La Purísima, Dancing at the Altar: The Construction of Revolutionary Hegemony in Michoacán, 1934–1940," *Everyday Forms of State Formation,* 247–64; Jospeh, "Rethinking Mexican Revolutionary Mobilization: Yucatán's Seasons of Upheaval, 1909–1915," 135–69; Joseph and Nugent, "Popular Culture and State Formation in Revolutionary Mexico," 3–23; Florencia E. Mallon, "Reflections on the Ruins: Everyday Forms of State Formation in Nineteenth-Century Mexico," 69–106; Daniel Nugent and Ana María Alonso, "Multiple Selective Traditions in Agrarian Reform and Agrarian Struggle: Popular Culture and State Formation in the *Ejido* of Namiquipa," 209–46; Roseberry, "Hegemony and the Language of Contention"; Derek Sayer, "Everyday Forms of State Formation: Some Dissident Remarks on 'Hegemony,'" 367–77; James C. Scott, "Foreword," vii–xii. Becker, Joseph, Joseph and Nugent, and I also explicitly engage the Subaltern Studies school.

51. Prakash, "Writing Post-Orientalist Histories of the Third World," 383–408; Rosalind O'Hanlon and David Washbrook, "After Orientalism: Culture, Criticism, and Politics in the Third World," *Comparative Studies in Society and History,* 34 (1992): 141–67; Prakash, "Can the 'Subaltern' Ride?" quotations on 158, 164, 184.

PART 3

History at A(nother) Crossroads

9

Is World History Possible? An Inquiry

Roxann Prazniak

U.S. educational and academic circles in the last decade of the twentieth century have brought forth curricular discussions that bear striking resemblance to those of the decade following World War II. Strengthened by the outcome of two world wars, the United States moved with unprecedented political leverage in the 1950s into a central position in the world economy. Like all newly arrived economic powers, the United States sought a cultural legacy appropriate to its new position. In academia, this move was made in the effort to define a single survey course that all college freshmen could take as a common foundation for an educated citizenry— thus was born the western civilization course. Today, five decades later, the limited scope of western civilization courses is readily debated, often with an eye toward replacing this requirement with world history or global history. As the United States takes the lead in movements toward new levels of global integration, academicians, with the support of corporate and government funding agencies, meet for workshops and conferences to articulate the forces that are bringing world history and global history into contemporary consciousness and, on this basis, to define the structure and content of world history courses. Just as western civilization was very much a creation of universities in the United States, so the contemporary moves in world history are primarily a U.S. phenomenon.

This chapter is a review of the state of the field in world history writing and teaching. It asks: Is world history possible, even while recognizing that it is already a practice? In many cases, the implementation of world history courses has run ahead of the academy's ability to offer a conceptual framework for their structure and content. Offering a rich and complex terrain on which to integrate cultural history, environmental history, and issues of societal diversity, the possibilities of world history are abundant, often seeming too abundant and, therefore, confused. While many proceed to teach and write in this area, there is little questioning with regard to the disturbing issues of power relations that underlie approaches to world history. As William McNeill has noted, leading organizations within U.S. academic circles "are presently fumbling around in search of a more adequate conceptualization of human history as a whole."[1] In many discussions, including McNeill's own, "time will tell" best describes the answer offered to difficult questions about the methods, purpose, and consequences of a world history approach. Time alone will not address the problems that require moral courage, responsibility, and imagination.

The primary organizers of current discussions on world history and global history are the World History Association, the Globalization Project at the University of Chicago, and the Global History series out of Columbia University. Scholars inside and outside these circles attempt comparative studies, world-systems analysis, and global contextualization in an effort to refigure our understanding of "human history as a whole."[2] High school and college teachers encourage students to think of the world's historical influences on their own family trees or the history of the oceans as a way to expand awareness to global dynamics. Proponents of world history recently helped save the World History Program at Northeastern University, which offers doctoral training in this area of study.[3] Through its myriad manifestations, the discourse on world history generates a range of assumptions that inform the present transition and consequently shape the future discourse. The purpose of this chapter is to reflect on the historical processes and their representations that might define a world or global history and to suggest that a genuine, fully evolved approach to world history is possible only if it is based in a critique of societal repressions and the possibilities that critique reveals.

WESTERN CIVILIZATION: U.S. DEMOCRACY IN THE ATLANTIC WORLD CONTEXT

Although now finding itself pushed out of the limelight, the western civilization course was the first post–World War II college course to construct a worldview for U.S. students and to give them a sense of place and direction in the international setting. Prior to World War I, English history had been the focus of European studies, and English institutions were examined as the origins of U.S. political history. History at the time was conceptualized primarily around national political developments. After World War I, when the United States emerged for the first time in its history as a creditor nation to England and France, academic emphases shifted. The distinctiveness of U.S. history became the new focus. Ties between U.S. and European histories were significantly underplayed. A third shift followed the second world war, when Western Europe once again lay in ruins, and the United States and the Soviet Union emerged as the only two world powers. With the advent of the Cold War, political democracy became the principal signifier of U.S. national identity in world affairs. In this global context, academicians at prestigious U.S. universities offered western civilization courses as a way for students to understand how the United States had come to be the legitimate heir of the European democratic tradition. From its origins in classical Greece through the Renaissance,

Reformation, and Enlightenment to the modern era, this steady movement toward democratic ideals, so the story went, pushed the United States to carry on the best of Europe's past.

In his study of the U.S. historical profession, Peter Novick writes that "in both its remote and immediate origins, 'Western civ' was a war baby."[4] Although, as Novick points out, such a course was first taught at Columbia University immediately after World War I, it was not until after World War II that western civilization courses became widespread. The Columbia course, titled Contemporary Civilization, was, as McNeill has noted, "an offspring of the World War I emergency course for soldiers, to teach them what it was they were going across the ocean to defend."[5] In the interwar years, the University of Chicago created a humanities course that linked history, literature, art, and music. Harvard's General Education Committee in 1945 issued a report strongly encouraging the introduction of western civilization courses on all college campuses. Just as the Columbia course had been designed to teach students why the United States joined in the first world war effort in Europe against the Germans, so the Harvard rationale for the new western civ course was the need to explain "why we fight" totalitarianism in the post-World War II period and to create a history of a free society that could be a "common learning" and basis for national unity.[6] The Rockefeller Foundation and Carnegie Corporation made funds available for many of these academic projects, including newly established area studies programs. Of particular interest to these granting agencies were studies cast in a framework of free world versus totalitarian societies.[7] In the aftermath of World War II, the point had to be made that not all who claimed the western legacy were democratic. There were different historical paths from classical Greece to the present and only some led to modern democracy. As the 1997 Ford Foundation White Paper on The Globalization Project at the University of Chicago points out, western civilization courses were designed to historicize and add temporal dimension to what had previously been taught as timeless values and truths in the classical tradition.[8]

Lest this should begin to sound too much like a conspiracy to use educational institutions for political purposes, in fact, the experience of the interwar and post-World War II years primarily illustrates the high levels of coordination among national, corporate, military, and academic interests that can be achieved without formal central planning mechanisms. The appearance of ideological control was of concern to those who participated in this process.

> The authors of the Harvard report, in proposing a course called "Western Thought and Institutions," noted that they had "considered the possibility of suggesting as a title for such a course 'The Evolution of Free Society,'" but that title, they explained, "carries with it implications of indoctrination which would be unacceptable to many."[9]

Pendleton Herring, president-elect of the Social Science Research Council in 1948, recommended that historians stress contrasts between the Soviet Union and the United States. In his words, the work of the historian was to "clear the contemporary minds for the tasks immediately ahead."[10] Noting that even though many of the western civilization courses designed to fulfill this explicit mission eventually evolved in other directions, Novick argues with abundant evidence that the measure of ideological control was significant. Projects that fit Herring's model were more likely to be funded, and scholars were informed that findings contrary to this political program might not be suitable for publication. One of the most poignant examples of this was the case of Merle Curti, who, in doing research on Radio Free Europe, discovered that, contrary to popular view, Radio Free Europe had received massive amounts of secret government funding. When it came time to put pen to paper for publication, Curti heeded the words of Conyers Read, then president of the American Historical Association, who in an address warned that "not everything which takes place in the laboratory is appropriate for broadcast on the street corners."[11] In a cold war, words and publications were weapons, and how you used them determined whether you were a patriot or the enemy. Curti, who had earlier challenged Read for abandoning critical thought, eventually wrote in his own book that Radio Free Europe was "supported by voluntary contributions."[12] As Novick concludes, "It was one of the many examples of the dilemmas involved in simultaneously mobilizing the West for worldwide ideological struggle, while parading disinterested objectivity as one of the West's distinctive values and institutions."[13]

The Ford Foundation White Paper, which looks back on the western civilization courses as infused only with an "ideology of historicization," does not reflect on the political relations internal to the past discussions of western civilization or the current discussions on world and global history.[14] Given the clear link between ideological pressure and academic self-censorship in the not so distant past, one would hope that those presently engaged in discussions on world history would not find it naive to suggest that political dynamics in the present ought to be consciously examined.

In the process of creating western civilization courses, U.S. academicians generated Eurocentrism to a much greater extent than Europeans ever did. Although some European academicians contributed to the discussion around the creation of western civilization courses in the 1950s, such courses were not introduced into European universities. The idea of one history that was a generic European story, let alone one that ended in the triumph of the United States, was anathema to the staunchly nationalistic French, English, Italians, Germans, and others. The western civilization course was, in effect, a world history course with the United States as the most recent bright light in the story of free society and the individual, distinct from the totalitarianism of first the Germans and then the Russians. Asia, Africa, Oceania, and Eastern Europe were defined in relationship to this central narrative of human social development, whether they were marginalized in that narrative, introduced as counter examples, or relegated to other areas for separate study.

WESTERN CIVILIZATION TO WORLD HISTORY

World history discussions in the United States have had their own unique origins in the particulars of U.S. history, but U.S. circles were far from the originators of the discourse. Outside Europe and the United States, world history has taken many forms. To some extent a world vision informs all human communities. Premodern written histories in India, China, Russia, Africa, and Central Asia organize the past primarily either as chronicle of state events or precedents for political and social guidance. A tradition of world-history writing in modern Europe, from Giambattista Vico to Karl Marx and Arnold Toynbee, sought to understand patterns of civilizations, in the world as they knew it, and the unique place of European history in that array. Once the United States claimed that mantle of uniqueness, it became the raison d'être of the western civilization course first and U.S. versions of world history second. On both sides of the Atlantic, Raymond Grew notes, world history in general can be seen as

> a natural product of modern ideas and experience, including the impact of imperialism (and the need to explain, justify, or criticize it); the related spread of capitalism and commerce (understood as both the product of history and also an engine of change); and the fascination with technology, which stimulated attempts to predict the future in visions both utopian and nightmarish. . . . The world such historians wrote about was European and North American, but the outcomes they predicted were global.[15]

As these forces of modernity continued to evolve, world history shaped by the U.S. experience took on its own nuances. Whereas world history of the nineteenth- and early–twentieth-century variety in Europe was characterized by a more homogeneous approach to groups and cultures and greater pessimism about modernity, world history as it progresses in the United States takes on an optimism and a penchant for diversity. It is no longer possible to speak only of great traditions and great men, as did the earlier articulations of world history. This greater inclusiveness speaks to a greater objectivity while at the same time making conceptual efforts more complex and vulnerable to moral fatigue. Even with such inclusiveness, does a world history funneled primarily through events originating in the nineteenth- and twentieth-century Euro-U.S. sphere provide sufficient clues about current dilemmas? So much that has faded or been lost through the impact of industrial technology may be fundamental to our understanding of the present and choices for the future.

World history, while not new, has entered a new and perhaps more globally conscious stage. For all of its complex incarnations, from ancient and medieval to modern historical renderings of the human place in the world, the most recent efforts to make our world comprehensible come at a time when humanity is more economically interconnected and yet self-consciously diverse than ever before. Difficult as it is for small communities to circumscribe their universe and organize around agreed-to social values and moral judgments, the possibility or even desirability of doing this in today's world is highly problematic. If efforts to write world history, even with the best of intentions, become little more than a nation-building process writ on a transnational scale, how will the "forgetting," which Ernest Renan and others since have noted as an essential feature to consensus building, apply to the imagined global community? Who will forget what? Will so many be willing to forget so much? Will the global economic engine be sufficient to bend national wills to one world historical narrative even if multiple points of view are allowed? What roles will those for whom national leadership does not speak play in the struggle to define the past and therefore the future? In a contemporary world that most world history writers describe as borderless, scores of groups from Ireland and Turkey, to Pakistan and Kosovo, fight major battles to protect divisions they consider very real and meaningful. To consider such issues simply a sign of backwardness is shortsighted, for they are consequences of the political present. A common story of humanity would need to examine the claims of dissenting groups in critical relationship to the dominant economic and technological innovations on which world history writing at present relies so heavily for its overarching framework.

World history teaching in the 1980s gained momentum in many respects by extending the original post-World War II project to introduce western civilization courses into the college curriculum. Times had changed and adjustments were required to maintain resonance with reality. Independence movements that were the consequences of colonial and imperialist ventures produced well-established nations that exercised their own claims to world memory. Within the United States, women and ethnic groups articulated challenges to national narratives in which they were excluded or marginalized. To address some of these circumstances, the American Historical Association held a joint meeting in 1982 with the U.S. Air Force Academy (USAFA) to discuss ways to improve world history teaching.[16] The USAFA had taught world history since the 1950s as a way of preparing its officers for foreign service. Those present remember this conference as electrifying, opening up a whole new area of academic research and teaching possibilities. Addressing the conference were such prominent historians as William McNeill and Philip Curtin. These historians, inspiring figures who in the 1970s had begun to challenge narrow, nationally based historical approaches with the insights of their macrohistorical studies, conjured up a project with radical potential that has yet to be realized and that often finds itself hijacked by inattention to issues of socioeconomic difference. Participants at the 1982 conference founded the World History Association that same year; the *World History Bulletin* was first published in 1983 and the *Journal of World History* followed in 1990. Regional, national, and international conferences regularly mark the success with which this effort has grown.

For practical reasons the USAFA moved directly to world history in the post-World War II period, creating a curriculum to which civilian academic interests found a link in the 1980s, when it seemed to many that western civilization courses had become problematic as representations of the world to which citizens should be educated. At the founding of the World History Association, Philip Curtin, then president of the American Historical Association, wrote that "not long ago world history and western civilization were synonymous," but now a new generation of scholars, many with specializations outside of Europe, were moving toward a more even-handed framework that departed in some ways from both area studies and an all-European approach.[17] Similarly, the current globalization project at the University of Chicago sees its Regional Worlds discussions as a "furthering and deepening of the historicization central to the Western Civilization course, and an equal furthering and deepening of the contextual and mutual understanding" among peoples of different societies.[18]

WORLD HISTORY VERSUS GLOBAL HISTORY

Participants in both the Chicago and the Columbia projects on global history mobilized their efforts in the mid-1990s in part to respond to some of the limitations they perceived in world history approaches. Recognizing the overlap between world history and global history, some have argued that there are also important distinctions between the two. Bruce Mazlish, a proponent of global history, defines the present stage in world-history writing as a continuing effort to transcend Eurocentrism and foster multiculturalism through greater inclusion of non-European voices from the past.[19] He finds this a valuable but limited goal that, in the end, is premised on the notion that a world perspective of human history is possible, a notion that global historians question. With a view toward modifying the world history project, Raymond Grew writes, "[T]he challenge of global history is to construct global perspectives." Grew's emphasis here is on a history that has multiple vantage points, a coexisting cluster of perspectives.[20] He contrasts this with world historians, old and new, who, in his view, basically attempt to discover a single perspective that he calls the "celestial perspective," modeled on the secularized theological view in western Europe and characteristic of nineteenth-century developments in European historiography.

The difference between world history and global history is to some extent a matter of degree, with both parties leaving the question of singular-versus-multiple perspectives more open than not at this point. World historians, as a group, unlike the global historians, may be more hopeful about eventually creating a thread through human history as compelling as the one constructed for western civilization, but any glance through the *Journal of World History* or world history conference proceedings indicates that approaches are at present all over the map, "fumbling" in a creative-chaos sense, perhaps. Participants in the Globalization Project at the University of Chicago speak of multiple geographies and multiple worlds in their proposal for an area-studies, regional-worlds approach. They suggest moving away from ideas of fixed civilizations and regions, seeing such concepts as, at best, heuristic devices for the study of global processes that yield patterns that are the result of our interests rather than the cause of our interests. This "constructivist" approach underlines the idea that histories are not facts but artifacts that come into focus and are always in the process of change relative to the "high-velocity, shape-shifting, fast-changing world in which we find ourselves."[21] There often seems little distinction between this and a multicultural approach in which different civilizational histories are sliced into sections of a world history volume. The Columbia Project on Asia in the core curriculum has produced three large volumes designed as teaching guides and source materials for representing Asian perspectives in the scheme of global history.[22] Each contains many interesting individual essays regarding Asian influences on the West and comparisons with the West. As a collection, however, these volumes do not come to grips with dialogues native to regions, both in the past and the present, that might challenge an emerging global framework. Both multiculturalism and post-modernism divert attention from the severe social and environmental problems embedded in the assumptions of a triumphant globalism.

The need to understand languages and social systems that are regionally based necessitates for both the world historian and the global historian a grounding in area studies as a foundation for detailing global processes. The World History Association, at the outset, sought to steer a course that would "keep the breadth of a world-historical perspective alongside the depth necessarily required for research in any particular field."[23] Ross Dunn, Kevin Reilly, McNeill, and others calling for world history immediately formed WHA ties with various area studies groups, including the African Studies Association and the Association for Asian Studies. Authors of the globalization project white paper at Chicago seek a new "architecture for area studies [that] is based on process geographies."[24] In this scenario, area studies remains a central focus of the globalization project efforts; at the same time, areas are no longer seen as having durable boundaries and enduring properties. Both also recognize that the areas as presently defined within U.S. academic circles may not match the way people of various regions would map their world. World historians attempt to overcome the fragmentation of the postmodern era through means as yet undiscovered, and global historians advise embracing fragmentation to transform it into a respect for unsynthesized multiplicity. Although the global perspective may appear to have greater space for critical perspectives to emerge, a self-reflective view of the power relations among which historians move is underdeveloped in both approaches.

In the search for overarching thematic structures with which to order representations of the past, both world historians and global historians are drawn to the twin poles of human rights and environmental issues. These are workable themes but only if handled critically, that is, by seriously considering the consequences of facts we find emotionally disturbing. Italo Calvino in his short story, "World Memory," creates a somewhat crazed historian who is charged, on the eve of the end of life on earth, with compiling a complete human history for transmission to outer galaxies. The historian has a deep need to suppress just one fact, his wife's betrayal of their marital bonds and his subsequent murder of her. This suppression leads him to reshape and eliminate other parts of the historical record. He comes to believe that the lie he has constructed is truer than the facts he has suppressed, because the lie is an expression of human passion, more fundamental than the accumulation of facts. In the end, he must also kill the person to whom he is telling his story.[25] Like Calvino's historian, the global or world historian chooses among the facts he will include and thereby excludes others that could serve as alternative starting points for reflection on the past and present. When there is no tomorrow, as in Calvino's literary sketch, the willful elimination of undesirable data may create interesting philosophical speculation, but when a future must be faced, the denial of stressful facts is debilitating.

Take one example from among the hard facts that do not fit our world story line of movement toward ever greater human fulfillment: it is often said that over-population in Third World countries is the leading problem of our times. In terms of use of world resources, however, it is the United States that is overpopulated, with 20 percent of the world's people using 80 percent of the world's natural resources. Each U.S. citizen equals sixteen persons in terms of impact on the world's environment, as compared with his Third World cousin. Who will make this a central narrative of the new world histories? To what extent will the perspective that structures Clive Ponting's *A Green History of the World: The Environment and the Collapse of Great Civilizations* become a fundamental organizing principle of our global story? Often included in the new world histories, environmental issues are at the same time pushed to the back, negating their power fundamentally to restructure our global narrative. With a "green" focus, great events and individuals of the past are often marginal to a story of how historically changing relationships to the natural environment have modified the life and death circumstances of all inhabitants.[26] Environmental history is one route by which we can begin to grasp sensed truths about our past and present that resonate both emotionally and factually. Work and leisure critically examined would provide a similar point of departure.[27]

BEYOND EUROCENTRISM

There is no doubt that the World History Association's first call to loosen the grip of Eurocentrism was an act of intellectual and scholarly liberation. Even more liberating would have been some reflection on how that grip was imposed to begin with, and how this understanding might factor into any new efforts to represent human history. At present, however, Eurocentrism is a false issue. Continued preoccupation with this problem masks an important shift that has taken place: Unlike the 1950s, when the transition to a western-civilization model was accompanied by cold war ideologies that confined intellectual inquiry, the present transition toward world or global history has a dynamic of almost unlimited comparative topics, decentered approaches, "shape shifting," and regional worlds strategies. This full sea of possibilities threatens to drown rather than simply suppress critical perspectives.

Best defined as ideology rather than geography, Eurocentrism deflects social realities that carry critical perspectives vital to full social analysis. Because of the daunting problem of selectivity, given an overwhelming amount of historical material and the claims of multiple groups, a common strategy in structuring world history texts is to accept an ideology of global economic and cultural integration under industrial capitalism as a primary organizing principal. Instead of giving equal focus to points of resistance and alternatives to the dominant Euro-U.S. narrative, world-history writing and teaching often offer a sense of diversity, an elaboration on patterns, without constructive critical reflection. This tends to be just as true for representations of European history in the world history story. Just as western civilization courses took one strain of themes—commercial individualism, legal rights, and political democracy—as their pivotal points, so U.S.-style world history continues to represent the past around the same themes. The Captain Swing raids in eighteenth-century England, the Chartist's view of the Opium War, the "isolationism" of the United States prior to World War I, and numerous other expressions of opposition to nation building in Europe and the United States, are world historical trends that challenge Eurocentrism. More than passing events that failed, dissenting social movements within the Euro-U.S. sphere underline the definition of Eurocentrism as ideology, not geography.

Initial efforts to structure mammoth amounts of material for world history textbooks were not cast very far from the western civilization model. Most world history texts juxtapose one civilization with another and then one national history alongside another. In this rearrangement, European history is decentered in some respects, but the themes of the European narrative still pervade the whole. European nations are no longer alone at the center of civilization but nationalism, as one theme from the European experience, still defines criteria for inclusion in these histories. The displacement of agricultural society, industrial urban growth, and capitalist economic relations are additional themes that set the standard for histories that could pose other questions and develop other themes. With issues and themes derived from the workings of European history, Eurocentrism is not transcended even when areas entirely outside of Europe are the focus of study.

To the extent that there is an international forum on these teaching issues, the *World History Bulletin* facilitates this discussion. Around the world, many world history courses are, it appears, national histories set in a world-history context. Curricula proposals for the teaching and practice of world history at Potchefstroom University in South Africa, for example, emphasize the "study of history of their country against the background of overseas events" and the introduction of students to "an understanding and appreciation of their heritage and that of other peoples and cultures."[28] World history in China today has moved from a Marxist framework that included China in a world pattern of development, to a curriculum in which China's national history gets the lion's share of coverage, separate from courses in world history that tell the story of the rise of the capitalist West. In a revealing statement, Dorothea Martin writes that "as world history in China becomes more reflective of the agenda of the reform-minded leadership in China, it begins to look more like world history elsewhere."[29] World history becomes the story of industrial capitalist integration with national variations. New Zealand proponents of world history argue that "a world history perspective can direct attention to these patterns of wider significance and thus enrich the national history."[30] Again, the placement of national events in a world context for the illumination of both defines the primary approach to world history. A final example from Romania stresses development of world history to show the Romanian people "as creators of an interesting civilization" and the "complex connections of the Romanian people with the history of the world."[31]

Conceptually similar to those just discussed, the relationship of U.S. history to world history has one significant difference. Rather than establishing its centrality in world or global history, U.S. world historians assume a universality to what they identify as their primary concerns. If ever a case could be made for ideology as superstructure rising to the occasion to reflect shifts in the economic substructure, the language of world history is surely one. "Things on the move" make up a major category for world history studies. These might be people, as in migrant labor, or water, seeds, and porcelain. With an emphasis on mobility and instability, the fragmentation of all phenomenon resonates with the view of history Karl Marx constructed to express the triumph of capitalism itself. He wrote:

> That which characterizes the bourgeois epoch in contradistinction to all others is a continuous transformation of production, a perpetual disturbance of social conditions, everlasting insecurity and movement. All stable and stereotyped relations with their attendant train of ancient and venerable prejudices and opinions, are swept away, and the newly formed becomes obsolete before it can petrify. All that has been regarded solid crumbles into fragments; all that was looked upon as holy, is profaned; at long last, people are compelled to gaze open-eyed at their position in life and their social relations.[32]

Does this "coincidence" of patterns between the global economy of capital and the architecture for new area studies/regional worlds suggest an insufficient critical perspective in current intellectual constructs? Where is the critical edge that challenges the injustices that give cohesion to the status quo? And finally, is education driven by ideological concerns acceptable under any condition? Is education for U.S. citizenship as it was conceived in the cold war era so different from education for students in the "first great age of microchip internationalism"?[33]

COMPARATIVE HISTORY AND WORLD SYSTEMS AS WORLD HISTORY

National narratives placed in the context of world developments, often narrowly defined as the spread of industrial capitalism, offer one widespread approach to world history teaching; others employ a comparative methodology in search of a promising strategy for world history. Philip Curtin, speaking in an interview in 1978, said of the Comparative World History project at the University of Wisconsin, Madison, that its informal motto had been: Study should be "interdisciplinary within the geographical area of specialization and inter-area within the discipline."[34] All study is comparative, in the sense that Benedict Anderson has discussed, but the explicit focus on a comparative approach has been an exciting and productive starting point for much of recent writing in the world history genre.[35] Richard Eaton, in an article on religious conversion in modern India, argues for comparative history as a vantage point from which to "help free the profession from the sort of nationalist or civilizational straitjackets that have bedeviled so much of history writing in the past. To the comparativist, the topic, the problem, or the process is the focus of attention, not the place."[36] Eaton's article focuses on the interaction between incoming and indigenous religious frameworks and shows that both parties to the conversion process experience change, the results of the conversion effort being shaped to a large extent by what the native culture brings to the encounter. It is the interactive aspect of the comparative approach that can open new space around topics, space in which the integrity of each element is valued as a critical resource in the human story. Comparative approaches have long been employed in historical analysis, but the present historical moment has brought forth a new concentration on comparative studies, suggesting one way to grasp processes beyond the patterns of state building that might help to conceptualize a world history.

The potential of comparative studies to challenge assumptions carried over from western civilization courses into world history is a crucial factor in moving toward a perspective that addresses a wider range of fundamental issues. Michiel Baud and Willem van Schendel, in their comparative history of borderlands, argue that "border regions have their own social dynamics and historical development," and, consequently, a world history viewed from the perspectives of the world's borderlands would pose some valuable but otherwise marginalized or unasked political and economic questions.[37] Peter Stearn places nationalism in a comparative context and in so doing opens even this concept to a fuller analysis.[38] The comparative approach is a good place from which to gather insight for the moral imagination required to lift historical analysis to a new plateau but does not in itself provide a conceptual framework for a single, coherent new story of humanity, if such is the goal.

From an implicit comparative vantage point, the writings of Immanuel Wallerstein and Fernand Braudel have inspired much work that focuses on interregional dynamics at work in the world economy and/or cultural spheres. Wallerstein's proposal—that there were no world economies before the sixteenth century—although since challenged, set the stage for examining history as structured by the dynamics of international trade and the division of labor that characterized the growth of capitalism. Braudel's work on civilization and capitalism from the fifteenth to the eighteenth centuries gave focus to the material aspects of culture that accompanied this world system in economics. Many have since argued that world economies, to be distinguished from empires, predated the European world system. Philip Curtin's *Cross-Cultural Trade in World History,* Janet Abu-Lughod's *Before European Hegemony,* Jerry Bentley's *Old World Encounters: Cross-Cultural Contacts and Exchange in Pre-Modern Times,* and *The World System: From Five Hundred Years to Five Thousand,* edited by Andre Gunder Frank and Barry Gills, are a few of the works that have argued that complex interregional trade networks centered outside of Europe and predating the fifteenth century flourished as world systems.[39] Frank's most recent work, *Reorient China,* argues not only that world economies structured history long before the sixteenth century but that European dominance has only been a reality since the late eighteenth and early nineteenth centuries. While his argument that China was the engine of the global economy for all but the last one hundred or so years provides some space for thinking about alternatives to European style modernity, his focus on global economic cycles does not raise the question of what China's alternative economic history might suggest by way of critique of the present. The political and social dynamics of a highly developed but not unchecked economic sector, such as that sustained in China over centuries, are valuable evidence of alternative past social formations. Not to be applied wholesale to current problems, China's historically shaped range of social possibilities offers ways to think about the costs and consequences of contemporary policies, both within and outside of China. Instead, in Frank's account, China uncritically becomes a maker of and heir to the transnational global present.

CONCLUSIONS

The possibilities of comparative history offer an array of themes and topics from which teachers and writers of world history can pick and choose, mix and match. Process-centered courses that question the categories in which we think offer ways to unfold the meaning of contemporary events and historicize them. Each approach still dances around questions of purpose and intent, and ultimately, I think, avoids moral choices that get made in the process of writing and living history that we are not confident about making an explicit part of our mainstream academic dialogue. Will global history courses really make the consistent effort to include in their course discussions activists from Third World countries, rural areas, and the urban centers of poverty, or will this be considered nonacademic, irrelevant to the dynamism of the times? The brave soul who got one line in the Ford Foundation White Paper—reminding us that peasants as agriculturists and taxpayers have been and still are the backbone of most civilizations, countries, regions, and worlds—will lose even that one line in the critical dialogue the paper proposes if the peasants and their advocates are not a major part of the Internet, lecture, and speaker component of the global history course. How much critical potential can these courses incorporate? Will the inclusion of voices from Taiwan, South Asia, and South

Africa provide the appearance of diversity but basically be a dialogue within the same social class, a global elite educated to a kaleidoscope of "process" geographies? In his reflections on the contradictory "ideas" of the Pacific Rim regions as both frontiers for capitalism and escapes from capitalism, Arif Dirlik argues for recognition of "diverse localisms that do not deny but take as their point of departure the common concerns of the globalized world."[40] Such common concerns would include labor issues for migrant workers across global economic boundaries and the integrity of land-based communities, whether they are found in Chiapas, Australia, or South Dakota.

Oddly enough, the serious inclusion of dissent and localisms may render the task of finding a human story less cumbersome and overdetermined. The hunger for a constructive "story of humanity" is fueled by a genuine need as well as marketing designs.[41] There is a powerful sense that something is wrong in our world, that something needs explaining, that we need to make sense of how we got where we are and where we are going. The narratives of unlimited progress through science, the exaltation of unchallenged individualism accompanying the triumphal march of national democracies, no longer tell the story we feel we are living. A focused view of dissent in the face of these dominant narratives may also give greater meaning to diversity. If one accepts the admittedly linear notion that a story with a plot is essential for our growth, the story of global economic integration leaves too much out in terms of costs to humanity and obscures with a wealth of intriguing topics the critique essential to making sense of our present and providing meaning for a future that will be humane rather than posthuman.

Would we be as quick to sign up for world citizenship if Saudi Arabia, Japan, India, or Africa held the preponderant position in the world? There is an abiding faith, as William McNeill has expressed, that humanity is in for some difficult times ahead and that "a clear and vivid sense of the whole human past can help to soften future conflicts by making clear what we all share."[42] Yet who will set the standard for world citizenship? Who will structure the story of humanity? William Green, in an essay on periodizing world history, declares that 1492 would have been a global, watershed date even if the Chinese had been the ones to discover the Americas rather than the Europeans! After writing about an evolutionary mainstream (Western Europe) that had more enduring, universal, and influential values that he says consequently define the core of world history, Green pauses only briefly to wonder if a world history written from an Asian perspective would be substantially less materialistic.[43] Periodization in world history is still wedded to the western civilization categories.

Ashis Nandy, in a discussion of history's "forgotten doubles," suggests that the nineteenth-century European view of history itself works against efforts to find a moral and just direction in the global setting. He reminds us that the historical concepts of a nation-state system that are responsible for 110 million man-made violent deaths in the twentieth century alone does not have much claim to strategies for just and peaceful living.[44] India's historical epics, Nandy points out, are more likely to end with a sense of ambivalence over the passage of a great era than with victory or conquest suggesting the triumph of one way over another. "Traditional India not only lacks the Enlightenment's concept of history; it is doubtful that it finds objective, hard history a reliable, ethical, or reasonable way of constructing the past."[45] Pulitzer Prize-winning journalist Ellen Goodman has written about a cultural shift in the United States in which she sees a greater tolerance for ambivalence, different from fatigue and confusion.[46] Will greater ambivalence produce greater strategies for just and peaceful living? Ambivalence connotes deep regard for the profound dilemmas of life. It can also cultivate its own varieties of injustice and violence.

In the late 1960s, the Rockefeller Report on the Americas considered both liberation theologians in the Catholic Church and activist students on college campuses to be "vulnerable to subversive penetration." The report's recommendation was increased military assistance and spending for the sake of "Western Hemisphere Security."[47] The connections among these levels of politics do not have to be seamless to constitute an effective obstacle to creative solutions for our present dilemmas. In addition, if an intellectual solution could be found to the problems of writing a contemporary history for global awareness, the administrative and fiscal hurdles would be formidable before the results could be translated into educational norms. William McNeill has noted the particular "intellectual and administrative circumstances of the 1930s that contributed to the very rapid propagation of courses" structured by the western civilization model.[48] A corporate-supported world history could not be critical, and a critical world history would not be sufficiently funded.

In a 1927 essay, Walter Benjamin pondered the Soviet Union and Western Europe through a comparison of two cities, Moscow and Berlin, representing the socialist and capitalist systems as they were taking shape. He wrote that the matter was not which reality was better than the other or which had the greater potential. He was impressed with some of what he saw in Moscow that winter, but he was also critical. What he knew he had to decide in assessing the present world condition was "which reality is inwardly convergent with truth? Which truth is inwardly preparing to converge with the real? Only he who clearly understands these questions is 'objective.'"[49]

We have lost a sense of this kind of truth grounded in humane action and social responsibility. Perhaps it lies buried in realities beneath fragmented postmodern heaps. If there is any "celestial perspective" or principle around which to organize multiple visions, it has roots in the realities that embody alternative ways of viewing the momentum of the present. Moral imagination, the wish/need for a coherent biography of humanity informed by a sense of social justice, a self-critical story of how we got to where we are and what options we might now create, can only have meaning if the story is grounded in local needs everywhere. As long as we veer away from analysis that carries connotations of Marxist categories and instead stress the seemingly neutral constructs of "contact" and "encounter," as many world historians do, I don't see how we can come to terms with the heart of our current social and intellectual crises.[50] A similar dead end awaits us if we fail to define moral commitments, because we consider them solely the purview of religious associations. As Gerrit Huizer, writing on social injustice, has noted, "The problem of the Indian peoples in Mexico and other Latin American countries was not that they lacked economic integration or acculturation. . . . The problem was that they had been integrated into the capitalist system for several hundred years through (class) exploitation or as a labor reserve."[51]

   In the late twentieth century both socialism and capitalism as originally conceived have run their course, leaving, it appears, only fascism as a still unexhausted ideology for approaching the problems generated by industrial and postindustrial technologies. Will more technology continue to seem the easy though costly answer to social problems and moral confusion? In the high-speed fragmentation of life and meaning, will inhumane elimination of difficult problems become an acceptable solution if presented as short-term nastiness for long-term good? This time, who will educate students to the dangers of a new totalitarianism that synthesizes Orwell's *1984,* Bradbury's *Fahrenheit 451,* and Huxley's *Brave New World?* The bitterness and tragedy of much of our history would have to be fully recognized before it could be turned toward alternative, sustainable, and humane visions, whether they be mosaic or celestial in nature. Work from this perspective could generate a foundation for historical understanding that would place center-front some difficult truths we already sense in the shadows of world news and daily life. Perhaps then we could begin a story of humanity that charts us away from what Thomas Berry has called a civilization that bases its economy on burning the timbers of its lifeboats.[52]

NOTES

   The final version of this chapter benefited from discussion with the participants and organizers of the conference, "Missing Chapter: The Historiographic Marginalization of East Asia," held May 3–4, 1999, at the Institut des Sciences de l'Homme, Institut d'Asie Orientale, Université Lumière-Lyon 2, Lyon, France.

   1. William H. McNeill, "The Changing Shape of World History," in *History and Theory* vol. 34, no. 2 (May 1995) p. 14.

   2. Among these authors are: Janet Lippman Abu-Lughod, *Before European Hegemony* (New York: Oxford University Press, 1989); Michael Adas, *Prophets of Rebellion: Millenarian Protest Movements Against the European Colonial Order* (Chapel Hill: University of North Carolina Press, 1979); S. A. M. Adshead, *Central Asia in World History* (London: MacMillan,1993); Jerry Bentley, *Old World Encounters: Cross-Cultural Contacts and Exchanges in Pre-Modern Times* (New York: Oxford University Press, 1993); Philip D. Curtin, *Cross-Cultural Trade in World History* (New York: Cambridge University Press, 1984); and Wang Gungwu (ed.), *Global History and Migrations* (Boulder, CO: Westview Press, 1997).

3. Pat Manning, "Northeastern's World History Ph.D. Program Will Be Continued," *World History Bulletin,* vol. 14, no. 1 (Spring 1998), pp. 19–20. According to this report, the administration's alternative to eliminating the entire history department was to continue on a trial basis a program in world history while ceasing to offer degrees in any other areas of history, United States and Europe included.

4. Peter Novick, *That Noble Dream: The "Objectivity Question" and the American Historical Profession* (Cambridge: Cambridge University Press, 1988), p. 312.

5. William McNeill, "The World History Survey Course," in Joe C. Dixon and Neil D. Martin (eds.), *1982 World History Teaching Conference* (ERIC document), p. 2.

6. Novick, *That Noble Dream,* p. 312.

7. Ibid., p. 310.

8. "Area Studies, Regional Studies: A White Paper for the Ford Foundation," The Globalization Project, (Chicago: University of Chicago, June 1997), p. 9.

9. Novick, *That Noble Dream,* p. 314.

10. Ibid., pp. 316–317.

11. Ibid., p. 318.

12. Ibid., p. 319.

13. Ibid., p. 314.

14. "Area Studies, Regional Studies: A White Paper for the Ford Foundation," p. 8.

15. Raymond Grew, "World Historians and Their Goals: Twentieth-Century Answers to Modernism," review article, *History and Theory* vol. 34, no. 4 (December 1995), pp. 372–373.

16. Joe C. Dixon and Neil D. Martin, "1982 World History Teaching Conference."

17. *World History Bulletin* vol. 1, no. 1, 2 (Fall/Winter 1983), 18. "Area Studies, Regional Studies: A White Paper for the Ford Foundation," p. 9.

19. Bruce Mazlish, "An Introduction to Global History," in Bruce Mazlish and Ralph Buultjens (eds.), *Conceptualizing Global History* (Boulder, CO: Westview Press, 1993), p. 3.

20. Raymond Grew, "On the Prospect of Global History," in Mazlish and Buultjens (eds.), *Conceptualizing Global History,* p. 237.

21. "Area Studies, Regional Studies: A White Paper for the Ford Foundation," pp. 2, 5.

22. Ainslie T. Embree and Carol Gluck (eds.), *Asia in Western and World History: A Guide for Teaching* (New York: M.E. Sharpe, 1997); Myron L. Cohen (ed.), *Asia: Case Studies in the Social Sciences: A Guide for Teaching* (New York: M.E. Sharpe, 1997); Barbara Stoler Miller (ed.), *Masterworks of Asian Literature in Comparative Perspective: A Guide for Teaching* (New York: M.E. Sharpe, 1997).

23. *World History Bulletin* vol. 1, no. 1 (Fall/Winter 1983), pp. 2, 8.

24. "Area Studies, Regional Studies: A White Paper for the Ford Foundation," p. 2.

25. Italo Calvino, "World Memory," in *Numbers in the Dark and Other Stories* (New York: Vintage Books, 1995), pp. 135–141.

26. Clive Ponting, *A Green History of the World: The Environment and the Collapse of Great Civilizations* (London: Penguin Books, 1991), pp. xiii–xiv. In a world history text as recent as *Traditions & Encounters: A Global Perspective on the Past,* by Jerry Bentley and Herbert Ziegler (Boston: McGraw Hill, 2000), environmental themes are mentioned only in passing while the emphasis on the interactions of regions yields a table of contents and consequently a basic frame of analysis that differs only slightly from the headings of current western civilization texts.

27. For current discussions, see Juliet B. Schor, *The Overworked American: The Unexpected Decline of Leisure* [New York: Basic Books, 1991] and Jeremy Rifkin, *The End of Work: The Decline of the Global Labor Force and the Dawn of the Post-Modern Era* (New York: G. P. Putnam's Sons, 1995).

28. Elize S. van Eeden, "An Approach to the Teaching of Universal/Global History Concepts in World History Practice in South Africa," in *World History Around the World*, a special issue of the *World History Bulletin*, vol. 14, no. 1 (Spring 1998), p. ii.

29. Dorothea A. L. Martin, "World History in China," in *World History Around the World*, p. 8.

30. Brian Moloughney, "Linking World and Nation: The Place of World History in New Zealand's Bicultural Environment," in *World History Around the World*, p. 10. 31. Mihai Manea, "Regarding Teaching World History in Romania," in *World History Around the World*, p. 11.

32. Karl Marx, *Manifesto of the Communist Party* (1848), pp. 48–49.

33. Ross Dunn, *World History Bulletin* vol. 1, no. 1 (Fall/Winter 1983), p. 9.

34. Philip D. Curtin, "Going Global," in Leonard Blasse, Frans-Paul van der Putten, Hans Vogel (eds.), *Pilgrims to the Past: Private Conversations with Historians of European Expansion* (Leiden: Research School, CNWS, 1996), pp. 36–37.

35. Benedict Anderson, *The Specter of Comparisons: Nationalism, Southeast Asia, and the World* (London: Verso, 1998).

36. Richard M. Eaton, "Comparative History as World History: Religious Conversion in Modern India," in *Journal of World History* vol. 8, no. 2 (Fall 1997), p. 243.

37. Michiel Baud and Willem van Schendel, "Toward a Comparative History of Borderlands," in *Journal of World History* vol. 8, no. 2 (Fall 1997), p. 212.

38. Peter N. Stearns, "Nationalisms: An Invitation to Comparative Analysis," in *Journal of World History* vol. 8, no. 1 (Spring 1997), pp. 57–74.

39. Abu-Lughod, *Before European Hegemony;* Bentley, *Old World Encounters;* Fernand Braudel, *Civilization and Capitalism, 15th–18th Century* (London: Fontana Press, 1979); Curtin, *Cross-Cultural Trade in World History;* Andre Gunder Frank and Barry Gills (eds.), *The World System: Five Hundred Years or Five Thousand?* (London: Routledge, 1993); Andre Gunder Frank, *Reorient China* (Berkeley: University of California Press, 1998); Immanuel Wallerstein, *The Modern World System* (San Diego: Academic Press, 1974/1989).

40. Arif Dirlik, "There Is More in the Rim Than Meets the Eye: Thoughts on the 'Pacific Idea,'" in Arif Dirlik (ed.), *What Is in a Rim?: Critical Perspectives on the Pacific Region Idea* (Lanham, MD: Rowman & Littlefield, 1998), p. 366.

41. Grew, "World Historians and Their Goals," p. 376.

42. McNeill, "The Changing Shape of World History," p. 26.

43. William A. Green, "Periodizing World History," in *History and Theory* vol. 34, no. 2 (May 1995), p. 111.

44. Ashis Nandy, "History's Forgotten Doubles," in *History and Theory* vol. 34, no. 2 (May 1995), p. 60.

45. Ibid., p. 59.

46. Ellen Goodman, "Media Diet," in *Utne Reader* (January–February 1999), p. 102.

47. Gerrit Huizer, "Social Movements in the Underdevelopment of Development Dialectic: A View from Below," in Sing C. Chew and Robert A. Denemark (eds.), *The Underdevelopment of Development: Essays in Honor of Andre Gunder Frank* (Thousand Oaks, CA: Sage Publications, 1996), p. 299.

48. McNeill, "The World History Survey Course," p. 2.

49. Walter Benjamin, "Moscow" in *Reflections: Essays, Aphorisms, Autobiographical Writings,* ed. Peter Demetz, trans. Edmund Jephcott (New York: Schocken Books, 1986), p. 97.

50. See, for example, McNeill's responses on these questions in a 1979 interview, "The Rise of the West in Retrospect," in Leonard Blasse, Frans-Paul van der Putten, Hans Vogel (eds.), *Pilgrims to the Past: Private Conversations with Historians of European Expansion* (Leiden: Research School, CNWS, 1996), pp. 62–64.

51. Huizer, "Social Movements in the Underdevelopment of Development Dialectic," p. 282.

52. Thomas Berry, *The Dream of the Earth* (San Francisco: Sierra Club Books, 1988).

10

Whither History? Encounters with Historism, Postmodernism, Postcolonialism

Arif Dirlik

Film analyst Vivian Sobchak writes, with reference to the film *Forrest Gump*, that it "stands as both symptom of and gloss upon a contemporary—and millennial—moment in which history (with either upper- or lower-case *h*, in the singular or plural) and historical consciousness have been often described on the one hand as 'at an end,' and on the other hand have been the object of unprecedented public attention and contestation."[1] Where the status of history is concerned, it is not too difficult to think of other paradoxes commonly encountered in contemporary discussions: history as the medium at once of discourses of domination and liberation; skepticism over the knowability of the past versus evidence across the disciplines of a preoccupation with historicity; an interpretive voluntarism against a sense of the persistent burden of the past—even a sense that the most important forces shaping human history may be beyond the control of human beings; and, most ironically, an enrichment in our understanding of the past even as we seem to be losing control over the methods, organization, and goals of historical knowledge.

Others could be named, but these will suffice for the moment to illustrate the theses I will take up in this chapter: that there is (once again) a crisis in history that is a product of factors that involve both complex considerations of history as discipline and epistemology, and the cultural meaning of history; that it is not clear whether the crisis signals a hopeless disintegration of history or a paradigm shift in historical practice; and that, whatever the outcome, the transformation of history as we have known and practiced it for the last hundred years or so does not imply either history's end or an end of the concern with the past. Postmodern history, if that is what it is, is most likely to be also posthistorical in the sense of containing history as a significant moment, which may serve as a reminder of the power of

history even in its negation. It implies also a significantly diminished cultural role
for history than it enjoyed under the regime of modernity.

The current crisis is not a crisis in the disciplinary practice of history as such—at
least, not yet. To be sure, during the past three decades, historians have faced challenges that continue to force rethinking both of history's relationship to the past
and narrower questions of method.[2] Some of these challenges have been mounted
from within the historical discipline. Such is the case with the linguistic or narrative turn in theories of history that was to end up questioning the possibility of historical truth, and the appearance of new social and cultural histories that were to
lead at once to the "thickening" (in the Geertzian sense) of historical description
and skepticism toward the possibility of holistic comprehension of the past. These
tendencies to postmodernity in history were reinforced by the appearance and diffusion of poststructuralism, resulting in a questioning of all the working concepts
of the historian from "space" and "time" to "subject," "context," and "event," also
underlining in the process the complicity of history in social and political power—
 to the point where it seems nearly impossible even to determine what is a significant historical problem, let alone how to deal with it. The proliferating claims on
the past of new social constituencies, already an important moment in the creation
of the new social history, has gained momentum since the 1980s as the assertion of
diasporic identities has further scrambled notions of what is a proper unit of historical analysis. The claims to different pasts, both at the national and the global levels, have issued, most fundamentally, in a repudiation of history as a cultural arti-
fact of the modern West, which must be rejected if other cultural traditions are to
acquire contemporary voices of their own. Finally, if historians could ever pretend
to monopolize overinterpretations of the past, that pretense seems less credible than
ever before as new visual and electronic media make claims on representations of
the past.

Historians have been able to absorb some of these challenges and have simply
ignored others. As Nancy Partner writes:

> [F]or all the sophistication of the theory-saturated part of the profession, scholars in all
> the relevant disciplines that contribute to or depend on historical information carry on
> in all essential ways as though nothing had changed since Ranke, or Gibbon for that
> matter; as though invisible guardian angels of epistemology would always spread pro-
> tecting wings over facts, past reality, true accounts, and authentic versions; as though
> the highly defensible, if not quite the definitive, version would always be available
> when we really needed it.[3]

How long this disciplinary resilience may last is an open question, for if there is no
apparent crisis in the practice of history, there is little question about a crisis in the
cultural meaning of history. George Iggers, himself a defender of the rationality of
history, observes perceptively, "The revolt against the conception of historical truth
and with it the belief in the applicability of rational criteria, say scientific or schol-

arly, to the investigation of the past cannot be viewed as a current in historical thought in a narrow sense but as part of a broad reorientation of modern consciousness under the changing conditions of modern existence."[4]

We might note, however, that while the current reorientation of historical thought may have roots in the past of European modernity or draw upon precedents from that past, it is the product more specifically of the social and intellectual ferment of the 1960s, draws upon a much broader range of cultural sources than European modernity, and is informed and shaped by novel technological transformations that produce not only new kinds of information and representations but also new meanings of being human. The historiographical reorientation of the last few decades, no less than the new social and cultural histories, was informed by the conviction, "[S]cholars should begin to take seriously the cries of the 1960s for 'involvement' and 'relevance' of history that militant social reformers were legitimately demanding of the academic community. Only a radical questioning of the cultural utility of history . . . can 'contribute to the salvation of the human *species* which it is our duty as thinkers to serve.'"[5] The turn to the Third World in the 1960s also initiated the assault on Eurocentric universalist conceptions and practices of history, although that itself would undergo a reorientation with the appearance of ideologies of globalization and multiculturalism in the 1980s. The transformation of Euro-America's place in the world, and with it of the historiography it informed, prompts Frank Ankersmit to observe "that autumn has come to Western historiography."[6] On the other hand, while modernist assumptions may still guide historical practice in the discipline, scholars find no shortage of postmodernist representations in the new visual media.[7]

Tracing debates over history in the 1960s and 1970s, Richard Vann concludes that, by the mid-1970s, "something like a paradigm shift had occurred; for the next twenty years historians' language, not explanation or causality [in other words, the relationship of historical to scientific knowledge], would be *the* topic around which most reflections on history would center."[8] The outstanding marker of this "paradigm shift" was Hayden White's *Metahistory*, "the most revolutionary book in philosophy history over the past twenty-five years,"[9] which was to bring to the center of attention an already proliferating concern with narrative. The "linguistic turn" would derive additional momentum from the rapid diffusion of poststructuralism in the 1970s and 1980s. The result was a reorientation in theory from a positivistic concern with history as a recuperation of the past to a concern with the ways in which the historian constructs the past.

The implications were to be far-reaching, if uncertain, in their practical consequences for historians. There may well have been a paradigm shift in the philosophy of history, as Vann suggests, but if we understand paradigm shift in the Kuhnian sense—as a new way of ordering knowledge or understanding—the new paradigm represented by the linguistic turn suggests most prominently a dis-ordering, or even the impossibility, of historical knowledge. This is the way White's "revolution" in historiography appears to Iggers. What Iggers has to say about White touches on several important aspects of the new revolution in history:

> The new emphasis on history as a form of literature is related to the reduction of history to language. Hayden White is . . . quite right in insisting that every historical text is also a literary text and that as such it is governed by literary criteria. But White goes beyond this to conclude that a historical text is in essence nothing more than a literary text, a poetical creation as deeply involved in the imagination as the novel. The history the historian writes is determined ultimately not by any reference to his subject of study but by literary decisions, by the limited choices permitted by such literary determinants as "emplotment" and "choice of tropes."[10]

Whether or not this is an accurate reading of what White does is open to question. Sidney Monas observes somewhat differently that White's point was that differences among the historians and philosophers of history he dealt with "were not to be explained in terms of who was right and who was wrong, who plugged in to 'objective reality' and who did not, but rather in terms of differences of temperament and the relationship of temperament to genre, mode, and emplotment. None of them used evidence 'improperly.'"[11]

In other words, the question is not whether historians may dispense with evidence, or engage in arbitrary manipulation of the past, but rather what, beyond evidence, makes for a work of history, especially a great work of history with seminal consequences for our understanding of the past. Ironically, White's work does not diminish but expands the role of the historian who now appears as the creator of history, the subject of the text, rather than a transmitter of past reality, a task best accomplished by absenting the author from the text.

Recognition of these points is important, because they point to the even more ineluctable question raised by the narrative turn: not the relationship between narrative and evidence, but the relationship between narrative (and by implication, evidence) and objective truth. The most significant consequence of the narrative turn is the affirmation of the possibility of multiple narratives on the same event(s) or past(s) that may have equally valid claims on the truth of the past, accompanied by a rejection of the professional historian's assumption that different claims to historical truth may be adjudicated on the basis of evidence alone. We may agree readily with Iggers' statement, "A historical text must be understood with reference to the context to which it refers and that this context contains an element of objectivity not fully identical with the subjectivity of the historian and an element of rationality that presumes elements of intersubjectivity in the methods of historical inquiry."[12] But that still leaves open the question of the historicity of history itself, and the possibility that historical "context" (no less than the historical "event") may be as much a product as a condition of history.

While most historians may write as if they are at the end of history, it is a presumption of modern "scientific" professional history in particular that, while the past as such may lie behind us, history—the effort to understand and write the past—is at all times a project that extends into the future. Like the "truths" of modernity, the truths of history are deferred truths, which means, on the one hand, that the future is likely to have a better access to truth than the present, and, on the other hand, that there is a built-in obsolescence to historical work at any one time. In the words of J. B. Bury, "This work [the work of history], the hewing of wood and the drawing of water, has to be done in faith—in the faith that a complete assemblage of the smallest facts of human history will tell in the end. The labor is performed for posterity—for remote posterity."[13] This faith in cumulative truth ignores that posterity's notions of time and space may well be quite different than those of the present in the same manner that the present differs from the past, or that the "hewing of wood" may result in the splintering of the truth of history, not its unification into one comprehensive whole. These are exactly the implications of recognizing equal or at least, comparable, validity to conflicting narratives on the past, which also would suggest that the future does not offer any guarantee of getting closer to truth.

The implications reach beyond the goals of history into its practice. The historian ceases to be *just* a rational excavator of the truth of the past and is rendered instead into the imaginative creator of the past whose "temperament," in Monas' term, becomes at least as important in the creation as claims to reason and method. Unlike, say, ideology, the temperament of the historian does not lend itself easily to analysis on the plane of rationality, but requires the confrontation of his or her subjectivity.[14] The new importance assigned to emplotment, structure of the text, and so forth, shifts attention from the context to which the work of history refers to the text as at least partially an autonomous entity to be read in its own right or in relationship to other texts. The analysis of text no less than the analysis of the author implies a shift in the direction of literary analysis away from strictly historical readings, which in the process renders history into a subspecies of literature.

What may be most important is that such questions are not narrowly epistemological questions but are epistemological questions with broad cultural implications. Unlike earlier discussions on historiography, which revolved around the status of historical versus scientific ways of knowing, and were conducted in a cultural vacuum, the turn to narrative almost imperceptibly shifted, portentous, questions between culture and history. Hayden White, from the beginning, practice trayed his undertaking as a cultural project; the critique of historical political involved questions not only of "historical culture," or the cultural contemporary implications of history, but also the relationship of history to historical to text. In the 1973 article referred to previously, he contrasted historical/cultural historical as "socially innovative historical vision," and continent than explanation to why "metahistorians" found an easier in Anglo-American contexts:

In Continental Europe, speculative philosophy of history is not only very much alive, the kinds of problems it poses and the questions it raises stand at the center of a debate over the purpose of historical inquiry and the cultural utility of historical consciousness. In part, this is due no doubt to the philosophical traditions prevailing on the Continent. Throughout the nineteenth century, European thought remained more metaphysical in its orientation than its British or American counterparts; European thinkers remained much less convinced of the power of science to substitute for metaphysics; but more importantly, perhaps, the Continental experience of the two world wars and of fascism served to give ethical thought and ontological inquiry a different orientation.[15]

White has also raised the question of culture as a delimitation on the options available to the historian. He wrote, more than a decade later, "[T]he plausibility of any given narrative account of real events resides [first] on the perceived adequacy of a given plot structure to the representation of the meaning of the set of events serving as the historian's referent," and second, "[T]he number of strategies available to the historian for endowing events with meaning will be coterminous with the number of generic story types available in the historian's own culture."[16]

The premise that history was conditioned by a cultural context that historians themselves served to shape placed the new turn in historiography squarely within post-1968 intellectual developments that would come to be associated with postmodernism and poststructuralism. The turn to narrative in historiographical discussions in the United States coincided with the questioning of history by Roland Barthes and the assault on "grand" or "master" narratives by poststructuralist thinkers such as Jean-Francois Lyotard, who would ultimately define postmodernism as the repudiation of master in favor of local narratives and stories and draw attention to the gaps and fissures in narratives as a better way of getting at the truth of the past than what the documentary evidence provided. While the common attention to narratives and representations easily leads to the confounding of the two developments, it may be best to think of them as independent developments within a common historical situation that intersected in the constitution of a new cultural context. Having said this, it is probably fair to observe that the new views of history propounded by White, Louis Mink, and others were to benefit enormously from the diffusion of poststructuralist ideas with which they overlapped, and increasing popularity of postmodernist representations of the past—just as they have facilitated the latter.[17]

Iro. by historians who refused to question the validity of claims to truth in history political to historical analysis of the problems thrown up by the social and selves tstances of the 1960s and 1970s, would in the end contribute themselves importantegration of history—and play their part in foregrounding the cultural cure and narrative in historical work. The new awareness of the late 1970s torical practice was quite evident in a volume published in the at Duke U. ers, a White critic, and Harold Parker, a historian of France ers has continued since then to pursue this question, which has acquired increasing attention from historians. The pursuit in itself does not point to "postmodernist" or "culturalist" intentions, because casting the net broadly over historiographies worldwide does not necessarily imply a resignation to inevitable diversity but may be motivated by a search for a renewed universalism that seeks to overcome the parochialism of an earlier Eurocentric universalism.[19] It is important, nevertheless, that even historians who defend an earlier historicism or remain committed to notions of historical truth regardless of cultural context, should do their share in raising culture as a problem both in and for history.

Even more important have been the consequences of the varieties of "new" histories that emerged from the 1970s that further undermined the notion of a coherent, integrated history but also broke down the notion of culture by radically historicizing it (in a spatial as well as a temporal sense). Inspired by the works of historians such as E. P. Thompson and Eric Hobsbawm, who already had introduced culture into Marxist analyses of social movements in the 1960s, new social historians dealing with labor movements as well as groups that had hitherto been left out of history—from women to ethnic groups to indigenous peoples—produced histories showing the importance of culture and history to the self-definition of these various groups. The "location of culture," to borrow Homi Bhabha's felicitous phrase, was moved from the national to the group level; more importantly, these groups were revealed to have a historical consciousness of their own that was bound with their particular experiences, which challenged not only the "sense of history" of the dominant groups in society but also that of historians who played important parts in the formulation and consolidation of dominant history. The question, of course, was how to integrate these proliferating narratives into a coherent whole, relate social to political and cultural history, and reconcile proliferating senses of history. The very deepening of historical knowledge and its extension beyond received boundaries, had by the late 1970s already led to complaints about "balkanization" of national histories.[20] The problem of coherence was visible also in community studies as well as the new "microhistory" inspired by anthropology, in particular Clifford Geertz's idea of "thick description."[21]

It is worth repeating here that, in all these cases, the problem was not merely a technical or theoretical problem of organizing disparate historical narratives but the confrontation of different historical epistemologies. "History from the bottom" revealed stories and histories that had been suppressed in earlier historiography but now came forth to make their own claims upon the past and to challenge the claims of historians—in effect confirming the abstract speculations of historians such as White or postmodernists such as Lyotard.[22] Poststructuralist assumptions—including the rejection of the distinction between reality and fiction—were explicitly adopted by the new cultural historians, which has led historians and philosophers such as Mark Poster and Frank Ankersmit to declare the arrival of postmodernity in history.[23] This time around, however, postmodernity is not a response to historians' failure but a product of their very success in getting at the truths of history, which prove to be too complex to be contained in systematic narratives or theoretical systems—or even a single epistemology. The proliferation of claims on the past means not only the proliferation of narratives within the historical profession but also that professional historians' narratives are reduced to only one set of narratives among others.[24] The question is no longer whether histories can be true in an objective sense, but whether truths may be containable in something called history.

This question has been brought to the fore dramatically with a new awareness of global transformations that has emerged since the 1980s. What we may describe as the replacement of the paradigm of modernization by a paradigm of globalization has many dimensions that range from the recognition of new groups, the empowerment of others, and questions about the nation-state as an appropriate political, economic, and cultural unit, to the disappearance of socialist alternatives to capitalism accompanied by, ironically, an erosion of a Eurocentric teleology of modernity (to be distinguished from the erosion of Euro-American political and economic power). These are the phenomena that inspired Francis Fukuyama's "end of history" thesis.[25] Fukuyama's ideological reasons for bringing history to an end are misguided, but there may be another reason, quite contrary to that of Fukuyama, for considering a possible end to history. I describe it simply as a sense of the reversibility of time that has accompanied the widespread rejection of the teleology of modernity and the many reversals in history that have accompanied it—most importantly in the case of the great revolutions of the last two centuries. Varieties of claims on history consigned to the past, rendered invisible or simply ignored under regimes of modernity have reappeared to haunt the contemporary world, propelled to the surface of consciousness by the reconfiguration of social and political relationships globally.

If postmodernism in history means anything, at the very least it points to a proliferation of pasts making claims on the present. Such proliferation is liberating to the extent that it enriches the repertory of pasts to draw upon in order to act in the present and imagine the future. But it can also be devastating in its consequences if it leads not to open-ended dialogue but to resurgent culturalisms that, against the evidence of history, insist on drawing boundaries around imagined cultural identities—not just to keep out what is constructed as foreign but, more seriously, to suppress the diversity within. The latter seems to be more possible in a world where identity is not the product of freewheeling negotiations but is subject still to the prerogatives of power of various kinds. Rather than usher in renewed hopes for alternative futures, the denial of the teleologies that have informed history instead has rendered the future opaque; as a chaotic present makes a mockery of any effort to contain the pasts it has unleashed, the future itself is caught up in the terrifying anxieties of the present, stripped of its power to inspire or to guide.

I offer two examples. First is the proliferation of "memory" literature since the 1980s. Historians have long taken memory as the raw material for history, as a way to get at the truth of the past. If the new historiography of the 1970s endowed memories with greater status, in its most recent appearance memory has emerged as a competitor with history, in opposition to the latter.[26] Memory may serve different purposes under different circumstances for different groups. The memory literature of recent years is connected most intimately with such traumatic events as the Holocaust or the Cultural Revolution in China. An event such as the Holocaust, White writes, may "escape the grasp of *any* language even to *describe* it and of *any* medium—verbal, visual, oral, or gestural—to *represent* it, much less of any historical account adequately to *explain* it."[27] Memories of traumatic events may in such cases well accomplish what history is unable to capture or explain. Memories may also serve to capture glimpses of the past for groups who have been erased from history. They also add moral force to history in the case of groups (such as the Japanese-Americans interned during World War II) seeking recognition of their grievances. Memory serves to bolster the self-images of newly empowered groups seeking to overcome their images as victims in history.

Loss of confidence in history may be most pertinent to the discussion here. Pierre Nora writes, "The loss of a single explanatory principle, while casting us into a fragmented universe, has promoted every object—even the most humble, the most improbable, the most inaccessible—to the dignity of historical mystery. Since no one knows what the past will be made of next, anxiety turns everything into a trace, a possible indication, a hint of history that contaminates the innocence of all things."[28] The decline of the hegemony of the past ("regime of discontinuity," as Nora puts it[29]) has allowed for a proliferation of memory that talks back—not just recent memory, where it is most visible, but also distant forgotten memories that have returned to challenge history. The result is a multiplication of "private memories demanding their individual histories."[30] If historians often have forgotten or suppressed memories not suitable for their purposes, memory often appears as if it is immune to the history or histories that constitute it. Ironically, the confrontation of memory and history seems also to promise abolishing the difference between the two. We may view the proliferation of memory as an indication of the impossibility of history. We may also view it as the proliferation of histories; many histories do not cohere and have no hope of doing so, which may be the price paid for "the democratization of social memory."[31]

If memories claim their own truths against history, they may seek also to reverse the latter to create a new history. In many ways this is happening with the populations of the now fallen Communist regimes, seeking to recuperate suppressed histories. But it is also happening with others, victimized by history, who seek to create new images of themselves once that history has been accounted for and recedes into distant memory. A Jewish rabbi, heading the struggle for compensation for lost Jewish property, aims "to reconstruct an image of Jewish life before the war, one that will drive out visions of emaciated concentration camp prisoners in their striped uniforms . . . to paint a picture of the Jew before the war properly, not as a victim but as a society."[32] On the other side of the world, peoples in the Pacific seek to forget their victimization by erasing memories of their colonization.[33] Indeed, replacing memories of colonization, victimization, and even the distinction between oppressor and oppressed is central to the project of so-called postcolonial criticism. We have moved here beyond the recuperation of "people without history" into history, or the complication of the past, to the reversal of received historical narratives, where the most important question guiding the rewriting of the past is the identity needs of the present.

The second example of reversal is the cultural reversal of what was earlier taken to be a relationship between the First and the Third Worlds as well as of peoples with or without states—especially of indigenous peoples, again a major preoccupation of postcolonial criticism. This reversal also implicates the reversal of historical judgment on what used to be called the "second world," the world of socialist revolutionary regimes that have disappeared from history, leaving behind not images of hope and liberation but of death and destruction. Their disappearance has also left the other two worlds face-to-face with one another, trying to renegotiate cultural relations in a new situation of "globality." History is central to such renegotiations. Historians of the advanced capitalist world seek to accommodate the new situation by a multiculturalist rewriting of history that seeks to write back into history those that had been left out of it, or condemned to backwardness, in the process also moving Euro-American modernity from the center to the peripheries of history—albeit also trying to salvage what is left of universalism, as in the case of the renewed preoccupation with world history. Such efforts to recuperate a declining cultural hegemony are not necessarily acceptable to the "Others" of Euro-American modernity. The Others reassert their own claims by reaffirming their own pasts; "traditions" relegated to the past by modernizationist history and rejected in the 1960s and 1970s by critical intellectuals as Eurocentric concoctions, are now upheld by the Others in claims to alternative modernities or alternatives to modernity. Indigenous peoples, whose silencing and oppression in the name of civilization have been global, similarly reassert their pasts against the claims on history of the "civilized" by denying history altogether. Indeed, the most radical challenge to history lies not in demands for alternative histories but demands for "alternatives to history" that have been voiced by widely different Third World and indigenous intellectuals such as Ashis Nandy in India and Vine Deloria Jr. in the United States. To quote Nandy:

> The historical mode may be the dominant mode of constructing the past in most parts of the globe but it certainly is not the most popular mode of doing so. The dominance is derived from the links the idea of history has established with the modern nation-state, the secular worldview, the Baconian concept of scientific rationality, nineteenth-century theories of progress, and, in recent decades, development.[34]

The end to such dominance, Nandy concludes, requires rejection both of science and history. These lines were published not in some offbeat journal but the same *History and Theory* that served as a medium for the "paradigm shift" of less than three decades ago. From its universalistic methodological claims of three decades ago, history has come now to be portrayed as a culturally bound epistemology that must be transcended for the "salvation of the human *species* which it is our duty as intellectuals to serve."

These reversals have good reason, and a great deal of merit, in forcing us to rethink history as a cultural product. But they also point in directions quite different than those that informed the histories of the 1960s and 1970s. Charles Maier writes of the proliferation of memory, "The surfeit of memory is a sign not of historical confidence but of a retreat from transformative politics. It testifies to the loss of a future orientation, of progress toward civic enfranchisement and growing equality. It reflects a new focus on narrow ethnicity as a replacement for encompassing communities based on constitutions, legislation, and widening attributes of citizenship."[35] Ethnicization is even more dramatically apparent in global cultural conflicts over the meaning and status of history. While the attack on history serves a sharply critical purpose in the hands of cosmopolitan intellectuals such as Nandy and Deloria, whose critiques are self-consciously posthistorical, it is equally open to appropriation for the most parochial and reactionary essentialisms and exceptionalisms.

At this point we are considerably past the postmodernist view of history as a "collage." In a world where the teleology of Eurocentric modernity is as much out of fashion as the utopias of yesterday, different temporalities coexist in shifting spatial configurations, rendering history itself into part of a collage that includes many different versions of the past. The collage itself is posthistorical; without history and the modernity that informed it and propelled it globally, there would be no collage but simply a scattering of times and places. But where does it leave us?

However welcome may be the abolition of the earlier hierarchies of history, there is a price to be paid for the liberation from the hegemony of history: loss of a vision of the future that may help make sense of the present and the past as well. Worse still, this loss of vision also leaves us at the mercy of forces of our own creation. Heilbroner, describing the present mood as "apprehension," writes, "If there was ever a time in which the shape of things to come was seen as dominated by impersonal forces, it is ours."[36] Is there any point to history when the only choices for the future may be either endless play or domination by such impersonal forces?

The historiographical "revolution" or paradigm shift of the 1960s and 1970s, whether by historians or metahistorians, was motivated by an urge to democratize history and in this has succeeded all too well—with the ironic consequence that it has contributed to the marginalization both of history and the historian, with consequences that are not necessarily favorable for democracy. The democratization of history may be visible most readily in the current productions of history for popular cultural consumption, which are also revealing of the predicament both of history and democracy. When a few years back historians objected to Disney's plans to build a U.S. history theme park in Virginia, Disney representatives responded that since history was all constructed, Disney had as much prerogative to construct the past as the historians who sought to monopolize it! The historian may object that there is a big difference between historians' construction of the past and a theme park construction that places Monticello next to McDonald's, commodifying an important marker of democracy no less than the past; but such objections carry less weight when the boundaries of interpretation have been blurred, and historians become complicit in the authentication of "popular" representations of the past.

The latter may be more readily observable in visual media such as film and television, which reach millions around the globe daily and are likely to become increasingly attractive even to professional historians who seek to get their message to broader constituencies than the few fellow-academics who are the consumers of written works. History on film may confirm, at least for the present, Ankersmit's claim that "representation" (analogous to art) expresses what the historian does better than interpretation or narrative (analogous to literature).[37] Film, Rosenstone argues, brings us a different, multimedia version of the past in blending reality and fiction, or actuality and simulation, "through poetic overlays of sounds, images, words and ideas."[38] History in the conventional sense, "words and ideas," may be part of the film but is now part of a larger language of representation that brings the truth of the past to life in other ways. Historians who are called upon—as consultants or actual participants—to authenticate film or television historical narratives similarly find themselves as part of a production of the past of which they are no longer subjects. In an article he wrote in 1967, the distinguished historian J. H. Hexter pointed to the "footnote" as a distinctive feature of historical writing.[39] In history on film, historians play the part of footnotes, inserted into the narrative to comment and elaborate on its complexities. The "footnoting" of historians could be taken to mean that historians are still indispensable to the authentication of the postmodern text.[40] However, it also implies a diminished role for the historian in the production of history. From a postmodernist perspective, there is nothing about film or television history that necessarily subverts historical understanding, or truth. But neither can we avoid the questions raised by the production of history in accordance with considerations in which marketability inevitably takes precedence over the pursuit of knowledge, and the public is most important in its role as consumer.

Not the least important of these questions is the complicity of such history production in the promotion of technological fetishism. There may be nothing postmodern about these representations of the past—unless we are prepared to take the postmodern back into the heart of modernity in the nineteenth century. The theme parks of the present have their predecessors in the World's Fairs of the nineteenth century, which also claimed to represent history in its totality; albeit in the service of the technological "civilization" of which the contemporary West represented the pinnacle.[41] The representation of the past on film is as old as the history of that medium; and historical fiction of which it may be a visual counterpart is even older. And, of course, even less is novel in the appropriation of the past for a variety of motives, from political to commercial, and democratic to antidemocratic. What may be novel is the disappearance of a counterpart to all of the above in transformative visions of the future and the attenuation of the conviction that knowing the past might have some value in their realization. As Lutz Niethammer puts it:

The inflation of the various "post" concepts might suggest that we are no longer able or willing to define the content of where we are and where we want to go; that we seek only to know where we come from. What used to appear self-evident or desirable has lost its innocence, and now words more or less fail us. "Posthistory" is the most far-reaching of these concepts, for it denies a future not only to one characteristic element of a phase of history (modernity, revolution, industry, etc.) but to the idea of history itself.[42]

Postmodernism proves to be highly liberating in some ways, self-destructive in others. Postmodernism without history is not only available for appropriation in diverse causes but may serve to undermine the democratic goals that informed its origins. Partner writes, "The danger inherent in capricious, opportunistic violations of the protocol of historicity is really not that millions of people will absolutely come to believe this or that, but that millions of people will come to be cynical, disabused and wary, to believe nothing and thus feel no connection with the polity at all."[43]

There is probably not much that historians can do about a problem of this magnitude and is broadly cultural and political. There may be little that is odd about manufacturing history in a world that is poised on the verge of manufacturing human beings. If historical time is generated by "the tension between experience and expectation," as Reinhart Koselleck suggests, it may become increasingly meaningless as "expectation" comes to mean little more than what is to be consumed next, accompanies visions of the future into oblivion, or disappears into everyday experience of an eternal present. Poster argues that this is in fact what is happening with the electronic media, which collapse notions of space and time and bring the future into the present.[44]

While there is no reason why historical practice should abandon its search for truth as historians have understood it over the years, there are very good reasons why they should not continue to pretend that the cultural challenges of the last three decades mean little for history or disavow the very real challenges of the present. Even as staunch a defender of history as Richard Evans is driven to conclude:

[P]ostmodernism in its more constructive modes has encouraged historians to look more closely at documents, to take their surface patina more seriously, and to think about texts and narratives in new ways. It has helped open up many new subjects and areas for research, while putting back on the agenda many topics which had previously seemed to be exhausted. It has forced historians to interrogate their methods and procedures as never before, and in the process has made them more self critical, which is all to the good.[45]

The challenge is to face up to the evidence that constructivism in history is here to stay, and construct out of the rich materials of the past possibilities for alternative visions of the future that are informed not only by age-old visions of human dignity and liberation but also account for problems thrown up by changing times. Such visions in the end will be convincing if only they are grounded in past and present realities, to the uncovering of which history may still have much to offer.

NOTES

This essay was written while I was a fellow at the Netherlands Institute for Advanced Studies in the Humanities and Social Sciences. I am indebted to fellow-fellow Eric Johnson for his critical suggestions as well as suggestions of works with which I was not familiar. I would also like to thank Henk Wesseling for his comments and encouragement.

1. Vivian Sobchack, "Introduction: History Happens," in Vivian Sobchack (ed.), *The Persistence of History: Cinema, Television and the Modern Event* (New York and London: Routledge, 1996). pp. 1–14, p. 3.

2. These challenges, their implications for history, and the methodological questions they raise have been discussed in a number of excellent collections. For prominent examples, see Robert A. Canary and Henry Kozicki (eds.), *The Writing of History: Literary Form and Historical Understanding* (Madison: University of Wisconsin Press, 1978); Henry Kozicki (ed.), *Developments in Modern Historiography* (New York: St. Martin's Press, 1993); Peter Burke (ed.), *New Perspectives on Historical Writing* (Cambridge: Polity Press, 1993); Frank Ankersmit and Hans Kellner (eds.), *A New Philosophy of History* (London: Reaktion Books, 1995). Also, Peter Novick, *That Noble Dream: The "Objectivity Question" and the American Historical Profession* (Cambridge: Cambridge University Press, 1988), provides interesting discussions of the impact of the new developments on historians on the United States. Dominick LaCapra and Steven Kaplan (eds.), *Modern European History: Reappraisals and New Perspectives* (Ithaca, NY: Cornell University Press, 1982), and Mark Poster, *Cultural History and Postmodernity: Disciplinary Readings and Challenges* (New York: Columbia University Press, 1997), offer important discussions of the relationship between poststructuralism and history. The most extensive defenses of history against postmodernism is to be found in Joyce Appleby, Lynn Hunt, and Margaret Jacob, *Telling the Truth about History* (New York: Norton, 1993), and Richard J. Evans, *In Defence of History* (London: Granta Books, 1997).

3. Nancy F. Partner, "Historicity in an Age of Reality-Fictions," in Ankersmit and Kellner, *A New Philosophy of History,* pp. 21–39, p. 22. Henry Kozicki writes, somewhat more smugly, that "despite current theoretical distractions the historical discipline is soundly based on traditional practices properly understood." Preface to Kozicki, *Developments in Modern Historiography,* pp. xi–xii, p. xiii.

4. George G. Iggers, "Rationality and History," in Kozicki, *Developments in Modern Historiography,* pp. 19–39, pp. 21–22.

5. Hayden White, "The Politics of Contemporary Philosophy of History," *Clio* III, 1 (1973), pp. 35–53, p. 53.

6. F. R. Ankersmit, "Historiography and Postmodernism," *History and Theory* vol. 28, no. 2 (1989), pp. 137–153, p. 149.

7. Partner, "Historicity in an Age of Reality-Fictions." See also Robert A. Rosenstone, "The Future of the Past: Film and the Beginnings of Postmodern History," in Sobchack, *The Persistence of History,* pp. 201–218.

8. Richard T. Vann, *"Turning Linguistic: History and Theory* and History and Theory, 1960–1975," in Ankersmit and Kellner, *A New Philosophy of History,* pp. 40–69, p. 69.

9. F. R. Ankersmit, "Historiography and Posmodernism," *History and Theory* vol. 28, no. 2 (1989):137–153, p. 143. The reference is to Hayden White, *Metahistory: The Historical Imagination in Twentieth Century Europe* (Baltimore, MD: Johns Hopkins University Press, 1973).

10. Iggers, "Rationality and History," p. 28.

11. Sidney Monas, "Introduction: Contemporary Historiography: Some Kicks in the Old Coffin," in Kozicki, *Developments in Modern Historiography,* pp. 1–16, p. 6.

12. Iggers, "Rationality and History," p. 19.

13. J. B. Bury, "The Science of History," quoted in Allan Megill, "'Grand Narrative' and the Discipline of History," in Ankersmit and Kellner, *A New Philosophy of History,* pp. 151–173, p. 159.

14. Linda Orr, "Intimate Images: Subjectivity and History—Stael, Michelet and Tocqueville," in Ankersmit and Kellner, *A New Philosophy of History,* pp. 89–107, p. 90. Contrast this, for example, with Jean Chesneaux, *Pasts and Futures, Or What Is History For?* (London: Thames and Hudson, 1978), where the argument proceeds on the basis of rationally comprehensible class and social interests in the shaping of history.

15. White, "The Politics of Contemporary Philosophy of History," p. 49. White also observed with enthusiasm that "on the continent, nothing is taken for granted, everything has been brought under question, even the utility of historical consciousness itself" (p. 52).

16. Hayden White, "Historical Pluralism," *Critical Inquiry* 12 (Spring 1986), pp. 480–493, p. 488.

17. Richard Vann, in his account of the changes, suggests independent developments. Vann, *"Turning Linguistic,"* p. 59. White obviously did not oppose "metanarratives" per se, and unlike Lyotard, who was driven by anti-Marxism, found critical inspiration in the Marxist tradition in Europe. White suggests in an essay, however, that it may be necessary to draw a distinction between "modernist" (which was the context for "metahistory") and "postmodernist" ways of historical narration: "After modernism, when it comes to the task of story-telling, whether in historical or literary writing, the traditional techniques of narration become unusable—except as parody." He also writes, with regard to certain types of "events," especially as they are presented on the electronic media, that it may be "impossible to tell any single authoritative story about what really happened—which meant that one could tell any number of possible stories about it." The distinction probably should not be carried too far, as it appears that White does not care to distinguish postmodernism too strictly from modernism, viewing it more or less as a development of the latter. See H. White, "The Modernist Event," in Sobchak, *The Persistence of History,* pp. 17–38, p. 24.

18. *International Handbook of Historical Studies: Contemporary Research and Theory* (Westport, CT: Greenwood Press, 1979).

19. I base this observation at least in part on my experience with conferences in which I have been a participant along with George Iggers, and a more explicitly unreconstructed (I say this with affection) universalist Jorn Rusen. For an example, see Rusen, "Some Theoretical Approaches to Intercultural Comparative Historiography," *History and Theory* vol. 35, no. 4 (December 1996), pp. 5–22.

20. Samuel P. Hays, "Theoretical Implications of Recent Work in the History of American Society and Politics," *History and Theory* vol. 26, no.1 (1987), pp. 15–31, p. 15. The same tendency has been visible within the history of the same group. For a discussion of

problems in integrating women's history, see Joan Scott, "Women's History," in Burke, *New Perspectives on Historical Writing,* 42–66. Novick, *That Noble Dream,* chap. 14, "Every Group Its Own Historian," provides a detailed account of these developments.

21. Giovanni Levi, "Microhistory," in Burke, *New Perspectives on Historical Writing,* pp. 93–113.

22. The reference here is to the works of historians such as E. Le Roy Ladurie, C. Ginzburg, R. Darnton, and Natalie Davis. How "stories" may help us get closer to the "truths" of the past and also subvert the truths of history, is the subject of Natalie Davis' *Fiction in the Archives: Pardon Tales and Their Tellers in Sixteenth-Century France* (Stanford, CA: Stanford University Press, 1987). For a recent example from my own field of Chinese history, see Roxann Prazniak, *Of Camel Kings and Other Things: Rural Rebels Against Modernity in Late Imperial China* (Boulder, CO: Rowman & Littlefield, 1999).

23. Poster, *Cultural History and Postmodernity,* especially the introduction, and Ankersmit, "Historiography and Postmodernism," and "Historical Representation," in F. R. Ankersmit, *History and Tropology: The Rise and Fall of Metaphor* (Berkeley, CA: University of California Press, 1994), pp. 97–124. It is an open question whether describing works such as the above as "postmodern" gives an accurate impression of their origins or merely appropriates them for the postmodern. The authors do not necessarily view their works as postmodern, clearly distinguishable from the modern, as do analysts such as Ankersmit and Poster. Richard Evans, in his extensive "defence" of history, points out rightly that many of the "postmodern" issues raised with regard to historical work long have been questions for historians. On the other hand, it may be suggested that whatever the inspirations at their source, such works do contribute to a discourse of the postmodern.

24. I am bracketing in the context of this discussion the obvious fact that history has never been the monopoly of professional historians. Historical fiction and histories produced by journalists are obvious examples. They have been joined in recent years by claims on a "better" telling of history by disciplines as far apart as economics, history, sociology, and literature. What may be important at the present are the explicit recognition of such claims, as well as the recognition of the claims on history by previously ignored and marginalized groups.

25. Francis Fukuyama, *The End of History and the Last Man* (London: Hamish Hamilton, 1992).

26. Jacques Le Goff, *History and Memory,* trans. Steven Rendall and Elizabeth Claman (New York: Columbia University Press, 1992), p. xi.

27. White, "The Modernist Event," p. 30. Emphases in the original.

28. Pierre Nora, "Between Memory and History: *Les Lieux de Memoire,*" *Representations* 26 (Spring 1989), pp. 7–25, p. 17.

29. Ibid., p. 17.

30. Ibid., p. 15.

31. Le Goff, *History and Memory,* p. 99.

32. Richard Wolffe, "Putting a Price on Barbarity," *Financial Times* (6–7 March 1999), p. 1.

33. Klaus Neumann, "'In Order to Win Their Friendship': Renegotiating First Contact," *The Contemporary Pacific* vol. 6, no. 1 (Spring 1994), pp. 111–145.

34. "History's Forgotten Doubles," *History and Theory* vol. 34, no. 2 (1995), pp. 44–666, p. 44. Deloria's rejection of history and science is even more total. See *Red Earth, White Lies: Native Americans and the Myth of Scientific Fact* (New York: Scribner, 1995). Such repudiations of history are "posthistorical" in the sense that they are mediated by the history that

they reject. This does not trivialize them but rather enhances their plausibility. If some Australian aborigines believe that the gods sent anthropologists to preserve the traditions of old, Turkish historians in the 1920s and 1930s used the scholarship of European Turkologists to create a national history. It would be wrong, also, to describe the repudiation of history by a Nandy or Deloria as backward looking, as they self-consciously take the present as their point of departure. I have elaborated these points most recently in "History Without a Center? Reflections on Eurocentrism," in Eckhardt Fuchs and Benedikt Stuchtey (eds.), *Historiographical Traditions and Cultural Identities in the Nineteenth and Twentieth Centuries* (forthcoming); "Reading Ashis Nandy: The Return of the Past, or Modernity With a Vengeance," in Vinay Lal (ed.), *Dissenting Knowledges, Open Futures: The Multiple Selves and Strange Destinations of Ashis Nandy* (Delhi: Oxford University Press, forthcoming); and "The Past As Legacy and Project: Postcolonial Criticism in the Perspective of Indigenous Historicism," *American Indian Culture and Research Journal* 20.2 (1996), pp. 1–31.

35. Charles Maier, "A Surfeit of Memory? Reflections on History, Melancholy and Denial," *History and Memory* 5.2 (Fall/Winter 1993), pp. 136–151, p. 136.

36. Robert Heilbroner, *Visions of the Future: The Distant Past, Yesterday, Today and Tomorrow* (New York: Oxford University Press, 1995), pp. 69, 13.

37. Ankersmit, "Historical Representation."

38. Rosenstone, "The Future of the Past," p. 213.

39. Vann, *"Turning Linguistic,"* p. 53.

40. I am paraphrasing here the concluding lines to Grafton's marvelous book on the footnote: "Footnotes guarantee nothing, in themselves. The enemies of truth—and truth has enemies—can use them to deny the same facts that honest historians use them to assert. The enemies of ideas—and they have enemies as well—can use them to amass citations and quotations of no interest to any reader, or to attack anything that resembles a new thesis. Yet footnotes form an indispensable if messy part of that indispensable, messy mixture of art and science: modern history." Anthony Grafton, *The Footnote: A Curious History* (London: Faber and Faber, 1997), p. 235.

41. Paul Greenhalgh, *Ephemeral Vistas: The Expositions Universelles, Great Exhibitions and World's Fairs, 1851–1939* (Manchester, UK: Manchester University Press, 1988), and Robert W. Rydell, *All the World's a Fair* (Chicago and London: University of Chicago Press, 1984). It is interesting that historians, but especially anthropologists, were enthusiastic participants in World's Fairs as, among other things, consultants directors, as they believed them to be golden opportunities for publicizing their work and disciplines.

42. Lutz Niethammer, in collaboration with Dirk Van Laak, *Posthistoire: Has History Come to an End?* trans. Patrick Camiller (London: Verso, 1992), p. 10. Note that "posthistorical" as the end of history is quite different from my use of the term above. Niethammer also traces the origins of the concept to right-wing German intellectuals of the 1930s. It was adopted subsequently—after 1968—by left-wing intellectuals.

43. Partner, "Historicity in an Age of Reality-Fictions," p. 39.

44. Poster, *Cultural History and Postmodernity,* pp. 67–70. Koselleck, quoted in Poster, p. 68. Poster views postmodernism as a resolution of problems presented by new sensibilities of time and space that are inextricable from the new technologies that provide their material context.

45. Evans, *In Defence of History,* p. 248.

Index

academia, academic, 5, 84n21, 221, 223–24, 226, 228; academic community, 90, 243; academic voice, 208; business, 9, 101; fellow-academics, 252; meaningful discussion, 200; Western, 8, 85, 87, 169. *See also* intellect, intellectual; scholarship, scholarly

Achebe, Chinua, 181n22

Adorno, Rolena; 200–201

aesthetic, 52, 67, 68

Africa, African, 5, 13–16, 89, 98, 104, 124n153, 157–73, 175, 177, 200, 224–25, 234; backwardness, 176, 184n45; diaspora, 201; Euro-African interaction, 164, 185n61; historians, 98, 99; initiatives and resistance, 180n13; North, 9, 12–14, 67–69, 73, 81n4, 82n5 studies association, 228; West, culture, 212n2

African-Americans, 123n140

Africanists, 98, 159

agencies, agents, 9, 16, 26, 29–31, 79, 85–87, 104, 208; funding, 221; human, 197; political, 162, 192; semiofficial, 81n2; state, 198; subaltern, 159, 198, 202

agenda, 79, 81, 142, 253; alternative/radical, 42; research, 82n6; of ruling class, 14

Ahmed, Aijaz, 40, 115n23

Ajayi, J. F., Ade, 162

Alarcon, Norma, 215n31

Algeria, 68, 80

alternative, alternatives, 3–5, 7, 12, 27, 38, 42, 142, 148–51, 191; answer, 209; approaches, 15, 69; building alternative political communities, 195; explanations, 126; futures, 248; global, 31; hegemonic, 196; historiographies, 8; method, 209; methodological, to Orientalism, 69; mode of development, 134; model, 68, 81; modernization, 135; modes of history, 18; past, 142, 148, 233; practices, 207; postcolonial, 31; revolutionary, 129; significant, 82n6; social scientific, 73; solidarity, 206; southern, 154n17; to traditional thought, 97; visions, 5, 253; ways of knowing, 18

America, American, 96, 137–38, 141, 245

American Historical Association: 14, 82n6, 224, 226, 227

American Historical Review, 17

American Historical Review Forum, 197

Americas, 51; Central and South, 200; North, 114n5

Amin, Shahid, 178n3, 208

anachronisms, 76, 78

analysis, 96, 98, 191, 192

Anderson, Benedict, 156n40, 172, 174, 232

Anderson, Perry, 71

Andes, 52, 53, 61n7, 201, 202;

259

Ankersmit, Frank, 243, 247, 252, 256n23
anthropologists, 92, 100, 102, 148, 164,
    199, 203, 257n34
anthropology, 202, 247
Apartheid, 163
approaches, 76, 228
Arab world, 68
Arabic, 34, 79
archeology, 12, 14, 49–51, 60, 61n2
architecture, classical styles, 61n2
archives, 41, 42, 49, 203–5; archival docu-
    ments, 50; British, 173; Conventional
    archival material, 180n14; local
    archival materials, 83n7; Ottoman
    financial, 77
Argentina, 201
Arrighi, Giovanni, 20n9
Asad, Talal, 74
Ashcroft , Bill, 30
Asia, 16, 34, 89, 124n153, 168, 177, 200,
    224; Asiatic mode of production, 71;
    East, 38; economic crisis, 5; Central,
    225; Columbia Project on , 228; histo-
    riographies of , 157; South, 10, 94,
    202, 233; Southeast, 34, 36; South
    Asianists, 159, 210 West, 9, 12–14, 67,
    69, 73, 81n4, 82n5;
Association for Asian Studies, 228
assumptions, 67, 71, 72, 79, 93, 205
Atkins, Keletso, 164
Australian aborigines, 257n34
authenticity, authentic, 52, 99, 142, 200
authenticate, 252
authenticity, 46, 175, 188n8
autonomy, autonomous, 16, 29, 69, 79,
    113, 158, 170, 176, 196, 245; commu-
    nities, 99; cultural, 175; economic,
    200; historical subjects, 197; organiza-
    tions, 193; political positions, 41; ter-
    rain, 95; unit, 129; of science, 82n5;
    for women, 207
Aymara people, 212n3

backward culture and values, 4, 87, 101
"backwardness" (blaming native traditions
    and culture), 37, 41, 111, 170, 250;
    African, 176, 184n45

Badillo, Jalil Sued, 60n1
Bagchi, A.K., 96, 97
Bahl, Vinay, 97
Bahujan Mahila Aghadi, 107
Balagopal, K., 93, 94
banditry, bandit studies, 128, 198
Bandung conference of non-aligned
    nations, 62n11
Bangalore, 107
"barbarous practices," 166, 184n45
Barlow, Tani, 143, 146, 147, 153n35
Barthes, Roland, 246
base-superstructure, 52
Baud, Michiel, 232
Bauman, Zugmut, 83n7, 102
Baxi, Upendra, 206, 208
Bayly, C. A., 195
Bengal, 91, 102, 170, 195
Benjamin, Walter, 235
Berlin, 235
Berry, Thomas, 236
Beverly, John, 215n31
Bhabha, Homi, 43, 165, 247
Bhadra, Gautam, 93
Bhagalpur, 96
Bhartiya Janta Party, 111
bias, 12, 70–71, 79
Bloch, Marc, 60n1
Boahen, Adu 161
Bodh Gaya in Bihar, 107
boundaries, 29, 31, 45, 51, 86, 129–31,
    141, 165, 167, 247–48, 251; *boundary
    2*, 202; marker, 50; European, defined,
    174; geographical, 34
Bourdieu, P. 111
bourgeois, 27, 107, 133, 137, 157, 194,
    196
Brass, Tom, 90–93, 109–10
Braudel, Fernand, 232
bridges, bridging, 19, 36–37, 70, 76, 79
Brumfiel, Elizabeth, 60n1
Buddhism, 20n4, 140;
Buell, Fredrick, 29–30
*Bulletin of Concerned Asian Scholars and
    Modern China,* 133
business management: 9, 85, 101,
    119n103

CPI(M), 115n23
Calcutta, 90, 196
Calvino, Italo, 228, 229
Canberra, 193
Cape Province, 163
capital, 12, 16, 19, 40, 103, 111, 135, 151
capitalism, 5–7, 10, 15, 18, 29–33, 37, 41–42, 86, 97, 101–3, 129, 132, 135–36, 147, 248; critique of, 9; Euro-American, 136, 153n12; global, 191; historicizing, 149; victory of, 18, 25; development, 157; knowledge, 111; paradigm of development, 149; pre-capitalist, 45; rise of the West, 230; transformations, 168; universality, 167
Captain Swing, 18th century, 232
cardinal values, 82n5
Carnegie Corporation, 223
Caribbean, 157
caste, 91, 95, 105, 165, 174, 193; -like, 175; relations, 206
Castro, Americo, 76
categories, 16, 27, 39, 92, 105, 145–46, 158, 164–65, 174–75, 186n68, 186n70, 233; conceptual, 168; implicit, 204; native, 182n38; social analysis, 11
categorization, 30, 208
Celik, Zeynep, 80, 81
Central American specialists, 202
"centrisms," 26, 35, 36
Chakrabarty, Dipesh, 45, 88, 93, 97, 101, 112, 159, 170, 177
Chandra, 208; "Chandra's Death," 206
Chatterjee, Partha, 31, 91, 94, 96, 174, 177, 192
Chicago and the Columbia projects, 227
children, 4, 5, 206, 207
China, Chinese, 5, 12, 13, 15, 37, 46, 52, 101, 125–32, 135–42, 147, 225, 231, 234; alternative economic history, 233; Confucian heritage, 34; cultural revolution in, 145, 249; history, 41, 69, 132, 136–38, 140, 147–49, 233; intellectuals, 61n7, 150; left, 195; Marxist historiography, 149; rural industrialization, 154n18; South, 129–30; world, 34

Chreten, Jean-Pierre, 183n40
Christianity, Christian, 61n2, 162, 171; doctrines, 170; messianic Christian cults, 183n40; Muslim and Christian communities, 76; organization, 120n113; politician, 173; symbols, 205
churches, 103, 104, 120n113, 216n31, 235
citizenries, 37
citizenship, 16, 177, 234
civil society, 39, 69, 155n33, 175
civil space, 83n7
civilization, 13, 49, 50, 51, 74, 94, 135, 221–23; critics of, 55; critiques of, 62n19; meaning of, 14
civilized Han world, 61n7
civilizing process, 51, 61n2; mission, 19
class, 9–12, 14, 19, 23n24, 32, 40, 50–51, 60, 86, 105, 133, 140, 144, 146, 153n12, 155n37, 162–69, 174, 193, 195, 200–201; analysis, 85, 96; Bengali middle, 91; *Bhadralok* (genteel), 97; classness, 110; consciousness, 90; dangerous, 104; exploitation, 236; landowning peasant class, 209; managerial, 85; middle, 102; production of, 30; -stratified, 50, 56; struggle, 59, 93; subaltern, 197; U.S. capitalist, 59; upper, 59; working, 15, 86, 99, 171, 175, 194, 195
classicism, classical, 50, 61n2, 222
Clendiuu, Inga, 205
Clinton, Bill, 104, 120n115
coercion, 167, 208
Cohen, Amnon, 78
Cohen, Paul, 132, 137, 138, 139, 141
Cold War, 144
Coleman, James, 188n82
collaborationism, 208
collaborators, 104, 207
colonization, colonialism, 5, 10, 16, 27–28, 79–80, 97, 144–46, 157–62, 165, 175, 194, 206–8: anticolonial intellectuals, 172; critique of neocolonialist, 195; culture, 13; empire, 39; forces, 204;

former colonial worlds, 200; goals, 199; internal, 44; intellect, 4, 32; interdependence between colonizer and colonized, 84n23; period, 88; recolonization of the world, 8; anticolonialism, 172, 189n97; violence, 166; of the world, 44

Comaroff, Jean, 100

Comaroff, John, 100

commodities: 9, 32, 106

communalism, communal, 87, 91, 174, 186n68, 195; discourse, 90; movements, 187n78; ethnic/communal, 207

communication, 106

communism, 53, 60, 135

Communists, 127–30, 153n12, 249; intellectuals, 155n37; movement, 115n23; party of India (Marxist Leninist), 90; and socialist movements, 73; victory, 132

community, 16–17, 51–52, 60, 90–91, 98–99, 101, 103, 107, 151, 160, 164–65, 170, 175–76, 201, 206, 209; academic, 90, 243; building alternative political, 195; business community in the U.S., 20n4; global, 226; land based communities in Australia, South Dakota, Chiapas, 234; native, 199; religious, 168; small, 225; studies, 247; suppression of, 156n41; of the victims, 158

comparative study, 76, 231–32

complicit, 9, 15, 39, 42

complicity, 94, 124n153, 207, 252; of history, 242; of intellectuals, 11, 15

conflicts, internal, 192, 204, 210

confrontation, 201, 204, 207, 247

Confucianism, Confucian, 5, 101, 128, 135–36, 140

confused, 221

confusion, 27, 45, 100, 156n40, 198

consciousness, conscious, 15, 28, 30, 40, 43, 47, 85, 91, 95, 97, 100, 131, 195, 197, 204–5, 221, 248; class-, 90; of China, 128; ethnic, 129; historical, 40, 42, 47, 241, 246–47, 255n15; of individuals, 107; modern, 243; of the past,

125; self-, 31, 67, 148; theory, 67, 76; unconscious assumptions, 68; unconscious theories, 75

conservatism, conservative, 8, 46, 105, 110, 133

consumerism, 38, 47, 102

consumption, 58, 59, 64n35, 151, 251

constructivist critique, 57

contradiction, 27, 31, 70, 155n37

"contact zones," 19, 36, 40

contemporary situations, 3, 42, 112

contestation, 241

contesting power, 98

Cooper, Frederick, 98, 111, 200

courses, 222, 224, 227, 233

Crecelius, Daniel, 72, 77

crisis: Asian economic, 5; of the capitalist, 103; in Chinese historiography, 15; contemporary, 18; in the cultural meaning of history, 242; of feudalism, 51; of historical consciousness, 19, 40; of historical thinking, 3, 8; in history, 241; of history, 8; of Indian state, 87; paradigm, 125; in the whole world, 4

critical thought, 204

critics, 55, 164, 215n31

critiques, 68–69, 82n5, 143–44, 195

Crummey, Donald, 168

culture, cultural, 3–13, 16–19, 27, 29–35, 39, 51–54, 79–80, 85, 95, 99–103, 109–11, 118n94, 135–36, 144, 151, 172–76, 199; assumptions of modernization, 132; backward, 87; -based explanations, 142; consumption, 251; crisis in the cultural meaning of history, 242; critics, 27, 47; diversity, 106, 121n121; elite, 17, 196, 202; expressions, 76, 86; hegemony, 34, 71, 153n12, 250; heterogeneity, 25; history, 86, 221, 241; homogenization, 25; identity, 45; imperial, 28, 93; "indigenous," 119n104; and language, 78; legacy, 221; local, 37; location of, 247; nationalisms, 147; new cultural context, 246; phenomenon, 74; popular, 209; production, 72; revolution, 127, 145, 209, 249; subaltern culture, 207;

terms, 165; theory, 40; translation, 55, 57; west African cultures, 212

culturalism, culturalists, 135, 136, 142–43; culturalistic, 132; intentions, 247; new culturalism, 43; premises, 153; resurgent, 248

Curti, Merle, 224

Curtin, Philip, 226–27, 232–33

Dahomey, 161

dalit, 106, 108

Daniel, James,

Darling, Linda, 77

Darwin, Darwinian theory, 50, 58, 188n80

Davidson, Basil, 161, 175

decolonization, 62n11, 88, 173, 175, 177

deconstruction, 47, 80, 82n5–6, 204, 209–10; deconstructionism, 99; of texts, 196; of Sa'id's Orientalist scholarship, 69

Delhi, 90, 119n103

"delinking," 37, 129

Deloria, Vine Jr., 250, 251, 257n34

democratization, 4

dependency, 193, 200; theory, 13, 16, 157, 159

Derrida, Jacques, 64n30, 193, 210, 211

development, 4, 15, 28, 40, 47, 52, 129, 149–50, 176; developing strategies, 100; economic, 62n11, 191; economistic developmental theories, 195; historical, 57; initiative, 167; ideology of, 26, 31; socialist development policy, 154n18; technological, 85

developmentalism, developmentalists, 31, 37, 39, 42, 171, 188n80, 200

dialectic, 36, 42, 93, 159

dialogue, 202, 204, 248

diaspora, 40, 46, 128, 130, 141

dichotomy, 7, 16, 133, 137, 158, 185n61

differences, 8, 11, 16, 34, 43, 86, 88–89, 96, 99, 100, 104–5, 113, 205; cultural, 39, 109, 151; gender-based, 60; interiorization of, 38; methodological, 50; notion of, 35

Dike, K. Onwnke, 104, 161

Dikotter, Frank, 140

Diouf, Mamadou, 162

Dirlik, Arif, 70, 99, 84n21, 234

discourse, 9, 12, 17, 27, 30, 32, 37, 71, 92, 109, 207–8, 211, 256n23; colonial, 144; communal, 90; conflicting, 198; contradictory, 155n37; counterhegemonic discourse, 169; derivative, 174; European, 164; future, 222; of imperialism, 38; nationalist, 156n41; official, 195; political, 73; of Third World, 150; of truth, 89; western, 9, 158, 169

discursiveness, 32, 150

Disney, 251

diversity, 106, 108, 110, 121n121, 248

"divide and rule" policy, 103

documents, 17, 49, 50, 196, 198, 205, 208

domination, 36, 95, 193, 207

Doumani, Bishara, 78

Duara, Prasenjit, 156n40

Durkheim, Emile 53, 54, 55, 59, 60;

Dutt, R.C., 88, 115n11

Earth, 4, 49

Eaton, Richard, 232

ecology, 150, 156n38, 200

economy, economic, 15, 30–31, 38–40, 129, 143–44; autonomy, 200; dependency, 193; development, 62n11; domestic, 150, 169; economists, 92; exploitation, 95; foundation, 56; global, 130, 150, 231; reconstruction, 62n11; social, 103; urban, 169

education, 51, 52

Einstein, Albert, 82n6

egalitarianism, 89, 112

Egypt, 52, 61n4, 68, 72, 79, 80

elite, 18, 26, 88, 194, 208; culture, 196, 202; group, 104, 193; Indian, 174; Interactions of, 197; metropolitan, 168; native, 46; Third World, 146

emancipation, emancipatory, 7, 17, 85, 99–100, 176, 179n12, 191, 210; liberating politics, 16; projects of, 7, 14; purposes, 197; reconstruction of an, 195

employment, 244–45

empowerment, 16, 36, 108–9, 132, 151, 153n12, 157, 248
Engels, Fredrick, 58
England, 79, 90, 222
English, 4, 224
"Enlightenment," 27, 33, 47, 88, 121n121, 150, 155n40, 223, 235; pre-, 169; rationalism, 33, 93
epistemology, epistemological, 3, 8, 43, 50, 87, 144, 245; history as, 3, 42, 43; history as discipline, 241; issues, 82nn5–6; modern, 70; questions, 69; single, 248
equality, 16, 106, 107, 177, 190n104
Escobar, Arturo, 42,
essential "difference," 121n121
essentialism, 37, 39, 73, 172, 178n4, 251
essentialized notion of culture, 40;
essentializing, racial, 187n76
ethic. *See shresta dharma*
ethnicity, ethnic, 11, 30–31, 60, 86, 101, 105, 129–30, 140, 144, 146, 155n37, 200, 247; Andean ethnic leaders, 201; linguistic and ethnic groups, 172; religious authority, 207
ethnicization, 25, 251
ethnocentrism, 9, 33–34
ethnography, 80, 164, 203
Euro-America, 18–19, 26–28, 30–34, 36, 243; cultural hegemony, 135; modernity, 250; heart of, 40; non-Euro-American societies, 133; spatiality, 38
Eurocentrism, Eurocentric, 9, 17–18, 25–36, 47, 94, 102, 132, 147, 192, 224, 229; as a concept, 27, 61n7; ideology, 230; erosion of teleology, 248; teleology of modernity, 251; universalism, 247
Europe, European, 11, 16, 18, 31–33, 44, 81, 149–50, 163–64, 171, 212n2, 255n17; colonizing culture, 79; Eastern, 7, 224; Europeanness, 80, 83n20; history, 16, 44, 190n104; Marxisms, 192; modernity, 166, 243; past, 223; pre-historic, 58; provincializing, 89; radio free, 224; Turkologists, 257; teleologies, 158; theories, 192; wages, 176;

Western, 67, 222, 235; world system, 233
Euro-U.S. narrative, dominant, 230
Evans, Richard, 253, 256n23
everyday life, 26, 31, 32, 60, 204
evidence, 12, 70–71, 73, 244; archaeological, 61n2; different kinds, 49; direct, 77; documentary, 246; empirical, 155n32; method of selecting, 75; read as, 67
exceptionalisms, 251
exploitation, 7, 95–97, 111, 205; global, 157; vocabulary, 145

"facts," 126, 145, 155n37, 229
Fanon, Frantz, 175, 176, 189n97
Faroqui, Suraiya, 76
fascism, 93, 94, 194, 246
"favorable market conditions, 104
fengjian and junxian, 140
feminism, feminists, 22n24, 26, 31, 45, 56, 91, 144, 215n31; movement, 107–8, 121n121; philosophers, 57; writings, 22n24. *See also* feminism, feminists; women
Ferguson, Adam, 52
feudalism, 51, 73, 209; antifeudal forces, 196
Feuerwerker, Albert, 153n14
Feyerabend, 149
Fields, Karen, 170
Findley, Carter, 75
Finley, Moses, 60n1
Flannery, Kent, 53
Fleischer, Cornell, 75
foragers, 52, 55
force, 104, 107, 110, 124n153, 251
Ford Foundation White Paper on the Globalization Project, 223–24, 233
formation of modern state, 51
Foucault, Michel, 59, 64n30, 96, 168–69, 193, 209–11; Foucaultism, 198; Foucauldian regimes of decentered power, 17
foundationalism, 27, 37, 39, 56, 146–47; concepts, 6; principles, 5; private foundations, 82n5

fragmentation, 128, 130, 134, 146, 228
Franciscan missionaries, 205
Frank, Andre Gunder, 6, 20n9, 233
freedom, 118n94, 126, 208
French administration, 172
France, French, 68, 74, 79–81, 162, 167, 172, 222, 224, 246; bourgeoisie, 209; labor system, 186n71; language, 173; political ideology, 185n57; revolution, 19n2, 194, 209
Friedman, Edward, 154n17
Friedman, Jonathan, 89
Fukuyama, Francis, 248
Fuller, Steve, 82
Functionalism, 31, 44
fundamentalism, 74, 107
future, 81, 136, 245, 248

Gandhi, Indira, 114n8, 195
Gandhi, M. N., 91, 150, 176, 186n68
Galindo, Alberto Flores, 201
Geertz, Clifford, 53, 247
Geertz, Ricouer, 96
gender, 11, 32, 39–40, 86, 99, 105, 108, 111, 133, 140, 153n12, 155nn37–38, 162–63, 169, 193, 206; analysis, 207; differences, 60; division of labor, 56. *See also* feminism, feminists; women
Genoveses, E. 93, 96
Germany, Germans, 53, 106, 209, 223, 224, 257n42
Ghana, 160, 173
Gibbon, A., 242
Gilbert, Joseph, 197, 202, 209
globe, global, 3–4, 29–32, 36–37, 89, 111–12, 125, 146, 151; capitalism, 3, 4, 13, 70, 103, 191; changing global situation, 145; commodity, 106; communication, 94; context, 136, 222; cultural conflicts, 251; destiny, 18, 26; economy, 130, 150, 231; exploitation, 157; forces, 99, 107; hegemony, 11; history, 17, 18, 103, 139, 221; ideology, 141; integration, 129; perspectives, 227; picture, 82n5; pillage, 134; power, 14, 70, 163; processes, 228; situation, 12; transformations,

248; transnational global present, 233; village, 8; watershed, 234. *See also* world
globalism, globalist, 18, 26–32, 38, 42,156n40; "age of globalism," 97; triumphant, 228
globality, 250
globalization, 3, 6, 7, 15, 25, 35, 38, 94, 103, 129, 147, 243; deglobalization, 111; Ford Foundation White Paper on The Globalization Project, 223; new, 12; paradigm, 248; project, 222, 227
Goodman, Ellen, 235
Gold Coast, 166, 173
Gonzalez, Rosalinda Mandez, 23n24
Gordon, Linda, 22n22, 115n10
Gramsci, Antonio, Gramscian, 17, 87, 174, 192–95, 198–99, 203, 207–11;
Great Britain, 44, 85, 93, 124n153, 167, 171
Greece, 61n4, 222
Green, William, 234
Grew, Raymond, 225, 227
Griffiths, Gareth, 30
Guatemala, 202, 216n31
guerrillas, 37, 90, 99, 173
Guha, Ramchandra, 97, 159
Guha, Ranajit, 17, 90, 93, 158, 165, 170, 196, 202, 211
Guinea, 176
Guomindang, 127–28, 131, 153n12
Guyana, 163

Hall, Stuart, 43, 44
Hammer-Purgstall, Joseph von, 68
Harare, 162
Hardiman, David, 196, 197
Harding, Sandra, 56
Harvard report, 223
Harvard school, 144
Harvard's General Education Committee in 1945, 223
Hastorf, Christine, 60n1
hegemony, hegemonic, 9, 34, 79, 80, 125, 167–69, 194–96, 208–10; assumptions, 71, 150; forces, 99; status, 155n37; paradigm, 70, 132

Heilbroner, 251
Herring, Pendleton, 223, 224
Hexter, J. H., 252
hierarchy, 11, 51, 94, 111, 207–8; com-
    plex, 163; disciplines, 14; of history,
    251; non-hierarchial cross-regional dia-
    logue, 192, 193
Hindu, Hinduism, 93–94; fundamentalist,
    107, 111 Hindutva, 107 scriptures, 5,
    102
historians, 12–13, 23n25, 41, 49, 50,
    92, 244–45, 251–52; concerns, 49;
    own culture, 53, 246; as "outsiders,"
    139
historical thought, 8, 18, 33, 125, 243,
    245; ahistorical attitudes and
    approaches, 68, 92, 192
historicism, 31, 136, 141, 146; *Positions,*
    148; positivist, 155n37
historicity, 3, 8, 26, 29, 42; denial, 140;
    Eurocentrism, 27; history, 244; nega-
    tion, 148; preoccupation with, 241;
    reassertion, 12
historicize, 30, 149, 233, 247
historiography, historiographical, 12–13,
    27, 81, 100, 125–26, 131–33, 156n40,
    158, 161, 194–95, 245; critical, 148;
    context, 192; developed, 157; new, 87;
    poverty of, 98, 173, 202, 203; prob-
    lems, 80; reorientation, 243
history, historical, 3, 9, 12–14, 16, 27,
    30–33, 39–42, 57, 68, 71–79, 97,
    115n10, 138–44, 241–53; aberration,
    127; ahistorical, 98; alternative, 148,
    250; ambiguous, 162; "antifoundation-
    list," 178n2; autonomous historical
    subjects, 197; "better," 112; Biblical,
    61n2; common, 36; defense, 256n23;
    different conceptions, 164; disavowal,
    26, 29, 30, 45; end, 21n11, 52, 248,
    257n42; environmental, 221; fiction,
    256n24; fictionalized, 96; forces, 104,
    124n153; from below, 86, 164; hege-
    mony, 47, 251; as invention, 148;
    legacy, 131; making, 157; materialist
    conception, 53; metahistory, 255n17;

modern, 27, 42; native, 150; outside,
    148; posthistorical, 251, 257n34; reaf-
    firmation, 42; remaking, 148; repudia-
    tion, 242, 257n34; of small-scale pro-
    ducers, 161; trajectories, 36, 130
Hobbes, Thomas 50, 58
Hobsbawm, Eric J., 86, 91, 198, 247
Hodgkin, Thomas, 161, 188n82
homogenization, 110, 129, 199, 134
Huang, Philip, 69, 149, 154n18
Huizer, Gerrit, 236
humans, humanity, 6, 8, 21n11, 204–5,
    226, 234–35, 241; abuse of human
    rights, 18; activity, 148; agency, 197;
    humanities course, 223; continuity of
    the human species, 82n5; emotions,
    100; endeavor, 82n5; future, 37; his-
    tory, 52, 222, 227, 241, 245; passion,
    229; progress, 27; rights, 18, 34, 150;
    social development, 224; social and
    humanistic sciences, 78; society, 52;
    species, 251; survival of humankind,
    82n5; vision of human dignity, 253;
    vision of human future, 37
humane action, 235
humane visions, 236
hunters, 52, 56
Huntington, Samuel, 45, 46, 55, 133, 135,
    153n12
hybridity, 10, 28, 34, 36, 39, 46;

"Ibadan" school, 161
ideas, 4, 30, 45, 169, 252; diffusion of
    poststructuralist, 246; free interplay,
    126; industry, 9, 21n15; liberal, 158;
    liberating, 148; poststructuralist, 57;
    private ownership of, 72; "reason,"
    174; study, 12; surveillance, control,
    and development, 169; utopian,
    154n18
identity, 8, 18, 26, 32, 40, 45, 51, 100,
    105, 109, 120n104, 124n153, 202,
    250; Chinese, 130; continental, 164;
    counter-, 203; fixed, 10; formation,
    27; indigenous, 20n4; mythic black,
    175; oppositional, 200, 201; politics,

21n10, 146; revolutionary, 135; subaltern, 17, 197, 207; victims, 51, 101

ideology, ideological, 41, 52, 183n38, 245; control, 223; liberal, 94; revolutionary, 42

Iggers, George, 242, 244, 246, 255n19

ignored and marginalized groups, 256n24

ignored questions, 51

imperial bureaucrats, 172

imperialism, 18, 28–30, 35, 37–38, 132–133, 137–38, 140, 142; critique, 144; imperialist culture, 93; imperialist/fascist, 94; postwar, 171; resistant to, 158

Inca, 61n7

Indic world, 34

India, Indian, 4–5, 9–15, 52, 85, 87, 94, 108, 119n104, 123n140, 192–95, 205, 208–9, 225, 234–35, 250; anthropologist, 100; colonial documents, 165; Council for Historical Research, 114n8; essential, 159; historians, 89, 159; history, rewriting, 17; modern, 232; nation, 186n86; National Congress, 174, 186n68, 195, 196; nationalism, 91; Oil Company, 102; peasant insurgency in colonial, 92; peasants, 97; psychiatrist, 175; religion and language, 91

indigenousness, indigenous, 5, 6, 28, 38, 45, 95, 108, 120n104; house, 80; languages or mythologies, 87; movement, 193; peoples, 151, 216n31, 247, 250

Indonesia, 200

inegalitarian values, 101

inequality, 7, 9, 11, 40, 105, 169; gender, 23n24; inherited, 150; racial, 111

inside, and outside, 126, 136, 141

institutions, 52, 68, 125–26

insurgent masses, 95

intellect, intellectual, 87, 102, 149, 175, 196, 203, 250–51; developments, 246; heritage, 73; history, 92, 183n41; local, 205; new generations, 209; orientation, 28; organic, 171, 194; output, 67; rela-

tions, "horizontal," 192; tendencies, 6. *See also* academia, academic; scholarship, scholarly

interdependence, 79, 80, 84n23

International Labor Organization, 122n131

International Monetary Fund, 6, 185n61

Internet, 4, 11, 233

interpretation, 12, 149; archaeologists', 55; art of (*Verstehen*), 57; interpretive frameworks, 51; "whig," 188n80

interregnum, 128

Iranian Revolution, 74

Iroquois community, 60

Islam, Islamic, 12, 67–69, 73–74, 135, 183n40; essentialized, 76; veiling in the Islamic world, 207; world, 34

Italy, Italian, 194, 209, 224

Ivory Coast, 166, 187n77

Jabal Nablus, 78

al-Jabarti, Abdul-Rahman, 72, 77

Jacobin party, 194, 195, 208

James, Daniel, 201

Jameson, Fredric, 187n74

Japan, 53, 82n5

Japanese-Americans, 249

Jefferson, Thomas, 60n2

Jerusalem, 78, 83n7

Jews, Jewish, 78, 249

Johannesburg, 164

John, Mary E., 108, 109

Kafadar, Cemal, 76

Kapitza, Sergei, 19n2

Kenya, 162, 172–73; historians, 162–63

Kikuyu traditions, 162

knowledge, 8–9, 68–69, 73–74; capitalist, 111; categories, 165, 177; form, 47; high, 205; historical, 241, 247; imperial cultural, 28; relativity of all, 196; scientific, 243, 245; true, 165

Koditschek, Theodore, 86

Korea, 130, 150

Koselleck, Reinhart, 253

Kozicki, Henry, 254n3

Kriger, Normal, 171
Kropotkin, 154n18

labor, laborers, 89, 151, 169–70,
    186nn70–71 division, 7, 14, 49, 50,
    56, 232; force, 59; historians, 73
Lalur, 96
Lancaster, Roger, 202, 216n31
language, 4, 10–12, 73–75, 78–79, 99,
    101; French, 173; Indian religion and,
    91; knowledge of, 8, 73; of self-deter-
    mination, 171; of solidarity, 177; of
    systems, 53; and textual construction,
    210; tools, 71; of world history, 231
Lat Dior, 162
Latin America, Latin American, 13, 16,
    17, 85, 89, 94, 98, 112, 163, 168, 174,
    191–92, 197, 211, 236; dependency
    theorist, 157, 159; history, 202; histori-
    ans, 210; Mexican revolution, 201;
    postmodernism in, 202; scholars, 97
Latin American Research Review, 17,
    197–98
Latin American Subaltern Studies (LASS),
    17, 192, 200, 202, 203. *See also* Subal-
    tern Studies
Latinos, 124n153
left, leftist, 89, 90, 94, 116n30
legacy, 31–32, 42, 131–32, 141–43
legitimacy, legitimation, 77–78, 104, 167,
    180n14
Lerche, Jene, 95
Levenson, Joseph, 127, 132
Levi-Straus, Claude, 74
Levy, Marion, 153n14
Lewis, Bernard, 78
liberalism, liberal, 16, 46, 177, 208; bour-
    geois, 137; dismissals of, 190n104; ide-
    ologies, 94; neo-liberalism 58; rela-
    tivism, 8; view, 164
liberation, 168, 179n12, 195, 251, 253;
    history as medium, 241; idea, 148;
    national, 200; project, 189n97; theol-
    ogy, 13, 193
liberationist, 175
liberalization, 107, 176
Lieten, G. K., 20n9

linguistics, 74, 199, 242; diversity, 178n6;
    nihilism, 204; oxymoron, 93; and tex-
    tual techniques, 209
literacy, 50
literary analysis, 245
literary criticism, 203
literary movements, 203
local, 7, 28–29, 151, 205–9; archival
    materials, 83n7; contexts, 186n68; cul-
    ture, 37; mobilization, 176; local
    movements, 150; narratives, 246;
    needs, 37; responses, 124n153; and
    subaltern cultures, 209
localism, diverse, 234
localities, 129, 155n37
localization, 4, 25, 129, 147
localized: differences, complexity, 31;
    movement, 172; sustainable technolo-
    gies, 151
location, 38, 146, 207, 247
Lomas, Clara, 216n31
Lowenthal, Richard, 139
Lyotard, Jean François, 246, 247, 255n17

MacFarquhar, Roderick, 127
Maharashtra, 106, 107
Maharashi Mahesh, 119n103
Maier, Charles, 251
Mallon, Florencia, 94, 157, 164
Mandala, Elias, 169
Mani, Lata, 206, 207
Maoist, 90, 154n17
Marcuse, Herbert, 94
marginalization, marginalized groups, 9,
    11, 86, 256n24
market, 30, 59, 167
marketability, 252
Martin, Dorothea, 230
Marx, Karl, 50, 55, 59, 89, 96, 225, 231;
Marxian concepts, 85, 191
Marxism, Marxists, 13, 27, 43, 85–87, 89,
    95, 115n15, 132, 139–40, 142–43,
    159, 191–92, 195, 210, 230 analysis,
    247; anti-, 255n17; approach, 16, 163;
    British, 44; categories, 87, 96, 196,
    235; historians, 13, 114n8, 139; histo-
    riography, 132, 149; history, narratives,

164; neo-Marxism, 73; new Marxist scholars, 21n9; post-, 11, 59, 143, 163; rediscovered, 200; theory, 163
master-slave dialectic, 93
material: context, 8, 257n44; culture, 118n94
materialist, conception of history, 53
materiality, 8
May, Hans, 106
Maya literati, 205
Mazlish, Bruce, 227
Mazumdar, Sucheta, 149, 156n39
McDonald's (fast food chain), 122n140, 252
McNeill, William, 221, 222, 223, 226, 228, 234, 234
media, 5, 242–42, 252
memories, 248, 249, 251;
Menchu, Rigoberto, 216n31
Meso-America, 2
Mesopotamia, 52, 61n4
metanarative, 5, 6, 8–10, 16, 86, 99, 101, 104, 146, 255n17; historical, 211; nationalist, 159, 162
methodology, methodological, 27, 39, 50–51, 75–77, 87, 137; alternative to Orientalism, 69; borrowing, 200; breakthrough, 165; criticisms, 198; modern standard historical, 72; post-modernist, 88; premises, 147; presupposition, 142; trap, 200
Mexico, 50, 201–2, 209; Indian peoples in, 236; southern, 53–54
Mi Sant Monastery, 99
Mishra, Girish, 195, 196
Mitchell, Timothy, 14, 79, 81
Mobutu, 176
modernism, modernists, 19, 27, 32, 35, 98
modernity, 5–6, 16, 25–26, 41–42, 97, 104, 121n121, 135, 137, 146, 150, 157, 159; Euro-American, 36, 250; European, 11, 26, 166, 243; fetishism, 141; meaning, 33; regimes, 33, 242; socialist, 151; teleology, 134, 248, 251
modernization, 127, 132–35, 176, 191; anti-modernizationist, 142, 147; Arabic as a language, 79; decolonization and, 62n11; discourse, 27, 37; narrative,

132, 137; older modernization theory, 153n14; paradigm, 128, 248; projects, 5, 6; teleology, 128
modernizationism, 128–29, 250
mode of production, 30, 212n2
moment of suffering, 92, 93
Monas, Sidney, 244
Monticello, 252
movements, 107, 160–63, 168, 170–73, 198–99, 207, 222; communal, 187n78; communist, 115n23; communist and socialist, 73; feminist, 43, 107, 108, 121n121; Indian National, 88; indigenous, 193; Islamic, 68; labor, 161, 176, 247; literary, 203; local, 150; nationalist, 89, 173; new social, 176; peasants, 91, 95; people's, 87, 90, 91; postcolonial discourse, 198; radical, 37, 150; religious, 161, 183n41; resistance, 99; revolutionary, 132; right-wing religious, 150; rural, 188n80; segregated, 108; social, 21n10, 173, 174, 192, 247; tribal resistance, 195; witchcraft eradication, 183n41
Muir, Robert, 121n115
Mukherjee, Anayna Reed, 94
Mukherjee, Ramkrishna, 92, 93
multiculturalism, multiculturalist, 6, 12, 32, 47, 106, 227–28, 243; lifestyle, 21n10; pluralism, 46; redefinitions, 40; rewriting of history, 250; sensitivity, 11; workforce, 9
multinational, 86; companies, 4; corporations, 101, 111; trade, 7
Muslims, 74, 80; brotherhoods, 173; and Christian communities, 76; historical experiences, 83n20; immigrants to France, 68 workers, 74. *See also* Islam
mythology, 13, 87

Non Resident Indians (NRI), 114n5
Nair, Rukmini Bhaya, 96, 97
Nanda, Meera, 120n104
Nandy, Ashis, 31, 250, 251, 257n34
Naoroji, D., 88, 115n11
narratives, 200; concern with the, 243; conflicting, 245; historical, 75, 164, 191, 247; nationalist, 195; unitary, 57

nation-states, 30, 111, 121n121, 83n7,
    151, 159, 172, 175, 188n81, 194, 248;
    nation-state system, 234
nations, national, 37, 44, 112, 128–29,
    135–36, 148, 156n40, 157; Alliance of
    People's Movements (NAPM),
    122n131; de-nationalization, 25;
    Endowment for the Arts, 81n2;
    Endowment for the Humanities, 81n2;
    form, 30, 37; histories, 13, 201, 231,
    247; idea of, 174; Indian people, 194;
    liberation, 200; Maoist notions, 154n17
    self-determination, 194; struggle, 171
nationalism, nationalist, 10, 31, 37, 87,
    146, 156n40, 160, 169, 177, 200,
    208–9; Asante, 173; Black, 215n31;
    Indian, 91; narratives fashioned by,
    156n40; secular, 170 discourses,
    156n41; elites, 194; historiography,
    151; narrative, 195; metanarratives,
    159, 162; movement, 89, 173
nationality, 99, 104, 105, 155n37
Naxalites, 90, 91, 107, 108, 195
Near East, 53, 75
negation, 148, 196, 242
"negritude," 172, 175
networks, 49, 159, 207
neo-Smithian "trade thesis," 62n17
New Zealand, 231
Nicaragua, 199, 202–3
Niethammer, Lutz, 252, 257n42
Nietzsche, Friedrich, 55, 59, 64n30
Nigeria, 166
nihilism, 70, 82n5, 204
Nora, Pierre, 249
Norris, Christopher, 94
North v. South, 9, 106, 212n2
Novick, Peter, 223
Nugent, Daniel, 209

objective reality, 244
objects of inquiry, 50
Occidental, 7; nihilist Occidental face, 10
Oceania, 224
Ogot, B. A., 162
O'Hanlon, Rosalind, 91, 93, 94, 96,
    178n2, 210, 211
Onselen, Charles van, 164

Opium War, 230
oppression, oppressed groups, 7, 18–19,
    35, 38, 92, 96–97, 145–46, 151, 175,
    201, 249; classes, 60; mass of people,
    104; peoples, 199
oppressiveness, 53, 208
oppressors, 200, 249; evil, 201; speaking
    of, 18, 35, 38; struggles against, 152;
    and suppression, 151; victims, 19, 35
Oriental, Orientalism, 4, 5, 13–15, 31, 36,
    40, 67–69, 73–75, 146, 147, 150, 151;
    postrevolutionary, 141; legacy, 141,
    143; neo-, 12, 73, 75, 78; nostalgia,
    141; paradigm, 73, 81n4; preoccupa-
    tion, 142; scholarship, 12, 15, 69, 73,
    81–82n4; Western, 67
originality, 72, 73
Ortner, Sherry, 94, 169
Oslo agreements, 78
"otherness," 164
Ottoman Empire, Ottomans, 68, 71,
    75–78, 83n20

Pacific Rim, 234
paradigm, 10, 12–13, 15, 27, 69–70, 81n4,
    87, 125–26, 131–32, 142, 149,
    153n12, 163, 192; approaches, 75;
    consequences, 155n32; historical, 41,
    131; market-economy, 156n39; mod-
    ernization, 128, 248; shift, 241, 243,
    250, 251
Palestinian term, 78
Pandey, Gyanendra, 91, 96178n3
paradoxes, 18, 25, 97, 241
Parker, Harold, 246
parochial, 10, 144
parochialism, 19, 40, 247
Partner, Nancy, 242, 253
Pasha, Defterdar, M., 73
past, 3, 28, 30, 38–42, 148, 242, 244–45;
    abuses, 19; consciousness, 125; con-
    struction, 11, 18, 251; domination,
    150; Europe's, 223; hegemony, 249;
    multimedia version, 252; new way of
    thinking, 18; popular representations,
    252; reassertion of alternative, 142;
    repertory, 248; rewriting, 250; study,
    152; uses, 19

patriarchy, 204–5, 207
peasants, 17, 51, 76, 78, 85, 104, 106, 135, 153n12, 194–95, 202; categories, 92; everyday forms of resistance, 198; Indian, 97; insurgency , 17, 92; movements, 9, 95; women, 151
pedagogy, 8, 75
people: of color, 12; history, 87, 92, 101, 110, 112 , 165; indigenous, 151, 212n31; movements, 87, 90, 91; nontribal, 95; oppressed mass, 104; poor, 101; protests, 91; struggles, 191
Perestroika, 19n2
Peron, Juan, 201
Persian Gulf begging sundicates, 4
Perusak, Darshan, 93, 95–96
Petras, James, 21n10, 121n110
philosophy, 12, 74, 113, 204
Pieterse, Jan Nederveen, 101, 105–6
Pinochet: 191
place, 68, 76, 251
plagiarism, 72
pluralism, 46, 56, 105
plurality of voices, 86
Pocock, J. G. A., 73
politics, political, 30, 33–34, 50, 146, 194–95; agency, 192; anticolonial, 160; of culture, 173; democracy, 89; distributional, 159; dominant groups, 51; economy, 30, 32, 35, 37, 39, 144; French political ideology, 185n57; hegemony, 17, 210; identity, 78; and intellectuals, 192, 211; of location, 98, 99, 146; scientists, 43 transatlantic racial, 173
poor, poverty, 4–5, 9, 95, 98, 109–10, 123n140, 163; farming communities, 164; people, 101, 104; women, 109; working, 112
populism, new, 109
Positions, 132, 142–43, 147
post, concepts of, 253
postcolonialism, postcolonialists, 3, 6–7, 10–12, 14–15, 17, 19, 27–29, 31, 33, 38–40, 47, 79–80; condition, 146; criticism, 28, 145, 146, 249; discourses, 70; discourse movement, 198; encounters, 142; Indian society, 193; intellectuals, 151; literary critics, 57; "modi-

fied postcolonial critiques," 143; repudiation in postcolonial criticism, 147; periods, 200
Poster, Mark, 247, 253, 256n23
postmodern, postmodernism, 3, 6–7, 10, 12, 14–15, 17, 25, 70, 79, 86, 94, 192, 198–99, 211, 212n3, 255n17; critiques, 203; era, 228; history, 241; label, 90; literary critics, 57; method, 197; pre-, 32; text, 252; turn, 18, 192, 201 in Latin America, 202 First World, 38; methodology, 88; methods and techniques, 98, 111; perspectives, 192, 252; refusal, 210; scholars, 88
poststructuralism, poststructuralists, 49, 97, 143, 192, 198, 199, 212n3; assumptions, 247; ideas, 57, 246; theory, 163
postwar historians, 144
power, 148–49, 158, 169, 211; and culture, 103; and domination, 38, 41, 60; hegemony, 69; powerlessness, 108
Prakash, Gyan, 17, 90, , 97, 116n30, 178n2
Prazniak, Roxann, 153n12
prejudices, 68, 70
premodern society, 50, 225
pre-modernity, 42
present, 3, 8, 28, 30, 40, 42, 245; origins, 146; and past, 145; presentism, 148; struggles, 152; uncertainties, 136; understanding, 25
primitivity, 4, 111, 158, 166
primordial: loyalties, 97; religion, 107; values, 101, 107, 111
privilege textual crticism, 203
privileging, 202
production, 56, 90
productive junior partner, 167
progress, 97, 167
progressiveness, 5, 99
proletarians, proletariat, 184n48, 209
proliferation of approaches, 125
property rights of native peoples, 61n2
Protestant Academy, 106
Protestant Ethics, 101, 137
provinicializing Europe, 47, 88, 89; and its history, 16, 111, 177
psychic security, 118n93

272

Index

psychologism, 32
psychologizing, 189n98, 190n98
punishment, 206

Qing, 127, 153n12

races, racial, 26, 30–31, 39, 104–5, 141,
164–65, 171, 173, 200
racism, 141, 157
radicalism, radicals, 6, 10, 37–39, 80,
142, 163–64; agenda, 42; change,
21n10; critique of Eurocentrism, 26;
essentializing, 187n76; historiography,
41, 150; history, 149; inequalities,
111; methodological individualism,
27; movement, 37, 150, 171; nationalist, 176; new, 151; politics, 197;
relativism and post structuralism,
49, 55; research agenda, 13; scholars, 138
Rande, M. G., 88, 115n11
Ranger, Terence, 98, 160
Ranke, 242
rational choice, 39, 43
rationalism, 93, 111
rationality, 52, 245
Raj, 87, 119n104
Read, Conyers, 224
Reagnomics, 85
"realities," 247, 252
reason and method, claims to, 245
reconfiguration, 40, 169
relativism, 8, 55
religion, religious, 30, 85, 101, 103–4,
107, 111, 161; ethnic/religious authority, 207; Western, 85
Renmin ribao, 127
representation, 145, 246, 252
repression, 50, 222
repressive antagonism, 160
resistance, 10, 16, 28, 35, 110, 124n153,
158, 160, 162, 167–69, 179n12, 194,
198, 199, 201, 209–10; active, 170;
genocide and, 61n2; movement (place
based), 99; tribal resistance movements,
195; use of concept, 159, 168; studies,
199, 203; subaltern, 207

revolution, revolutionary, 14, 37–38, 41,
97, 127, 130–37, 142, 153n12,
155n37, 169, 194, 248, 253; anti-,
145–46, 149; dislodging of, 131; historiography, 128, 133, 151, 251; ideolo-
gies, 42; incipient revolt, 95; industrial,
53; modernization, 147; myth, 209;
open, 206; paradigm of, 15, 126, 132,
137; post-, 42, 141, 145, 148–49, 201;
teleology, 131, 148
Rhodesia, 160, 179n10
Rifkin, Jeremy, 103, 120n115
Right, new, 85, 109
Robertson, Roland, 28, 29
Rockefeller Foundation, 223
Rockefeller Report on the Americas
1960s, 235
Rodney, Walter, 163
Romania, 231
romanticism, neo-romanticism, 96
Rome, 61n4, 61n2
Rosenstone, A. Robert, 252
Rowbotham, Sheila, 122n131
Royal Commsion on Labour in India
MCMXXX, 97
Rozman, Gilbert, 153n14
Rudolph, Llyod, 133
Rudolph, Susan, 133
Rusen, Jorn, 255n19
Rushdie, Salman: 10, 74
Russia, 4, 53, 111, 224, 225

Sachs, Jeffery, 4, 5
Sahelian Sokoto, 161
Sahlins, 101
Sa'id, Edward, 12–15, 67–69, 75, 81n4,
82n6
San community, 60
Sangari, Kumkum, 105, 121n121
Sarkar, Sumit, 93
Sartre, Jean-Paul, 80
Sati, 119n104, 120n104, 206
Scarnecchia, Timothy, 162
Schendel, Willem van, 232
Schmidt, Elizabeth, 169
scholars, 17, 87, 99–100, 81, 143, 153n12,
168, 177, 191, 197, 208, 243; African,

159; Chinese, 101; European, 163; Latin American, 97; literary, 182n38; new, 69; postmodernist, 88; progressive, 16, 191, 192; radical, 138; South Asianist, 210; struggles of, 211; U.S., 94; western, 88; western mainstream, 115n10

scholarship, scholarly, 12, 67–70, 72–74, 76, 78, 80, 81n2, 144; endeavors, 82n5; tradition, 72, 157, 164 academic, 5; alternative model for, 81; diploma mill industry, 9; of European Turkologists, 257n34; historical, 143; in human and other sciences, 82n5; individual creators of the, 15, 69; new, 82n6; Orientalist, 81n4; radical, 142; scholastic questions, 155n33; social utility of, 14; twentieth-century standards of, 72. *See also* academia, academic; intellect, intellectual

schools, 89, 144, 161, 163

Schrecker, John, 140

Schwartz, Benjamin, 132

science, scientific, 19n2, 27, 33, 39, 67, 82n5, 202–3, 242–45; and rational society, 4; and technological knowledge, 5; truths, 42; western superiority, 6

"scientificity," 39

scientist, 149, 165

Scott, James, 168, 170, 198, 200

Scottish Enlightenment, 52

Searle, Eleanor, 76

Seed, Patricia, 198, 200, 201, 202

semiotics, 17, 197, 202

Sen, Amartya, 118n94

Senegal, 162, 172

Shaw, Stanford, 68

Shetmajur Shetkari Shramik Aghadi, 107

shresta dharma (supreme ethics), 102

Simmel, George, 59

Singapore, 5, 130, 135

Singer, Amy, 77, 78

Sivaramakrishnan, K., 95, 96, 101

Skinner, William, 140

Skurskie, Julie, 188n89

Slatta, Richard, 198, 199

slavery, 93, 184n45

Smith, Adam, 52, 54, 55

Smith, Anthony D., 174

Smith, Carol, 202

Sobchak, Vivian, 241

social sciences, 27, 37, 38, 74, 75, 81n2, 82n5, 132, 137; Research Council, 223

social scientists, 144, 178n6

social theory, 20n2, 27, 28, 40, 60

socialism, socialist, 18, 25, 50, 94, 133–35, 156n39; alternative, 248; communist socialist movements, 73; development policy, 154n18; modernity, 151; non-, 41; nonsocialist states, 201; program for women, 44; society, 196; systems, 235

society, social, 30, 50–52, 54, 56, 74–76, 112, 198, 223, 242; alternative, 233; bias, 71; categories, 38; civil, 152n2, 154n33; disparity of , 68; economy, 103; egalitarian, 89, 112; engineering, 168; formations, 159, 208; goal, 82n5; and humanistic sciences, 78; ideologies, 8, 149; immediate social utility, 81n2; Islamic, 67; justice, 100, 235; memory, 249; movements, 21n10, 173, 174, 192, 247; networks, 170; new social constituencies, 242; "other," 40; "peripheral," 163; power, 149; responsibility, 110; revolution, 194; role of science in, 82n5; science theory, 37, 39; scientific endeavors, 82n5; scientific terms, 80 socialist, 196; societal repression, 222; stratified, 107; Third World, 147; traditional, 133

sociology, 72, 175, 210

solidarity, 196, 206–7

Somalia, 98, 160

sources, 71–72, 74–76, 80–81, 203–5; indigenous, 12; of meaning, 86; oral, 180n14; primary Ottoman Turkish, 83n20

South v. North, 9, 106, 212n2

South-South exchanges, 157, 211, 212n2

Soviet Union, 20n2, 59, 62n11, 74, 175, 191, 222–23, 235

space, spatial, 30, 37–38, 45, 202, 242, 247; assumptions, 27; civil, 83n7; fragmentation, 130; political, 78; relations, 56;

shifting spatial configurations, 251; teleology, 128; temporal and, 26, 31, 134,
136; time and, 68, 245, 253; thinking
of, 19; third, 39; webs, 37. *See also* time
Spalding, Karen, 60n1, 201
Spanish, 205
spatiality of globalized capitalism, 12
spatialization, 38
Spivak, Gayatri, 40, 45, 96, 166, 183n44,
197, 204, 210
state, 202; emerging nation, 61n2; formation, 14, 31, 50; modern European,
51; -based societies, 50; -building, 161,
176; and religion, 104
Stearn, Peter, 232
Steward, Julian, 52, 53
strategies, 155n32, 197, 205, 246
Strauss, Levi, 96
structure, structural, 36, 73, 75, 85–86,
146, 160; adjustment programs, 179n6
alternative, 149; challenge, 32; changes,
90; contexts, 141; democratic, 103;
established, 71; hegemonic, 89; modernity, 42; new global power, 67; patrimonial social, 175; political economy,
39; power, 30, 32, 46; restructuring (or
reinvention) of life, 148; symbolic, 165
structuration, 28–29
subaltern, 47, 183n44, 193, 195–97, 201,
206–10; agency, 159, 198, 202; category, 16, 158, 210; communities,
206–8; consciousness, 196, 200; identities, 17, 197, 207; methods, 192; original subaltern group, 203; subalterns'
stories, 100
Subaltern Studies, 3, 9, 16–17, 85, 87,
90–94, 157–59, 164, 168, 177,
191–94, 198–200, 203; collective, 88;
historians, 156n40, 186n68; historiography, 6; Latin American Subaltern
Studies (LASS), 202; perspective, 205;
post-, studies, 97; reception, 84n21;
scholars, 166, 169, 193, 210; school, 6,
14, 15; strategy, 112; voices, 88
subalternists, 11, 94, 208
"subalternity," 146, 157, 166, 177
subject, 204, 207, 242
subjectivities, 8, 38, 45, 82n5, 101, 104,

120n104, 135, 146, 150, 244–45;
recovering subaltern subjectivity, 197;
subjective notions, 109
subliminal methods and messages, 20n4
subordinated groups, 55, 87
superstitions, 19n2, 119n104
superstructure, 52, 231
suppression, 141, 156n41
surveillance, 206–7
sweatshops, 4–6, 20n5
Syria, 78
systems, 53, 104, 207, 235

Taiwan, 127, 130, 135, 233
Tanzanians, 163
Tarde, Gabriel, 59
tat tvam asi ("thou art that"), 102
technology, technological, 150–51, 252,
255 developments, 85; innovations,
226; and scientific knowledge, 5; transformations, 243
techniques, 137, 202–3
teleologies, 19, 27, 45, 136, 148, 151; erosion of a Eurocentric, 248; of Eurocen-
tic modernity, 251; European, 158; of
modernity, 134, 248; of modernization, 128; temporal, 126, 131
temporalities, temporal, 42, 127–28, 136,
247; fragmentation of, 130; mapping of
the world, 140 new assertion of, 38;
reworking of, 27 teleologies, 126, 131
Teotihuacan, a city in central Mexico, 56
territorialization, 172, 187n77
text, textual, 67, 76, 92, 96, 99, 203,
209–10, 230, 244–45; analysis, 17, 98,
192, 196, 198–99, 203, 205; constructed, 203, 205; deconstruction of,
196; dialogue between, 76; postmodern, 252; reading against the grain, 17
truth, 92
Thatcher, Margaret, 58
Thatcherism, 85; post-, 43, 44
theological view, 227
theories, theoretical, 11–12, 14–15, 27,
38–40, 53, 67, 70–71, 78, 137, 200,
204; categories, 201; traditions, 192 of
class struggle, 195; contemporary, 28;
constructivist critiques of the, 60; con-

sumption, 64n35; conscious, 67, 76; critical, 210; cultural evolutionist, 54; Darwinian, 58; dependency, 16, 163; of development and underdevelopment, 7; of dogma, 73; "drain," 88; European, 192; gay, 144; globalization of social, 28; grand, 29, 86; implicit, 50; Malthusian, 58; older modernization, 153n14; other, 8; pluralism, 56; poststructuralist, 163; for the Three Worlds, 29; of "underdevelopment," 163

Thiong'o, Ngugi wa, 180n17

Third World, 3–6, 9–10, 13–14, 26, 28, 37–38, 47, 50, 62n1, 74, 79, 109, 115n10, 124n153, 128, 133–34, 137, 145–47, 150, 163, 178n2, 192–93, 197, 200–201, 229, 233, 243, 250; areas, 212n2; discourses, 150, 151; intellectuals, 14, 19, 147, 192; Marxism, 142; people, 187n74; regions, 193; states, 188n81; studies, 143 Third Worlders, 19, 37, 40

Three Worlds, 7, 8, 37

Thompson, E. P, 86, 91, 247

Thomas, Cal, 103, 104

Tiffin, Helen, 30

time, 43, 68, 222, 242; place, 76, 251; social context, 76; space, 245, 253, 257n44; thinking of, 19; timelessness, 30. *See also* space, spatial

Tipps, Dean, 133

totalitarianism, 223, 236

totalizing interpretations, 125

Toure, Sekou, 176

Toynbee, Arnold, 225

trade unions, 167, 171, 176

tradition, 120n104, 135

transformations, 42, 168, 248

translocal communication, 105, 106

transnational: capital, 113; capitalism, 147; corporations, 45; domination of capital, 40; economic, 102; feminism, 216n31; 1global present, 233; multicultural capitalism, 103; structures, 26, 36

transnationalism, 38

transnationalization, 40

tribalism, 172

tribes, tribal, 95, 104, 108, 160, 165; resistance movements, 195 imagined Africa of, 167, 174

true knowledge, 165

truth, 42, 89, 148, 244–45, 248; conception of historical, 242; enemies of, 257n40; of history, 247

Turkey, 34, 83n20, 257n34

unequal power relations, 80

United Kingdom, 43, 74

United States, 43, 74, 85, 90, 92, 103, 118n93, 122n140, 127, 164, 200, 212n2, 221–24, 246; academic circles, 228; Air Force Academy (USAFA), 226; anthropologists, 52; business community in, 20n4; capitalist class, 59; cultural shift in, 7; historians, 141; Institute of Peace, 153n16; literary and scholarly production, 67; newspapers, 78; postcolonialists in, 27; Republican Party, 110; scholar, 94; television in, 4; universities in, 221

universalist, 255n19; conceptions, 243

universalistic metanarrative, 86

universalism, 247

universality, 167, 168, 170

universalization, 35, 188n81

universalized, 135; historical claim, 30

universalizing, 171; pretensions, 158

universe, 92, 225

University of Chicago, 223, 227;

Upadhaya, Carol, 109

Upanishads, 102

utopia, 4, 154n18

values, 68, 82n5, 101, 107, 111

Vandana, Shiva, 116n32

Vann, Richard, 243

vedic insights, 102

Vico, Giambattista, 225

victims, victimization, 51, 96, 208, 249

Vidal, Hernan, 203

Vietnam, Vietnamese, 137–38, 150

Vietnam War, 19n2

Vilas, Carlos, 203

Virginia, 251

Vishwakarma puja, 102, 119n104

vision, 37, 157, 251, 253

voices, 10, 86, 88, 99, 208
volunteerism, 120n115, 121n121
Vornov, Anatoly, 4

Wacquant, J. D. Loic, 111
wages: 16, 166–67, 170, 176
Wallerstein, Immanuel, 232
Walter, M., 7
warlords, warlordism, 128, 131
Washbrook, David, 93, 96, 178n2, 210, 211
Weber, Max, 137
Weberian, 93, 101
Wei-ming, Tu, 141
West Asia and North Africa, 67, 69, 73, 81n4, 82n5
West, Western, 5, 7, 9–10, 39, 68, 85, 88; civilization, 50, 74, 221–24, 227, 229, 234; discourse, 158, 169; -educated people, 171; history, 138; humanism, 94; impact, 16; "leftist," 179n12; mainstream scholars, 115n10; non-, 5, 9, 102, 121n121, 157; "sinified" intellectuals, 141; social sciences history, 44; world, 112
White, Hayden, 244, 245, 249;
White, Luise, 169
Willis, Paul, 110
Winent, Howard, 9
Wolfe, Patrick, 115n15, 124n153
Wolof kingdom, 162
women, 4–5, 12, 23n24, 45, 105–9, 115n10, 150–51, 162–63, 167, 169–70, 206–7, 247; Indian, 204; non-Western, 121n121. *See also* feminism, feminists; gender
workers, working class, 15, 85–86, 96, 99, 103, 157, 171, 175, 194–95, 202; African, 167, 170; authentic voices, 88; Commercial Workers' Union, 163; culture, 135; identity, 111; migrant, 122n140; Muslim, 74; youth, 110
world, 167, 221–22, 229 Arab, 68; as a better place, 52; bread for the, 120n113; capitalist system, 104; citi-

zenship, 234; colonial, 200, 207; contemporary, 42; First, Second, Third, and Fourth, 47, 93, 70, 109, 250; historians, 236; modern, 50; New, 52, 229; Old, 52; order, 106; present, 80; regional, 227; rest of, 70; shaping, 42; temporal mapping, 140; Western, 112; World's Fair, 252, 257n41. *See also* Earth; globe, global
World Bank, 6, 108, 123n140
World Bank Report, 109
World Health Organization, 5
world history, 11, 17, 21n11, 124n153, 221–22; in China, 229–30; Journal of, 226–27; periodization in, 234; population, 4
World History Association (WHA), 222, 226–29
World History Bulletin, 226, 230
World History Program, 222
'World Memory," 228
world order, 28–30
world systems, 222, 231, 233; analysis, 37, 133, 153n14; capitalist, 135; variety of, 33
World War I, 167, 222–23
World War II, 3, 7, 27, 39, 86–88, 132, 137, 159, 186n70, 200, 221–23, 249; post World War II, 3, 173, 222–23, 226
writing, 14, 50, 52, 203; American, 137; of history, 91; progressive, 108; women's, 96; world history, 221
Wylie, Alison, 57

Xiaoping, Deng, 131

Yellow Emperor, 128, 130, 141
Yellow River, 99, 113
Yellow Sea, 129–30
Yucatan, 205

Zedong, Mao, 127, 150
Ziclinsky, Christopher, T., 5
Ziyang, Zhao, 130
Zolberg, Aristide, 174

About the Contributors

Rifa'at Ali Abou-El-Haj is professor of history and teaches in the program of philosophy, interpretation, and culture at the State University of New York, Binghamton. In 1996–1997, he was Ertegun Visiting Professor at Princeton University. His training is in the history of modern Europe and the Near East. He has published three books and more than thirty articles, some appearing in Arabic, French, and Turkish.

Vinay Bahl is associate professor of sociology at the Pennsylvania College of Technology. Her training is in modern Indian history and sociology with special focus on industrialization, work, gender, and culture. She is the author of *The Making of the Indian Working Class: The Case of the Tata Iron and Steel Company 1880–1946* (1995) and a book chapter in *Congress and Classes: Nationalism, Peasants and Workers* (1988). She has published fifteen articles on the subject of the working class, industrialization, women, and caste.

Fredrick Cooper (Ph.D., Yale, 1974) is Charles Gibson Collegiate Professor at the University of Michigan, where he teaches in the department of history, the Center for Afro-American and African Studies, and the Residential College. He specializes in twentieth-century African history, the history and anthropology of colonialism, labor history, the study of slavery and emancipation, and the relationship of the social sciences to decolonization. He is the author most recently of *Decolonization and African Society: The Labor Question in French and British Africa* (1996), coauthor of *Beyond Slavery: Explorations of Race, Labor and Citizenship in Post-Emancipation Societies* (2000), and coeditor of *Tensions of Empire: Colonial Cultures in a Bourgeois World* (1997) and *International Development and the Social Sciences: Essays in the History and Politics of Knowledge* (1997).

Arif Dirlik is a professor of history and adjunct professor of anthropology at Duke University. His most recent publications include *Postmodernity's Histories: The Past*

277

As Legacy and Project (2000), *Postcolonial Criticism in the Age of Global Capitalism* (2000) (in Chinese), *The Postrevolutionary Aura* (1999) (in Chinese), *Waking to Global Capitalism* (1999) (in Korean), and *The Postcolonial Aura: Third World Criticism in the Age of Global Capitalism* (1997). He is also the editor most recently of *What Is in a Rim? Critical Perspectives on the Pacific Region Idea* (1998), *Chinese on the American Frontier* (2000), *Critical Perspectives on Mao Zedong's Thought* (1997) (with Paul Healy and Nick Knight), *Places and Politics in the Age of Global Capital* (2000) (with Roxann Prazniak), and *Postmodernism and China* (2000) (with Zhang Xudong).

Peter Gran is professor of history at Temple University. He has published *Islamic Roots of Capitalism: Egypt 1760–1840* (1979 and 1998, also in Arabic) and *Beyond Eurocentrism: A New View of Modern World History* (1996). He has published articles on Islamic history and political economy.

Florencia E. Mallon teaches modern Latin American history at the University of Wisconsin, Madison. Until 1996, her main research focus was nineteenth-century Peru and Mexico. Since 1996, she has been researching the relationship between the Mapuche indigenous people of southern Chile and the Chilean state, focusing on the twentieth century. She is currently editing and translating the testimony of Rosa Isolde Reuque Paillalef, *When a Flower Is Reborn: The Life and Times of the Mapuche Indigenous Community of Nicolas Ailio and the Chilean State, 1906–1999*. She has published two books, the most recent of which was the prize-winning *Peasant and Nation* (1995), and more than thirty articles.

Thomas C. Patterson is professor of anthropology and history at Temple University. He has published more than a hundred articles, notes, and reviews dealing with archaeology, class and state formation, contemporary social theory and the historical development of archaeology and anthropology, and anthropology as a profession in the United States and Latin America. He has published *The Inca Empire* (1991), *Inventing Western Civilization* (1998), and *Making Alternative Histories: The Practice of Archeology and History in Non-Western Settings* (coedited with Peter R. Schmidt) (1995).

Roxann Prazniak is Elliott Professor of History at Hampden-Sydney College. She is the author of *Dialogues across Civilizations: Sketches in World History from the Chinese and European Experiences* (1996) and *Of Camel Kings and Other Things: Rural Rebels against Modernity in Late Imperial China* (1999).